Cheating on Tests

How to Do It, Detect It, and Prevent It

✦ ✦ ✦ ✦

Gregory J. Cizek
*University of North Carolina
at Chapel Hill*

 **LAWRENCE ERLBAUM ASSOCIATES, PUBLISHERS**
1999   Mahwah, New Jersey   London

Lawrence Erlbaum Associates, Inc., Publishers
10 Industrial Avenue
Mahwah, New Jersey 07430-2262

Cover design by Kathryn Houghtaling Lacey

Library of Congress Cataloging-in-Publication Data

Cizek, Gregory J.
    Cheating on tests : how to do it, detect it, and prevent it / Gregory J. Cizek
        p. cm.
    Includes bibliographical references and index.
      ISBN 0-8058-3144-4 (cloth : alk. paper). — ISBN 0-8058-3145-2
    (pbk. : alk. paper)
    1. Cheating (Education). 2. Educational tests and measurements. I.
    Title.
    LB3609.C47 1999
    371.26—dc21   99-20275
                                                              CIP

Books published by Lawrence Erlbaum Associates are printed on
acid-free paper, and their bindings are chosen for strength and durability

Printed in the United States of America
10 9 8 7 6 5 4 3 2 1

✦ ✦ ✦ ✦

Contents

❖ ❖ ❖ ❖

Preface

I must reveal some previously unconfessed personal behavior related to the topic of this book. Like the notorious habits of Chicago voters, I began cheating early and often. In 1970, I was in seventh grade at St. Antoninus, a Catholic elementary school located in suburban Cincinnati, Ohio. It is easy for me now, as a professor of education, to see that I cannot be held completely responsible for cheating. Infinitely more culpable were the curricular materials used at my school. I blame SRA.

My school had a terrific academic reputation and produced solid academic success. The competent faculty, composed of Dominican Sisters as well as lay teachers, was respected by the students. The facilities were adequate and well maintained. Parental support for academic achievement was noteworthy. An ethos of high scholastic expectations was palpable. The only flaw, as I see it, was the curriculum. Specifically, the SRA reading laboratories, or "SRA Labs" as we called them.

SRA is the acronym of a company, Science Research Associates, that produced instructional materials for use in schools. The SRA reading materials were part of our language arts curriculum. The Labs consisted of a paperboard box, with dimensions of approximately 18 × 18 × 18 inches. The box housed a series of 100 or more color-coded cards and card-stock strips. Approximately a dozen or so of the cards were color-coded Aquamarine, a dozen Lavender, a dozen Magenta, and so on. (Remember this, because the color coding of the SRA system was a key factor in my cheating.)

The SRA cards (called "Skill Builders," I think) provided individual instruction in various language arts skills or concepts. For example, a Skill Builder might provide instruction and practice on the concept of synonyms and antonyms; another might cover identifying main ideas in a passage. Each Skill Builder also had, on the back of it, a self-test over the skills or principles the card addressed. Students wrestled with the Skill Builders one-on-one, working only within the Skill Builders of a certain color.

The color-coding scheme represented various levels of challenge, although students weren't supposed to know this. At that time—the 1970s—it was becoming inappropriate to overtly recognize gradations of academic accomplishment. For example, labeling the levels with ascending numbers or terms now commonly used in competency testing, such as *Basic, Proficient,* or *Advanced,* was seen as potentially damaging to students' self-concepts. So curriculum producers used colors, or animals, or geometric shapes, or virtually any other symbolic system to which no order or rank could be inferred. Of course, we all knew that Aquamarine was intended for use only by the marginally literate. Even if you started working on the SRA materials at the Aquamarine level, you wanted liberation to Lavender as soon as possible. Gold was the level that few students attained but to which nearly all of us aspired. Working on a Gold Skill Builder was a badge of honor and symbol of status.

The fact that the SRA materials were centrally located meant that a student had to get up from his or her desk, go to the front of the room, remove a Skill Builder, then parade back to his or her seat with a Skill Builder of an easily discernible color flapping away for all to see. Students then worked on the color-coded materials at their desks; here, too, the teacher or a fellow student could readily recognize your skill level at a glance. The prominently displayed color-coding feature was considered to be beneficial for teachers who wanted a facile method of keep tracking of achievement in language arts. It was also probably considered to be a good thing by students who were working at or near the Gold level. It was considered to be a particularly embarrassing thing for denizens of the lower levels, like Aquamarine.

The key to progressing through the various color levels was successful performance on a certain number of individual Skill Builder tests within each color category. The tests consisted, usually, of a passage of text, followed by mostly multiple-choice questions related to both the text and the skills that the student had practiced in a particular Skill Builder. On completing the test, a slender strip of color-coded card stock was available for use in checking his or her answers. A predetermined percentage correct was set as the pass–fail mark on individual Skill Builders; passing a certain number of Skill Builder tests permitted progress to the next color level. Because the entire system was intended to be individualized and self-paced, the checking of color-level tests was done independently by the students and the honor system was used. Our teacher monitored this from her desk by observing students who were checking their tests to see if they were doing any erasing during the checking.

After checking, there were only two possible outcomes. If a student's record showed too many failed self-tests at a given color level, he or she could begin to work again through additional Skill Builders at that level or he or she could choose to drop down a color level or two and acquire missing prerequisite skills. If a student passed the requisite number of self-tests within a color level, he or she would color in a block by his or her name on a large wall chart that illustrated the standing of the entire class. The student would then begin working on Skill Builders at the next color level.

The second key factor that contributed to my cheating was that my school, St. Antoninus, was coeducational. This fact, and the fact that I was—like any adolescent boy—a hormonally unstable mass of repressed self-uncertainty, is inexorably intertwined with my motivation for cheating. I don't recall for certain, but I think my first significant other was a willowy, intelligent, inimitable young lady named Cherie. Somehow she transcended the homogenizing effect of the plain white shirts and blue plaid jumpers that made every seventh-grade girl except her appear to be identical.

I doubt that Cherie knew of my feelings. I wanted desperately to impress her, but lacked the means that so many of my classmates possessed. Phil lived in the great neighborhood. Steve was the captain of every sports team and dashingly handsome. Pete could play "House of the Rising Sun" on his guitar; he even had his own band. Scott was the head altar boy. "The Fish" had a minibike. Dave had a mustache. I decided that my best hope was to appeal to Cherie's academic side, passing myself off as an intellectually stimulating left-brain companion. In my mind, the sequence of events could be accurately predicted: Guy falls for girl. Guy reaches Gold level in the SRA Labs. Girl falls for guy. Surely Cherie would develop an abiding admiration and affection for any guy who could rise up through the levels of the SRA colors at a breathtaking pace. I would be that man.

It is important to mention, however, that I was not one of the most gifted students of the language arts, and cheating played a definitive role in my plans for personal happiness. I quickly discovered that, although the teacher kept a careful eye out for the acts of erasure while students checked their tests, she was nearly oblivious to what occurred when students were actually taking the tests. It was a time-saving and inconspicuous matter to procure the corresponding answer key when visiting the SRA Lab to get the test in the first place. The answer keys were small and, because of the color coding, blended in nicely with the test booklets for each level.

Using the answer keys made the entire language arts curriculum a thoroughly enjoyable experience for me. I ascended through the SRA colors at an incredible pace. The wall chart showed that I attained and retained the position of second in the class for the entire year. (Cleverly, I ascertained that being first would arouse suspicion. Besides, the student at the head of the pack, Roger, was regarded by some as an egghead. Although I wanted to appear talented, I reasoned that a person perceived as having *too much* intellectual prowess might be judged socially undesirable.)

As it turned out, Cherie was not nearly so impressed with intellectual prowess as I speculated she would have been. At the end of eighth grade, the students at my school all went separate ways for high school, and I have no idea what happened to Cherie. On a more practical note, I maxed out the seventh-grade SRA Lab Skill Builders before the end of the school year, only to discover that the publishers had arranged things so that a student couldn't just relax then; they had produced an eighth-grade SRA Lab that awaited Roger and me. I learned more about language arts than might have been expected of a student who simply copied answers from the answer key without the burden of having to actually work through a Skill Builder or read the passages, but I certainly learned less than I would have had I actually done the work. Because the teacher never detected my misbehavior, I also learned that it is entirely possible to get away with cheating on tests.

In the academic pursuits that followed my seventh-grade year, I also learned that I was not the only one who cheated. I discovered methods of cheating that were considerably more sophisticated than the comparatively crude system I had used. Today, as a professor of educational assessment, I find myself in the ironic position of working at an academic enterprise that is seriously threatened by cheating. Although I teach teachers about the nuts and bolts of testing, I also give tests. Although

I speak to my classes about the problem of cheating, I must also be on guard for it. Although I consider cheating to be one of the most serious impairments to obtaining accurate information about students' accomplishments, I must face the stark reality that it is as ubiquitous on the testing scene as Number 2 pencils.

The balance of this book is an attempt to bring together what is known about cheating on tests. The first chapter provides an overview of the problem, a definition of cheating, and an explanation of why attention to cheating is important. Chapter 2 describes how researchers study the problem, documents the extent of the problem at various levels of the educational system, and reviews what is known about why cheating occurs. Chapter 3 provides a catalog and classification of ways to cheat. Methods used at all levels of the U.S. educational system are illustrated—from elementary school to professional licensure and certification in fields such as medicine, law, and business. This chapter might be seen as a sort of how-to-do-it primer, ripe for abuse by the nefariously minded. However, the purpose of the chapter is not to provide tools for the potentially wayward but to inform educators about the ways in which cheating can occur, much as methods of counterfeiting are studied by agents of the U.S. Treasury Department.

The fourth chapter examines cheating by educational professionals, with a focus on attitudes of teachers and others toward the problem. Because what constitutes cheating is not defined consistently across cultures, chapter 5 summarizes what is known about cheating from studies done in other countries. International comparisons of student achievement in math and science are prominent these days; an international perspective on how cheating might contribute to "achievement" is probably in order as well. Various factors associated with cheating are examined in chapter 6. Chapter 7 gives the reader an overview of the ways in which cheating is currently detected, covering both observational and statistical approaches. Chapter 8 presents a review of the sundry approaches to responding to cheating at various levels of the educational system. Chapter 9 suggests ways in which cheating can be prevented and includes examples of academic dishonesty guidelines and honor codes. In chapter 10, legal issues related to accusations of cheating are examined; summaries and key principles that can be derived from leading court cases involving cheating are presented.

The final chapter provides a summary, conclusions, and recommendations for educators and others concerned about cheating. This chapter situates the issue of cheating in the context of the current ethos about educational testing; it looks at the role that systemic reforms can play in reducing cheating, including suggestions to affect fundamental changes in educational attitudes and perspectives regarding the role of testing.

To conclude this preface, I will again confess some personal thoughts. This book would not be possible without the broad participation required in the task of assembling such a book. Lawrence Erlbaum Associates (LEA) has a long and successful history of publishing important works in the field of education. I am indebted to Lane Akers of LEA for his keen insights during the conceptualization of this book and his enthusiastic encouragement at every stage of its production. The book clearly benefited from the editorial work of the copyeditor, Brendan MacBryde, and Book Production Manager, Robin Marks Weisberg. I appreciate the assistance of Dr. David J. Weiss of Assessment Systems Corporation, who provided a review copy of that company's cheating software, Scrutiny!

My work on this book was greatly facilitated by the help of Professor Michael LeBlanc of the State University of New York at Oswego who provided insights on statistical methods of detecting cheating. Dr. Diana Pullin of Boston College, an early mentor and loyal friend, generously shared her expertise related to legal issues. Vidya Ramaswamy, a graduate assistant and doctoral candidate in educational psychology at the University of Toledo, spent hours combing through university libraries in two states. Donna Stein provided some creative tips during the preparation of the manuscript. Deborah Wilson, Yu Lei, and Barb Monger helped with graphics and illustrations.

I happily acknowledge support of numerous colleagues at the University of Toledo College of Education, specifically, Professors Lynne Hudson, Stephen Jurs, and David Bergin. Professor Hudson, Associate Dean for Graduate Studies, is an unrelenting supporter of scholarship and service. I have solicited her wisdom and thoughtful advice at many junctures and she has given freely. Professor Jurs is a professional mentor and personal friend. In matters related to educational testing, statistics, evaluation, and research, I think he is always right. Professor Bergin provided valuable assistance and expertise in the area of educational psychology and motivation; his familiarity with the research in his field is encyclopedic. I am grateful for the helpful criticisms and suggestions provided by the reviewers of this book, Dr. David J. Martin of Texas A&M University and Professor Robert Frary, who is based at Virginia Tech University and is among the most prolific and insightful contributors to what is known about cheating. I also benefitted from discussions with and information provided by Dr. James Wollack of the University of Wisconsin. I take full responsibility, however, for any errors of conceptualization, analysis, or interpretation that remain in this volume.

Certainly, this book would not have been possible were it not for the individual research efforts of many scholars whose work is cited herein. As an area of study, cheating is a comparatively narrow and—I believe—undervalued endeavor. Because of this, the present volume may not stand on the shoulders of scholars popularly regarded as giants, but they are, at least in my opinion, very tall people. Some, notably Donald McCabe, Stephen Davis, John Houston, and William Kibler, have made numerous contributions to what is known about the topic. As I performed the task of compiling and synthesizing their work and the contributions of others, I was reminded of Felson's law, which addressed another form of cheating: "To steal ideas from one person is plagiarism; to steal from many is research."

I also appreciate the contributions of many students and fellow professors to the chapter on cheating methods. Naturally, they all insist that they never actually cheated themselves, but *someone else* told them about the methods they suggested.

Finally, I have no idea if I will ever write another book. It makes sense to me, therefore, to acknowledge important influences in my life that made writing this book possible. First, I recognize that the discipline, persistence, and self-confidence required to attempt this task was instilled in my life early on. This kind of support from my parents, Roger and Helen Kabbes, has been invaluable. I also acknowledge the support of my wife, Rita, for her endless encouragement and confidence in me, and our children, Caroline, David, and Stephen, who I join in thanking God for showering his blessings on the U.S. educational system and in pleading his continuing favor.

—*Gregory J. Cizek*

✦ O N E ✦

An Introduction to Cheating
The Wrong and the Short of It

Ten minutes cheating is better than two hours studying.
—Orlando, Florida student, quoted in Cumming (1995, p. B2)

This is a book about cheating on tests. It's a pretty safe bet that most readers of this book have done it, or at least we've all seen it occur. Has anyone not been tempted? A crib sheet, two taps on the desk means B, a casual glance across the table toward another student's answer sheet—such actions are commonly known as cheating.

At least, sometimes it's called cheating. I remember overhearing a superintendent at a school administrators' conference tell a story about how his students' answer sheets on a high-stakes test were carefully examined for "stray marks" before being sent to a computer service for optical scanning and scoring. "Stray marks," he related with cocktail in hand and a wink of the eye, "were things like wrong answers."

Most of the time, however, no one likes to think about cheating, to talk about it, or to consider its causes, results, remedies, or recourses. So we don't call it anything. In an era when nearly every aspect of testing is open to intense scrutiny by legislators, policymakers, educators, parents, and advocacy groups, cheating remains a taboo topic. Perhaps we avoid talking about cheating because we want to avoid confusion with that "other" kind of cheating, as in "cheating on one's spouse." (Although, in that other sense, a book on "cheating in the classroom" would probably sell a considerably greater number of copies.)

But this book is about cheating on tests—from the fill-in-the-blank variety that teachers use with their kindergarten students, to the fill-in-the-blue-book essay examinations in high school social studies classes, to the fill-in-the-bubble type used for licensure and certification of adults seeking entry or continuing credentials in medical, business, and legal professions. Grade school students and their teachers take state-mandated competency tests, adolescents face tests to acquire a driver's license; physicians take board exams, and lawyers take bar exams. The facts are these: Everyone takes tests; most of us have cheated; and we are all affected by cheating. This book examines these facts in depth.

Before proceeding, however, two caveats are in order. First, throughout this book the term *test* will be used as a synonym for *quiz, assessment, examination,* and sometimes *assignment,* when the assignment is intended to be completed under independent conditions. Specialists in the field of educational measurement might recoil at this blurring of distinctions between concepts. However, in the interest of clarity and accessibility to a wide audience, I have taken some liberties with these terms, and readers should continually strive to conceptualize *test* as an extremely broad concept. For some readers, the term might call to mind a specific test question format, such as multiple choice. As used in this book, the term *test* is not nearly so limited. Although a test might consist of multiple-choice items, I use the term to encompass essays, matching items, oral interrogations, projects, and so on—any format that is used to gauge a person's knowledge, skill, or ability in a given area.

As it happens, multiple-choice formats have dominated the test-making proclivities of teachers, testing companies, and organizations that award credentials over recent decades. Consequently, much of the research on cheating has been in the context of multiple-choice tests, and much of what has been proposed for detecting, preventing, and responding to cheating on tests is embedded in the milieu of multiple choice. Scarcely enough research has been done regarding cheating in any format; terribly little is known about cheating in the context of alternative assessment formats, such as portfolios. As a result, many of the examples and illustrations in this book are necessarily drawn from the context of traditional testing, although consistent attempts are made to extend the principles and findings to all types of tests.

A second caveat relates to the narrowly circumscribed focus of this book, which is limited to cheating on tests, and does not include consideration of other forms of academic dishonesty. For example, cheating can be defined to include plagiarism,[1] padding bibliographic notes, cooperating on homework assignments, or other forbidden actions. However, this book does not address these other forms of cheating. Nonetheless, although this book deals almost exclusively with cheating on tests, the content of several chapters will be useful for addressing problems such as

---

[1]Another variation of cheating consists of taking research materials with the intention of preventing others from having access to the materials. In higher education, a common practice (particularly in law schools) is "razoring" journals—that is, cutting out pages—so that other students cannot read an assigned article or must rely on a reduced set of materials when preparing a report. For some reason—either a nefarious one or simply to save on copying charges—one journal article that was sought for this book was razored out of the journals in three different libraries.

plagiarism, including the sections dealing with correlates of cheating behavior, honor codes, and legal issues.

In the balance of this chapter, a definition of cheating is provided along with a broad overview of the problem it poses for educators and others interested in meaningful test results. A few humorous euphemisms for cheating are passed along, followed by presentation of a more serious rationale for why detection and prevention of cheating are important. The chapter concludes with an explanation of exactly how researchers are able to study the problem of cheating or estimate the frequency with which the behavior occurs.

WHAT IS CHEATING?

In this book, a straightforward definition of *cheating* is used. The definition adopted is that found in *Merriam-Webster's Collegiate Dictionary* (1993), which defines cheating as "depriv[ing] of something valuable by the use of deceit or fraud"; and "violat[ing] rules dishonestly (as at cards or on an examination)" (p. 195). In an educational context, this definition is readily adapted to testing. A long-standing tradition in education holds that knowledge is valuable. Long-standing societal mores include holding those who possess knowledge in greater esteem than those who do not. Cheating can be seen as an attempt, by deceptive or fraudulent means, to represent oneself as possessing knowledge. In testing specifically, cheating is violating the rules.

A minor squabble has occurred regarding the concept of cheating as notions of effective teaching and learning practices evolve. For example, some have questioned whether what is known as cooperative learning is too much like cheating. When this question is examined in light of the straightforward definition of cheating presented here, the simple answer is "no." In cooperative learning, where students work together to achieve common goals, knowledge is the property of the group; no misrepresentation or deprivation has taken place. Further, no rules are violated—in fact, quite the opposite. In cooperative learning contexts, the rules explicitly encourage collaboration and sharing information.

By contrast, there are many occasions when a teacher or credentialing agency seeks information about individual—not group—mastery of knowledge or skill. A third-grade teacher wishes to know whether each child knows that the product of 7 and 6 is 42, not that someone in the class does. (The same can probably be said about the parents of students in that class!) At a personal level, as a prospective candidate for radial keratotomy, I would be interested knowing that my ophthalmologist can perform that procedure independently. I would be distressed to learn that my physician was certified to perform the procedure in a group effort, especially if the group wouldn't be around when I needed my surgery.

Of course, cheating can still occur in group contexts. A teacher might assign a final project to be completed in the same groups as were constituted for the purpose of cooperative learning, with the condition that each group complete its project independently. If groups were to violate these rules, cheating has occurred. The bottom line is this: Rules usually exist regarding acceptable behavior in the context of tests used for educational evaluation or professional credentialing. The rules might be announced verbally by a teacher, printed on an examination booklet, spelled out in a Code of Academic Conduct, or contained in course information packets. When these guidelines are violated, it's called cheating.

A KINDER, GENTLER CHEATING

At least in this book it's called cheating. Most readers have probably encountered euphemisms designed to diminish or disguise an action that, if called by its ordinary name, would be the object of opprobrium. People often attempt to couch critical comments in kinder, gentler phrasings that veil their intended meaning. For example, a grade school teacher can say of a student who doesn't get along with others that he or she "works well independently." A high school counselor, in a letter of recommendation for college can state, "Of all the students I have known, this one really stands out in my mind." An employer can write a letter of reference that says, "You'll be lucky if you are able to get this employee to work for you." Politicians admit to having "inappropriate relationships" that are, in fact, cheating (in the other sense).

Cheating on tests has its own euphemisms. In the classic studies on honesty by Hartshorne and May (1928), the behavior of a child who cheated by removing a blindfold to surreptitiously score higher on a dot-drawing task was called peeking. Cheating has been kindly referred to as "falsely reporting success." One textbook for teachers provided some delicately worded remarks for them to use when reporting cheating to a child's parents. For the child who cheats, it is advised that the teacher tactfully note that the student "*uses all available resources in obtaining answers* [italics added] but *needs help in controlling resourcefulness* [italics added] during testing" (Linn & Gronlund, 1995, p. 339). One classroom teacher referred to cheating as "inappropriate self-administered rewards." Another referred to it as "intentional knowledge appropriation." Cheating was actually made to sound like somewhat of a good thing when described as "an adaptive form of behavior resulting from acceptance of institutionalized goals, but not the institutionalized means" (J. Harp & Taietz, 1966).

I found a chapter in a child psychiatry book to be the mother lode of cheating euphemisms. Its author provided a history of how cheating has been viewed, beginning with the conception of cheating as a sin and continuing through cheating as a crime and as a sickness (Mechling, 1988). However the author quickly moved to modern conceptualizations. In the context of sports, cheating prompts "metacommunication" when players engage in "innovative behavior not unambiguously forbidden." Better yet, cheating can be seen as a type of expertise in the form of "knowing how to circumvent the rules and gain a tactical advantage." The author cited the work of ethicists who term cheating "a special form of bracketed morality." Cheating is viewed as deviant—but explainable—when viewed as "a neurotic response created by the nature of our civilization" or as a form of "deliberate human resistance against late capitalism."

Euphemisms make cheating sound infinitely better. Or, if not an innocuous behavior, cheating can be referred to as an affliction. Mechling (1988) also referred to cheating as a member of the class of actions called *transcontextual syndromes*. If not totally acceptable, at least cheating sounds excusable if a person suffers from transcontextual syndrome. According to Mechling, transcontextual syndromes also include plain stuff, like play, humor, and metaphor, and he viewed cheating as qualitatively better than these. He described cheating as not mere play but as a form of *deep play*. If, as Mechling asserts, examinations closely parallel games, then certain "paradoxes of communication" are involved that prompt cheating. Examinations, after all, afford "plenty of room ... for *expressive behavior or 'style'*" (p. 360).

The result of these paradoxes is that "the total experience may promote creativity" (Bateson, quoted in Mechling, 1988, p. 358).

Euphemisms for cheating are also institutionalized. For example, a large testing company where I used to work always shied away from actually implying that someone had cheated on one of its tests. The company would document "test administration irregularities"; that phrase always sounded to me like a condition that could be remedied by including more fiber in the diet. The company's staff would investigate "achievement similarities not attributable to chance"; that wording sounds like something we would want students to do—that is, accomplish something other than by luck alone.

All of the doublespeak can, apparently, muddle one's thinking. In my opinion, the Most Muddled Award goes to an English teacher whose article attempted to illustrate how cheating was actually an illustration of commendable teaching and learning practices, such as "negotiation," "collaborative problem solving," and a demonstration of students' "production ability under time pressures." The teacher, who had left the room during an examination (more on that misstep in a subsequent chapter of this book), experienced an epiphany as he approached the classroom door on his return. (The article does not say what the teacher was doing during his absence, although it may be relevant in determining whether the epiphany was chemically induced.) Looking through the window of the classroom door, the teacher noticed several students cheating—copying answers, discussing options, trading information. Momentarily, the teacher considered actions that would respond to the cheating. For an unexplained reason, however, the teacher suddenly saw things differently:

> I realized I wasn't looking at cheaters; I was looking at collaborators. I wasn't looking at students copying answers; I was looking at students solving problems. I wasn't looking at rapscallions sabotaging the educational system; I was looking at students preparing for successful lives in the real world. (K. Davis, 1992, p. 74)

At first blush, it is easy to laugh at some of these nonsensical euphemisms. At second blush, attitudes such as that expressed by the English teacher are reprehensible and antithetical to the ethical values all teachers—knowingly or unknowingly—inculcate. It is cynical to believe that becoming adroit at cheating prepares a student for successful life in the real world. We must hope that such a belief is unfounded. Although the euphemisms may be humorous, the consequences of cheating are serious.

CHEATING AND THE CONCEPT OF VALIDITY

I suspect that most readers would readily acknowledge the self-evident wrongness of cheating. For the rest—it is hoped that this is a minuscule percentage—a brief digression into the consequences of cheating from a more dispassionate, scientific perspective is presented. To adequately understand the consequences of cheating from such a perspective, some detail regarding the psychometric concept of validity is in order.

Validity is perhaps the single greatest concern in any testing situation. Validity is the degree to which evidence supports the conclusions (technically, "inferences") made about a person's knowledge, skill, or ability. These inferences are normally based on a less-than-ideal amount of information about the person. For example, teachers are evaluated based on the observations of a principal or peer, who watches perhaps only a single lesson or two. It is risky to make judgments about the teacher on the basis of a single lesson or two. The teacher may be having a bad day, the students may be inattentive because it is the day before a vacation, the teacher may have chosen a lesson that is too challenging or not challenging enough, and so on. However, it is often too costly or simply not feasible to gather additional information. Nonetheless, it is necessary to consider the validity of the conclusions about the teacher's skill, perhaps especially so when based on such a limited amount of information.

A *test* is commonly defined as a sample of behavior obtained under controlled conditions. The validity, or meaningfulness, of test results is the extent to which a person's performance on the sample of test questions can be used to make conclusions about his or her overall competence in the area of interest. For example, a teacher might want students to be able to name all of the elements in the periodic table, given only the two-letter symbols for the elements. In practice, however, a teacher might construct a test that lists only 10 of the symbols. Without explicitly saying so, what the teacher really wants to do is to make an inference about the students' knowledge of the entire domain of elements from their performance on the sample of 10, that is, to infer that students who identify 10 of 10 correctly have probable mastery of all of the elements in the periodic table, that students who identify 5 of 10 have mastery of about half of the elements, and so on.

These notions of validity as "accuracy of inferences" and "sufficiency of evidence" are central in modern psychometric theory (see, e.g., Messick, 1989). Those who administer tests and use test results may not be conscious of the desired inferences, though many testing specialists would argue that they should be. For example, a teacher might wish to make the inference that a girl who can correctly identify at least 20 of 26 letters in the alphabet is "ready" for kindergarten; a college admissions director might wish to infer that a high school student who scores at least 1,200 on the Scholastic Assessment Test (SAT) is likely to succeed in his freshman year at that college; a state regulatory agency charged with oversight of dental practice might wish to infer that a woman who scores at least 85% correct on a licensure examination is likely to provide competent, safe, and appropriate services to her patients. In each of these cases, the number or percentage correct gets all the press, but it is the inference that is the heart of the matter.

In all of the preceding cases, the validity (i.e., the correctness or accuracy) of the inference is threatened if, for example, a parent mouths the letters for the child behind the teacher's back, if the high school student pays a confederate to take the test in his place, or if the woman had obtained a copy of the dental test beforehand. Each of these actions involves cheating—violating the rules or standard conditions for the test. Even for nonpsychometricians, it is easy to see how the accuracy of the desired inference is degraded when the rules are violated. A child may be judged ready for kindergarten when she is not; the consequence for the little girl may be a year (or more) of frustration, withdrawal, or feelings of failure. The high school student may be admitted to a college for which he is not adequately prepared; he may also be preventing the admission of a more qualified student. Licensing a dentist who is incompetent or unsafe is, well, ouch, I really don't even want to think about that.

There is also some evidence that cheating on tests taken during a student's schooling is related to cheating that occurs later in life. For example, one study of 60 students in a master of business administration (MBA) program found that those students who admitted to having engaged in cheating behaviors in school were more likely to report having engaged in dishonest behaviors on the job (Sims, 1993). Additional information on the correlates of cheating—that is, relationships between cheating and student characteristics and situational variables—is found in chapter 6 of this book.

Rightly or wrongly, test scores are also used as indicators of instructional quality and, when aggregated, suggest inferences about educational institutions and programs. For example, when physician residents take medical board examinations, high failure rates can be attributed, in part, to curriculum deficiencies, lenient grading, or other inadequacies in the residents' training—especially if the failing examinees generally performed well on examinations administered during their training. If cheating is the real reason for the residents' good performance on in-training examinations and subsequent poor performance on board examinations, these facts can reflect badly—and inappropriately—on the residents' training institution.

There are also undesirable side effects of cheating on those who don't cheat. In an analysis of cheating among engineering students, Todd-Mancillas and Sisson (1987) noted that dishonest examination behavior places those who do not cheat at a disadvantage when it comes to grades, admission to graduate programs, applications for scholarships, and the job hunt. In an article focusing on communications students, Todd-Mancillas (1987) suggested that academic institutions that do not control cheating may suffer as well; the author noted that employers who are dissatisfied with the on-the-job performance of graduates with (inappropriately obtained) high grade point averages may discount the abilities of subsequent graduates from the institution.

Teachers, schools, and agencies responsible for testing programs take great pains to ensure valid inferences. Psychologists carefully study the development of children to determine which readiness tasks predict success in kindergarten. High school curricula are studied and groups of teachers are impaneled to help determine the content of college admissions tests. Activities called *job analyses* or *role delineation studies* are conducted to identify the knowledge and skills required for safe and effective practice of dentistry. Such studies might involve surveying hundreds of practicing dentists to determine the procedures they perform most frequently, identifying the activities they engage in that are most critical to successful treatment of patients, or even directly observing the daily work of dentists to carefully delineate their essential functions.

Examinations based on curriculum reviews, job analyses, or expert judgment are then developed by personnel with expertise in the area to be tested and who have some knowledge about the principles of sound testing. Great expense is involved in editing and reviewing examinations for clarity, absence of bias, appropriate reading level, and so on—all designed to enhance the validity of the inferences based on test results.

A WEAK LINK IN THE VALIDITY CHAIN

In my experience at a national testing company, extreme security measures were established to prevent the likelihood of any person obtaining illicit access to an examination. This was done, of course, to heighten the degree of confidence in inferences made from test scores. Employees were trained to keep tests in the development stage secure at all times. Draft copies of tests were not to be left exposed on a desk during the day; they were locked in fireproof cabinets at night. Test questions and answer keys could not be kept together. Paper copies of test materials were shredded; even the bags of shredded nothingness were kept in a locked room until they could be securely disposed. I remember one particularly interesting discussion of whether to permit experts to send potential test questions to the company by fax. After all, if the sender misdialed, a faxed test question might mistakenly be sent to who knows where!

I concluded that my employer had enough obsessive–compulsive security systems in place to prevent any cheating at the front end of the testing process. The back end, however, was another story altogether. A week or two before a high-stakes test meant for, say, dentists, the highly secure testing materials would be packaged up (numbered and shrink-wrapped) and shipped to 100 or more testing sites around the country. On arrival at all these locations, the materials would be received by someone in a mail room and stored. Later, the tests would be checked in by a test supervisor. The day of the examination, test takers would sit next to each other, monitored only by people called *proctors*, who, despite their best intentions and some training, were generally underprepared, under compensated, overwhelmed, and seriously outnumbered.

I have learned that a proctor is someone who (usually) is a graduate student and who earns slightly more than minimum wage for walking around or sitting in a crowded room, trying desperately to avoid confronting two highly anxious dentists who are copying from each other. I have also observed that graduate students in the area of testing—that is, those who know something about testing, validity, and cheating—are underrepresented in the field of proctoring. It seems that proctors are most often derived from areas such as marketing, communications, general studies, or "undeclared major."

In summary, the contrast is astounding. The scrupulous and secretive security measures adhered to by those who develop tests are juxtaposed against the throw-it-to-the-wind reality of what happens to the tests when they leave the comfort of their maternal homes. As the confession of the English teacher who left his classroom during an examination illustrates, the same reality applies to the classroom testing that I witnessed in the large-scale testing industry. Although carefully constructed to yield valid inferences, serious threats to validity occur whenever tests are actually administered. It is during the administration of a test—at any level of the educational system—that cheating becomes the most serious threat to validity in testing today. Because tests are used to assist in making important decisions about people, the legal system, test makers, and test administrators have demanded much more attention to validity than ever before. To be concerned about validity in testing demands attention to the problem of cheating. To begin attending to cheating, we must first understand the extent of the problem, which is the central topic of the next chapter.

✦ T W O ✦

Frequency and Perceptions of Cheating

Samantha Kane, a petite, vivacious ninth-grader at a Los Angeles County high school strolls through her favorite shopping mall one school night. "Everybody does it," she says when asked about cheating. She holds up her left hand and proudly displays minute abbreviations of the 50 states inked on her palm for an exam earlier in the day. "I don't feel guilty," she says. "I feel good because I'm going to get a good grade."
—D. Levine (1995, p. 66)

As it turns out, Samantha's observations, published in an article entitled "Cheating in Our Schools: A National Scandal" (D. Levine, 1995), are remarkably accurate. Research on the frequency of cheating reveals that, in the elementary school years, a minority of students report cheating on tests, but by the time they reach high school and college nearly everyone is doing it. Not surprisingly, the desire to get a good grade is a common reason for cheating. In the sections that follow, the methods used to study the extent of cheating are reviewed. Then the frequency of cheating at various levels of the U.S. educational system is examined and comparative data are reviewed that illustrate the differing perceptions of cheating held by those who give tests and those who take them. The chapter closes with a summary of students' self-reported reasons for cheating.

HOW CHEATING IS STUDIED

Undoubtedly, all parents have heard the line "But everyone does it!" when confronting a child about some undesirable habit, behavior, or action. In many cases, everyone really isn't doing it; the claim that they are is intended to excuse the behavior or reduce the punishment. However, in the case of cheating, it turns out that nearly everyone really is doing it.

Of the fairly limited amount of research on cheating, the frequency with which it occurs is the most thoroughly studied aspect. In the next chapter, various research studies are reviewed that document the occurrence of cheating at various levels of the educational system. A preliminary concern that must be addressed, however, relates to how the problem of cheating can even be studied. After all, a researcher or teacher can't simply ask people who have just taken a test, "Who cheated?" Because cheating (to some extent) still has a negative stigma, students are not likely to "fess up." Researchers have devised some remarkably clever—and accurate—procedures for estimating the extent of cheating.

The most common method used to investigate the frequency of cheating actually does involve asking students to confess using a survey. Using necessary disclaimers regarding confidentiality and anonymity, and appropriate procedural designs, researchers have been able to gather reasonably accurate information regarding the frequency of cheating, who does it, the kinds of cheating behaviors used, and so on.

A second method of investigating cheating developed from social science researchers' experiences asking about other sensitive topics. Researchers have learned that people tend to underreport behaviors that are socially unacceptable. One way to get people to respond truthfully about negative, illicit, or stigmatized attitudes and behaviors is to ask them not about their attitudes or behavior but about the attitudes or behavior of their friends. For example, social scientists have found that people who are reluctant to confess their own racially prejudiced attitudes are considerably freer about reporting on the prejudicial opinions of their associates. Researchers have also discovered that people commonly hold the same views on many issues as their friends or are at least more willing to truthfully report a friend's position than their own. Accordingly, conclusions about a person's attitudes are frequently more accurate when based on how the person reports on a friend's opinion than on self-reports about his or her own attitudes.

A third, seemingly obvious, method for studying cheating is simple observation. Unfortunately, inferring cheating from behavior is fairly inaccurate. For example, a student who is observed to be staring for several minutes at another student's paper immediately prior to recording an answer may be suspected of cheating. On the other hand, it is entirely reasonable that the student may not have seen the other student's paper at all but had merely been resting his or her eyes for a few moments, or contemplating his or her own response to a question, or daydreaming about the coming weekend, or a host of other explanations. Because concluding that cheating has occurred from student behavior is what is termed *high inference*, direct observation is probably the least frequently used method of investigating cheating.

A fourth collection of methods for investigating cheating relies on more elaborate experimental designs. For example, some studies have estimated the incidence of cheating by giving students a test while a bogus answer key is left unattended. The incidence of cheating is determined by the extent of agreement between students' answers and the phony answer key. Another common research design involves a clever ruse: A test is administered, the test is collected and scored without making any marks on the students' answer sheets, and the scores are recorded. The next day, the teacher announces something like "There was not enough time to grade the tests" and that they will be distributed for students to score their own tests. In these cases, cheating is defined operationally as the differences between the (secretly) known scores and the scores students award themselves. Spiller and Crown (1995) identified some of the earliest studies of cheating as operationalizing cheating by returning misgraded tests to students and noting the proportion of students who failed to report the error to the instructor. (Presumably, the misgrading is in the student's favor.) Spiller and Crown observed that this strategy for studying cheating "received the most attention in the first half of the century but was rarely used in the past thirty years" (p. 764). Indeed, studies that define cheating in this way have virtually disappeared (perhaps because that specific behavior is no longer commonly considered to be cheating).

Another clever design was implemented by Houser (1982) in a study involving cheating by elementary school children. Houser developed a one-page story about rain forests, which was followed by a 20-item multiple-choice test. Each of the 20 items had five answer choices. Unbeknownst to the students, for 7 of the items, all five answer choices were shams—either all five choices for an item were correct or all five options were factually incorrect. Students were then directed to correct their own tests using an answer key provided to them. For each of the sham questions, the so-called answer key was essentially a randomly selected letter. The probability of answering one of the seven items correctly is sheer chance—in this case, 1 out of 5, or .20. The total expected score for a student on the seven sham items is simply the sum of the seven probabilities, or in this case, 1.4. Houser found, however, that the students' scores on the sham items were substantially greater than chance; students tended to get about four of these items correct.

One of the earliest technologically aided methods for studying cheating was described by Zastrow (1970), who studied cheating among graduate students in a social work program. Zastrow's description of the experimental design is both elaborate and ironic in that the research method used to determine the frequency of cheating seems to rival in sophistication the methods used by students to cheat. A description of Zastrow's method follows:

> During the semester they [the students] received three unannounced quizzes. Each quiz was two pages in length, with the pages stapled together. On the first page were true–false questions, with the answers having to be recorded in a designated space to the left of each question. On the second page was an essay question. Upon completing the quizzes in class, Ss [students] were instructed to separate the two pages and hand in the second page in order to allow the instructor to grade the essay question.… The Ss were then informed to take the first page home; grade it (indicating which true–false questions they answered incorrectly); and return it to the instructor within a 6-day period. The correct answers were relatively easy to locate since the questions were taken directly from the required textbook for the course.

> Unknown to the Ss, the back of the first page of each quiz contained a white, invisible coating of powdered lead carbonate. When the students answered the true–false questions on the first page, an invisible impression from the white powder was transferred to the second page. Immersing the second page into an atmosphere of hydro-

gen sulfide gas caused the white powder to turn dark brown; thereby revealing a visible copy of what was recorded on the first page. (pp. 157–158)

A final group of methods used to investigate cheating relies on statistical investigations of students' answers to test questions obtained in real testing situations. These methods are used after a test has been given and involve, primarily, investigations of the similarity in students' responses. Using well-established statistical tools, one can quantify and express the degree of similarity of responses as a probability that the answers were produced by the students independently—that is, without cheating by collaboration or copying. Using these methods, one can then estimate the percentage of certain types of cheating within a group of test takers, without reliance on the students' willingness to admit the behavior. (Additional information on statistical methods of detecting cheating is provided in chap. 7.)

Overall, despite researchers' progressive acumen in designing innovative ways of measuring cheating, simply asking people about their cheating behavior is, by far, the most prevalent approach. For this reason, it is important to investigate the accuracy of results obtained using survey methods. The dependability of self-report survey methods has been examined using combinations of the methods described previously. In a study by Erickson and Smith (1974), 118 college students were given a test on which an opportunity to cheat was provided; 43% of the students took advantage of the opportunity. The students were then asked whether or not they had cheated. The researchers found (not surprisingly) that no student who did not cheat falsely reported that he or she did. They also found that the highest rates of self-reported cheating were among those students who actually did cheat. In similar studies, the same general conclusion has been replicated: Self-reported incidences of cheating appear to be reasonably accurate estimates of how often the behavior actually occurs.

An interesting caveat to this conclusion is beginning to emerge in studies that use the randomized response technique (RRT) for studying controversial subjects. RRT, introduced by Warner (1965) is increasingly being used because it provides respondents with a considerably greater assurance of anonymity and, therefore, reduced motivation to falsely report their attitudes and behaviors. A commonly used modification of the RRT procedure (introduced by Greenberg, Abul-Ela, Simmons, & Horvitz, 1969) involves pairs of questions, one innocuous and one pertaining to the sensitive behavior being investigated.

To use the paired-question RRT technique, respondents are provided with pairs of yes–no questions. One question of each pair asks respondents about something for which there is a known probability. This question is called the *benign* or *A question*. Popham (1994) suggested that such a question might be along the lines of "Were you born in any of the following six months: January, March, May, July, September, or October?" (p. 413). In a sample of reasonable size, the known probability of being born in one of these months is .50. The other question in each pair—the *sensitive* or *B question*—might ask respondents if they have engaged in sexual intercourse in the past week.

Students are also provided with a method for determining which of the paired questions they will answer. The method might be as simple as a flipping a coin, in which the probability of flipping heads or tails is also .50. Respondents flip their coins before answering each question to determine whether they will answer the A or B question. If the coin comes up heads, the student is directed to answer the benign A question; if tails, the student answers the sensitive B question. Popham

(1994) described how the data are then analyzed to determine the frequency of sensitive behavior:

> Because half of the responses should have been made to each question [in the pairs] ... and because half of the responses to the benign question should have been yes and half should have been no ... it is possible to estimate students' responses to the sensitive question. To illustrate, suppose 1,000 students had supplied responses and there were 700 yes and 300 no responses. We could first calculate that 250 yes responses and 250 no responses should have been made to Question 1, the benign question.... That leaves a ration of 450 yes responses and 50 no responses to the sensitive question. Therefore, we can conclude that 90% of students responded affirmatively to the sensitive question. (p. 413)

Research on the RRT procedure has found that, because investigators have no way of telling whether a person has answered the A or B question, respondents are more likely to answer truthfully. In the end, the researcher obtains a fairly good estimate on both items—the uninteresting fact of students' birth months and the more interesting data on the frequency of their sexual activity.

One study by investigators from the University of Maryland and the Federal Bureau of Investigation's Academy at Quantico, Virginia, compared self-reported cheating using RRT and a simple anonymous questionnaire (Scheers & Dayton, 1987). The authors found that RRT yielded higher estimates of the frequency of cheating than the anonymous questionnaire, ranging from 39% to 83% higher, depending on the question. The authors concluded that surveys—the primary method used in gathering information on cheating—are inadequate for that purpose. Thus, if anything, the frequency of cheating might actually be underreported in the studies described in the next section, which focuses on the extent of cheating on tests.

SO HOW OFTEN DOES IT OCCUR?

Nearly every research report on cheating—whether the data were obtained by a carefully designed study, a survey of self-reported behavior, an RRT approach, or questionnaire regarding perceptions of cheating on the part of another—has concluded that cheating is rampant. Researchers have examined cheating at all levels of the U.S. educational system, from the crude crib noting and peeking of early elementary school years to sophisticated high-tech cheating observed in licensure and certification testing for adults. Comparatively less research has been done on the extent of cheating at the extremes, that is, in the early elementary years and in the professions. A moderate amount of research has been done on high school cheating; a considerable amount has been done using samples of college students and faculty.

One reasonable hypothesis for this disparity in the research is that ethical considerations and requirements of informed consent impinge on the ability to conduct research with very young children, whereas the supply of college-level psychology students willing to participate as research participants is legendarily endless. It is also possible that elementary school cheating is seen as, well, elementary. Copying the spelling of the word *chlorophyll* on a weekly spelling test is probably not viewed as a serious validity concern or as a threat to the public's safety or welfare. No student's diploma hinges on this bit of knowledge. At the other end of the spectrum, there are some potential explanations for why little research has been done on the problem of cheating on licensure and certification tests for adults. Perhaps it is because the security precautions taken to deter cheating on such tests are more substantial than at other levels, or because the research would be so difficult to conduct, or because those public and private organizations responsible for awarding licences and credentials simply don't want to know about the extent of the problem, fearing legal and other consequences. Nonetheless, word gets out, and cheating incidents at this end of the educational continuum often receive the greatest amount of exposure in the national media.

Attempting to summarize the research on the occurrence of cheating is an apples-and-oranges endeavor. Researchers do not define cheating in the same way; various surveys have questioned students about their behaviors, or their perceptions, or their opinions about the behavior of others; evidence on the frequency of cheating comes from a mix of questionnaires, experiments, and longitudinal data collections. Even when comparing the results of reasonably similar research designs, we find that the phrasing of a survey item can make the results difficult to compare and interpret. For example, two studies might involve random samples of undergraduate psychology students attending large Midwestern public universities. However, one researcher might ask about the frequency of cheating over the students' college careers, and another might be concerned only about cheating in the current year or current semester.

Despite these difficulties, the following sections will attempt to summarize what is known about the frequency of cheating across the levels of the U.S. educational system. Results are provided separately for elementary-school-age students, high school students, and college students. Relevant information about the design of individual studies are presented whenever it was available so that the most accurate picture of cheating can be obtained. And what a picture.

Cheating in the Early Years

Only a handful of studies have examined cheating on academic tasks by elementary school students. One early study recorded cheating by 12% of a group of third-grade students (James, 1933). A later experiment conducted by Houser (1978) involved 297 girls and 289 boys enrolled in fourth-, fifth-, and sixth-grade classes across several suburban public schools near Los Angeles. The students in Houser's study were instructed to read a story and respond to seven test questions, which the students would then self-score using a scoring key that had been attached to the test while the teacher was out of the room. Unknown to the students was the fact that the seven questions were part of an experimental design and that none of the questions had a single correct answer. Thus, students would be able to answer the questions correctly only by sheer luck or by using the attached key. Statistical analysis showed that the percentage of items answered correctly significantly exceeded chance, and the researcher concluded that over half of the elementary school students had cheated. Houser remarked that the fairly extensive degree of cheating was surprising, especially given that the children had been explicitly informed that their performance on the test would not count and would not be reported to their teachers.

A report by Brandes (1986) documented the extent of cheating by public school students in California. Brandes mailed a survey to sixth graders attending 45 California elementary schools. The students were assured of anonymity, and the schools were chosen to be representative of low-, average-, and high-scoring schools on the California Assessment Program's mathematics test. Responses were received from 1,037 students and their teachers—a response rate of 77%. Brandes found that 38.6% of elementary school students admitted copying at least once from another student during at test; 15% reported doing so a few or many times. Using crib notes to cheat on a test was confessed by 10% of students who said they had done so "a few" or "many" times; 72% said they had never done so. Unfairly attempting to gain access to test materials before a test was the least frequent type of cheating among the elementary students surveyed; slightly less than 1% of students reported doing this "many times" and only 10.5% said they had gained inappropriate access to test materials "once" or "a few times."

As would be hypothesized, a different picture emerged when students were asked whether they had seen another student cheat on a test: Brandes (1986) found that 29.6% of sixth graders said they had witnessed cheating "many times," 40.5% said they had observed cheating "a few times," and 15.7% said they had observed cheating by a classmate only once. Opinions were fairly uniformly distributed when the sixth graders were asked how their classmates would feel about a student who cheated. Most respondents thought their classmates would not care (38.9%); fewer thought that they would dislike it a little (35.6%) or very much (25.5%).

A study by Evans and Craig (1990a) involved 158 seventh- and eighth-grade public school students who were queried about their perceptions of cheating. Evans and Craig found that 63.5% of this group perceived cheating as "a serious problem" at their school. More than 65% of the students agreed or strongly agreed with the statement that students in a class usually know when cheating is going on. A similar study by the same authors (Evans & Craig, 1990b) surveyed 358 middle schoolers and yielded similar results.

Feldman and Feldman (1967) studied the frequency of "unplanned cheating that is done individually" (p. 957) by elementary school students. The experiment involved permitting students in a seventh-grade social studies class to score their own tests according to an answer key that the teacher had written on the blackboard. Unknown to the students, the tests had already been scored by the teacher. During the self-scoring, the teacher was "unexpectedly" called away from the classroom, leaving the students unattended. Cheating was defined as the number of students who changed answers to test questions while the teacher was out of the room. Of the 81 students, 23 incidents of cheating were recorded—nearly 30% of the students.

Finally, a retrospective study by Schab (1969, cited in Bushway & Nash, 1977) asked older students to report when they began cheating. Approximately 24% of girls and 20% of boys reported that they began cheating in the first grade, although many students began cheating in later elementary school. Thirty percent of girls and 24% of boys reported that they began cheating in the seventh or eighth grade.

Overall, the results of studies of cheating in the early school years are reasonably consistent. They reveal that approximately one third of elementary-school-aged students report cheating personally and that students believe cheating by others is even more frequent. Students generally view cheating as a problem in their schools. Regrettably, little research related to cheating on tests has been conducted with very young children, although, as is seen later, researchers have studied correlates of cheating behavior on other (i.e., nonschool-testing) tasks involving young children. Disconcerting as it might be that such a substantial proportion of elementary students report cheating, the problem becomes even more pronounced in high school.

Cheating in High School

The research on cheating at the high school level is more abundant, just as is the behavior itself. Several large-scale studies have been conducted, and apparently, Samantha is right, or nearly so: Almost everybody is doing it. A high percentage of admitted cheating is a consistent finding of research on cheating at the high school level. The problem is also perceived to be pervasive by the students themselves. In one telephone survey involving a random sample of more than 1,300 respondents, students were asked to rate the severity of "students cheat[ing] on tests and assignments"; 68% classified the problem as very or somewhat serious (J. Johnson & Farkas, 1997, p. 42).

McLaughlin and Ross (1989) surveyed 130 public high school students in Tennessee. The researchers first asked students to judge various activities as cheating or not cheating. For most of the cheating behaviors, students were apparently cognizant of their impropriety. Ninety-nine percent of the students recognized copying during an exam as cheating; 95% classified arranging to give or receive signals during a test as cheating; 92% said that it was wrong to look at notes during a test. Only 30% said that copying an answer mistakenly left on the board was cheating; 29% saw preparing for a test using an old test paper (that only a few students had) as cheating. In an interesting proof of the proverb "It is better to give than to receive," 95% said asking someone else for a test answer was cheating, whereas only 87% thought that giving someone else an answer was cheating.[1]

McLaughlin and Ross (1989) also asked students to rate the seriousness of the cheating behaviors noted earlier using a scale ranging from 0 (*not serious*) to 5 (*very serious*). Mean ratings of seriousness for all behaviors ranged from 1.6 to 3.6. Even ratings for forms of cheating such as copying during an exam—recognized as clearly wrong by the students—were only rated near the middle of the seriousness scale. Perhaps most disconcerting were students' responses to a hypothetical question about how frequently they would participate in the behaviors if they were sure they would not be caught. On a scale ranging from 1 (*never*) to 4 (*always*), the average frequency of participation was consistently in the *seldom* to *often* range.[2]

Brandes (1986) who collected data on sixth graders as reported earlier, also studied cheating at the high school level. She surveyed 2,265 California public secondary school students (16.9% seniors, 76.3% juniors, and 6.7% sophomores). The

---

[1] Perhaps the greatest such "giving" ever recorded is mentioned in Hollinger and Lanza-Kaduce's (1996) study, which cited an early study by James (1933) in which 94% of high school students admitted allowing someone else to look at their test during an examination. Interestingly, in James' study, 80% of the students' teachers admitted to having done the same.

[2] I recognize the inappropriateness of averaging ordinal data, as was done in the study summarized here. However, when faced with the decision to exclude a study in an area where there are comparatively few (i.e., high school-level cheating), I decided to err on the side of inclusion. In this, and other cases, I try to provide cautions and additional information where appropriate.

survey questioned students about the frequency with which they engaged in various behaviors, permitting responses of *never, once, a few times,* and *many times.* Results showed that 73.5% of the students reported using crib notes at least once, 75% admitted copying from another student, and 96.7% reported seeing another student cheating. Comparatively smaller percentages reported using pre-arranged signals to communicate answers during a test (37.5%) and gaining unfair access to test materials before a test (41.5%). When asked about how their classmates would feel about a student who cheated, 75.3% said that their classmates wouldn't care, 21.6% thought that their classmates would "dislike it a little," and only 3.2% thought that their classmates would dislike it very much.

The studies by Evans and Craig (1990a, 1990b) and by Feldman and Feldman (1967) mentioned earlier also included high school samples. Evans and Craig administered a 120-item questionnaire to 305 (1990a) and 1,405 (1990b) senior high school students. Findings from the smaller sample revealed that 77.3% of this group perceived cheating to be a serious problem in their school. Overall, 88% of the students agreed that students in a class usually know when cheating is going on. Similar results were observed in the larger sample. Feldman and Feldman, whose experiment involved permitting students to score their own (previously scored) tests according to an answer key written on the blackboard, replicated their study using 12th-grade English students. Of the 73 seniors, 33 cheating incidents (45.2%) were recorded—up from the 28.4% of Grade 6 students.

One large-scale study was reported by Schab (1991) who synthesized results from surveys administered to high school students that spanned three decades: 1969, 1979, and 1989. The 1969 survey was administered to 1,629 students, the 1979

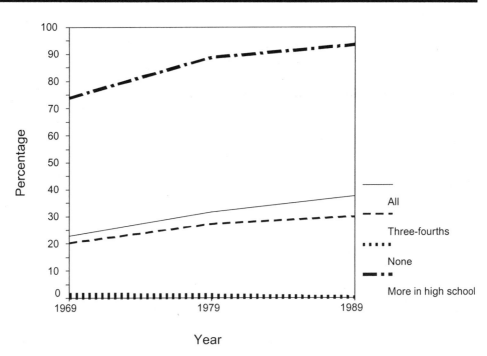

FIG. 2.1. Perceptions of students cheating in high school.

survey to 1,100 students, and the 1989 survey to 1,291 students. Figure 2.1 shows the increasing perception of cheating.

As shown in Fig. 2.1, an increasing percentage of students estimated that "three-fourths of the students in their high schools were guilty [of cheating]" (Schab, 1991, p. 840), with the percentage of students who responded affirmatively to this question beginning at 20.3% in 1969 and climbing to 27.2% in 1979 and 29.9% in 1989. The percentage of students who reported that "all [students] cheated at some time or other" also rose across the years, whereas a consistently minute percentage of students said that they did not believe there was cheating in their schools. When asked to compare their elementary and high school experiences with what they thought the frequency of cheating in college might be like, students overwhelmingly thought that there was more cheating going on in high schools.

More recent data on high school cheating has been collected in several large-scale surveys. S. F. Davis, Grover, Becker, and McGregor (1992) asked more than 6,000 students from a variety of collegiate settings if they had cheated in high school or college and whether they believed it is wrong to cheat. Rates of reported cheating in high school ranged from 51% for women at a small state university to 83% for men at a large state university. Across all locations, the percentage of students who stated that it is wrong to cheat was never below 90%. Nonetheless, 76% of the students overall admitted cheating; 80% of those who cheated said that they copied from another student or used crib notes during a test. In a study by S. F. Davis and Ludvigson (1995), 71 samples of college students from 11 states ($N = 2,153$) were asked if they had cheated in high school. In each sample, more than 70% said "yes," with more than 80% of those who admitted to cheating in high school saying they had done so on several occasions. Another survey of college students that asked about students' high school cheating found that only 15.5% of students said they did not cheat in high school (Baird, 1980).

A consistent source of national data on cheating in high school is found in annual reports produced by Who's Who Among American High School Students. This source is particularly interesting because the organization's annual survey includes the responses of approximately 3,000 respondents, who, according to the organization, are high-achieving, A- or B-average, 16- to 18-year-olds. The 1995 report summarized data collection over 25 years. In 1983, when students were first asked if they cheated in high school, 70% indicated that they had. In both 1993 and 1994, the figure had risen to 78% (Who's Who Among American High School Students, 1995). The surveys for 1993 and 1994 asked students to estimate how frequently cheating occurred at their schools and whether or not respondents had specifically cheated on a quiz or test. For some questions, the results were presented separately by subgroups of interest, including sex, school type, and community type. A summary of these results is shown in Table 2.1 and Table 2.2. Although no tests for statistically significant differences between subgroups were conducted, the 1993 and 1994 results reveal that the specific behavior of cheating on a test is common in all groups.

The Who's Who Among American High School Students surveys also provide a sense of good news–bad news. On the positive side, results from the 1997 survey reveal that 76% of students say they have cheated, signifying that a trend of increasing cheating (or, at least, increased admission of cheating) may have stabilized. However, the magnitude of this figure remains alarming considering that the students sampled are putatively regarded as the United States' best and brightest. Also on the

TABLE 2.1

Percentage of High School Students Responding "Yes" to the Question
"Have You Cheated on a Quiz or Test?"

	Sex		School Type			Community Type		
Year	Male	Female	Public	Private	Parochial	Urban	Suburban	Rural
1993	41.5	39.8	41.2	34.9	41.9	39.1	43.9	38.0
1994	42.2	44.5	44.4	36.0	51.7	45.6	46.2	41.9

Note. Adapted with permission from *Attitudes and Opinions From the Nation's High Achieving Teens: 25th Annual Survey of High Achievers* (pp. 12–15), by Who's Who Among American High School Students, 1994, Lake Forest, IL: Author.

TABLE 2.2

Percentage of High School Students Responding "Never Happens," "Pretty Rare,"
"Fairly Common," and "Almost Everybody Does It" to the Question
"How Common is Cheating at Your School?"

Year	Never Happens	Pretty Rare	Fairly Common	Almost Everybody Does It
1993	0.5	18.8	70.0	10.1
1994	0.2	10.3	54.8	34.2

Note. Adapted with permission from *Attitudes and Opinions From the Nation's High Achieving Teens: 25th Annual Survey of High Achievers* (pp. 12–15) , by Who's Who Among American High School Students, 1994, Lake Forest, IL: Author.

negative side is the finding that the percentages of students who said "Almost everyone is doing it" in response to a question about how common cheating was at their school jumped to 34.2% in 1994 from just 10.1% in 1993. In 1994, the survey asked students, for the first time, a question designed to find out why they had cheated: 66% simply said that "it didn't seem like a big deal" (Who's Who Among American High School Students, 1994, p. 12). The authors of the report concluded that "young people today are simply emulating the adult behavior they see all around them" (p. 12).

Cheating in College

For many college students, the college years mark both the full entry into adulthood and a time of liberty, exploration, and creativity. The freedoms to explore, create, and invent are cherished by college students, faculty, and administrators on campuses across the country. Students' inquisitiveness and interests in careers begin to peak, as does, apparently, the frequency of their cheating. And, as seen in the next chapter, their methods of cheating demonstrate their creativity and ingenuity at every turn. A great deal of literature documents that creativity, and a similarly substantial amount of research—reviewed in the following sections—documents the extent of cheating on U.S. campuses.

Frequency of Cheating in College: 1940s–1960s.   Data from early studies on cheating in college show that a smaller percentage of students admitted to cheating in the past than do so today. An early experimental study by Drake (1941) revealed a cheating rate of 23% in a group of college students. Drake studied 126 students in a women's college who were given six weekly tests in an unnamed subject. Using the method of returning previously scored tests to the students for self-grading, Drake found that 30 of the students cheated on at least one of the tests, 7 students cheated on four of the tests, 1 student cheated on five tests, and 1 student cheated on all six. The overall rate of 23% may have been the low watermark as far as cheating in U.S. colleges and universities. By the 1950s and 1960s, admitted cheating rates had climbed to 38% and 49% (Goldsen, 1960).

A particularly fascinating study of cheating was conducted in the 1960s by Hetherington and Feldman (1964), who studied what they called "opportunistic individual cheating" and "planned independent cheating" (p. 212) in 78 college students (39 male, 39 female) from two child psychology classes. The research design involved three situations. In the first situation, the researchers used five students who were not enrolled in the course as research assistants. These confederates attended classes frequently enough to be regarded as peers by the other students. However, their main role was to observe and record various types of cheating during the first 1-hour examination of the semester from widely dispersed locations in the classroom. The examination consisted of 90 objective items (e.g., multiple choice and true–false). The examination conditions were marked by a purposefully unobservant professor, a situation that, to coin a malapropism, might be called *inattentive proctology.* The student observers recorded all instances of copying, use of crib notes, permitting others to copy, and so on. For this part of the study, cheating was defined to have occurred if two observers witnessed an improper behavior. Test papers were then collected and, as in other studies, passed back for scoring by the students themselves, who were unaware that the papers had already been scored.

The second situation involved administration of an essay examination consisting of two questions, which the instructor told the class would be taken from a list of five essay questions distributed in advance of the examination. Students were to complete the examination in blue books—so called because these small booklets, readily available for purchase in college bookstores and designed for short essay examinations, have pale blue covers. However, to ascertain the degree to which students might complete, say, all five essay questions in advance in a substitute blue book and submit only those containing the two assigned examination essays, the blue books distributed for students' use were inconspicuously marked before being distributed for the examination. In this situation, which could be called *substitutio examinus*, cheating was defined as turning in a substitute blue book.

The third situation involved an oral examination in which students were individually asked questions by the professor in his or her office. After asking an individual student a couple of very difficult questions, the professor was "unexpectedly" called out of the room, leaving the course textbook conspicuously lying among other books on the desk (and with its position inconspicuously marked so that it might be readily determined if the book had been moved). In this situation, the *peekinheimer maneuver*, cheating was recorded as having occurred if the position of the book was noticed to have changed on the professor's return to his or her office.

Hetherington and Feldman's (1964) results reveal that the incidence of cheating may have been increasing in the 1960s. Across the three situations, 46 of the 78 student (59%) cheated in some fashion, although perhaps it is more accurate to say that 59% were *detected*. Cheating was most frequently observed in the inattentive proctology and substitutio examinus situations, in which an equal percentage (50%) cheated. The peekinheimer maneuver was used by only 22% of the students. Overall, only 10% of those who cheated in any situation limited their cheating to just one of the three situations.

During the period spanning from the 1940s to 1960s, in which studies of college cheating developed from surveys to more experimental designs, a clear pattern of increasing frequency of cheating can be discerned. During this period admitted or observed cheating increased in nearly the same fashion as the decades were passing, with a high of nearly 60% found by Hetherington and Feldman (1964). Beginning in the late 1960s, studies of college cheating began to focus on how college student cheating might be predicted or at least related to student characteristics and situational variations. However, a wealth of studies continued to document the frequency of occurrence.

Frequency of Cheating in College: 1970–Present.

With the dawn of the 1970s, the admitted cheating percentage also reached the 70s. And just as the frequency of cheating has increased, so has the number of studies attempting to document the extent of the behavior. The studies have produced evidence using three types of research designs: single-time-point surveys, trend studies, and experiments. Because of the sheer number of studies that have been conducted, it is not practical to review the details of each. Instead, a listing of the major studies since 1970 is presented in Table 2.3.

Table 2.3 reveals that the percentage of students who admit to cheating in college is remarkably and uniformly high. However, one of the weaknesses in the plethora of surveys on cheating is that students are usually only asked if they have engaged in cheating. Extremely little is known about how often students cheat. Even less is known about how much cheating occurs when a student admits to cheating. For example, 90% of students admitting to copying one answer on one test during their college careers suggests an entirely different problem than if 90% of students admitted to copying more than half of the answers on at least one test each semester. One of the studies listed in Table 2.3 addressed this issue, although the results are not as cleanly interpretable as might be hoped. Baird (1980) also asked students to rate how frequently they engaged in specific forms of cheating. Using a 3-point scale (1 = *never*, 2 = *occasionally*, 3 = *often*), Baird found that the most frequently used method was obtaining test information from other students (M = 2.69), allowing someone else to copy work (M = 2.66), and copying someone else's work (M = 2.12).[3] Although these means are high (i.e., all represent more than occasional cheating) no specific definitions of *never*, *occasionally*, or *often* were given.

Specific information is available, however, regarding the types of cheating behaviors engaged in by test takers. An extensive list of individual test cheating

---

[3]These results confirm those reported by another study previously cited in which a greater percentage of students reported allowing students to copy from them than reported copying from another student—the "more blessed to give than to receive" hypothesis.

TABLE 2.3

Cheating in College, 1970–Present

Citation	N	Description	Study Design	Findings
Sherrill, Salisbury, Horowitz, and Friedman (1971)	193	Undergraduates, large state university	Experiment	Using the grade-your-own-test procedure, Sherrill et al. found that, over the semester, 66% of the students cheated at least once on three tests; of these, 32% cheated at every opportunity[a]
C. P. Smith, Ryan, and Diggins (1972)	112	Two urban colleges	Single survey	91% said they had cheated while in college; 70% of men and 63% of women said they had cheated on at least one exam within the last two semesters; men reported cheating in an average of 25.5% (SD = 26.5) of their courses; women admitted cheating in 17.6% of courses (SD =17.0)
Houston (1976b)	323	Psychology students; one class	Statistical detection	Students seated next to each other had significantly more wrong answers in common than those not seated near each other;[b] Houston estimated that nearly 2 of every 15 wrong answers were probably exchanged between students
Baird (1980)	200	87 men, 113 females	Single survey	75.5% admitted cheating in college; 43.0% admitted cheating in one or more of their current courses; cheating on quizzes and tests was more common (42.5% and 58.5%, respectively) than cheating on midterm or final examinations (28.5% and 27.5%, respectively)
Singhal (1982)	364	Agriculture, technology, and engineering students	Single survey	56% admitted cheating; 2% said they did so "on a regular basis" (p. 776); the most common form of cheating on tests was the use of crib notes (24%); the most popular form of any kind of cheating was copying a homework assignment or lab report
Stern and Havlicek (1986)	314	Midwestern university	Single survey	82% admitted academic misconduct
Haines, Diekhoff, LaBeff, and Clark (1986)	380	Undergraduates, small state university	Single survey	54.1% admitted cheating in the current academic year

Study	N	Population	Method	Findings
S. F. Davis, Grover, Becker, and McGregor (1992)	6,000	35 colleges	Single survey	Admitted cheating ranged from a low of 9% reported by a sample of women at a small, private, liberal arts college to a high of 64% reported by men at a small regional university
Jendrek (1992)	776	Undergraduates, medium-sized university	Single survey	74% indicated that they had witnessed cheating during an examination; 47% said they had observed cheating between two and five times; the longer the student attended college, the more likely he or she was to observe cheating (61.9%, 75.6%, 80.9%, and 82.8% for freshmen, sophomores, juniors, and seniors, respectively)
Greene and Saxe (1992)	87	Undergraduates	Single survey	Students' own incidence of admitted cheating (81%) was not as high as the perceived incidence of cheating by others (99%)
Kerkvliet (1994)	443	Economics students at two large universities	RRT survey	42% admitted having cheated on at least one examination
Graham, Monday, O'Brien, and Steffen (1994)	48	Midwestern community college and private Catholic college[c]	Single survey	Overall admitted cheating incidence of 89.9%; specific behaviors included giving test questions to a student in a later section (46.2%), allowing a student to copy on a test (23.5%), and copying during an exam (26.0%)
Davis and Ludvigson (1995)	2,153	Juniors and seniors	Single survey	Follow-up study drawn from S. F. Davis et al. (1992) participants; between 42% and 64% of respondents from various institutions reported having cheated in college
Spiller and Crown (1995)	24	Studies	Trend study	Studies published between 1927 and 1986 showed substantial variation in reported cheating rates, ranging from 8% to 81% with an average of 40%; Spiller and Crown concluded that cheating frequency was not related to the year a study was conducted
Hollinger and Lanza-Kaduce (1996)	1,672	Large southeastern university	Single survey	68.1% admitted to cheating at least once during one 15-week semester; 26.3% admitted copying from another student during an examination; 22.1% knowingly permitted another student to copy from them; 10.4% used crib notes; 5.2% obtained and studied from an illegal copy of an examination[d]

(continues)

TABLE 2.3 (continued)

Citation	N	Description	Study Design	Findings
Mixon and Mixon (1996)	157	Business students	Single survey	62% reported they had observed cheating on an examination in college; 37% admitted having cheated themselves; 25% said that they knew someone who routinely cheats
Diekhoff et al. (1996)	474	First-year sociology and psychology students	Single survey	Diekhoff et al. administered a survey identical to that of Haines et al. (1986) at the same institution; 61.2% of students said they had cheated—an increase of approximately 13% since 1986. Copying from another student's exam was the most popular form of cheating (25.5%), followed by letting someone else copy (16.5%), using cheat sheets (13.5%), and studying a stolen examination (4.6%).

[a]In a related study, the "contagion of cheating" was investigated by Walker, Wiemeler, Procyk, and Knake (1966). The researchers set out to estimate the frequency of cheating in a class of 22 introductory psychology students using the method of allowing students to score examinations themselves that had, unknown to the students, been previously scored by the researchers. However, the Walker et al. study is unique in that the researchers repeated the experiment on successive tests throughout the semester. On the first test, 23% of the students were observed to have cheated; the percentage grew to 64% on the second test and 86% on the third test. Walker et al. (1996) surmised that, left unchecked, "cheating seems to be contagious" (p. 360).

[b]To rule out the possibility that students seated next to each other may have responded similarly simply because friends tend to sit near each other and may have studied the same way, Houston's analysis was based on random seating assignment.

[c]One problem with this estimate is that the study included behaviors such as "using a paper for more than one class" and "not contributing a fair share in a group project" (Graham et al., 1994, p. 256), which almost certainly inflated the overall cheating rate to nearly 90%.

[d]The Diekhoff et al. (1996) and the Hollinger and Lanza-Kaduce (1996) studies mark the only occasions in which receiving assistance (copying from another student) is reported to be done more frequently than giving assistance (allowing another student to copy). These findings may be anomalous. Or, as these data are among the most recent to become available, it is possible that a cultural transition is being witnessed—from the 94% of students who reported giving answers in the James (1933) study to the "it may be more blessed to receive than to give" philosophy of the 1990s.

TABLE 2.4
Student Reports of Specific Cheating Behaviors
and Student and Faculty Perceptions of Misconduct

Type of Cheating	% Students Who Have Done This	% Who Indicate that the Behavior is Cheating	
		Students	Faculty
Asking another student for the questions to a test that he or she has taken but you have not yet taken	76	45	87
Copying from another student during a quiz or examination	71	96	99
Permitting another student to look at your answer sheet during a quiz or examination	65	86	98
Asking another student for the answers to a test that he or she has taken and you have not yet taken	53	63	93
Previewing an examination from an illegal "test file"	41	57	94
Delaying taking an exam or turning in a paper late with a false excuse	41	71	90
Copying from a crib sheet during a closed-book test or quiz	24	96	99
Marking two answers on a hand-scored answer sheet when the directions permit only one	24	65	70
Claiming to have handed in a paper or examination when you did not	10	94	97
Taking an examination in place of another student	6	98	97
Getting an advance copy of an exam by having a student who is not enrolled "sit in" for the exam and not turn in the paper	4	93	96

Note. Adapted with permission from "Academic Misconduct: Results of Faculty and Undergraduate Student Surveys," by E. B. Stern and L. Havlicek, 1986, *Journal of Allied Health*, 15(2), pp. 133–136.

behaviors was assembled by Stern and Havlicek (1986), who included the list in a 52-item survey administered at a large Midwestern university in 1983 and 1984. The first two columns of Table 2.4 show a partial list of the behaviors included by the researchers (namely, those that involve cheating on tests) and the percentage of students who admitted to engaging in them during their college careers. As a review of the first two columns highlights, these examination cheating behaviors appear to be fairly common.

A few of the many surveys of college cheating have related incidence of reported cheating and college major. Meade (1992) surveyed 6,000 students at 31 prestigious universities in which students were asked if they had cheated at any time during their college career and found that business students reported the highest percentage of cheating (87%), followed by engineering students (74%), science majors (67%), and humanities majors (63%). In one of the largest studies of its kind, Bowers (1964) surveyed 5,280 college students and ranked the incidence of cheating among them: business (66%), engineering (58%), education (52%), social science (52%), art (50%), history (43%), humanities (39%), and languages (37%). Of the 157 business students surveyed by Mixon and Mixon (1996), only 37% reported they had cheated on an examination in college. Overall, these studies provide a rough, though fairly consistent picture: The order for frequency of reported cheating among the various college majors, from greatest to least, is (roughly) engineering, science, humanities, education, art, social sciences, history, languages, and economics. The discrepant results for cheating by business students—87%, 66%, and 37%—make them either the most or least frequent offenders, or perhaps simply the most variable in their truthfulness.[4]

Trends in College Cheating.   As other social problems have increased over recent decades, it has been hypothesized that cheating on tests would not be immune to such changes. To address this hypothesis, a 30-year study of cheating designed to monitor the frequency of cheating by undergraduate college students was conducted by McCabe and Bowers (1994). Initial data were collected in a survey administered to 5,422 students from 99 colleges and universities across the United States during the 1962–1963 academic year. Follow-up data were collected during the 1990–1991 academic year from 6,096 students at 31 schools across the country. To make the comparisons as equivalent as possible, McCabe and Bowers reduced the data to form subsets of male juniors and seniors drawn from small- to medium-sized, selective, residential institutions. Although McCabe and Bowers did not report an overall rate for cheating on examinations, the percentage of students engaging in specific test-related cheating is provided in a report by McCabe and Trevino (1996) based on the same data. Table 2.5 shows the percentages of students admitting to specific cheating on tests in the 1961 and 1991 samples. The table reveals that the admitted frequency of engaging in the three specific forms of cheating has increased markedly, in contrast to the fairly steady rates of cheating reported in other written work between 1961 and 1991 and cited by McCabe and Trevino. Reviewing the 30 years of data, S. Cole and McCabe (1996) concluded that "the number of students admitting to any form of cheating on tests, examinations, or major written

---

[4]The results shown here for various college majors are intended only as a humorous interjection. However, researchers have attempted to seriously answer the question of which subject areas elicit the most cheating. A study published in 1938 by W. W. Ludeman (cited in Schab, 1969) listed the following high school subjects in order of amount of cheating (greatest to least): mathematics, English, history, Latin, economics and sociology, and science. Schab's later research generally confirmed the earlier results. Schab (1969) noted that "mathematics still retains its supreme position as the course in which the most cheating is attempted" (p. 39). His research resulted in the following ranking: mathematics, history, science, English, and foreign language.

TABLE 2.5

**Student Reports of Specific Cheating Behaviors,
1961–1991**

	% Students	
Type of Cheating	1961	1991
Copied from another student on a test or exam	26	52
Helped another student to cheat on a test	23	37
Used crib notes to cheat on a test or exam	16	27

Note. From "What We Know About Cheating in College: Longitudinal Trends and Recent Developments," by D. L. McCabe and L. K. Trevino, 1996, *Change, 28*(1), p. 31. Reprinted with permission of the Helen Dwight Reid Educational Foundation. Published by Heidref Publications, 1319 18th St. N.W., Washington, DC 20036-1802. Copyright © 1996.

assignments had changed only modestly over three decades," although they also noted "significant changes in selected forms of cheating," including "modest to significant increases in individual forms of cheating on tests and examinations" (p. 69).

Another avenue to investigate perceived changes in cheating was pursued by R. B. Ludeman (1988), who surveyed a random sample of chief student affairs officers at 153 two- and four-year public and private institutions and asked them to describe their institutions' current experiences with academic dishonesty compared with 10 years previous.[5] A majority of the respondents (63%) said that their institutions had experienced about the same amount of academic dishonesty, 29% indicated that there had been an increase in academic dishonesty, and 8% said that there had been a decline. A similar finding that chief student affairs officers perceive continuing problems with academic dishonesty was reported by Aaron and Georgia (1994).

PERCEPTIONS OF CHEATING

Students and teachers have been questioned about their perceptions of cheating at both the high school and college level. Not surprisingly, students and their teachers differ in how they view cheating—including their perceptions regarding both the frequency and the seriousness of the behavior—with teachers tending to believe that cheating happens less and that is a more serious offense. The differences are strikingly portrayed in the report by Lispon and McGavern (1993) concerning cheating at the Massachusetts Institute of Technology (MIT). The authors quoted one faculty member and one graduate teaching assistant regarding their views:

Faculty Member: I think you should bear in mind that many students—I hope and believe most—could never

---

[5]The survey asked about all forms of academic dishonesty; it was not limited to cheating on tests.

	dream of cheating no matter what the pressures, opportunities or incentives.
Graduate Teaching Assistant:	Copying is so common at MIT. I think students even forget that it is cheating. (Lipson & McGavern, 1993, p. 4)

Perceptions of Elementary and Secondary School Students and Their Teachers

Only two studies have directly compared the perceptions of students and their teachers at the middle school and high school level. In one study, 130 high school students and 10 of their teachers were asked to classify 10 test-related behaviors as cheating or not cheating. The behaviors included actions such as copying during an exam, looking at notes during a test, and giving an answer to another student. The groups were also asked to rate the seriousness of each behavior on a scale ranging from 0 (*not serious*) to 5 (*very serious*). For all 10 behaviors, the percentage of teachers classifying the behavior as cheating exceeded the percentage of students who did so; in 7 of the 10 cases, 100% of the teachers agreed that the behavior constituted cheating. Similarly, the teachers' ratings always reflected a greater seriousness in their attitude toward the behaviors than the students' ratings did (McLaughlin & Ross, 1989).

Evans and Craig (1990b) administered a 120-item scale to 358 middle schoolers, 1,405 high schoolers, and 107 teachers from a suburban school district in Washington state. The instrument consisted of four subscales designed to measure different aspects of cheating.

The first subscale assessed the extent to which cheating was believed to be a problem. Overall, 61.0% of students viewed cheating as a serious problem compared with 69.5% of teachers who said so—a statistically significant difference. However, although students at both grade levels tended to see cheating as a more serious problem than their teachers, the perceptions were not the same for middle schoolers and high school students. The difference between middle students and their teachers was substantial (61.4% vs. 50.1%); the perception gap narrowed between high school teachers and their students, with 70.0% of teachers and 71.3% of students perceiving cheating to be a serious problem.

However, teachers and their students had similar perceptions about other aspects of cheating. Analyzing the responses to the first subscale item by item, Evans and Craig (1990b) concluded:

> A majority (51% or more) of both teachers and students in all schools agreed that students usually know when cheating occurs in class, rarely complain to fellow students whom they know are cheating, and typically do not report cheating to their teachers. Similar agreement held for the notion that students who cheat usually see nothing wrong with it. (p. 46)

The second subscale attempted to determine whether differences existed between students and teachers regarding what constitutes cheating. The scale required students and teachers to rate 24 items describing various behaviors with regard to whether the behaviors were cheating. Although high school students appeared to be no more knowledgeable about forms of cheating than middle schoolers, analysis of the responses again revealed significant differences between students and their teachers, with teachers having "a more advanced understanding of cheating" (Evans & Craig, 1990b, p. 47), Evans and Craig also noted that there was

> considerable uncertainty about specific attributes of cheating, especially regarding student exchange of test information. For example, teachers were stronger and more uniform in their understanding that cheating includes giving as well as receiving unauthorized advance test information. (p. 47)

Perceptions of College Students and Their Professors

As in the middle school and high school case, college students and their instructors tend to view cheating differently. For their part, students tend not to view cheating as very serious. In his survey, Baird (1980) asked whether students disapproved of cheating: 40% said they did not, 29% of those who admitted cheating said they never felt guilty about it, and 75% said that cheating was "a normal part of life." When asked how they would react to observing another student cheat on a test, 80.5% of the students in Baird's study said they would do nothing; only 1% indicated that they would report the incident.

Knowlton and Hamerlynck (1967) surveyed students from a small liberal arts college ($n = 165$) and from a large metropolitan university ($n = 533$) about their own frequency of cheating and their perceptions regarding how much cheating in general occurred at their schools. At one of the schools, the authors found that 81% of the students admitted cheating during their college careers and 46% admitted cheating during the semester just completed. They found that students who reported greater frequency of personal cheating also tended to perceive more cheating by others. Another interesting difference in perceptions was revealed: Knowlton and Hamerlynck (1967) observed that "the data suggest that the deviant [i.e., cheating] individual's estimate may have been *more accurate* than that of the non-deviant" (p. 384).

Sherrill, Salisbury, Horowitz, and Friedman (1971) confirmed these results to some extent. They asked about the perceptions of cheating in two groups: those who had been identified as cheaters in an experimental phase of the study (described earlier) and those who had not cheated when given an opportunity to do so. Sherrill et al. (1991) found that cheaters' estimates of the amount of cheating were much higher than noncheaters, although both groups' perceptions of the amount of cheating "were appreciably lower than the actual incidence of cheating" (p. 508).

The research of Stern and Havlicek (1986), in addition to examining the extent to which students admitted to certain cheating behaviors in college, asked students and their instructors to classify a list of behaviors as constituting or not constituting academic dishonesty. The last two columns of Table 2.4 illustrate the discrepancy between student and teacher perceptions. For every type of cheating studied, professors were more likely to label them as cheating compared with their students. These results are nearly identical to those observed in a previous study of 802 students and 678 faculty at Iowa State University (Barnett & Dalton, 1981).

A similar study was conducted in which all faculty and a sample of 131 undergraduate students at a small independent university were surveyed. Both groups were asked to rate the dishonesty of 18 behaviors on a 6-point scale, ranging from 0 (*not at all dishonest*) to 5 (*very severe dishonesty*). Although not included as a rating point on the scale, a midpoint of 2.5 might be considered to be *moderately dishonest*.

By this criterion, there was some agreement on the part of faculty and students: All of the examination-related cheating behaviors were rated to be at least moderately dishonest by both students and faculty members. However, as in previous studies, students were much less harsh in their judgments, with students' mean ratings lower than faculty ratings for every examination-related cheating behavior. For example, students rated the severity of "receiving the questions for an exam from an unauthorized source prior to taking it" to be 3.86, whereas faculty members pegged that behavior at 4.73, on average. "Helping other students by giving them questions to an exam" was rated 3.20 by students compared with the faculty's mean of 4.33. "Using cheat notes during an exam" received an average rating of 4.18 from students and 4.79 from their instructors (Sims, 1995, p. 236).

Faculty members ($n = 48$) at a private Catholic university were unanimous in classifying 11 behaviors as at least somewhat severe forms of cheating. One hundred percent of faculty viewed the following 8 behaviors to be cheating: looking at notes during a test, arranging to give or receive answers by signal, copying during an exam, asking for answers during an exam, taking a test for someone else, giving answers during an exam, allowing a student to copy on a test, and finding a copy of an exam and memorizing the answers. For 3 other behaviors—getting answers from a student in an earlier section, giving test questions to a student in a later section, and using an old test to study without the teacher's knowledge—the percentages of faculty who viewed the behaviors as cheating were 92.9, 86.8, and 66.0, respectively. In every case, the majority of students also viewed these behaviors as cheating; however, the percentage of students rating them as such never equaled or exceeded faculty members' perceptions. Student ratings for these behaviors ranged from 99.6% to 93.5% (Graham, Monday, O'Brien, & Steffen, 1994). In an interesting twist, Graham et al. also asked students to rate how severe they thought faculty perceptions of each behavior would be, and they asked faculty to do the same regarding student perceptions. As expected, for all 11 behaviors, faculty members underestimated how severe students thought the cheating behaviors were. Students, however, were remarkably accurate in their estimates of how severe faculty considered the behaviors to be.

One exception to the general pattern of student and teacher perceptions is the work of Livosky and Tauber (1994), who surveyed students ($n = 446$) and faculty ($n = 97$) from a public university and a private university, both located in Pennsylvania. Their survey described 10 potential cheating situations involving in-class examinations, for which respondents judged (yes or no) whether or not the situation constituted cheating. Situations ranged from merely planning to cheat, to cheating when an occasion to do so presented itself (so-called opportunistic cheating), to actually carrying out a plan to cheat (i.e., intentional cheating). Livosky and Tauber found that students tended to be more strict in their judgments about cheating. For example, students, to a greater degree than their professors, perceived the mere preparation of a cheat sheet with only the intent to use it as an example of cheating; students were also more likely than faculty to classify making plans to sit next to someone with an intention of copying during an exam as cheating. On the other hand, students and faculty members were nearly equally likely to view other behaviors as cheating; for example, 94% of faculty and 96% of students classified as cheating the actions of a student who makes elaborate plans to sit next to another student and is seen repeatedly looking at the student's answer sheet during an examination. (Livosky and Tauber did not ask the seemingly quite interesting follow-up question regarding why the other 6% of the faculty members did not consider such behavior to be cheating!)

Overall, the research on perceptions of cheating portrays a fairly clear picture. Compared with their instructors, students tend to view cheating as more common, less serious, and more justified. Most of the studies of students' and instructors' views have examined these differential perceptions at a single time point. This general conclusion must be qualified, however; at least one study (Sims, 1995) examined the differential perceptions over time and found that the gulf between faculty and student perceptions of cheating tends to narrow as students approach graduation from college.

STUDENTS' REASONS FOR CHEATING

As one would probably suspect, there is essentially one major reason why students cheat. Perhaps this is one of the instances in which research was unnecessary because the findings would be obvious: Students cheat, primarily, to get a better grade. Of course, there are other reasons for doing so. (My own desire to be noticed in seventh grade comes to mind.) And, with the passage of time, new reasons for cheating have emerged that were not present or noticed by research conducted before 1980. For example, Covington (1992) suggested that students' desire to maintain a positive self-image can lead to cheating. According to Covington, students who expend much effort to perform a task on which they subsequently fail are confronted with the discomfiting possibility that the failure was caused by a lack of ability. As a hedge against this potentially threatening blow to self-image, students sometimes cheat. A fuller description of relevant research on the reasons students give for cheating is briefly reviewed in the following sections.

Reasons Given by High School Students

Some of the earliest research on reasons for cheating was published by W. W. Ludeman (1938) in his "Study of Cheating in Public Schools." W. W. Ludeman found that high school students named the desire to get better grades as their primary reason for cheating. Subsequent research has confirmed that wanting good grades is the number-one reason for cheating among high school students; however, additional reasons have also emerged.

Four reasons were identified by Trabue (1962). According to Trabue, students cheat because of (a) a need to meet external pressures (such as grades), (b) the overly difficult nature of assignments or tests, (c) the overly easy nature of the work, and (d) their feelings that some school-related tasks seem meaningless. Two of these factors—meaninglessness and difficulty of tests—were also revealed in the third subscale used in Evans and Craig's (1990b) study of middle schoolers and high schoolers. Comparing students' and teachers' perceptions of cheating, these authors found that "students generally agreed—but teachers did not—that teachers who are unfriendly, boring or dull, and have high expectations for student performance are more likely to encounter classroom cheating" (p. 48).

A survey of 200 seniors attending a Garden City, New York, high school found that although most students did not believe cheating was justified, those who did—55% of the boys in the study and 33% of the girls—believed that "it was justified when success or survival was in jeopardy" (Cornehlsen, 1965, p. 107). Students comments recorded by Cornehlsen revealed the same focus on grades, difficulty of the work, and parental expectations. Cornehlsen provided the following examples:

- "Marks are more and more necessary for college."
- "Many teachers are unreasonable about assignments. If they are unfair and pile on the work, your have to cheat in order to survive."
- "Some tests are unfair. They don't cover what you have learned."[6]
- "There is too much emphasis on the marks you get rather than what you know."
- "Parents keep pushing. They are not satisfied with less than a B average." (p. 107)

Finally, in a survey of 1,629 high school students in Georgia, Schab (1969) found that fear of failure was given as the main reason for cheating, followed by student laziness and the need to satisfy parental demands for good grades. Interestingly, students in Schab's study also cited the ease with which cheating could be accomplished as a major reason. Being high school students, they also mentioned cheating as helping to fulfill a need to get into college. Bushway and Nash (1977) reviewed numerous studies of cheating and found that many of them "stated that pressure to get grades to gain admittance to college or pressure to maintain their existing average caused many students to cheat" (p. 628).

Reasons Given by College Students

Research on the reasons college students give for cheating reveals the same two primary reasons as mentioned by high school students: concern about grades and time pressures. Attempting to interpret the results of his experiment (described earlier), Drake (1941) conjectured that "the crux of the situation is the competition for marks" (p. 420) and found that students "tend to cheat in proportion to their needs" (p. 419).

The survey conducted by C. P. Smith, Ryan, and Diggins (1972) was among the first to directly ask college students why they cheated. Students were asked to rate various pressures that might influence them to cheat on a scale ranging from 1 (*weak pressure*) to 9 (*strong pressure*). The pressures rated as strongest by male students in the study included (in decreasing order): graduate school requirements, competition for grades, heavy workload, and insufficient study time. Female students cited the same factors, but in a slightly different order.

Given a list of eight choices (and permitted to indicate more than one reason), students in the research conducted by Baird (1980) identified competition for grades as the primary reason for cheating (35%). Not enough study time finished second (33%), a heavy workload was the third most frequently cited reason (26%),

---

[6]This comment—that the test didn't cover what a student has learned—is a particularly intriguing one. I have found that there are at least three reasons why this could be the case. First, the student did not learn much. Second, the student did not learn what had been intended by the instructor. Third, the test really is "unfair."

The first possibility may be related to intelligence, effort, aptitude, learning style, persistence, quality of instruction, or a host of other issues. In any case, a test that revealed what a student did not know would not in itself be the problem but an indicator of a different problem. The second possibility is one that teachers can do something about by continually communicating expectations and monitoring that students understand these expectations. Additional information related to this idea is presented in chapter 11. The third possibility is that there are ambiguities or other test construction errors that lead to a student failing to perceive that something that they have learned was being elicited by the test question. Although a complete treatment of strategies for constructing valid tests is beyond the scope of this book, some information on this possibility is also provided in chapter 11.

and "other" was fourth (22%). Two years later, research confirmed that grades were the primary motivation for cheating, finding that "sixty-eight percent [of students surveyed] believed cheating was a direct result of competition for grades" (Singhal, 1982, p. 779).

G. E. Stevens and Stevens (1987) investigated cheating among 210 business students and identified 14 different categories of reasons for cheating. However, the most important explanations of cheating were students' beliefs that "cheating required less effort and that it was perceived as the best way to get ahead" (p. 27). The authors also discovered students' most important reasons for not engaging in cheating: the individual student's personal values and philosophy. It also is interesting to note also Stevens and Stevens' finding that, for those behaviors "viewed as basically unethical or highly unethical, students report that they practice these behaviors infrequently if at all" (p. 27). (Of course, one might surmise, with tongue in cheek, that the correct interpretation of this finding is uncertain, given the information presented previously in this chapter regarding the self-reported cheating behavior of business students.)

Following up on the work of Stevens and Stevens (1987), Payne and Nantz (1994) analyzed quantitative data from a survey of student beliefs and conducted focused interviews of 19 college students. Their survey revealed that 40% of students admitted cheating at least once on a test and 46% admitted cheating on a quiz. Their interviews helps shed some light on students' reasons for cheating and their understanding of the concept:

> In our interviews, however, social accounts that either were not included in the Stevens and Stevens survey, or were not highly rated in it, received considerable expression, particularly peer pressure, selective definition of cheating, and the placing of blame on teachers and classroom settings.... According to many students, there is a significant difference between cheating on exams ("blatant" cheating) and other forms of academic cheating (often viewed as less serious, or "not really" cheating). (Payne & Nantz, 1994, p. 93)

A questionnaire about students' reasons for cheating was administered to students following Zastrow's (1970) ingenious "powdered lead carbonate in an atmosphere of hydrogen sulfide gas" study to determine the frequency of cheating. Zastrow found that the primary reason given by the group of graduate students was "pressure to obtain good grades" (p. 158), although many students also identified what Zastrow termed "handicaps" as reasons for cheating. These included pressures created by time spent working at part-time jobs, participation in extracurricular activities, and being unprepared for the test. Reasons that centered on course instructors were also given, including "poor instructors," "unannounced tests," and "inadequate time to complete tests" (p. 159).

An abundance of reasons for cheating were studied by Haines, Diekhoff, LaBeff, and Clark (1986) in their investigation of *neutralization*. Neutralization refers, essentially, to denial of responsibility for improper actions because of the improper actions of others. Put another way, in the minds of some students, two wrongs really do make a right, or at least come out to be a wash. The top 10 neutralization reasons[7] showing the greatest differentiation between cheaters and noncheaters from the Haines et al. study are shown in Table 2.6.

---

[7]These reasons shown in the table are ranked according to the degree to which the reason differentiates between higher frequency and lower frequency of students' self-reported cheating behavior.

TABLE 2.6
Top 10 "Neutralization" Reasons for Cheating

Rank	Reason
10	People sitting around me made no attempt to cover their papers.
9	Don't have time to study because I am working to pay for school.
8	In danger of losing scholarship because of low grades.
7	Everyone else seems to be cheating.
7	The course material is too hard.
5	The course information seems useless.
4	The instructor doesn't seem to care if I learn the material.
3	A friend asked me to cheat and I couldn't say no.
3	The instructor left the room during the test.
1	The instructor assigns too much material.

Note. Adapted with permission from "College Cheating: Immaturity, Lack of Commitment, and the Neutralizing Attitude," by V. J. Haines, G. M. Diekhoff, E. E. LaBeff, and R. E. Clark, 1986, *Research in Higher Education, 25*(4), p. 347.

In fact, some evidence suggests that students view cheating as necessary beyond merely neutralizing. For example, research by Greene and Saxe (1992) showed that most students believed that others benefitted more from cheating than they did. Also, related to the "contagion of cheating," another researcher found that students report beginning to cheat when they see "lazy students getting better grades through cheating" (Moffatt, 1990, p. 5).

Research by Genereux and McLeod (1995) distinguished between reasons given by college students for two kinds of cheating: planned and spontaneous. Although the order of the reasons given for these types differed, the five major reasons were the same: (a) the perception that the instructor didn't care, (b) dependence of financial aid on a student's grades, (c) unfairness of examinations, (d) a lack of vigilance on the part of the instructor, and (e) the impact of course grades on the student's long-term goals.

Finally, one researcher asked college students why they permitted other students to copy from them during an exam, which at most colleges and universities also is considered cheating. It is only somewhat comforting that cheating for cash was cited as a reason by less than 8% of the students surveyed in this research. A sample of some of the other reasons discovered by S. F. Davis et al. (1992) is shown in Table 2.7.

CONCLUSIONS

What can be concluded about the frequency of, perceptions about, and reasons for cheating in high school and college? At least one confident observation can be made: This is not a case in which the research evidence presents a murky picture.

First, when students claim that "everyone's doing it," they are only slightly exaggerating. Surveys of students consistently reveal that 50% or more of students

TABLE 2.7

Top Reasons for Letting Other Students Copy During an Examination

Rank	Reason
1	He was bigger than me.
2	I knew they needed to do good in order to pass the class. I felt sorry for them.
3	I wouldn't want them to be mad at me.
4	She was damn good looking.
5	Because they might let me cheat off them sometime.
6	No particular reason. It doesn't bother me because I probably got it wrong and so will they.
7	I knew they studied and knew the material, but test taking was really difficult.
8	Just to do it. I didn't like the teacher, and I knew if I got caught nothing would happen.

Note. Adapted with permissin from "Academic Dishonesty: Prevalence, Determinants, Techniques, and Punishments," by S. F. Davis, C. A. Grover, A. H. Becker, and L. N. McGregor, 1992, *Teaching of Psychology, 19*(1), p. 17.

admit to cheating on examinations or other assessments. The percentage begins at a fairly high level in middle school and high school. The proportion of students who admit to cheating on tests is even higher in college samples. Research on the accuracy of self-reported cheating reveals that the startlingly high percentages admitted by students are probably correct. Some research even suggests that the levels may actually be underestimated. Findings from experimental studies—those in which an "opportunity" to cheat presents itself—also provide support for the accuracy of self-reported survey data. When structured conditions are established in which the potential to cheat is present and the action of cheating can be reliably detected, a great percentage of students choose to do so.

Some writers have claimed that levels of cheating are high and climbing higher. There is certainly evidence of the former. Concerning the latter, trend studies of reported cheating have yielded mixed results, with some showing increasing cheating and others revealing that the proportion of students who admit to cheating has reached a plateau. In any event, one conclusion from the trend studies is clear: All agree that the proportion is high and not going down.

The perceptions students and their instructors have regarding cheating are accurate in some respects and inaccurate in others. Students tend to see the pervasiveness of cheating about as it is. Even students who do not admit to cheating themselves perceive that there's "a whole lotta cheatin' goin' on." Their instructors tend not to see—or choose to report—the same levels of cheating behaviors in the classroom. Also, instructors tend to be off the mark when compared with how their students view the seriousness of cheating. The consistent finding is that teachers view cheating—from trivial to major—more seriously than their students do.

The relevant research has also borne out what might have been guessed about the reasons students cheat. They do it, primarily, to get higher grades. This is true at the elementary, secondary, and postsecondary levels. The concern about higher grades might, in turn, be motivated by other factors, such as desire to get into a college or a graduate program or the desire to get a good job. A second commonly asserted reason for cheating is that school tasks are too difficult or too time-consuming. Although these assertions are, to some extent, distinct from grades as a reason for cheating, there is obviously considerable overlap. The commonly cited reasons of "not enough study time" and "heavy workload" seem related, not distinct, factors. The overlap may, in truth, be even greater. For example, a student who was unconcerned about grades would not necessarily begrudge a difficult assignment or worry about a lack of study time. Thus, it is reasonable to speculate that the diversity of students' reasons yielded by various studies of cheating can probably be lumped into the single category of grades.

In this chapter, conclusions about the reasons students cheat were derived from students' own explanations. However, a more thorough immersion into what motivates students to cheat and factors related to the extent of students' cheating behavior is reserved for a subsequent chapter on the correlates of cheating. In the next chapter, however, we take a minor diversion and turn our attention to the methods students use to accomplish the (frequent) feat.

✦ T H R E E ✦

How to Cheat

A Compendium of Methods

**FIG. 3.1. Ring around the scholar. From FRANK & ERNEST.
Copyright © United Feature Syndicate. Reprinted by permission.**

This chapter presents everything I know about the methods used to cheat on tests. Which is not to say that it is comprehensive. *Au contraire.* I suspect that what is documented here is the tip of the iceberg. Methods used to cheat on tests are like snowflakes: There is an infinite number of possibilities.

The possibilities are, however, related to the type of testing being considered. For the past 50 years or so, most of the tests given in elementary schools through the college level and beyond have used objective-type question formats. These formats usually require the test taker to simply select the best or correct answer from options that are provided to them; examples of these formats include multiple-choice, true–false, and matching. Test makers, test administrators, and test takers all have a considerable amount of experience with these formats. Hand in hand with the development of objective formats has been the development of creative ways to cheat on them. Because of the sheer longevity of objective formats, cheating methods associated with them have had time to develop as well.

Over the past 5 to 10 years, educators have witnessed the introduction (or reintroduction) of alternative testing formats, for example, performance assessment and portfolios. The technology of these formats is not nearly as advanced as that of objective formats. Consequently, the methods of cheating on these assessments are also less well developed. In a later chapter, we see that alternative assessment formats may also be less susceptible to cheating, though researchers have not yet addressed that issue. Some of the cheating methods described in this chapter are useful almost exclusively on objective-type tests. Others are used exclusively for essay tests or other formats. A few can be adapted to nearly any format.[1]

THE RISKY BUSINESS OF DOCUMENTING CHEATING METHODS

Numerous aspects of human personality, intelligence, physical skills, and so on are found to be distributed normally. This means, for example, that a small proportion of adults are very tall, a few are very short, but most of us are about "average." So, too, with the creative component of cheating methods: A few of the methods are simplistic; a few are brilliant; most are remarkably ordinary. I suspect that only those who choose the rather simplistic methods are likely to get caught. Those who devise the most creative methods become the stuff of urban legends. Users of mundane methods probably slog through the educational system little noticed. This is not particularly a good thing, but it is the reality of the situation.

This chapter focuses on how cheating occurs. There are, of course, at least two risks in including such a chapter. First, and most obvious, is the risk of influencing those who *take* tests—that a catalogue of methods might fall into the hands of wayward students who will use the methods described for ill-gotten gain. Those concerned about the validity of test results would hope that a compendium of methods wouldn't fall into students' hands at all. Perhaps such a chapter might even influence students who are not particularly apt to cheat to begin engaging in the behavior on seeing the myriad methods and learning (in subsequent chapters) about the minuscule probability of being caught and the generally ineffective responses even for those who are caught.

A second risk is that those who *give* tests might be adversely affected. Once one comprehends the pervasiveness of cheating and having some exposure to the breadth of possibilities described in this chapter, the tendency to see cheating everywhere would be understandable. As Drake (1941) suggested, the teacher knowledgeable about cheating could turn into "a martinet during examinations, constantly on the alert for signs of dishonesty" (p. 418). As regards the trust and mentoring relationship between student and teacher that is deemed facilitative to learning, such a predilection would be highly undesirable.

The risks notwithstanding, this chapter on methods of cheating is included because—I believe—the potential benefits outweigh these risks. First, as demonstrated by the research reports summarized in the preceding chapter, cheating is so

---

[1]For most of the methods described in this chapter, distinctions as to whether a particular method is more useful for one format or another are not made. The type of testing to which the method applies is usually obvious.

prevalent in schools that it is hard to see how it could become more so. The "ceiling" for admitted cheating is 100%. No studies have reported a figure that high, though we are approaching that figure. The fear that cheating might increase is similar to worrying about grade inflation. As grade point averages (GPAs) rise near the top of the grade scale, the tiny room left at the top of the GPA scale makes it difficult to claim that any additional inflation has occurred. Once everyone is awarded an A, grade inflation essentially disappears as a concept; even the ability to detect further inflation is lost. So, too, with cheating. Given the state of affairs, it is hard to imagine—even if a chapter on methods did influence some students to cheat—that the increase would be noticeable.

In any case, it is not necessary to accept the hypothesis that the net result of presenting methods of cheating will be an increase in the behavior. Broad knowledge about methods of cheating should benefit those who must guard against it. Thus, any possible increase in cheating by those who take tests is, to an unknown extent, at least partially offset by a concurrent increase in the likelihood of perceiving cheating by those who give tests. The theory is analogous to the training of U.S. Treasury agents to spot counterfeit currency. The agents first become thoroughly familiar with the genuine article, but their training is supplemented on a continuing basis by exposure to the methods and intense scrutiny of the products of those who bang out bogus bills. By the same token, teachers and others who give tests may, as a result of exposure to the methods of cheating, be better prepared to prevent and detect the behavior, resulting in a consequent *reduction* in its frequency of occurrence.

As regards the second risk—that some teachers might become jaded and perceive cheating behind every bush—this is certainly a possibility. On the other hand, it is hoped that those who give tests will become more suspicious—in a *healthy* way—and become more attentive to preventing, detecting, and responding to cheating. Above all, it would necessarily be a good thing if the concern about cheating led to changes in classroom environments—changes that promoted an atmosphere more conducive to learning and in which students perceived that cheating would only impede their path toward acquisition of knowledge and skills that they valued.

A TAXONOMY OF EDUCATIONAL CHEATING

The variety of methods of cheating can be classified into three primary domains: (a) cheating by taking, giving, or receiving information from others; (b) cheating through the use of forbidden materials or information; and (c) cheating by circumventing the process of assessment. Simple examples of each domain include, respectively, copying from another student during a test, use of a "cheat sheet," and a student's arranging to take a test at a time other than the regularly scheduled time. As listed, the order of the domains probably also represents their relative frequency of use; that is, a sideways glance at a classmate's paper is more common than the use of crib notes, which is more common than attempting to take an examination at a later date.

There are, of course, methods that cross the boundaries. For example, a fairly common method used by college students involves leaving a notebook, textbook, or even an accomplice in a rest room. During an examination the student asks to be excused to use the rest room—a request that few instructors would deny. Once there, the student can review notes or textbooks or discuss the matter with the accomplice. This method involves all three domains: the use of unauthorized materials, receiving information from others, and taking advantage of the circumstances of testing.

There could also be subclassifications within the three domains. For example, the use of forbidden materials or unauthorized information can be accomplished by means of paper copy, electronic devices, clothing, bodily inscription, and so on. In the following sections, cheating methods within each of the three major domains are presented. Some of the methods used for cheating have attained legendary status; three such stories are presented in a subsequent section of this chapter. A final section looks at some of the ways advanced technology is being used to cheat on tests and other academic tasks.

Giving, Taking, and Receiving

Cheating occurs when, contrary to established rules, one person gives information to another person during a test. As the studies in the previous chapter have demonstrated, most students and their teachers perceive the person who gives information willingly, the willing recipient, and the person who takes information without the knowledge or permission of another to be guilty of cheating. The following situations show some of the variety of ways that giving, taking, and receiving (GTR) is accomplished. The methods are presented, roughly, in order of least to greatest sophistication, though such ordering is purely subjective.

GTR1:   A student looks at another student's test paper, answer sheet, or work during a test.

GTR2:   A student drops his or her paper on the floor, permitting another student to look at it.

GTR3:   Two or more students drop their papers on the floor at different times. Unknown to the instructor, who does not see which student's paper was dropped, the recipient who picks up the paper is not the one who dropped it. Instead, the student looks at the other student's paper, then drops it again, in order that the giver can reclaim it.

GTR4:   A variation of GTR1 involves a group of students who, either through friendship or compensation, collude to seat in such a way as to coordinate copying when an instructor permits students to choose their seats. A student of mine told me about a technique known as the "Flying V" or the "Power Wedge" formation shown in Fig. 3.2. The information giver—considered by the others to be a good source of information—sits in the seat marked "G"; the receivers sit in seats marked "R," with other, uninvolved, students in the remaining seats.

GTR5:   A giver and receiver communicate with sign language. One interesting variation of sign language cited by DePalma (1992) is the use of different colored M&Ms to signal answers to multiple-choice questions.

GTR6:   A giver and receiver share an eraser or other permissible item that is passed back and forth with answers or information written on it.

GTR7:   Two or more test takers devise a code for transmitting answers and a method for doing so. For example, clicking pens, taps of the foot, po-

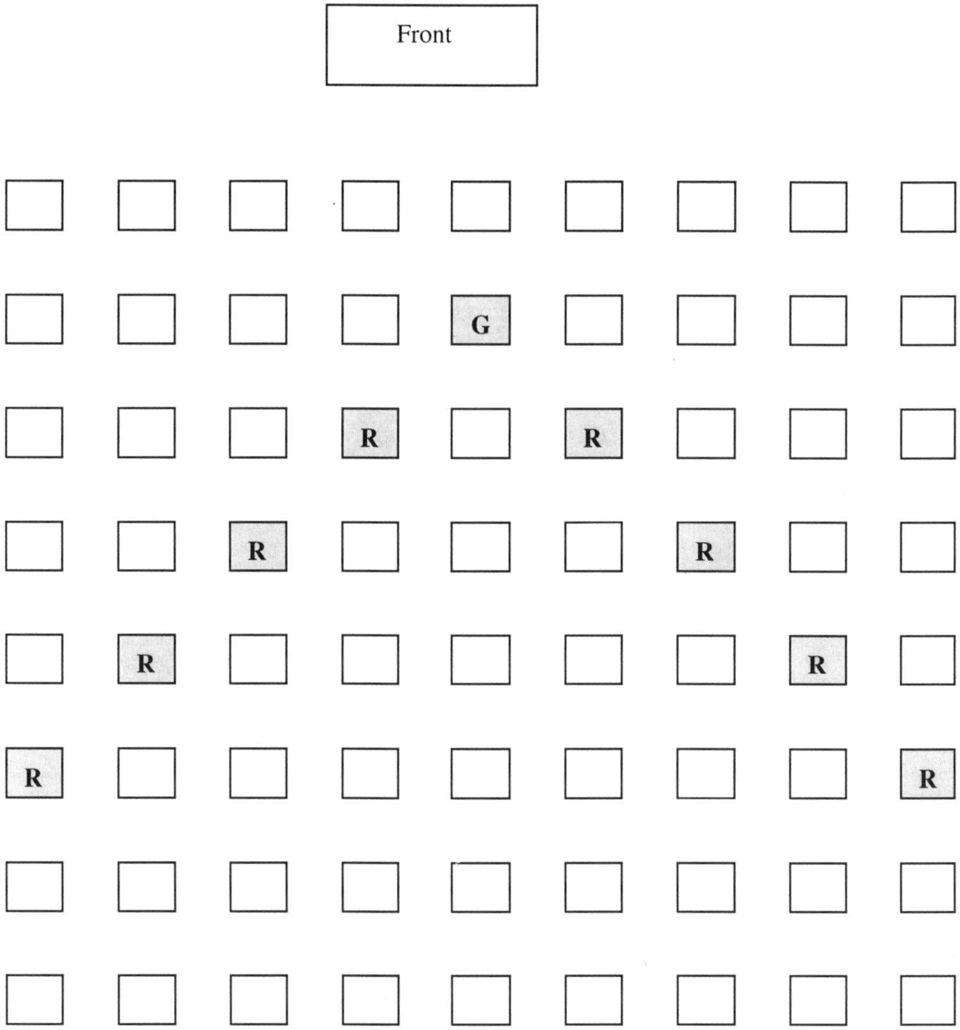

Front

FIG. 3.2. The "Flying V" copying formation.
G = giver of test information; R = receiver of test information.

sition of the hands on the desk, and so on. A couple of particularly good systems involve a giver placing an eraser or other object in a predetermined corner of his desk to indicate an answer to a multiple-choice item: upper left corner is A, upper right corner is B, and so on. For true–false tests, variations involve the giver rubbing one eye for true, the other for false; holding a pencil vertically for true, horizontally for false; moving right foot forward for true, left foot for false, and so forth. (One student told me of cheating that involved the giver simply tipping her head slightly to the left or right.)

GTR8: Several high-tech versions of GTR7 exist. For example, a code is devised using the four corners of cinder blocks, bulletin boards, or ceiling tiles and a small laser pointer, some of which are made to look like an ordinary pen. The giver uses the pointer to point to a corner of a bulletin board, wall tile, and so on, with each corner predetermined to represent an answer. One student told me of a particularly humorous situation in which the answers were pointed out using the letters that appeared on a poster behind the desk (and view) of the instructor.

GTR9:   A small mirror is useful for the occasional emergency when (ostensibly) a contact lens irritates the eye. While holding the mirror up to the face and pretending to fuss with the eye, the test taker uses the occasion to view the test paper of a person located behind her.

GTR10:   A student sits near the back of the testing room. When the student has a question, he or she takes the long walk to the front of the room where (usually) the instructor is seated. On the way, the student views the work of other students.

GTR11:   Using the same approach as GTR10, a student engages the instructor in a conversation about, for example, an unclear test question. During the conversation, the student views the work of students who have already turned in their work, which is readily observable on the instructor's desk.

GTR12:   A student sits near the door or window of the classroom so that he or she can obtain assistance from an associate outside the room. (I learned of this method from a student from Bangladesh, who told me of her experience taking a high school examination: "While taking the examination, I kept hearing noises, and the person in front of me kept looking out the window. When I listened carefully, I kept hearing the names of Mughal emperors and the British Lords who ruled East India. I realized that the person in front of me was whispering 'Battle of Plessy' to a companion lying outside beneath the window. The companion was, in turn, telling her the events, dates, and major figures of the war.")

GTR13:   A fast-working and better prepared student who will give information completes a test quickly and, during the test, writes as many answers as possible on a scrap of paper (best if crumpled or wadded up), eraser, and so on. One or more students who will receive information work during the test on questions they know. When finished, the fast-working student turns in his or her test, delivering the scrap of paper or eraser to the receiver, depositing it in a garbage can for the receiver, or simply dropping it on the floor near the receiver's seat.

GTR14:   The giver takes two copies of a test, two answer sheets, or simply uses a blank sheet of "scratch paper." The two pieces of paper are placed on top of each other as the giver works through the test, taking care to press firmly when writing words, numbers, letters, or filling in the bubbles on an answer sheet. The apparently blank sheet is then passed, dropped, or in any way delivered to the receiver. The use of firm pressure results in an impression on the blank sheet which can be "read" by another student when held at an angle to light, felt with the fingers, or simply revealed by sketching with a soft pencil. (This method works particularly well with bubble sheets requiring the receiver to merely fill in the bubbles for which there is an impression.)

GTR15: Although I have not personally seen these in action, I understand that there are small devices called Newtons made by the Apple Computer Company, which are about the size of a calculator. With one of these devices, students are capable of sending and receiving information between each other. An issue of *American Teacher* ("New Age of Stealth Cheating," 1995) warned teachers about a similar device made by the Sega toy corporation designated the IR7000, a calculator–organizer that enables students to send infrared messages to each other across the classroom.

Using Forbidden Materials

There are many occasions in which it is desirable for a student to use resources when taking a test. Such an occasion is involved in a course I regularly teach, for which certain equations, charts, and tables are provided in the textbook. In many cases, memorization of the formula or table is not nearly so important to me as knowledge of how to *use* the formula—or even which formula to use. In these cases, I usually permit students to use their books or notes, or I provide a sheet with all of the information, or I permit students to create and use their own pages containing any formulas, equations, and so on, that they deem necessary for a test. I do this when I believe that the resources provided would ordinarily be available to anyone actually working in the field. For example, when I want to determine how much longer a given test would need to be made in order to achieve some predetermined reliability, I look up the Spearman–Brown formula. When I need to do this calculation, I look up the formula. For students in my classes, I only expect them to know when the Spearman–Brown formula is appropriate for a given situation. If a calculation is necessary, they simply decide which formula is appropriate and refer to a reference source to find the formula.

On the other hand, there are times when a person who gives a test expects the test takers to know certain, factual information or rules without having to look them up. For example, suppose that an air traffic controller directed a pilot to enter an airspace 10 miles east of an airport at an altitude of 10,000 feet. The pilot, currently at 30,000 feet, 90 miles east of the airport would calculate that he must begin a descent on reaching a distance of 50 miles from the airport. The competent pilot correctly applies certain rules (e.g, a descent rate of 500 feet per mile) and knowledge about fuel economy (it is preferable to remain at a higher altitude to minimize fuel consumption) to determine—without referring to a manual—what action must be taken.

Much testing at all levels of the American educational system is, necessarily, designed to assess students' knowledge of basic facts, ability to apply rules, or, in the case of essay items, oral examinations and performance tests to determine whether the student can construct a response relying on information assumed to be mastered previously. The storehouse of previous knowledge that a student possesses comes into play when the overall quality of the student's performance is evaluated. To expand the storehouse, students frequently rely on sources of information that they do not truly posses, as in the case of crib notes, cheat sheets, and so on. When the test giver seeks an understanding of the extent of students' independent knowledge or skill grounded in the students' particular storehouse of information, outside sources of information or other materials—what are called in this section *forbidden materials* (FM)—are disallowed during testing.

Obviously, making the formal announcement that students are forbidden to use certain materials during an examination is an altogether different matter than ensuring FMs are not used. The following list does not address the variety of materials that might be used but *how* students secrete those materials into the testing environment.

FM1:   The infamous crib sheet or cheat sheet is a widely known method of cheating. Small bits of paper or other material containing information are found on or in, for example, the pocket of a calculator; between the lines of a calculator instruction booklet; taped underneath the brim of a baseball cap; under the crystal face of a watch; long narrow strips of paper, tightly rolled and inserted into the barrel of a clear plastic ball point pen; slips of paper inserted into a bag of potato chips or other food; taped to the inside surface of the free end of a belt; pinned under the flap or between the pleats of a skirt (girls); pinned to the underside of a necktie (boys); pinned to the inside of a long, exposed shirt tail, or inside the bib portion of bib overalls, or inside a coat (girls or boys); placed in a roll of toilet paper for use during an excused trip to the rest room (I have heard this particular method referred to as "taking a number three?"); and simply underneath the person (sitting on a cheat sheet is probably the most common form of concealment).

FM2:   Scrap paper is frequently permitted for students's use in writing a draft essay response, performing calculations, or sketching out ideas. (Apparently) plain white paper can be transformed into a cheat sheet by writing out volumes of information with a ball point pen that has run out of ink. The impressions are rarely visible unless a person views the paper from a certain angle.

The same method can be used to inscribe information onto the cover of a notebook, which is left, closed, on the desk or on the floor nearby. The impressions are more easily viewed if the cover of the notebook is dark blue or black.

FM3:   A variation of FM2 is to "write" information on the blank scrap paper using White Out.

FM4:   Information can be written on something other than a cheat sheet. For example, it can be written on personal articles, such as prescription glasses; inside the lenses of mirrored sunglasses; on keychains, backpacks, or Band-Aids or other bandages; on the surfaces of a beverage can, on a watchband; on an arm, leg, hand, or foot cast; and on white adhesive labels (like those used as mailing labels) attached to the bottom of a student's own shoe or the bottom of a nearby classmate's shoe. Information can be written on masking tape (the wider the width, the greater the amount of information possible) and worn around the wrist under a long-sleeved shirt. This method makes it considerably easier to write the material legibly than methods in which information is written directly on the skin.

Information can also be written on articles that would ordinarily be permitted during an examination; it can be written on the six sides of an eraser, each side of a pencil, the case for a calculator, and so on.

FM5: Information can be written on the desktop, floor, chair in front of a student, or other location. Pencil is preferred for writing the information because it can be easily removed with a swipe of the finger or hand. The information is usually written immediately prior to the examination. The information can even be written in plain sight on the top of a desk surface and covered with an object, such as a book, a purse, scrap paper, a calculator, or the test itself. One student told me that she witnessed information written extensively on the top surface of a desk close to the edge nearest the student (a girl) who simply leaned forward and rested her breasts on top of the desk whenever the teacher walked nearby.

FM6: A stylistic variation of FM5 is when a student writes the information on the back of a chair prior to an examination. Because classrooms in many schools and universities are not locked at all times, the student simply inscribes the information after hours and arrives early enough for the test to be assured of a seat with a view. It is difficult to accuse a student of cheating when the forbidden information is not on his own desk.

FM7: Information written on a desktop need not even be actually written. Using the eraser end of a pencil, information can be recorded on a desk surface in such a way that it is only visible to the person taking the test.

FM8: In courses where a reference or textbook is permitted for answering questions on a test, additional information can be written in the book, usually using pencil, but inscribed so faintly that it can only be detected by someone who knows that it is there. For example, a student told me of a foreign language class in which examinations consisted, in part, of students translating selections of literature that appeared in the assigned textbook. These were simply translated before the examination and written between the lines in the textbook in a *very* light manner.

FM9: Information can also be written directly on the body, with the surfaces between the fingers a preferred location. Pencil does not work as well on skin as on other surfaces and tends to dissolve if written on a spot where perspiration occurs. Ballpoint pen ink is preferred, though it can be difficult to remove in a hurry when confronted about potential cheating.

One student told me that an individually packaged moist towelette can be saturated with fingernail polish remover or other solvent for those times when the possibility of being confronted arises. Another told me that female students have carefully etched information onto the underside of long fingernails.

FM10: For essay examinations, an extra blue book can be used either for submitting a previously written essay or simply to contain a wealth of information.

Several methods of writing information on various surfaces are so clever as to be distinguished from the others with their own entries, FM11–FM16.

FIG. 3.3. The "info flower"
(illustration by Deborah Wilson).

FM11: A Russian student told me of a method used to hide FM, called *shparglka* in her native tongue. The information is written on a piece of stiff card stock, such as a 3 × 5 card. One corner of the card is punched with a hole, through which one or more rubber bands are attached. The loose end of the rubber band is fitted around the forearm or elbow and the entire apparatus is concealed beneath a long-sleeved shirt. When needed, the person can pull the card from under the shirt and access the information. When finished or when needful, the card is simply released and whisked back up under the shirtsleeve by rubber-band action.

FM12: Another student told me about how a paper flower can be decorated around the edges with all sorts of information (see Fig. 3.3). The "info flower" is then worn as a helpful fashion accessory.

FM13: One of the most clever ideas I have encountered is writing information on tissues. Holding the tissue up to the face allows the reader to gain access to the forbidden information. Subsequent blowing of the nose, sneezing, clearing the throat, or coughing into the tissue then wadding it up virtually ensures that it will not be inspected if cheating is suspected. Similarly, one student told me of an elementary school teacher who permitted students to chew gum in class. A student in the class would write information on gum wrappers. If worried about detection, the student simply deposited the chewed gum into the wrapper, which was never searched. Alternatively, students simply write the information on the stick of gum itself and rewrap it. During an exam, a piece of gum is unwrapped, the information is reviewed, and the gum is chewed, destroying any evidence.

FM14:   A female student told me how a quite large piece of paper could be covered with a substantial amount of information, then folded in a fan-shaped or accordion manner and taped to the inside surfaces of the thighs. When information was needed, the female student—wearing a dress—would simply raise the dress sufficiently to expose information. The student reported that the technique was especially effective in courses taught by male teachers who would not ordinarily be looking for cheat sheets in that area and would be reticent to confront a student about such a suspicion.

FM15:   The cheating shirt is a T-shirt with as much information as possible simply written on it in plain view. The information is written (typically) on the back of the shirt in a decorative or abstract way or combined with unrelated symbols, colors, or words so as to make the relevant information unnoticeable–"the forest for the trees" phenomenon. The shirt is worn by one student; the student behind the student wearing the cheating shirt is the beneficiary of the information. An extension of the concept is to prepare several identical cheating shirts to be worn by a group of students.
Some students have also created posters and hung them on examination room walls prior to a test. This method is most likely to be successful in large college lecture halls where the walls are usually covered with a melange of posters and advertisements anyway. The poster appears to be indistinguishable from a legitimate ad or announcement but contains information in various locations or encoded in such a way as to be virtually undetectable.

FM16:   Because many teachers permit students to have small bottled water containers during a test, an ingenious method of accessing forbidden material was developed by one student who, prior to an examination, carefully removed the label of the bottle, copied valuable information onto the inside of the label, and reapplied the label to the clear plastic bottle. The result was a functional water bottle, with an unremarkable outer label surface but an inner surface that contained information that could be viewed by a person who knew it was there.

FM17:   At the elementary level, at which students are often tested on their ability to perform calculations, calculator watches can be used. At any level, programmable calculators and date books can store a wealth of information. An article in the *Journal of Chemical Education* even named names, citing models such as the Sharp Electronic Organizer Model YO–110 as capable of storing the complete set of notes for most chemistry courses (Eaton, 1995).

FM18:   In large classes or classes in which the instructor permits listening to music during a test, students wear headphones and listen to tapes played on a Walkman. The tape, however, is one on which that student has recorded any desired information. Even in classes in which the use of personal stereos would not be permitted, the device itself is easily hidden under clothing and an earpiece concealed under long hair. One student told me of a classmate who, rather than memorize a speech as required, used this method to deliver a previously recorded speech.

FM19:   Because security is often more lax in elementary and secondary schools, students can, prior to a test, remove test materials from a classroom, a file cabinet, or a teacher's desk or briefcase. Teacher's frequently leave instructor manuals or test-bank disks where these can also be taken or copied. At the college level, the problem of student access to these materials was even the subject of a study by Oles (1975). Using a catalog for the current semester, Oles determined which introductory courses were using textbooks for which an instructor manual and test bank would likely be available. Oles then typed out a crude letter on a Xerox copy of university letterhead requesting the materials for 23 textbooks. Oles signed a fictitious name to each letter, listed a P.O. box number for the return address and mailed the letters to the publishers. Seven publishers did not respond, but 12 of the 16 who did (75%) sent the test manuals.

FM20:   In some cases, an instructor develops two forms of an examination to thwart cheating; half the students get Form A and the other half get Form B. Students sometimes gain access to one of the forms (using any of the variety of other methods of gaining access to forbidden materials) and make a list of answers to be used when the testing period arrives. If the student receives the same form as the one he obtained improperly, he fills in the answers according to plan. However, if the student had obtained an advance copy of Form A but was given Form B in class, the student simply records Form A on his answer sheet as the form he was given.

FM21:   At all levels, even locked rooms containing test materials are frequently readily accessible. In modern or remodeled buildings with so-called drop-in ceiling panels, it is possible to gain entry to a locked room simply by removing one or more panels and climbing in. Of course, this activity represents not only access to FMs but also criminal activity. One ironic example of FM21 was recently reported by the headmaster at Marist Catholic School in DeKalb County, Georgia. Apparently, two upperclassmen stole a key, gained access to a restricted area where tests were kept, then took, copied, and distributed copies of examinations for physics, chemistry, and—yes—religion classes (Loupe, 1998b).

Circumventing or Taking Advantage of the Testing Process

The third class of cheating methods involves taking unfair advantage of the person(s) giving a test or of the circumstances of the testing process. For example, students can take advantage of vague, ambiguous, or uncontrolled test administration protocols, their instructor's willingness to help, or expected social norms of polite behavior. Many of these methods involve cheating *after* a test has been given. In all of them, however, taking advantage of the process (TAP) can result in an inappropriate test score.

TAP1:   An elementary school teacher told me of a cheating method that, until discovered, was used for several months in her second-grade class. The teacher had a work basket into which students placed tests and assignments on completion. One 7-year-old would sometimes deposit her paper into the work basket without her name on it and return to her seat. Moments later, she would rise and go again to the work basket, take a paper out of the basket, and head back to her seat. When asked by the teacher what she was doing, the student indicated that she had forgotten to put her name on her paper. However, unknown to the teacher, the student had not removed her own paper from the work basket, but another (higher achieving) student's paper. She then simply erased the other student's name, wrote in her own, and redeposited the paper.

TAP2: Because teachers rarely make copies of students' papers before grading them, a student can alter their responses *after* a test has been graded. Then, because teachers also rarely can recall the answers all students made, the student simply claims that the paper was misgraded. Realizing that the papers were graded under time pressures, many teachers apologetically acknowledge the "mistake" and change the student's score.

TAP3: On a test of two pages, students can separate the pages and turn in only one of the pages. Bronner (1995) told how, at the end of a test, a student then took the other page, which contained several questions for which she did not know the answer, and went out into the hall to quickly look up the answers. Completing the page, the student then put it on the floor, stepped on it a few times to give it the appearance of being trampled and asked a friend to take it back into the room to the instructor, with the claim that the paper had been found out in the back of the room. Bronner reported that the student received an A on the test.

TAP4: In large classes, particularly at the college level, a student simply has any other well-prepared student go to class on the day of an examination and take the test for him. Or, if the student suspects that his absence from class might be noticed, the student and the substitute both attend the examination. The student works (but not too hard) on a test and turns in a paper without a name on it. The substitute works conscientiously and turns in a test with the student's name on it. (A less frequent variation of this occurs at all levels and involves twins who substitute for one another.)

TAP5: Several students have told me that it is not uncommon for a student who has not prepared for a test to simply not turn in the test or an answer sheet at the end of the test period. When the teacher returns the graded tests and the student does not get one, the student—with mortified expression—wonders how the teacher could have lost his test; after all, the teacher certainly recalls the student being there on the day of the test and working steadily through the test period, and often the reasonable recourse seems to be to allow the student to retake the test. The method does not necessarily ensure a higher grade for the student but, with the additional time to prepare for the test, certainly helps.

A variation of this method is recounted by Bronner (1995, p. 33), who told of a college student who faced two essay questions for a final examination for which responses were to be written in separate blue books. Skimming the two questions, the student realized he was prepared to answer the second question but knew nothing about the first one. As Bronner told the story, "The student labeled his second blue book 'II' and began it with what appeared to be the last sentence or two of the answer to the first essay question. Then on the second page of the second blue book he wrote '2' for the second essay question and a beautiful answer to it." According to Bronner, the student turned in only the second blue book and received a passing grade for the course, in addition to an apology from the instructor for losing the student's first blue book.

TAP6   A student in an early class period will claim that her row was one test short or one answer sheet short. Teachers who, because of time pressures, may not be sure of the exact count or do not want to delay the test to get to the bottom of the matter, usually just pass out the requested materials. If it is an extra copy of the test, this can be removed from the classroom and shared with another student; if it is an extra computer scoring bubble sheet, the method described in GTR14 can be used to prepare a duplicate answer sheet for another student to use in preparing a cheat sheet.

TAP7:   It is not uncommon for an instructor to leave the room during a test, perhaps to talk with a colleague in the hall, respond to a (sometimes planned) disturbance outside the room, use the rest room ... whatever. During this time, students in the class give and receive information.

TAP8:   Related to GTR11, a student discusses an examination item with an instructor while the instructor is grading papers turned in previously by other students. Although related to GTR11, this method is markedly better because of the fact that the papers being viewed have already been corrected.

TAP9:   Even if no papers are around to see, some students are particularly adept at asking questions to gain an advantage. For example, during an examination students engage teachers in extended conversations about a question that seems "unclear" and probe for elaborations by their teachers that, ultimately, provide enough information for a student to answer that question or some other one. Teachers rarely refuse to give this kind of assistance.

TAP10:   In a variation of GTR14, rather than making an impression on the paper, a giver takes two answer sheets and actually completes both, omitting to fill in his name on one of them. The receiver feigns working throughout the examination period. The giver turns in both sheets at a time when many students are turning in their papers. The receiver simply leaves the examination. Later, when grading the papers, the instructor notices one paper without a name on it and assumes that it must be that of the receiver.

TAP11:   A fairly common method of cheating, especially at the elementary school level, involves true–false tests in which students are directed to mark T or F in response to a statement. When answering the question, students can superimpose a T on an F or make a rather flourished script T, indistinguishable from a script F, which the teacher may interpret as a correct answer, giving the student—as people of good will are apt to do—the "benefit of the doubt."

TAP12:   On tests consisting of several pages stapled together, some teachers score the tests by marking the number of questions a student answers incorrectly at the bottom of each page, then adding up the deductions and subtracting from the total possible number of points. Realizing this, some students simply remove one or more pages from the inner part of the test. When the teacher adds the points off, the missing pages are inadvertently counted as if the student had correctly answered all questions on the missing pages.

TAP13   One of my all-time favorites involves cheating in a terribly simple manner—and one in which the student need not even cheat on the test itself. A number of students have told me that, because teachers often leave their grade books in places where students have access to them, a student can simply wait until the teacher is away and make changes directly in the grade book. Changing, for example, a D to a B is a simple matter whether the entry is in pencil or ink (likewise for numerical entries), and because teachers usually return graded tests to students, there is no way to determine what the original grade was. Changes are even less likely to be noticed if the teacher uses an electronic grade book.

TAP14:   In primary and secondary schools, teachers often use student aids. It is not uncommon for teachers to ask the student aids to make copies of tests prior to giving them or to correct tests already given. The student aid can make a few "extra" copies of the test to assist others in preparation or copy the answers for use by other students who take the test at a later time. At the college level, student aids or other employees in print shops where examinations are duplicated can provide unauthorized advance access to tests. In one 1992 case, officials at Louisiana State University uncovered an examinations-for-sale operation, which resulted in the arrest of a university employee ("LSU Discloses Cheating Plot," 1992).

TAP15:   Many teachers also use student aids to grade tests. Because teachers rarely audit the grading done by the aids, it is possible for student aids to mark a paper with a grade that is unrelated to—and better than—the student's actual performance.

TAP16:   A variation of TAP15 occurs in the classrooms of teachers who ask students to exchange papers with each other for grading. As the teacher calls out the correct answers, students are supposed to mark the questions answered incorrectly by their peers. Again, because teachers rarely audit these corrections, students bargain with each other and agree to mark fewer incorrect than they ought.

TAP17:   In addition to allowing students to correct each other's papers, many teachers also give take-home tests, with directions that they be completed independently. One of my own children brought home a take-home test that had accompanying instructions strictly forbidding use of the textbook or other materials and prohibiting students from discussing the test with each other. It is doubtful that the explicit directions dissuaded many students from cheating.

TAP18:   Teachers sometimes unwittingly assist cheating by leaving information written on a chalkboard, posted on a bulletin board, and so on. A student told me of a music teacher who wanted her students to be able to identify the intervals between two notes aurally. The teacher called a student up to the piano, struck two notes (one at a time) on the piano, and asked the student to identify the interval. It wasn't

until an exceptionally large percentage of the students demonstrated their keen ears that the teacher realized they were simply
looking at her fingers as she played the notes to determine the intervals.

TAP19: Answer keys from computer-scannable forms are often discarded
after read into scanners. Students know that the garbage can near
the scanner is frequently a rewarding depository of information. In
addition to the answer keys, refuse containers can contain ditto
masters used to print tests, draft versions of upcoming tests, and old
or previous versions of tests. (Even the dumpsters outside the buildings of large testing companies are sometimes rifled for shredded
test materials that, potentially, could be painfully reconstructed.)

TAP20: Computer-scannable answer sheets permit another type of cheating. After answer sheets are optically scanned, instructors often return them to the students. At that point a student can change one or
more of the filled-in bubbles and can claim that "the machine must
have made a mistake." In most cases, there is a computerized record
of the student's responses, which makes the student's claim easy to
refute. However, students can also make very light responses on the
answer sheet or leave blanks for items. When the answer sheets are
returned, the student can fill in the missing marks very lightly and
claim (plausibly) that the scanner did not "see" the marks.

TAP21: At the college level, examinations are often duplicated in large university print shops, also staffed to a great degree by student workers, who are able to make extra copies for sale or friendship.
Financially able students have also purchased advance copies of
tests from regular employees and have paid teaching assistants to
grade tests "favorably."

TAP22: A method useful on an essay test—even one in which each student
receives a different question—begins when a student simply copies
the topic or question on a scrap of paper. The student then asks to go
to the rest room—a request that teachers rarely deny—and walks to
the front of the room to ask a question or goes to the wastebasket to
throw something away. The purpose of the trip is simply to deliver
the topic to an associate. The associate might write both essays in
class and submit both or write both essays in class and return one to
the receiver.
In one variation of this method, the associate may not even be in
class but may write the essay in or near the rest room and provide it
to the receiver when he or she makes a second trip to the rest room.
In another variation, one student copies answers or information
onto a piece of paper and deposits it in some predetermined location
in the hallway, restroom, and so on. A second student then goes to
the restroom and retrieves the information. Each of these variations
takes advantage of the fact that teachers almost never deny students
a request related to a restroom "emergency."

TAP23: Most students know that it is a great inconvenience for a teacher to
make up different versions of the same test. A simple method of
cheating is simply for the student to be absent on the day of the test.
At minimum, the student obtains extra time to prepare. At best, the
teacher administers the same test when the student returns from his

or her absence but, because by that time the class has moved on to another topic, directs the student to take the test in the hall, the library, or some other (usually unproctored) location where the student can access otherwise FMs.

THREE ADDITIONAL CHEATING METHODS:
TWO APOCRYPHAL, ONE DOCUMENTED

In addition to the methods listed above, there are countless others and variations. Some of the most innovative methods have been crafted as narratives, told and retold as they are passed from generation to generation of test takers. Some of these narratives about cheating—especially the stories of those who escape detection—have a certain aura about them, like time-tested campfire tales, bedtime stories, or parables. The following sections present three such stories, two of which cannot be easily proven to be factual and one that was recently documented in newspapers and magazines around the United States.

Two Cheating Narratives: Tigger and Walter

Stories of vast files, retained in fraternity houses and containing copies of every examination ever given on a campus, are a standard bit of college-life folklore. This method of cheating was not mentioned in the lists presented earlier, but there is little doubt that it is a popular method within the Greek campus subculture. Two stories involving fraternity cheating were published by Mann (1987), who, claiming that the stories were true, described in detail how two fraternity members cheated using methods that would fall under the TAP category.

In his first story, Mann acknowledged the extensive files maintained by a fraternity. One of Mann's fellow students—nicknamed Tigger—was absent from class on the regularly scheduled day of the final examination in statistics and faced a make-up test. Mann reported that, fortunately, the fraternity had copies of eight of the nine versions of the make-up exam known to be used by the professor. Tigger boned up on the eight available versions but, on showing up at the professor's office for the make-up test, the predictable occurred: He was given the one version that had not been available. Tigger was apparently a quick thinker, however. After a minute or so scanning the test, Tigger approached the professor with a serious countenance. Mann recorded his classic words: "Sir, I cannot in good conscience take this examination because I have seen it before." The professor accepted the examination in return and gave the student a different version that, of course, was one of the eight with which Tigger had familiarized himself. Mann (1987) also recorded the words of the professor on Tigger's completion of the exam: "You are the most honest student I have ever known. Please let me know if you ever need a letter of recommendation" (p. 124).

Mann's (1987) second story involved a final examination in Renaissance history for which a student named Walter Hines was remarkably underprepared. The essay test was to be completed within a 3-hour final examination period, using blue books provided by the professor. Hines began to panic at the sight of the questions and began writing in his blue books. At this point, it will suffice to allow Mann's recounting of the narrative to speak for itself:

"Dear Mother, I just finished my final examination in Renaissance History. Since the professor says we must stay in here another hour until the end of the test period, I thought I'd write you a letter...." After three hours Hines handed the professor the letter to his mother which was in one blue book, took the other blue book and... raced to Wilson Library, filled in the other blue book with the right answers to the exam, sprinted to the post office on Franklin Street, [and] mailed the exam to his mother in Camp Hill. (pp. 125–126)

Later that evening, the professor—sounding irritated—telephoned Walter immediately with questions about Walter's examination:

"You handed to me a letter your wrote in a blue book to your mother. What is going on? Where is your examination? [Walter] told the professor he'd turned in the letter by mistake and mailed his mother the examination by mistake and that he'd get her to mail the professor the examination by registered mail and this is his mother's telephone number and would he please call her collect? It worked. (Mann, 1987, p. 126)[2]

The Great Time Zone Heist

Surely one of the best cheating stories is one that also happens to be true and has been thoroughly described in the popular media. The story is that of one Po Chieng Ma, also known as George Kobayashi, a resident of Arcadia, California.[3] Ma, a 46-year-old entrepreneur, started a company called the American Test Center, which offered assistance to Chinese and Taiwanese immigrants seeking to perform well on a variety of tests, including the Graduate Record Examination (GRE), Graduate Management Admissions Test (GMAT), and the Test of English as a Foreign Language (ToEFL). The company flourished between 1993 and 1996.

Ma's company hired "crack test takers" to sit for examinations administered at New York City area test sites. The test takers would memorize test questions and answers then telephone the information to Ma in Los Angeles, where, taking advantage of the 3-hour time zone difference, he would aggregate the information and encode the answers into the sides of soft, wooden Number 2 pencils. The pencils—among the most expensive writing instruments known—were then sold to test takers in the Los Angeles area at a cost of up to $9,000, although for some test takers, the fee also included transportation to the test site by Ma's wife and another associate.

Ma's pencil-selling business was halted when the operation was discovered in 1996 by a test taker turned government informant. As a result, Ma was arrested and charged with 1 count of conspiracy and 70 counts of mail fraud. According to the indictment prepared by a U.S. attorney in Manhattan, it was believed that the scam was used for every administration of the GRE, GMAT, and ToEFL between June 1993 and October 1996. In 1997, during a recess in his trial for mail fraud in New York, Ma fled to Vermont and was apprehended as he attempted to cross the border into Canada. Ma subsequently pleaded guilty in January 1998 to conspir-

---

[2]The same story is retold by Bronner (1995), who attributed it to a source who told the story to him in 1967. According to that source, the student's name was Jack instead of Walter; the mother lived in Boston, not in Camp Hill; and the incident occurred on the West Coast, at San Jose State College. Except for a few details, the stories are the same.

[3]The description of this incident is drawn from King (1997).

acy, obstruction of justice, and bail jumping. In response to the discovery of fraud, the test scores of several hundred test takers have been investigated or canceled.

CHEATING METHODS
AND ADVANCED TECHNOLOGY

Previously, the capabilities of various calculators, organizers, and hand-held computers were mentioned as facilitating certain kinds of cheating. In addition to programmable calculators, other electronic devices, such as pagers, can also be used for cheating. Numeric devices can be used to communicate a question number and correct answer. For example, the series "13 21 34 44 52" consists of pairs of numbers; the first number in each pair is the test question number, the second number corresponds to a letter (1 = A, 2 = B, 3 = C, and so on). On alphanumeric pagers, the communication can be simplified to "1C 2A 3D 4D 5B." A reporter for the Hartford, Connecticut, *Courant* investigated cheating in that state's schools and found that pagers are becoming one of the easiest ways to cheat on examinations; a student who has already taken a test can simply telephone another student's pager and key in the answers. The receiving student is notified of incoming answers by the silent pulse of the pager, giving the device its nickname—the "vibrating crib sheet" (Stansbury, 1997b, p. 1).

Cheating for the 21st Century

Programmable calculators and pagers are now, by most standards, comparatively low-tech cheating strategies. At the 1997 meeting of the National Council on Measurement in Education (NCME), Gregg Colton, a security expert for Schroeder Measurement Technologies of Clearwater, Florida, provided a glimpse of some higher tech forms of cheating that are presently possible. Colton's presentation covered the latest in audio, video, and other technology.

Microrecorders. Colton (1997) listed two recording devices that are small enough to permit concealment yet sensitive enough to permit a test takers to whisper test questions onto tape for use by one or more other examinees. One of the devices is "small enough to be covered by a normal business card" and features "a tiny tie clip microphone extension." The other device—even smaller—offers "an auto reverse mode, dual tape speeds for up to 3 hours of continuous recording, variable voice activation control, auto shut-off, and a highly sensitive built-in microphone" (p. 4).

Still Cameras. These devices can be used to photograph entire test booklets during an examination. Rather than relying on memory as Ma had done, actual photographic copies of examination pages can be mailed, faxed, or E-mailed anywhere. The devices are concealed in wristwatches, tie pins, cigarette lighters, and so on. In a packet of materials distributed at the NCME meeting, Colton (1997) illustrated a wristwatch camera developed in Germany (it keeps time and has chronograph and alarm functions, too) that uses seven-exposure, 35mm black-and-white film cartridges. The German manufacturer sells the watch for less than $300 and had reportedly sold over 58,000 in the previous 2 years. Colton also described a cigarette lighter, measuring approximately 4-inches × 1-inch × 0.75-inch and weighing 62 grams. The lighter-camera uses 12- or 24-exposure cartridges and sells for less than $400 (p. 4).

Audio and Video Transmitters.   Colton (1997) reported that audio transmitters are available that are about the size of a dime; video transmitters about the size of a quarter are also available. Either of these devices can be made to fit in a pager, a baseball cap, or a necktie; sewn into a jacket or vest, or concealed in an eyeglass case worn in the shirt pocket. Colton demonstrated a combination audio and video system that consisted of a pinhole camera worn as a tie pin (cost: about $150) that could be used by a test taker to transmit images of a test booklet to an assistant up to 20 miles away. A companion earpiece (the size of a hearing aid) can be worn by the test taker to receive answers to the televised questions.

Ultraviolet Pens.   This device can be used to write out the contents of an entire test onto plain "blank" paper. The writing can only be seen when viewed under an ultraviolet light source. Colton (1997) reported that sales of the $9 pens exceeds 19,000 per year in the United States (p. 7).

World Wide Web.   Finally, an additional way in which technology has facilitated new ways of cheating involves the World Wide Web. Many Web sites provide instruction or resources for potential cheaters. Most of these sites do not directly provide the means of cheating on tests; the information they contain usually advances plagiarism. However, other sites contain test preparation materials—usually offered for sale—and suggest that the purchaser will surely score higher if the materials are used. Although some of these sites offer legitimate test preparation services, others offer materials, like those of Ma's, which were obtained from tests that would not ordinarily be released for purposes of advance preparation.

A starting point for finding Internet resources for test preparation is the Yahoo! directory, under the subheadings Business and Economy: Companies: Education: Test Preparation. At the time this chapter was written, there were over 100 entries, advertising assistance for a variety of tests, including exams for firefighters, postal workers, anesthesiologists, engineers, electricians, social workers, nurses, and customs brokers. The entries ranged from the exotic (help preparing for the Vestibular—the university entrance examination in Brazil) to the parochial (preparation materials for nearly all of the large-scale admissions examinations used in the United States). More extensive cheating resources are made available at individual Web sites. The following annotated list provides just a sample of what is available. For each entry, the universal resource locator (URL) is listed at the end in brackets.

- The Evil House of Cheat: This site provides detailed descriptions of specific ways to cheat on examinations. Like many of the other cheating sites, however, its primary focus is on-line term papers. It provides access to nearly 10,000 term papers and links to other cheating resources, including one called The Cheat Factory, which offers access to a library of term papers that users may access in exchange for submitting a term paper of their own. In terms of status in the arena of Internet cheating resources, The Evil House of Cheat claims to be "leading the industry since 1995." [URL: www.cheathouse.com]

- Cheaters [*sic*] Heaven: The misspellings alone are probably enough to cause potential cheaters to avoid this site. Their boast: "This site will definately [*sic*] show you how to cheat in exams." [URL: www.geocities.com/televisioncity/set/8027]

- Cheater's Paradise: This site consists of links to other cheating sites, humorous anecdotes about cheating incidents, and specific suggestions for how to cheat on tests. The sponsors claim that the site has been the subject of "over 30 awards and reviews" (without details regarding what the "awards" were for). [URL: www.jaberwocky.com/cheat/]

- Papers Online: Sponsored by an organization called "Collegiate Care Research Assistance," this site includes a searchable file of research papers or will produce a paper written to the customer's specifications. Visa, MasterCard, American Express, and Discover cards are accepted. [URL: www.papers-online.com/]

- School Sucks: This is probably the most popular and notorious of the cheating resource sites. According to one report, the site generates 40,000 hits per day. The sponsor of this site, 27-year-old Kenneth Sahr, boasts that it has the most up-to-date resources and instant downloads. In addition to English language resources, term papers in Russian and Hebrew are also available. It is promised that the site will soon offer resources in 15 languages.
  The large number of hits on the School Sucks site mean megarevenues. Estimates of total revenue include income from advertisers who pay $20 for every 1,000 times that pages with their advertisements are viewed. (Doing the math, that's $800 a day from just one advertiser.) There's also a two-tiered fee system: Users can pay a one-time fee of $15 for "30 Megabytes of papers" or choose a monthly subscription plan permitting year-round access for $6.99 a month. [URL: www.schoolsucks.com]

Although sites promoting cheating clearly outnumber those providing information about preventing it, there are a few resources available to assist test givers to maintain and promote integrity in testing.

- The Mining Company: This site, primarily for secondary school teachers, provides links to "sites to help curb cheating." [URL: 7-12educators.miningco.com/msub15.htm]

- Center for Academic Integrity: According to information at this site, "the Center for Academic Integrity was founded in 1992 to help colleges and universities develop a viable network for sharing information about academic integrity policies and procedures by providing a forum to identify, affirm, and promote the values of academic integrity among students." The Center's site provides information about an annual conference, research on academic integrity, a listserv–discussion forum, and links to other resources. [URL: www.academicintegrity.org]

- Duke Honor Council: One of a number of institutions in higher education that have honor codes (see chap. 9), the Duke University Honor Council maintains a Web page of information and links to other institutions with honor codes and organizations that promote academic integrity. [URL: www.duke.edu/web/HonorCouncil/]

- Urban Legends Reference Page: This site contains a taxonomy of urban legends, a portion of which is devoted to examination lore and the history of stories involving clever cheating techniques. However, also included are a number of legends in which the instructor prevails against would-be cheaters using ingenious cheating-prevention techniques. The site is maintained by Barbara and David P. Mikkelson. [URL: snopes.simple-net.com/index.html]

CONCLUSIONS

An almost limitless number of possibilities exist for giving and receiving information prior to or during an examination, even when such communication is forbidden. Information can be secreted into an examination in ways that are nearly impossible to prevent and equally difficult to detect. Additionally, many of the circumstances encountered either in the normal course of human relations or those specific to the testing process can be used to the advantage of a person who purposes to cheat on a test. The methods range from the mundane method of looking at another student's work without permission to advanced approaches using technologically sophisticated apparatus. In the following chapter, we examine the fact that "it's not just the kids" who engage in cheating.

✦ FOUR ✦

Cheating in Postgraduate and Professional Contexts

Dear Dr. Cannell:

As a teacher, I have been repeatedly astounded in recent years concerning what is going on in testing. I think you would be absolutely flabbergasted if you knew how much cheating now takes place on the various achievement and basic skills tests in public schools. One of our elementary schools was recently named by Instructor [magazine] as one if its top ten elementary schools in the nation. Yet it is common knowledge among the teachers, principals, and supervisors that this school took twice as long as usual to administer the Stanford Achievement Test because they spent the morning teaching the test and the afternoon giving it…

—Letter from a teacher (reproduced in Cannell, 1989, p. 13)

In the previous chapter, the extent of cheating on tests was presented. However, the focus of that chapter was on cheating among grade school students, high schoolers, and college undergraduates. Unfortunately, cheating is not limited to those groups. In this chapter, cheating in the professions is examined. In particular, plenty of evidence exists concerning cheating by professionals—architects, physicians, dentists, and so on—in the context of their in-training, licensure, and certification examinations. Perhaps more disconcerting is the prevalence of cheating by teachers in the form of inappropriately assisting their students on various tests. In the following sections, the available data on these phenomena are presented and summarized.

59

CHEATING IN THE PROFESSIONS

Many professions use licensure or certification testing to help promote safe, competent, or effective practice by those in the profession. For example, potential doctors who have completed an undergraduate degree face examinations throughout their formal medical school training. After medical school, physicians take examinations to obtain a license to practice in states across the United States. Subsequently, they may take board exams that test their competence to practice in a medical specialty, such as ophthalmology, otolaryngology, or urology. The tests frequently have a multiple-choice component, and high standards are set for passing the tests.

Two things are clear. First, passing a multiple-choice examination does not guarantee that a physician will be safe, effective, or wise when it comes to removing someone's cataracts, adenoids, or kidney stones. Such tests rely on the logic of what is "necessary but not sufficient" for competent practice. By testing a physician's knowledge of various medical problems and procedures, it can be ascertained fairly confidently whether the physician knows what to do. How the physician actually performs in daily practice is another question. Logic dictates, however, that a physician who knows what to do is considerably more likely to perform acceptably than one who does not.

Second, when a test is used as part of the process for determining whether a physician possesses the requisite knowledge, some people will attempt to cheat on it. It seems disconcerting that some physicians who do not have the necessary level of knowledge–one hopes not your physician or mine—may have passed a licensing or credentialing examination by cheating. Neither is it consoling that similarly unqualified physicians may have passed the same examination without cheating—simply by guessing correctly in a few cases, taking the test repeatedly, or whatever. All things considered, however, it is probably safest to choose a board-certified otolaryngologist to remove your tonsils than one who has not passed that specialty's examination.

A similar context applies in many other professions that offer licenses or credentials that can be obtained, in part, by passing a test. These tests are called *high stakes*. A high-stakes test is one for which passing or failing results in serious consequences. For example, passing a state's real estate licensure examination permits the examinee to engage in representing buyers and sellers in real estate transactions—a potentially lucrative livelihood. On the other hand, failing the test means that a person's desired employment or career opportunity may be essentially closed off. High-stakes tests are contrasted with *low-stakes tests* in which the consequences are not as serious. For example, many second-grade students take weekly spelling tests, for which the teacher might demand, say, 80% correct in order for a student to proceed to the next spelling unit. A student who fails such a test does not likely face consequences any more serious than, perhaps, having to restudy the spelling words and retake the test.

Cheating on examinations in the professions is evident because the tests are predominantly high stakes in nature. The medical professions have generated the most literature on the problem of cheating in the professions for two reasons. First, medical programs are highly selective and competitive, perhaps influencing some physicians-in-training to cheat. Second, the medical professions have traditionally taken a serious approach to the problem of cheating—investigating, sanctioning, and taking strong measures to prevent it. More recently, cheating by teachers has received increased attention. Although improprieties by members of these two professions are frequently covered in newspapers, magazines, and on television, they are not the only ones.

Cheating in Medical School

On finishing an undergraduate degree, many college graduates seek admission to medical school. The admissions process is highly competitive and is assisted by use of the Medical College Admission Test (MCAT), a standardized testing program administered by the Association of American Medical Colleges. Once admitted to medical school, potential physicians face a rigorous curriculum and more competitive assessments and in-training examinations. Outstanding performance in medical school helps ensure a student's selection into a prestigious residency program. Because the stakes in certifying the competence of a potential physician are comparatively high, those involved in assessment programs for physicians place a high premium on valid testing.

Although in-house studies of cheating and strict codes of academic honesty are prevalent among medical schools, there are fewer published reports of findings related to cheating. One early study found that cheating continues to occur in medical school training programs, nearly to the extent that it does in college. The survey included 448 students at two medical schools. Most of the students (87.6%) admitted cheating while in college, and 58.2% admitted doing so in medical school, with the percentage increasing as students moved from their freshman to senior years (Sierles, Hendrickx, & Circle, 1980).

More recently, out of a national sample of 2,459 second-year medical students, 12.5% agreed with the statement that "Everyone cheats in medical school at one time or another," another 29.7% agreed that "cheating is a normal outgrowth of the competitive nature of medical school," 32.4% said that "not a single exam goes by without someone cheating on it," and 59.3% thought that cheating is impossible to eliminate in medical schools (Baldwin, Daughtery, Rowley, & Schwarz, 1996, p. 269).

Medical students were asked to indicate whether they had personal knowledge of several specific cheating behaviors in a study by R. E. Anderson and Obenshain (1994). Of the 174 respondents, 21.8% said they had seen another student copy on an examination, 19.3% had permitted another student to copy from them, 13.0% admitted looking at another student's examination and keeping his or her answer if it was the same as the other student's, 8.7% had "personal knowledge" of crib sheet usage, and 2.3% knew of one student taking an examination for another. These data are highly similar to the results obtained by Baldwin et al. (1996), who also asked students about specific cheating behaviors.

Sierles, Kushner, and Krause (1988) studied a first-year medical school class in depth, administering surveys about cheating that included questions about whether the students had cheated on specific examinations in behavioral science, physiology, and neuroscience. In the initial survey involving 143 students, 86.2% of the medical school students admitted cheating in college and 22.1% admitted cheating in medical school. However, on a follow-up survey asking about cheating on individual medical school examinations, the number of students admitting cheating decreased dramatically. For example, 11 students admitted to cheating on the behavioral science exam; only 1 admitted cheating on the physiology test. The researchers also asked students if they had observed cheating during examinations. Fifteen said they had witnessed cheating on the behavioral science examination; of these, 12 said they did not report the incident, 2 said they reported it, and 1 who said that he or she had observed cheating did not answer the question about whether he or she had reported the matter. Overall, the comparatively low rates of admitted and observed cheating in this study may be partially attributable to the design of the study: Students had been asked to record identification numbers on their surveys. Or, as the authors found in the written comments of some students, there may be a reluctance among medical students regarding admitting or reporting cheating.

At the end of the second year of medical school, medical students are given the U.S. Medical Licensing Examination (USMLE) administered by the National Board of Medical Examiners (NBME). Another high-stakes examination, the results on the USMLE can determine whether a student continues into the third year of medical school, and can help or hinder a student's chances of being accepted into a desired residency program. In August 1997, however, the NBME was forced to put the scores of more than 20,000 medical students on hold, pending an investigation into cheating on the test. The president of NBME, L. Thompson Bowles announced that "some examinees could have had access to the exam before the administration of the test" ("Suspected Cheating," 1997, p. 5) and that researchers were working to isolate the tests of potential cheaters. Although it is believed that the number of students who actually cheated was small, and NBME has had cheating problems in the past, Bowles noted that past problems were nothing of this magnitude.

Overall, cheating in training programs for the medical professions appears to be about as common as in other areas. Although we might wish that no physician was ever licensed on the basis of an inappropriately obtained test score, such is not the case. On the positive side, research indicates that medical students apparently know that cheating is wrong (when presented with lists of dishonest behaviors, medical students tended to recognize them as wrong; Simpson, Yindra, Towne, & Rosenfeld, 1989) and medical schools continue to work to find ways of preventing cheating. An article on cheating that appeared in the *Journal of Dental Education* summed up the state of affairs succinctly: "Responses indicated that students felt cheating was not justifiable, but also suggested that students might benefit from ethics courses" (Warman, 1994).

Cheating by Teachers and Administrators

A majority of U.S. states now require some kind of competency testing for students. The mandated tests frequently cover core subject areas, such as reading, mathematics, and science, and may be administered to all students in all grades or to samples of students in a few grades. In addition to state-level mandates, many local school districts also have student proficiency testing programs. The tests may be commercially produced, such as the Iowa Tests of Basic Skills (ITBS) or the Stanford Achievement Test, which are designed to measure students' relative standing compared with performance across the country, or they may be developed by a state's department of education specifically to measure learning outcomes deemed valuable within the state.

These tests can also be high stakes as far as students are concerned, such as when a certain level of performance on a test is linked to promotion from grade to grade, high school graduation, or acquisition of their first driver's license. However, the stakes can also be high for educators themselves, such as when the results are used to judge whether acceptable student progress has been made and whether to administer financial rewards or penalties to teachers or districts or when the results become fodder for media reports and comparisons of school quality. Although the stakes on these tests are intended to be greatest for students, secondary uses of test results can cause a spillover of concern into school district management and teachers' classroom practices.

Cheating in the Classroom. Student competency testing began its heyday in the 1970s, but concerns about the honesty of teachers began much earlier. A study conducted in the late 1920s examined the test cheating behaviors of 110 women enrolled in college-level education courses who were about to begin their student teaching. To determine the extent of cheating, the researchers used a technology of the time (a thin paraffin sheet under the students' answer sheets) and an enduring study design (self-grading of tests). The paraffin sheet left a record of students' original answers on the back of their tests, enabling researchers to determine if students changed answers during self-scoring. The researchers reported that 26 changed 1 to 2 answers; 4 students changed more than 10 answers (Atkins & Atkins, 1936).

Few studies like the one by Atkins and Atkins (1936) have been conducted with prospective teachers. Many more studies involving practicing teachers began to be conducted in the 1980s, as researchers began investigating the unintended consequences of the mandated tests. The director of testing for the Austin, Texas school district candidly observed the following:

> teachers cheat when they administer standardized tests to students. Not all teachers, not even very many of them; but enough to make cheating a major concern to all of us who use test data for decision making. (Ligon, 1985, p. 1)[1]

As the competency testing movement gained momentum in the 1970s and a greater number of states mandated testing of students, teachers began to experience increasing pressure for their students to perform well on the tests. The sources of pressure on teachers are many and, combined with teachers' own personal beliefs and training, affect what teachers do in the classroom generally and in their approaches to preparing students for high-stakes tests in particular. Figure 4.1 illustrates the sources of pressure and how these combine with other factors to influence instruction and assessment.

---

[1] A number of commentators have debated what constitutes cheating practices vis-à-vis teachers' efforts to raise students' scores on standardized or other externally mandated tests (e.g., Cohen & Hyman, 1991; Mehrens & Kaminski, 1989). Clearly, a continuum of behaviors exists, ranging from clearly acceptable to clearly unethical. In this chapter, I have, for the most part, tried to avoid demarcating the two ends of the continuum. When a behavior seems clearly unethical—such as telling students answers to a test question or changing students' answer sheets—I (and perhaps the majority of educators) feel comfortable labeling the behavior as cheating. Other behaviors—such as intensive practice on content known to be covered by a test—can be seen as simply good teaching and the intended alignment between curriculum, instruction, and assessment, and I do not lump them in with behaviors that clearly represent cheating. In summarizing research on the issue, I submit the researchers' definitions, descriptions, and conclusions, realizing that the reader may define all, some, or none of the behaviors listed as cheating under various conditions.

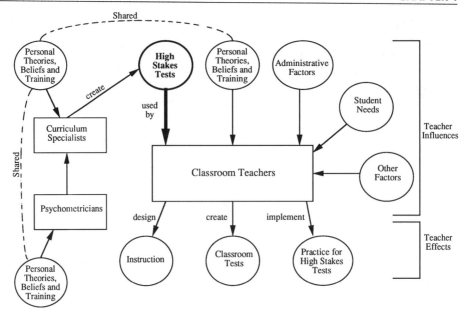

FIG. 4.1. Model of influences and effects of high-stakes testing on teachers. From "Rethinking Psychometricians' Beliefs About Learning," by G. J. Cizek, 1993, *Educational Researcher, 22(4)*, p. 7. Reprinted with permission.

The sources and intensity of the pressures perceived by teachers as well as their responses to those pressures, have been studied by Shepard and Doughtery (1991), who surveyed teachers in two large school districts. They found large proportions of teachers reporting pressure to improve students' scores, with the pressure coming from all directions: 17.1% identified parents as a source of "substantial" or "great" pressure, 24.4% identified other teachers, 56.3% identified principals, 65.9% identified the media, and 78.9% said that district-level administrators and boards of education were the source of the pressure (Shepard & Doughtery, 1991, p. 14). In the same study, 31.5% of the teachers surveyed reported spending 2 or more weeks giving students old forms of standardized tests for practice.

One study investigated suspected cheating in the Chicago public schools (Perlman, 1985). Forty schools were included in the study, 23 of which were included because of their status as "suspect" schools and 17 were included as comparisons. The suspect schools were identified as such because of their unusual patterns of score increases in previous years, unnecessarily large orders of blank answer sheets for the ITBS, or tips reported to the Chicago Schools Office of Research. After finding a high percentage of erasures and other anomalies on one administration of the ITBS among seventh and eighth graders, a second form of the test was administered in the 40 schools under more controlled conditions. Perlman found that, even accounting for the reduced level of motivation students would have had on the retesting, "clearly the suspect schools did much worse on the retest than the comparison schools" and suggested that because of weaknesses in the design of the research "it's possible that we may have underestimated the extent of cheating at some schools" (pp. 4–5).

Several attempts have been made to quantify the extent of cheating by teachers and to identify the kinds of behaviors that constitute inappropriate test administration practices. In one study, Kher-Durlabhji and Lacina-Gifford (1992) asked 74 preservice teachers to indicate how appropriate they believed certain behaviors to be. Only 1.4% thought that either changing answers on a student's answer sheet or giving hints or clues during testing were appropriate, and only 2.7% agreed that allowing more time than allotted for a test was acceptable. However, 8.1% thought that practicing on actual test items was okay, 23.4% believed rephrasing or rewording questions to be acceptable, and 37.6% judged practice on an alternate test form to be appropriate.

These beliefs of preservice teachers probably translate into actual classroom practices. North Carolina teachers in Grades 3, 6, 8, and 10 were asked to report how frequently they had witnessed certain "test irregularities." Overall, 35% said that they had observed cheating by either personally engaging in inappropriate practices or being aware of unethical actions of others. The behaviors included giving extra time on timed tests, changing students' answers on their answer sheets, suggesting answers to students, and directly teaching sections of a test. In nearly every case, however, the teachers reported that their colleagues engaged in the behaviors from 2 to 10 times more frequently than they had personally. Other practices uncovered revealed flagrant to subtle cheating. More flagrant examples included the case of students being given dictionaries and thesauruses by teachers for their use on a state-mandated writing test. One teacher said that she checked students' answer sheets "to be sure that her students answered as they had been taught" (Gay, 1990, p. 99); other teachers reported more subtle strategies, such as "a nod of approval, a smile, and calling attention to a given answer" were effective at enhancing students' performance (p. 97). A 1989 survey of teachers in Memphis revealed extensive cheating on the California Achievement Test, including one case in which a teacher displayed correctly filled-in answer sheets on the walls of her classroom (Toch & Wagner, 1992).

A large sample of third-, fifth-, and sixth-grade teachers in two large school districts was asked to describe the extent to which they believed specific cheating behaviors were practiced by teachers in their schools (Shepard & Doughtery, 1991). Their responses, shown in Table 4.1, indicated that a wide range of behaviors are perceived to occur at least occasionally, although for all of the behaviors listed but one, a majority of respondents said that these behaviors occurred rarely or never. A second observation that leaps from Table 4.1 is the remarkable extent to which teachers report that they have "no idea how often this occurs." The phenomena of teacher isolation and lack of collaboration on issues of assessment have been described elsewhere (see Cizek, Rachor, & Fitzgerald, 1996); these factors may also contribute to abuses in test administration.

A study involving 186 teachers from Georgia found that elementary school teachers were more likely to report using inappropriate methods to increase their students' test scores, that the degree of pressure to raise scores that teachers perceived was positively related to the extent of inappropriate practices, and that teachers were less likely to report engaging in behavior considered to be cheating (Monsaas & Engelhard, 1991).

Predictably, tolerant beliefs regarding inappropriate testing practices have led to serious consequences for teachers who have been caught engaging in such practices and to prominent coverage in print and broadcast media. In 1989, a teacher in South Carolina was fired when she admitted giving exact test questions and an-

TABLE 4.1
Percentage of Teachers Who Believed a Test Administration Practice Occurred at Their School

Behavior	Never	Rarely	Often	Frequently	No Idea
Providing hints on correct answers	28.5	20.8	16.9	5.8	28.0
Giving students more time than test directions permit	38.0	19.7	15.2	4.4	22.7
Reading questions to students that they are supposed to read themselves	38.8	22.2	11.9	2.2	24.9
Answering questions about test content	43.2	20.5	8.9	2.8	24.7
Changing answers on a student's answer sheet	58.4	7.8	5.5	0.6	27.7
Rephrasing questions during testing	36.3	20.8	16.1	1.9	24.9
Not administering the test to students who would have trouble with it	50.7	15.8	7.5	5.8	20.2
Encouraging students who would have trouble on the test to be absent on test day	60.1	10.8	5.5	1.9	21.6
Practicing items from the test itself	54.6	12.5	8.0	3.3	21.6
Giving students answers to test questions	56.8	11.6	6.4	1.9	23.3
Giving practive on highly similar passages as those in the test	24.9	15.8	10.5	19.7	19.1

Note. Reprinted with permission from *Effects of High Stakes Testing on Instruction,* by L. A. Shepard and K. C. Doughtery , 1991, p. 18.

swers to a high-stakes test for her students to practice with several days before the test was to be given (Canner, 1992). An analysis of several dozen Los Angeles schools revealed that the performance of their students on the California Assessment Program (CAP) tests may have been partially attributable to cheating by teachers when the percentage of erasures and changed answers on students' answer sheets was found to be significantly higher than would be expected (Aiken, 1991). Nationally, a 1990 broadcast of *60 Minutes*, titled "The Teacher is a Cheater," advertised the teachers' misdeeds involving student testing.

Perhaps the mother of all cheating scandals occurred in 1996 in Fairfield, Connecticut, and involved one of the school district's most respected and award-winning schools, Stratfield Elementary. The school district comprises nearly 7,000 students and was widely considered to represent educational excellence. In particular, Stratfield Elementary was twice singled out (in 1987 and 1994) to receive Blue Ribbon awards for excellence from the U.S. Department of Education. In 1993, Stratfield was honored by the magazine *Redbook* as one of the best elementary schools in the country. In 1995, the school's high test scores won it a $15,000 achievement grant.[2] The performance of Stratfield's students was so good that, between 1990 and 1992, composite ITBS scores for the school's third and fifth graders never fell below the 98th percentile.

Perhaps too good. When the 153 third- and fifth-grade students' answer sheets for the January 1996 administration were sent to Riverside Publishing Company in Chicago for scoring, an analysis turned up an extremely high rate of erasures. Not just erasures, highly unusual patterns of erasures. The analysis showed that 89% of the erasures were from a wrong response to a correct one, and the rate of erasures at Stratfield was up to five times greater than other schools in the same district.

Because of the highly unusual patterns, Stratfield students were retested in March 1996, using an alternate form of the ITBS. The district widened its probe into the matter and instituted a public relations campaign to control damage to its image in what was being dubbed Erasergate.[3] The retesting resulted in scores that were significantly lower on the March 1996 administration, and forensic experts were called on to examine answer sheets under microscopes and investigate such things as the differential tendencies of adults and children when filling in answer-sheet bubbles. Although it was never proved that cheating had occurred, Stratfield's principal resigned and admitted that he had taken some of the questioned tests home overnight but only to alphabetize them (Weizel, 1997). One observer familiar with the evidence concluded that the probability of tampering was "95% certain" but that officials would "never find the smoking eraser" (Lindsay, 1996, p. 29).

In a case that rivaled Stratfield's Erasergate in its sensational coverage, cheating that involved both teachers and students shocked the nation in 1995. Steinmetz High School had been a participant in an Academic Decathlon, in which students from schools across the United States vied to win state academic competitions and advance to a prestigious national event. The victory in the 1995 event in Illinois by Steinmetz High School was challenged by a previous state champion, Whitney Young High School. Apparently, the Steinmetz scores were unusually high and included 6 of the top 12 individual scores in mathematics.

An investigation into the Steinmetz victory revealed cheating in the 1994 competition by the high school's Decathlon team coach, who also taught English at the school. The teacher admitted to cheating in 1994 by feeding answers to team members during the competition, although he denied cheating in 1995. Officials representing the academic competition asked the team to take what they called a "validation test" as a means of verifying the team's outstanding performance. When team members refused, their champion status was revoked. Subsequent investigation of the 1995 event resulted in allegations that a Steinmetz student had obtained a copy of the test in advance and given it to the team's coach, who in turn duplicated and distributed it to team members. And, in another twist to the case, it was discovered that, during the 1995 competition, "a Steinmetz student appar-

---

[2]The material presented in this and following paragraphs regarding the Fairfield, Connecticut schools is drawn from information on the scandal published by Lindsay (1996).

[3]Apparently, the damage was severe. Lindsay (1996) reported that the district hired a person named Thomas Failla, the same media consultant who managed, for the Union Carbide Company, public relations in the aftermath of the Bhopal, India, chemical spill, which killed more than 2,000 people in 1984.

ently took the name tag of a judge in the speech contest, posed as the official, and awarded his highest score to a classmate" (L. Harp, 1995, p. 14).

Cheating in the Principal's Office.   It is not only teachers that feel pressures to improve students' test scores using both appropriate and inappropriate methods. Whereas teachers report that principals are a source of pressure, principals in turn report that they, too, feel pressure to increase scores. In fact, such pressures, combined with pubic demands for better performance and increased accountability, affect principals, central office administrators, and board of education members as well. Numerous instances of cheating by administrators have been publicized across the country.

For example, the principal of Cherokee Elementary School in Lake Forest, Illinois, was suspended, demoted, and eventually took a new job as a principal in Kansas City, Missouri, as a result of an investigation into extraordinarily high scores by her students on the *Stanford Achievement Test*. A court-appointed hearing officer found that Linda Chase had distributed to teachers materials covering content that would be on the *Stanford* and actual copies of the test itself. She was also accused of encouraging teachers to cheat, instructing them to erase and correct answers that students had written in their test booklets before they were sent in for scoring, and erasing all answers on a math test that had not been completed by a student so that it would be invalid and not counted in the school's average ("Cheating Scandal," 1992).

In another case, the superintendent of the Barker, New York school district resigned following a cheating scandal in that district. The superintendent and a principal were alleged to have told teachers at an elementary school to correct wrong responses on the answer sheets of third graders who had taken the New York Pupil Evaluation Program tests.

In April 1996, the Chicago school district investigated a curriculum coordinator who purportedly copied and distributed the ITBS to teachers at Clay Elementary School. The teachers were believed to then have led students in practicing on the same version of the test that was to be used in the district. Also in 1996, an elementary school principal at Kaaawa Elementary School in Oahu, Hawaii, reportedly asked her staff to fill in computerized test answer sheets with correct answers in cases in which students had not finished in the allotted time. The principal was not fired for her behavior, but state officials notified the principal that they "didn't feel it was appropriate" (Lawton, 1996, p. 5).

An abundance of inappropriate practices were uncovered in Georgia, including allegations that teachers used copies of an upcoming test for "drill and practice," allowed students to use their history textbooks for reference on the social studies portion of the Georgia High School Graduation Test (GHSGT), gave students the topic for the writing test portion of the GHSGT the day before the test, and distributed the words that would appear on the vocabulary portion of a test in advance (Loupe, 1998a)

There are two obvious problems with these kinds of cheating: (a) they make students' scores less valid and (b) they render conclusions about aggregate student performance meaningless. There is another, perhaps even more serious, problem: Many educators do not view these practices to be inappropriate. For example, Popham (1991) surveyed teachers, administrators, superintendents, and school board members from the Midwestern United States and California regarding their views on the appropriateness of what he called "test preparation practices." These included allowing students to practice for an upcoming standardized test using materials from the test that would be administered. In addition to stereotypical differences in perceptions between Midwesterners and West Coast residents, Popham found fairly broad acceptance of behaviors that clearly undermine both the intent of the mandated tests and the interpretability of test results (see Table 4.2).

Not only have educators been found to cheat on tests by helping their students to attain inappropriately high scores, but cheating has also been documented on the tests educators take themselves. In 1997, nearly 200 of those who took a test required to become assistant principals had their scores canceled because they had been exposed to a "study guide" that contained at least some of the answers to questions on the actual test. Additionally, three administrators had their state certification revoked and others who had been promoted to administrative posts were demoted pending their retaking of the test (Williams, 1997). In another case, school officials were implicated in an investigation of 600 alterations in the transcripts of nearly 300 students at Brea Olinda High School in Orange County, California. Like Stratfield, Brea Olinda had previously been honored as a Blue Ribbon school by the U.S. Department of Education (Cumming, 1995, p. B2).

ASSORTED CHEATING

Obviously, medicine and education are not the only professions affected by cheating. With regularity, newspapers and television news broadcasts carry stories of cheating that seem shocking because of their magnitude or sophistication or simply because they violate consumers' expectations that credentials, licenses, or certificates are all earned in an honest fashion. The following examples are intended to highlight the fact that butchers, bakers, and candlestick makers—virtually all professions that attempt to assure the competence of those they credential or license to practice—are equally as susceptible to the temptation of unethical test-taking behavior.

Pilots

In 1990, a newsletter of the National Organization for Competency Assurance reported that the friendly skies may be friendly but perhaps not as safe as the public would hope. The newsletter article also demonstrated the fallacy of the common perception that multiple-choice or other objective-type examination formats are uniquely susceptible to cheating. In this case, cheating had been detected in the performance examinations of pilots, providing an ironic twist to another airline slogan that "*some* people just know how to fly." The newsletter reported the following:

> A recent investigation of pilot testing procedures has determined that serious flaws may exist in the current system. Critics contend that because the examinations require an in-flight practical exam administered on a one-to-one basis, the examiners have incentives to give easy, cursory tests that fail to identify incompetent pilots. Examiners are paid based on the number of tests they administer.... Evidence has already been uncovered indicating that an examiner awarded some licenses without even testing the candidates in the air. ("Systematic Flaws Found," 1990, p. 3)

TABLE 4.2

**Percentage of Teachers and Administrators Who Considered
a Test Administration Practice Appropriate**

	Midwest			California		
Behavior	Teachers	Administrators	Teachers	Principals	Superintendents	Board Members
Student practice with previous test form	34	47	57	25	60	68
Student practice with current test form	14	17	36	6	17	21

Note. From *Defensible/Indefensible Instructional Preparation for High-Stakes Achievement Tests,* by W. J. Popham, 1991, p. 2. Reprinted with permission.

Marines

The U.S. Marines recruiting campaigns have advertised that they are looking for a "few good men." A scandal at the U.S. Naval Academy demonstrated that they may be hard to find. The heavily publicized and thoroughly investigated event involved cheating by midshipmen on an engineering final examination in 1992, with repercussions lasting for years afterward. Twenty-six midshipmen were expelled from the Naval Academy, and more than 50 more were punished for their role in illegitimately obtaining and using a copy of the final examination prior to the test (Blum, 1994).

Cosmetologists

According to a report published in the *New Orleans Times–Picayune*, the Louisiana Inspector General found that "cheating on state cosmetology exams went unpunished, even when aspiring manicurists were caught red-handed" (E. Anderson, 1996). The report indicated that no one was nailed, even though the cheating was flagrant. Apparently, the cosmetologists refused to finger their colleagues. Authorities couldn't break the cheating ring, perhaps because the cheating methods were so polished… (sorry).

Attorneys

In 1988, a woman named Laura Salant was sentenced to 3 years of probation, fined $2,500, and ordered to serve 2,000 hours of community service for her role in cheating on the California bar examination. Salant's husband, Morgan Lamb, had previously failed the bar examination and turned to cheating, convincing his wife to impersonate him and take the test for him. Salant registered for the test as a male candidate under her husband's name and was admitted to the test with an identification card showing a picture of her as a man, with hair pulled back and thick eyebrows painted onto her forehead. Her performance on the test placed her third among 7,688 attorneys who attempted the exam. However, examination supervisors became suspicious and questioned the score of "Mr. Lamb," observing that he appeared to be approximately 7 months pregnant at the time of the test (Norris, 1988).

Stock Brokers

The regulatory arm of the National Association of Securities Dealers (NASD) licenses people who engage in the buying and selling of securities using, as part of the process, an examination program. The NASD is the parent organization of the Nasdaq stock exchange. To participate in the buying and selling of securities on the Nasdaq, securities brokers and dealers are required by U.S. law to be a member of the NASD; currently, the NASD comprises more than half a million members. Members of the NASD are qualified following passage of an examination covering such topics as federal securities law, tax law, investment banking, and the rules of financial responsibility.

In 1997, the NASD's regulatory subsidiary announced that 20 registered representatives had been fined, censured, and barred from practice after it concluded that they had payed imposters to take an NASD qualification examination for them. Twenty-one additional representatives had already been disciplined as a result of the investigation into suspected cheating on the test. The NASD said that the 20 were assessed more than $650,000 in fines and were required to forfeit an additional $1.2 million in commissions ("20 Are Disciplined," 1997).

Police Officers

A federal grand jury recently widened an investigation into test cheating by Detroit police officers. The test, which was administered in April 1997 to more than 2,000 officers, is designed to assess officers attempting to qualify for promotions within the police force. An investigation was begun when two sisters, Officers Priscilla and Veronica Robinson, allegedly obtained a copy of the test in advance and used the test to score over 190 out of a possible 200 points. Those who prepared the test indicated that "scores above 150 defied probability and were strong evidence of cheating" ("More Detroit Police," 1997, p. 12). The officers, 8-year veterans, were subsequently fired. However, the investigation was widened in an attempt to identify the source of the test and the possibility that several other officers who had obtained unusually high scores—all of whom worked in the offices of the police chief, executive deputy, or mayor of Detroit—had been beneficiaries of advance information as well.

Firefighters

According to the *Los Angeles Times*, in June 1996 nearly 80 members of the Los Angeles Fire Department had to retake a section of the examination required for promotion to captain because of suspected cheating (Wilgoren, 1996).

Reverends?

A case involving divinity school students at the Yale University Divinity School demonstrates that all professions are susceptible to the temptation to cheat and that, again, cheating is not limited to multiple-choice tests. The 1995 scandal at Yale concerned violation of the rules for a take-home midterm examination in a course called New Testament Interpretation. In mid-October, the examinations were distributed to the 110 students enrolled in the course. Students were to spend only 1 hour on the test, no books or collaboration were permitted, and the exam was to count for 15% of the student's grade.

Showing unique interpretations of New Testament ethical guidelines, many students apparently disregarded the directions. Teaching assistants for the course who graded the examinations reported unusual performance by the students. A news account of the scandal that appeared in the school newspaper reported that "under normal circumstances, 20–25 percent of students receive honors [grades]. On this exam, class members said they thought that the number was closer to 40 percent" (Sullivan, 1995, p. 1). On the basis of the information from the assistants, the professor confirmed that "some of the exams were too long for an hour's worth of work, and others were simply too polished" (p. 1) and recommended that the students do penance for their infractions.

Taxi Drivers

Finally, in a news account that surely goes a long way toward explaining the legendary driving skills of taxicab operators in New York City, the *New York Times* reported that a 5-month probe of taxi licensing operations revealed widespread cheating. Apparently, proctors and other taxi drivers collaborated in a scam that charged prospective licensees a fee of $1,500 to help them cheat on the taxi operators examination (Christian, 1998).

CONCLUSION

In elementary and secondary schools, students report that they cheat on examinations because of pressure or desire to get good grades. In college, cheating on tests continues, prompted in many cases by a continuing quest for high grades and supplemented by the knowledge that superior performance in college can help gain admission to graduate school or land a sought-after position in a competitive job market. However, the temptation and pressures to cheat on tests continue after formal education stops, and cheating has been documented in licensure, certification, and credentialing programs across the United States. For some, the pressures to cheat are related to the desire to gain a competitive advantage. Others, such as teachers, report that they cheat out of a desire to help the children they serve, or to protect themselves from unwanted intrusion into their professional practice by those whom they believe do not understand the demands or context of their jobs (see M. L. Smith, 1991).

If travelers seek assurance that the knowledge and skills of pilots are up-to-date, some form of incorruptible performance assessment is necessary. Investors who risk their earnings in the stock market want some guarantee—if not a financial return, at least that their transactions are being handled in a competent fashion. A community rocked by criminal activity would surely wish that those charged with investigating and apprehending crooks did not themselves attain rank or status by fraudulent means. If the American public is to have confidence that educational standards are being met, some valid gauge is needed.

Attending to the wishes of these various constituencies for accurate information about those who are awarded licenses or credentials can be accomplished through testing. Ensuring that test results are meaningful is, of course, again primarily an issue of validity, as is the degree to which correct decisions are made in awarding or denying licenses or credentials. As we have seen, such decisions—in order to avoid capriciousness or arbitrariness—usually include some type of objective examination process. The key validity concern is the accuracy of inferences made about the knowledge, competence, or safety based on an individual's score on an examination. Examinations need not rely on multiple-choice formats, although in recent years multiple-choice tests have dominated the licensure and certification field because of their comparative advantages in terms of efficiency and objectivity. In any case, cheating as a threat to valid inferences extends to performance assessments, essay examinations, portfolios, and all other forms of testing.

Regardless of the testing process used, and despite precautions and conditions instituted to prevent cheating, those who—for whatever reason—want to circumvent the process can attempt to do so by cheating. The problem is not, however, a uniquely American one, as we see in the next chapter.

✦ F I V E ✦

Cheating in Other Countries and Cultures

FIG. 5.1. The "Cheating Garment." Used with permission from the Gest Oriental Library and East Asian Collections, Princeton University.

Up to this point, information about the extent of cheating, perceptions of cheating, and cheating methods presented in preceding chapters have focused on the problem as it exists within the borders of the United States. Far from being a parochial problem, however, cheating occurs around the world. The phenomenon has been studied by researchers interested in comparisons between cheating in the United States and other countries. Apparently, students who smuggle cheat sheets into examinations or wait longingly for another student to leave an answer uncovered are as common abroad as in the United States.

In the following sections of this chapter, research on the methods and frequency of cheating in other countries is presented, as is research on the perceptions of cheating on the part of test takers and test administrators in other countries. Cultural differences in perceptions of cheating among the diverse cultural and ethnic groups within the United States is also examined.

CHEATING AROUND THE WORLD

In other countries, cheating has a longer history than in the United States, if only because the United States is younger than most nations. It has been reported that persons who sought to take civil service examinations more than 1,000 years ago in China were searched for crib sheets before being permitted to take examinations which were "conducted in individual cells from which candidates could not budge for three days" (Brickman, 1961, p. 412). Brickman also described the elaborate "cribbing garments" worn by the Chinese test takers, now displayed in the Gest Oriental Library at Princeton University and shown in Fig. 5.1. The garment dates to the late 19th century and measures approximately 29 inches long by 25 inches wide with 39-inch long sleeves, and contains more than 700 complete compositions composed of nearly half a million characters inscribed carefully on its fabric. According to Brickman, the cribbing garment

> was rented to those who intended to cheat. When sewn into the coat, the garment could be smuggled into the cell and the candidate could copy at leisure and without fear of detection, any number of the 722 essays based on the Confucian writings. (p. 412)[1]

More recently, an article in the *Chronicle of Higher Education* described the elaborate methods developed by cheaters in Saudi Arabia—and the elaborate system of proctors (called *invigilators*) designed to deter the practice of cheating on tests (Caesar, 1983, p. 64). A delightful story about an Australian student named Tommy Taylor is presented in a book titled *Taylor's Troubles* (Tarling, 1985). Tommy, an inveterate cheater, describes the pervasiveness of cheating and tells some of his personal cheating philosophy and problems in a candid interview.

---

[1] In the course of conducting research for this book, I viewed the cribbing garment at the Gest Library and received extensive background information and commentary on the use of the garment by Martin Heijdra, curator of the Chinese and East Asian collection. Heijdra rejected the notion that the garment was actually used for cheating. He believed that, because the compositions written on the garment are responses to very low order questions and because the responses would be easily recognized by anyone scoring the examination, the garment was probably not used for cheating. He hypothesized that the garment was probably worn for good luck, inscribed as it is with the "wisdom of the ages" so to speak. Heijdra also noted that very few such garments were produced; instead of purchasing or constructing one's own garment, it was more likely that the garment was simply "rented" by successive waves of test takers.

Everybody cheats in exams, except the girls, but I reckon that I am the best cheat of all time. My first rule is never to cheat so I top the class. If I ever come top in anything it's because I worked. Cheating into first position isn't fair, because the people who come first work really hard for it. But I reckon that anyone ought to be allowed to cheat into a pass or maybe even get a B. It was actually John Finlay who told me that cheating took as much skill as studying, so now I reckon I deserve whatever I get.

Everyone cheats differently. Copying is the stupidest way of going about it....Teachers get very upset when they mark papers which are identical.

Greg cheats by bringing in books. I don't like his style at all. It's too bulky. One day he got caught, but he said that he had forgotten to leave them outside the exam room. Mr. Cooper let him off. The twins cheat themselves into high positions. Peter got himself into third place for Maths, and that made Jenny pretty mad because she was fourth and had worked hard.

Everybody cheats around here—not counting the girls—but I reckon my system is best of all. I have copied all the answers on bits of paper and they are inside my socks. I pull them out one at a time, copy them onto the question-sheet, put them back, then if teachers see me copying from the question-sheet, they can't think I've been cheating. It looks as if you've been scribbling on the sheet to get your thoughts together. The only trouble with my system is that my socks are so full of cheat-notes that I limp. Clayton Smith can always tell when I'm going for an exam because I can hardly walk through the door. "Hey, Taylor!" he yells, in front of the teachers, "how's your feet?"

"Sssh!"

"Oh sorry. I forgot. Today must be our English exam—you're limping." (Tarling, 1985, pp. 61–62, cited in Godfrey & Waugh, 1996, p. 16)

A Sampler of Student Cheating in Other Countries

Tommy's story may be charming in its candor. But the fact that he was a student at a highly conservative, independent religious school in Australia demonstrates that no school system can be inoculated against the problem. A number of other nations have experienced more serious cheating incidents than those described by Tommy. The following news reports illustrate the ubiquity of the problem of cheating.

Dateline: Israel.   A news story from August 1990 described the circumstances surrounding the West Bank Matriculation Examinations (WBME), a high school test administered to approximately 14,500 students each year in Israel. The challenge to both Palestinian students taking the test and those in charge of security for the test was daunting, as administration of the WBME was caught up in regional political discord. According to the news report, the test was disrupted when "gangs of youths distributed photocopies of correct answers, shouted solutions from megaphones, and forced teachers to aid pupils during the actual examinations" (Weil, 1990, p. 7).

Dateline: Kashmir Valley, India.   Students in the Kashmir province of India had used none-too-subtle means of cheating on their 10th-grade examinations. In 1990, teachers reported that the students "came to the exams with AK-47 assault rifles, pistols, and hand grenades. PhDs were doing exams for 16-year-olds, and no one dared complain." The newspaper noted that, "understandably, invigilators preferred to stay well away from the exam halls" and that "the few students who tried to manage without cheating were jeered out of the schools" (Adams, 1992, p. 9). In response to the troubles of 1990, the Kashmiri Board of Education ran advertisements on television and radio warning that similar incidents would not be tolerated for the 1991 examinations and invoked penalties that included cancellation of test scores for all students at an examination center if even a single incident of cheating was observed. Apparently, the warnings succeeded. According to news reports, "The mountains ringing the city may be once again ringing with gunfire, but this year's students can be sure they were given a fairer chance to prove themselves than last year's" (Adams, 1992, p. 9).

Dateline: Australia/Malaysia.   A high-priced plot to cheat on an examination at Deakin University in western Victoria, Australia, was uncovered in 1993. Five Malaysian students, enrolled in a bachelor's of business degree program at their home institution in Malaysia, Penang College, were participating in a special program that permitted them to complete the degree at Deakin University. To ensure satisfactory performance on a final examination at Deakin, the students pooled their money to purchase airfare for one of the group to fly back to Malaysia and obtain a previously scored copy of the final examination that had been mailed back from Deakin (Maslen, 1993).

Dateline: South Africa.   With the downfall of apartheid, an increasing number of South Africans are seeking entrance to colleges and universities. To identify the most meritorious applicants, the country established school-leaving examinations in 1996 that provide information about qualifications for admission. Inevitably, as competition for admission increased, so too did the prevalence of cheating. Education officials in South Africa revealed widespread cheating on the tests and indicated progress on developing "cheat-proof exams." In the meantime, officials moved to implement stiff penalties for those caught cheating. These include, for students, a waiting period of 1 year before being permitted to take the test again and, for teachers who abet cheating, fines and imprisonment (MacGregor, 1997, p. 17).

Dateline: Brazil.   With the government's restructuring of the *vestibular*—the high school examination that qualifies students for placement in government or private universities—a wave of cheating swept the country. The tests are given at highly secure, government-approved test sites. Nonetheless, authorities in São Paulo caught one student impersonating another; in Goiás, federal authorities canceled the vestibular after arresting a man possessing copies of the test and answers prior to the examination. In Curitiba and Passo Fundo, authorities reported on the activities of the so-called vestibular mafia, which arranged for one knowledgeable candidate to sit for the test and to transmit answers to other candidates also taking the test who had paid the requisite fee (Haussman, 1988).

Dateline: Nigeria.   Investigation of cheating at three universities in Nigeria revealed widespread cheating on examinations. The three postsecondary institutions were located in the Rivers state of Nigeria and included the University of Port Harcourt, Rivers State University of Science and Technology, and the Rivers State College of Education. The investigation concluded that "examination malpractices ... have been extraordinary in Nigeria in recent times" (Akaninwor, 1997, p. 276). A typology of cheating practices was developed, including the following:

- *Bullets*: tiny folded pieces of toilet paper containing samples of major points in a course which are catapulted to students inside an examination room.
- *Dubbing*: the use of head scarves, skirts, or facecaps to conceal source materials during a test.
- *Tattooing*: the writing of vital information on body parts.
- *Walkie-talkies*: an arrangement in which examination questions are smuggled out of the examination room to helpers who solve problems then whisper them to students in the room.
- *Giraffe system*: weak students strain their necks to catch a glimpse of material they want to copy from better students.
- *Contracting*: involves the assistance of an examination proctor who substitutes examination answer sheets for a fee. (Akaninwor, 1997, p. 277)

Dateline: Russia. According to a 1998 Associated Press account published in the *Philadelphia Inquirer*, cheating is widespread in Moscow universities. Although most students still rely on old-fashioned cheating methods, higher technology has been adapted by those who can afford it. At Moscow State University, cellular phones and pagers are being used by cheaters, facilitated in part by a unique method of testing used there. A common testing practice in Russia is for instructors to distribute a list of numbered essay test questions prior to an examination from which students will respond to a subset on the day of the test—the idea being that students will prepare for all of the questions and enhance their learning. On the day of the test, students line up to draw a card, on which the number of their essay question is printed. Because the lining up and drawing of cards is a time-consuming process, cheaters lag toward the end of the line and wait to draw their card until one of the earlier students completes his or her essay and prepares to leave the examination room. At that point, the cheater signals the question number to the student who is leaving who then arranges to have the complete text of an answer sent by means of a pager to the candidate. Apparently, there is ample evidence of this form of cheating. According to the Associated Press report,

> at Moscow's Vessolink pager service, operators say that during exam times they receive a large number of unusually long messages. On a regular day, operators type out one- to two-line messages, but university testing periods bring on an avalanche of six-, seven-, and even 10-line messages. "Normally, a message longer than 200 or 300 characters is very rare," said Anatoly Kopylov. "But during exam period, we have a lot of these messages, and even longer ones of up to one thousand characters." (S. M. Brown, 1998, p. F6)

Dateline: Ireland. Two students were expelled from the University of Dublin for obtaining and using prior copies of an examination in experimental physics. When the cheating was first suspected, university officials required all students to retake the examination. Although most students who retook the test showed improved performance, the two students who were suspected of cheating did con-

TABLE 5.1

Examples of Irish Primary Certificate Examination Compositions, 1946–1948

A Bicycle Ride (1946)

I awakened early, jumped out of bed and had a quick breakfast. My friend, Mary Quant, was coming to our house at nine o'clock as we were going for a long bicycle ride together.

It was a lovely morning. White fleecy clouds floated in the clear blue sky and the sun was shining. As we cycled over Castlemore bridge we could hear the babble of the clear stream beneath us. Away to our right we could see the brilliant flowers in Mrs. Casey's garden. Early summer roses grew all over the pergola which stood in the middle of the garden.

A Day in the Bog (1947)

I awakened early and jumped out of bed. I wanted to be ready at nine o'clock when my friend, Sadie, was coming to our house. Daddy said he would take us with him to the bog if the day was good.

It was a lovely morning. The sun was shining and white fleecy clouds floated in the clear blue sky. As we were going over Castlemore bridge in the horse and cart we could hear the babble of the clear stream beneath us. Away to our right we could see the brilliant flowers in Mrs. Casey's garden. Early summer roses grew all over the pergola which stood in the middle of the garden.

A Bus Tour (1948)

I awakened early and sprang out of bed. I wanted to be ready in good time for our bus tour from the school. My friend, Nora Greene, was going to call for me at half-past eight as the tour was starting at nine.

It was a lovely morning. The sun was shining and white fleecy clouds floated in the clear blue sky. As we were going over Castlemore bridge in the horse and cart we could hear the babble of the clear stream beneath us. From the bus window we could see Mrs. Casey's garden. Early summer roses grew all over the pergola which stood in the middle of the garden.

Note. From *Critical Issues in the Curriculum: Eighty-Seventh Yearbook of the National Society for the Study of Education* (p. 94), by L. N. Tanner (Ed.), 1988, Chicago: University of Chicago Press. Reprinted with permission.

siderably worse. Apparently, the two students shared information about the test with others: At the expulsion hearing for the two students, "evidence was given to show that in conversation with other students, their predictions of the questions which would or would not be set showed an unusual accuracy" (Walshe, 1988, p. 10).

Madaus (1988) provided an illuminating example of how students pass along information about test content in the context of the Irish Primary Certificate Examinations administered during the 1940s. As Table 5.1 shows, memorization of stock responses, passed from student to student, can be adapted to nearly any essay test question.

Although Madaus described examinations administered in the 1940s, the same effect has continued to be witnessed to the present. For example, a 1989 article described cheating on the General Certificate of Secondary Education (GCSE) examinations in Great Britain. The article reported that "pupils are supplied with the mark scheme [for essays] which gives detailed information and leaves little opportunity for the pupil to show his or her ability" (Nash, 1989, p. A1).

It's Not Just the Lads

As in the United States, cheating on examinations is engaged in by persons in graduate professional programs, teachers, and other adults. In some countries, concerns abound regarding the integrity of their entire educational systems. A sampling of a few of these cases follows.

Dateline: Cuba.   Widespread corruption involving teachers at the Guiteras pre-university school in Havana facilitated a cheating scandal in Cuba. Ten teachers and the deputy head of the school received jail sentences ranging from 6 months to several years for accepting bribes ranging from hundreds to thousands of dollars to help students pass examinations. In addition to cash payments, the bribes also included gifts, such as alcohol, perfume, clothes, shoes, calculators, watches, and videos. In exchange, the teachers falsified examination scores, substituted good papers for poor ones, and, in one case, permitted a student to work on an examination away from the school—at a teacher's home (P. Smith, 1987).

Dateline: Canada, Mexico, Caribbean, and the United States.   Graduates of foreign medical schools are required to take an equivalency examination administered at 54 locations across North America in order to be licensed to practice in the United States. However, 10,000 of the approximately 17,000 physicians who took the examination in July 1983 were asked to retake the test in November of that year when it was determined that between 3,000 and 4,000 students may have had prior access to the test. A report of the incident revealed that, on the day of the examination, "some disgruntled test takers produced exact copies of the test, which they claimed had first been bought by one person for $50,000 and then sold for lesser amounts to others" ("Cheating Found," 1983, p. 20).

Dateline: Bangladesh.   In 1995, 4,000 students were expelled and 50 teachers were fired for their parts in a pervasive cheating scandal. According to a researcher at Macquarie University in Australia, cheating in Bangladesh has been marked by horrifying brutality: The 50 fired teachers were released for suppling test answers to students; 1 teacher who had spoken out against the cheating was hacked to death by students. Education officials in Bangladesh called cheating "a national vice" (Maslen, 1996, p. 16).

Dateline: Great Britain.   Two recent cheating scandals have been uncovered in Great Britain. The first involved the inaugural administration of national tests for primary school students (the so-called KS2 tests for 11-year-olds). According to published reports, cheating was "rife" on the national tests, as teachers coached pupils, gave examination questions for homework assignments, wrote answers on chalkboards during the tests, and allowed students to work on the examinations longer than the allotted time limit. The degree of cheating was unexpected but attributed to a large degree to the fact that test results would be used as a basis for development of school performance reports (Hofkins, 1995). In another case, this one involving postsecondary educators, the British Business and Technology Education Council released 39 inspectors–that is, examination supervisors—and another 99 resigned after it was discovered that they had been too lax on cheating (Tysome, 1994).

Dateline: India.   Bhopal University officials concerned about widespread cheating took drastic measures to ensure valid testing. A newspaper account reported that "policemen were stationed at intervals of every few yards to keep mischief makers at bay outside examination halls. Windows were guarded to keep students' friends from sneaking answers to them on slips of paper" (Bhargava, 1987, p. 37). The police were unable, however, to prevent all cheating; allegedly, the examination results for the daughter of the state's education minister were "manipulated" to yield a more favorable outcome than she had earned. At another Indian university, Rajasthan College in Jaipur, students were reported to have not even bothered to take examinations. The college has been accused of selling medical degrees to students for $625; the college also sold students degrees from other colleges in other states.

Cross-Cultural Research on the Frequency of Cheating

Most of the published English-language research on the frequency of cheating in other countries has involved comparisons of survey data collected in U.S. and foreign colleges and universities. In one study, a small group ($N = 49$, 10 men, 39 women) of undergraduates enrolled at Charles Sturt University in New South Wales, Australia were asked about their cheating behaviors and their responses were compared with a large sample ($N = 2,153$) of U.S. college students. The survey revealed that a smaller percentage of Australian students admitted that they had ever cheated: 53% admitted cheating in high school and only 4% admitted cheating in college, compared with 78% and 49%, respectively, for the U.S. students (S. F. Davis, Noble, Zak, & Dreyer, 1994).[2]

In another comparison study, 100 female Israeli students at a teachers college in Tel Aviv were compared with 100 female U.S. students enrolled in a college of education in Illinois. Both groups were asked to describe their frequency of cheating, which included copying from another student during an examination and letting another student copy, as well as their feelings about cheating. The authors concluded that

> Israelis report more cheating and are less negative toward cheating than their American counterparts. It is important to stress that we cannot answer the question of whether Israelis cheat more than Americans do, only that they are more willing to report that they do so. (Enker, 1987, p. 323)

Evans, Craig, and Mietzel (1993) compared cheating in groups of high school students from the United States, West Germany, and Costa Rica. All students were drawn from primarily middle-class socioeconomic strata; the 87 U.S. students attended a public high school, the Costa Rican sample consisted of 114 students from an academic public school in that country, and the 121 German students were drawn from four public schools at the *gymnasium* level. All students answered a language-appropriate version of a 109-item questionnaire developed previously.

---

[2]The data gathered by Davis et al. (1994) were reported separately for U.S. and Australian men and women. To derive the aggregated percentages given in this paragraph, I multiplied percentages for men and women in each country by their respective sample sizes and divided by the total number of respondents in each country.

Results included a greater perceived occurrence of cheating by the Costa Rican students, followed by U.S. and German students. (To some extent, this result may be related to the fact that German students ranked lowest, too, in acknowledgment of specific behaviors as cheating, with Costa Rican students next and U.S. students scoring highest in recognition of given behaviors as cheating.)

One large-scale study examined cheating solely within a large English university. The study involved 943 students enrolled in 19 major disciplines (e.g., chemistry, psychology, engineering, education, art, health services, and social work). Students were surveyed regarding whether they had engaged in any of 21 specific cheating behaviors. Of these, several dealt with cheating on examinations. In the sample, the greatest percentage of test-related cheating (29%) involved "coming to an agreement with another student or students to mark each other's work more generously than it merits" in a situation in which student grading is permitted (Newstead, Franklyn-Stokes, & Armstead, 1996, p. 232). Thirteen percent admitted copying during an examination without the other person realizing, 8% admitted using crib notes, 5% reported collaborating with another student to communicate answers during a test, and 1% reported taking an examination for another student. These results mirror results from an earlier study by the same authors involving 112 psychology students from "one old and one new university" in England (Franklyn-Stokes & Newstead, 1995). In that study, 20% of the students admitted copying, 13% admitted using crib notes, 6% confessed to collaboration during an exam, and 0% reported taking an examination for another student.

In another study—this one conducted using the responses of 800 secondary school students in Senegal—a survey asking students to describe how often they cheated found that "10.4% of the pupils cheat regularly and 26.2% do so occasionally" (Vandewiele, 1980, p. 208).

Cross-Cultural Research on Perceptions About Cheating

A study conducted in Russia in 1991 tapped the perceptions of 248 second-year or higher students attending four Moscow institutes. They included the Plekhanov Institute of National Economy, the Moscow Regional Institute of Physical Culture, the Moscow Pedagogical Institute, and the All-Union Institute of Textile Industry (Poltorak, 1995). Students were asked whether specific cheating behaviors were "acceptable in your peer group." Overall, 91.0% of the students viewed the use of crib sheets as acceptable; 81.6% said "peeping at someone's exam" was acceptable, and 86.1% perceived using lecture notes or notebooks during an exam to be appropriate when such aids are not permitted (Poltorak, 1995, p. 236). Students were also asked whether they considered the same activities to be cheating. In general, the percentages of students who said that the activities constituted cheating closely paralleled the percentages who said that the behaviors were acceptable. For example, in comparison to the 91.0% of students who said crib sheets were perceived to be acceptable, 87.0% also considered the act of using a crib sheet to be cheating.

Poltorak (1995) also examined the Russian students' perceptions on the basis of their gender and found interesting differences between male and female students. Regarding the activities of using forbidden notes and purchasing assignments, Poltorak observed that

94.1% of males in comparison with 81.8% of females claimed that "using your own lecture notes or notebooks on exam" was a normal activity. This type of cheating is more difficult to perform than cribsheets. Therefore, males may associate it with masculinity, i.e., "to have the guts" to actually bring the whole notebook in to a classroom and use it without teacher's [sic] noticing. Such "masculinity" is seen also in the fact that 46.3% of males, in compare [sic] with only 17% of female respondents, claimed buying papers and homeworks as acceptable. If there was any segment of Russian society to develop commercial skills first, it was those who were traditionally the bread-winners in family: men. Therefore, men were much more likely to get involved into the scheme of buying, even in education, than females. (p. 235)

The earlier cited studies by S. F. Davis et al. (1994), Newstead et al. (1996), and Evans et al. (1993) on the frequency of cheating also examined students' perceptions. At the college level, Davis et al. found that U.S. students were more likely than Australian students to perceive cheating as improving their examination scores (64% vs. 57%). The survey administered by Newstead et al. asked English students to rate, on a 1- to 7-scale, whether specific actions constituted cheating, with 7 indicating the firmest conviction that a behavior was cheating. Their analysis revealed that students generally acknowledged the listed behaviors as cheating, with all of the mean perception ratings exceeding the scale midpoint of 4. The researchers also queried students regarding their perceptions of why students cheat or do not cheat. As has been found in studies involving U.S. students, the English students cited time pressures (21%), the desire "to increase a mark" (20%), and the fact that "everybody does it" (16%) as the three primary reasons (Newstead et al., 1996, p. 233). Interestingly, the top two reasons given for not cheating were "it is immoral or dishonest" and the "situation did not arise or was not applicable to my course," which tied with 20% of students citing each of these as their reason (p. 233).

In their comparative study of U.S., Costa Rican, and West German high school students, Evans et al. (1993) found that Costa Rican students tended to be more aware of cheating in their classrooms and that a greater proportion of U.S. students perceived specific behaviors as constituting cheating compared with the Costa Rican or German students. Evans et al. (1993) noted that

the most striking differences [between the three countries] concerned items about plagiarism (e.g., quoting verbatim without citation) and passive cheating (e.g., letting a peer copy from one's own paper and taking advantage of teacher errors in scoring marking, or grading to secure a higher evaluation than would otherwise result). On both these counts, German students were less likely to classify such behavior as cheating than were the two other groups. (p. 591)

A subsequent survey involving samples of 17- and 18-year-old students from six countries (Australia, Austria, Costa Rica, East Germany, West Germany, and the United States) was expanded to develop a construct that Waugh, Godfrey, Evans, and Craig (1995) called *anticheating perceptions*—an index of the extent to which students perceived cheating to be wrong and their opposition to cheating behaviors. Aggregation of responses to several items on the survey and the statistical technique of Rasch modeling[3] of the data resulted in the ranking of students on

---

[3] An explication of the Rasch scaling technique is beyond the intended scope of this book. Interested readers are referred to the work of Wright and Masters (1982).

the construct. The authors concluded that significant differences in perceptions of cheating existed among the groups, falling along the following continuum from strongest to weakest anticheating perceptions: Australians, Costa Ricans, Americans, East Germans, Austrians, and West Germans. The authors provided a cultural rationale for the ordering that reads like a cross between armchair cross-cultural psychology and a travel brochure for a vacation in Australia:

> The West Germans—with their strong work ethic to succeed and achieve together—fell at one end of the continuum. The Australians—with their fair go mate syndrome, a wonderful outdoor sunny climate, and an easy attitude to work, with an expectation of personal achievement—fell at the other end. Anti-cheating perceptions of students in other countries fell between these. The logic for this is that West Germans and Austrians exhibited some confusion between collaboration and cheating in the pursuit of success because this is part of the national stereotype in which they learn and work…. East Germans will have their pursuit of success tempered by the socialist perspective, with less confusion between collaboration and cheating…. USA students value personal freedom with personal pursuit of success in the "American Way" meaning that the stereotype is that anyone can achieve in a "fair" America if they are prepared to work. Costa Ricans, with their moral principles pervading the achievement of success, will be less likely to confuse collaboration with cheating. (Waugh et al., 1995, p. 79)

A comparison between students' perceptions of the extent of cheating and the admitted frequency of cheating was made by Franklyn-Stokes and Newstead (1995), who found a very strong correspondence between students' estimates of the percentage of cheating by others and self-reports of actual cheating.[4] The researchers also compared students' perceptions of cheating with those of faculty members ($n = 20$) and found significant differences between the two. Faculty tended to perceive cheating as more serious that students did and to believe that it occurred less frequently.

Undergraduate education students ($n = 436$) from England, Grenada, Jamaica, Mauritius, and Nigeria were surveyed by Stanton (1980) regarding a variety of situations in which moral judgment was required. Two of the situations presented to the students described cheating on a test and cheating at a game. Three findings related to cheating on tests are relevant here: (a) among all national groups, there was considerable consensus that cheating on a test was an "undesirable behavior"; (b) there was no significant difference between the perceptions of males and females from any of the countries studied[5] regarding the desirability of cheating; and (c) in only two countries (England and Nigeria) were perceptions of the acceptability of cheating on a test related to cheating in another context (i.e., in a game), with those differences observed only in men.

Higher education in Saudi Arabia is rapidly expanding, both in terms of physical facilities and access. However, cheating on examinations is a rising problem as well. Perceptions of cheating by students in the Saudi Arabian higher education

---

[4]The researchers found the rank order correlation between perceptions and reported behaviors to be .79. Additional information regarding the meaning and interpretation of correlation coefficients is presented in chapter 6.

[5]Stanton was only able to study male–female differences in England, Mauritius, Nigeria, and Grenada; the Jamaican sample did not include any male respondents.

was studied by Khashan (1984) at the King Saud University College of Science and College of Administrative Science. Of 420 students surveyed, 55% said that they would transfer information to a friend during an examination. Khashan observed that, "in Saudi culture, students appear to have only a vague idea of what constitutes cheating and plagiarism. The way these concepts are understood in the West does not apply in the Saudi Arabian context" (p. 24).

To some extent, the opposite conclusion regarding Arab students' perceptions of cheating was offered in the work of Sumrain (1987), who surveyed 280 Arab and U.S. students. Sumrain found no statistically significant differences between the students' perceptions regarding whether specific behaviors constituted cheating, although the mean ratings of the Arab students were lower (on a scale for which lower ratings indicated less agreement that a given behavior was cheating). On the other hand, Arab students' views regarding appropriate punishment were statistically different from those of U.S. students, with the Arab students less severe in their recommended punishments. One major difference in Sumrain's study, however, may contribute to a difference in findings between it and that of Khashan: In Khashan's study, all of the Saudi Arabian students were surveyed at an institution in their native country, whereas all of the students surveyed by Sumrain were then attending a university in the United States and may have had greater exposure to U.S. culture and academic mores.

Several cultural differences were observed in the study of Senegalese secondary school students reported by Vandewiele (1980), whose survey included a majority of students from the Wolof ethnic group. When students who had admitted to cheating were asked to give their reasons for doing so, the Senegalese students cited laziness (44.6%), protestation against parental pressures and expectations (29.0%), doubts about the teacher's ability (6.0%), an environment in which everyone cheats (2.8%), and the desire to get a degree as fast as possible (2.3%) as the primary reasons. This finding contrasts sharply with the finding that the desire for higher marks or grades has been identified as students' primary reason for cheating in most other studies. Further, Vandewiele found that although 42.2% of the Senegalese students denounced cheating, cultural forces and pressures created by examinations caused some dissonance for the students. Vandewiele found that, on one hand, "solidarity, a supreme virtue with the Africans, inclines them to turn a blind eye on their colleagues' cheating"; on the other hand, a spirit of competition in the schools and the strict moral code of the Wolofs served to stigmatize the practice of cheating (p. 209). Along these lines, 51.9% of the students reported that they "felt embarrassed when other students cribbed from them" and reported that "I would feel ashamed to be in his shoes" (p. 209).

CULTURAL DIFFERENCES
WITHIN THE UNITED STATES

The United States has increasingly become a more multicultural nation. The U.S. higher education serves not only native-born American students but also naturalized citizens and students from nearly all countries wishing to share in the benefits and opportunities that an advanced education can provide. Particularly in areas such as the sciences, agriculture, medicine, and engineering, the U.S. system of higher education has helped prepare students from other nations to assume leadership roles on graduation and return to their native countries. This growing ethnic and cultural diversity has prompted a few researchers to examine the relationship between ethnic identity, cultural values, and cheating.

Cultural differences in how cheating is perceived among international students can create perplexing issues for school administrators in the United States. A case study of an actual cheating incident at a university, given the fictitious name "Uni" for the sake of confidentiality, illustrates the problem. At Uni, more than 50 students from the country of "Jaxar" (also fictitious) who were enrolled in the university's MBA program, were accused of cheating. When confronted about cheating on an examination—passing notes, signaling, looking at each other's papers—the students acknowledged the activities but disagreed that they should be classified as cheating. The students were subjected to disciplinary sanctions, which were appealed by the students and their families. Central to their argument in the appeal was the notion that

> the behavior was accepted in Jaxar; in fact, Jaxar families encouraged it in their sons studying in the U.S. They viewed the behavior as "helping each other—as required by their culture." As explained by everyone from Jaxar, each person was viewed as a "brother" in an extended family (the country was ruled by a hierarchical structure dominated by a few families). Each "brother" was expected to assist other brothers, especially those who needed help in understanding the course material or in passing the exams. (Cordiero, 1995, p. 28)

Cultural differences have been documented not only in international students within the United States, but also among American students of differing cultural heritage. For example, Sutton and Huba (1995) compared the perceptions about cheating of African American ($n = 161$) and White ($n = 161$) students enrolled in a large, public university in the Midwestern United States, and found considerable agreement that specified behaviors constituted cheating. The students agreed that taking an exam for another student, copying from another student without his or her knowledge, giving answers to another student during an exam, arranging to give or receive signals during an examination, and using unauthorized materials during an exam were "definitely cheating" (p. 23). When students' judgments about the propriety of these activities were examined separately by ethnicity, no significant differences were found. These students were also asked to give their perceptions regarding the pervasiveness of the same behaviors. The data in Table 5.2 confirm other reports about how widespread cheating appears to be on U.S. college campuses. However, of the behaviors listed in Table 5.2, significant differences were noted between African American and White students on only one activity—getting questions or answers about an exam from someone who had already taken it—with African American students perceiving that the behavior occurred more frequently than did White students.

Sutton and Huba also asked students to give their perceptions of when cheating was justified. Notably, 73.5% of the students indicated that "cheating is never justified under any circumstances" (1995, p. 26), and no difference was observed between African American and White students at this level. However, support for that global principle broke down somewhat when students were presented with narrower, more specific circumstances. Table 5.3 shows the percentages of students who agreed or strongly agreed that cheating would be justified in given situations. Differences between the groups were also noted at this level. Significant differences between African American and White students are marked in Table 5.3

with asterisks; in each case, African American students were more likely than White students to agree that cheating was justified in the given circumstance.

Another study compared the perceptions of 42 U.S. undergraduates with those of 38 Spanish-speaking and 26 Arabic-speaking English as a second language (ESL) students.[6] The study asked the three groups to rate three types of cheating on tests (using crib notes, copying, and allowing copying) along two dimensions (right–wrong and moral–immoral). The authors found that all groups rated the behaviors as wrong, with the use of crib notes rated most wrong and allowing another student to copy from one's paper judged least wrong. On the Moral–Immoral scale, all three groups rated the behaviors toward the immoral end of the scale, although "Spanish-speaker ratings were generally more neutral ... than were those of the other two groups" (Kuehn, Stanwyck, & Holland, 1990, p. 315).

Two qualitative studies have illustrated cultural components to perceptions of cheating among American students at the high school level. In the first study, P. A. Cordiero and Carspecken (1993) studied 20 highly successful Hispanic students in their junior and senior years. They reported, "Causing us some surprise, this research revealed extensive cheating on the part of the 20 students" (p. 286). The authors attributed the cheating to the students' desire for scholastic success, with

TABLE 5.2

African American and White Students' Perceptions of Frequency of Cheating on Examinations

Behavior	% Responding "A Great Deal" or "A Fair Amount"
Getting questions or answers about an exam from someone who has already taken it	60.9
Copying from someone's exam paper without his or her knowledge	51.0
Arranging to sit next to someone in order to copy from his or her exam paper	46.5
Using unauthorized notes during an examination	37.5
Giving answers to other students during an exam	32.6
Arranging with other students to give or receive signals during an exam	11.8
Taking an examination for another student	8.1

Note. From "Undergraduate Student Perceptions of Academic Dishonesty as a Function of Ethnicity and Religious Participation," by E. M. Sutton and M. E. Huba, 1995, *NASPA Journal, 33*(1), p. 29. Reprinted with permission of the National Association of Student Personnel Administartors (NASPA).

---

[6]One obvious difficulty with the design of this study is that the responses of all Spanish-speaking and all Arabic-speaking students were combined. Thus, for example, natives of Spain, Mexico, Belize, and Cuba would be lumped together in the analysis, as would speakers from all Arabic countries, despite potentially significant cultural differences.

TABLE 5.3
African American and White Students' Perceptions of Justifiability of Cheating

Statement: Cheating is justified ...	% Responding "Agree" or "Strongly Agree"
In order to receive a better course grade	12.8*
When a friend asks for help during an exam	13.4*
When a person needs to keep a scholarship	18.9*
When a person needs to pass a course to stay in school	20.5*
When a person needs to pass a course for graduation	23.6*

Note. From "Undergraduate Student Perceptions of Academic Dishonesty as a Function of Ethnicity and Religious Participation," by E. M. Sutton and M. E. Huba, 1995, *NASPA Journal, 33*(1), p. 29. Reprinted with permission of the National Association of Student Personnel Administrators (NASPA).

$^* = p < .05$.

success in school being "a way to demonstrate the capacity to rise out of low socio-economic status" (p. 287).

In the second study, Hemmings (1996) observed six high-achieving Black students in their junior year at an urban high school. Hemmings described cheating as the "pragmatic means for students with limited resources to pass their courses" (p. 40), in which cheating and sharing information was viewed not as inappropriate but as a responsibility. At one of the schools, students would

> participate in elaborate cheating networks in which one or two students provided answers to homework and tests to other members. The ethic governing these arrangements was simple: Students who were the strongest academically were morally obligated to pass along answers to the weakest. (p. 40)

At the other school, the high-achieving students were identified as an elite group, involved in a special "Program for the Academically Talented," although the students also participated in cheating networks. When Hemmings (1996) asked one of the students why they cheated so much, the student replied, "We're not cheating. We're helping each other out!" (p. 43).

CONCLUSION

There are a few parallels that can be drawn between what research in the United States has found regarding cheating and what cross-cultural research has yielded. First, anecdotes and research results from around the world suggest that cheating on examinations is a universal phenomenon. Students of all nationalities tend to judge cheating behaviors for what they are, and they tend to judge cheating less harshly than their instructors, who view cheating as a more serious offense. International studies of cheating also share methodological similarities—weaknesses, actually—with studies conducted in the United States, in that the data are primarily self-report data, collected by means of anonymous surveys of high school or college students, that depend on the cooperation and honesty of volunteer respondents.

However, cross-cultural studies reveal substantial differences in the way cheating is defined, perceived, and practiced. Anecdotes regarding systemic corruption of some educational systems notwithstanding, one difference is that there appears to be somewhat less cheating engaged in (or admitted to) outside the United States. None of the studies conducted in other nations approached the recent U.S. rates of 80% or more of college students admitting to cheating. It may be that U.S. students are either the most dishonest in the international community studied—or simply the most honest about their dishonesty.

The results also suggest that any cross-cultural differences in reported cheating behaviors should be interpreted with great caution because cheating is defined differently in various countries. These differences may be related to educational practices prevalent in each country. Several studies have noted differences such as reliance on more cooperative or more competitive learning environments; both within and outside the United States, differences may also be related to cultural conceptions of appropriate circumstances for giving and receiving assistance.

Second, studies of student perceptions of the acceptability of cheating reveal that, in many other countries, cheating is considerably more acceptable than in the United States. The study by Khashan (1984) captures this point, finding that, in Russia, even students who recognize behaviors as inappropriate in an academic context nevertheless judge the behaviors as acceptable. Khashan's work also illustrated gender differences in perceptions of cheating, which are surely related to cultural influences. Khashan's summary is probably an adequate summary of the bulk of the cross-cultural studies: "The way these concepts [i.e., cheating] are understood in the West does not apply in the Saudi Arabian context" (p. 24).

Given the increasing diversity of American society, the issue of cultural differences in perceptions of cheating is not one that can be readily ignored by those responsible for assessment programs wholly within the United States. The author of the case study involving students at Uni reported that the institution upheld disciplinary actions against the Jaxar students, concluding that a single ethical standard for academic integrity must be applied uniformly to all students (W. P. Cordiero, 1995). However, the outcome of any particular case is less of an issue than the bigger question of how to maintain the validity of inferences from test scores. As the United States moves toward a more thoroughly multicultural society, those who are responsible for giving and interpreting tests will need to become more aware of such cultural differences. At all levels of the educational system, those interested in preventing cheating—and preventing cases like the one at Uni from becoming occasions for litigation—will also benefit from understanding the differing perceptions about cheating that test takers of different cultural backgrounds bring with them to a test.

✦ S I X ✦

Correlates of Cheating

his chapter presents what is known about the correlates of cheating. When social scientists speak of correlates, they mean those variables—personal attributes, background characteristics, or situational factors—that have been shown to be related in some way to one or more other variables. In the literature on correlates of cheating, some researchers have referred to these variables as *determinants* of cheating. This term, however, connotes that cheating on tests is predestined or causally linked to factors that may or may not be under the test taker's control. To avoid this deterministic implication, I use the term *correlates* throughout this chapter, regardless of how the variables have been described in the original research.

Although inferences of causality are inappropriate based on the literature of cheating on tests, the notion of correlates does suggest the potential of *predictability*. That is, knowledge of some variable or constellation of characteristics can enable fairly confident predictions about whether cheating is likely to occur, the amount of cheating a student is likely to engage in or admit to, or the student's perceptions of cheating.

More than 100 correlates of cheating on tests have been studied. All of the usual suspects regularly included in social science research have been studied, including age, gender, intelligence, and socioeconomic status (SES). In addition, other student background characteristics have been examined, such as birth order, employment status, and fraternity and sorority membership—as have a number of personality correlates, such as extroversion, alienation, and need for approval. Variables related to the context of instruction and testing, such as instructor characteristics, class size, and test difficulty also have been examined for their possible relationship to cheating.

Correlates of cheating can be grouped along the lines suggested in the preceding paragraph, and these groupings serve as an organizing framework for this chapter. The first grouping consists of student demographic characteristics. This grouping includes background characteristics of test takers—variables over which they have no control, such as sex, age, and so on—and descriptive variables, such as employment status, academic major, GPA, and so on.

A second grouping consists of psychological constructs. In psychology, the term *construct* is used to refer to characteristics that exist only in the sense that they can be labeled, observed, and (sometimes with imprecision) measured. For example, the characteristic of intelligence is a construct. Strictly speaking, intelligence does not exist but is a convenient label that can be used and understood as a descriptor of behavior; it can also be roughly measured using tests that reflect social and scientific notions of the behaviors that constitute intelligent activity. Research on the correlates of cheating has included constructs such as intelligence, honesty, neuroticism, extroversion, and so on. This category of variables is the second most frequently researched.

A third grouping consists of variables related to classroom instructional and environmental factors. This category includes variables that describe educational aspects such as the classroom seating arrangement, class size, and the formats used for testing. These classroom environment factors are largely under the control of the instructor. However, this category also includes characteristics of instructors and teachers, such as classroom management styles and attitude toward cheating.

The fourth and final grouping, called "other" for lack of a better name, is simply a collection of correlates that don't readily fit into the preceding groupings. For example, school size has been studied as a correlate of cheating. This variable is not, however, a characteristic of the test taker or the test giver, nor can it be thought of under the control of either one. This grouping represents the smallest portion of the research on cheating.

STUDENT DEMOGRAPHIC CHARACTERISTICS

By far, the majority of the research on cheating on tests has examined variables that would fall in the student demographic characteristics category. This is not because of the large number of possible demographic variables but because relatively few student characteristics have been included in nearly every study of correlates. The most frequently studied correlates include "the big five": gender, achievement (represented by grades or GPA), age (or grade level in school), membership in a fraternity or sorority, and religiosity. The following sections summarize the research on these and other demographic correlates of cheating on tests.

Gender

Of all the demographic characteristics of test takers that could be related to cheating, gender has been the single most studied variable. One of the most consistent findings is that the incidence of self-reported cheating behavior by elementary school-aged students is about the same for boys and girls. Few studies have been conducted in which boys and girls were observed in academic testing situations. However, numerous studies have examined cheating in other, related contexts, such as observing the behavior of individual children who are given directions not to "peek" at information that would be helpful to complete a task or observing the extent to which a child cheats when playing a game, completing a puzzle, or working through a maze.

This relationship was first observed in the classic studies by Hartshorne and May (1928), which showed no differences between girls and boys on various tests of honesty. A study by Coady and Sawyer (1986) involving 80 second- and third-grade students also reported no significant differences between the boys and girls in a context in which there was a temptation to cheat. Krebs (1969) studied cheating on tests in a sample of 132 sixth graders; here again, there were no significant differences between the incidence of cheating for boys and girls. Anderman, Griesinger, and Westerfield (1998) found no significant differences in self-reported cheating in a sample of 285 sixth-, seventh-, and eighth-grade boys and girls. The few studies in which gender differences have been revealed provide contradictory findings: Hetherington and Feldman (1964) suggested that there may be slightly more cheating by girls in elementary school, whereas Lobel and Levanon (1988) found more cheating by elementary school boys.

Overall, it is likely that no real differences in cheating exist at the elementary school level. However, it is also clear from studies of cheating involving high school students that gender differences begin to emerge in subsequent years. Most investigators have reported a greater incidence and admission of cheating by male students in high school (see S. F. Davis et al., 1992; Schab, 1969). Feldman and Feldman (1967) described the transition of gender differences in cheating, finding that female students were more likely to engage in cheating in elementary school, although male students eventually surpass female students by the senior year in high school.

At the college level, a fairly consistent finding has been the comparatively greater frequency and admission of cheating by men, although this relationship has been evolving. Nearly all of the studies of cheating before 1980 showed more cheating for male college students. For example, in a study of 200 college students Baird (1980) found that "males admitted cheating in more of their courses than did females. They admitted cheating on more types of tests, and admitted using a greater variety of cheating methods" (p. 519). Baldwin et al. (1996) found more men admitted to cheating in high school, in college, and at every level of medical school. The greater rate of cheating by men has been confirmed in other studies ranging from smaller scale studies of college students involving less than 100 students (e.g., Hetherington & Feldman, 1964) to large-scale surveys of more than 6,000 students (e.g., S. F. Davis et al., 1992).

Although studies of self-reported cheating behavior at the college level tend to reveal a greater percentage of men who admit to cheating on tests, there are at least four caveats to this general conclusion. First, the proportions of male and female students *who get caught* cheating may be about equal, or at least the jury is still out on that question. One study of 311 accounting and economics students examined the demographic characteristics of students and cheating that were identified by using self-scoring of quizzes; the researchers found no significant differences between men and women (Nowell & Laufer, 1997). Another study of *reported* cheating incidents involving 943 college students in Great Britain found that reported incidents more commonly involved men (Newstead et al., 1996).

Second, female college students may engage in cheating as much or more than men under certain conditions. One study of adolescents found that women were as likely as men to cheat when the behavior was prompted by a desire to help another student, as opposed to motivated by personal gain (Calabrese & Cochran, 1990). Currently, it is unknown whether this finding also applies to the college level.

Third, as a variable, gender interacts with other variables that have been studied in relation to cheating. For example, in subsequent sections of this chapter, characteristics such as "motivation to avoid failure" and "self-esteem" are reviewed for their association with cheating behavior. In some cases, there are interaction effects between the variables; that is, the relationship of the variables to cheating depends on the gender of the student.

A final caveat: Although men have, for years, admitted to a greater amount of cheating in college, there is evidence that the "cheating gap" is narrowing and that parity between men and women is rapidly approaching. This recent development was summarized in one of the largest and most comprehensive studies of cheating at the college level, in which the authors concluded that:

> some important changes [in college-level cheating] appear to be taking place along gender lines. The increases in cheating observed at the nine state universities studied by McCabe and Bowers in 1993 were driven by increased cheating among women. While 59 percent of the women at these schools in Bowers' 1963 sample reported at least one incidence of test cheating, this had grown to 70 percent by 1993. For men, test cheating was essentially unchanged. (McCabe & Trevino, 1996, p. 32)

This observation is corroborated by findings over the past several years of no significant differences between the admitted cheating rates of men and women (e.g., Diekhoff et al., 1996) and, in at least one case, of significantly greater cheating by women (Graham et al., 1994).

Achievement

Achievement or performance in any area can only crudely be reduced to a single index. In the U.S. educational system, achievement is often summarized using grades, such as the familiar A to F scale in elementary schools and the 0.0 to 4.0 scale in colleges, or in other ways (e.g., percentages). A considerable amount of research has examined the relationship between achievement and cheating on tests, using grades or GPAs as the variable of interests. Because much of the evidence on the relationship between achievement and cheating is expressed using the procedure known as *correlation*, a brief explanation of that concept follows.

A correlation is a statistical index, symbolized by the letter r, that expresses the strength of the relationship between two variables.[1] Correlations can range from $r = 1.00$ to $r = -1.00$. An r of 1.00 would mean that the variables are perfectly related: High values on one variable are perfectly related with high values on the other variable, as low values on one are associated with low values on the other. For example, a correlation near 1.00 exists between height and weight for humans: Taller people tend to weigh more, and shorter people tend to weigh less. An r of -1.00 also means that the variables are perfectly related but in an inverse manner. For example, there is a perfect negative relationship between class attendance and class absence. That is, students who have high attendance are (by definition) those with

---

[1]Although obvious, it may be worth mentioning that it is from the statistical term *correlation* that we get the notion of "correlates"—things that are related to each other.

fewer days absent, whereas students who have poorer attendance have greater days absent. In the middle of the range between -1.00 and 1.00 is the correlation of $.00$, which can be interpreted to mean that there is no relationship between the two variables.[2] The larger the absolute value of the correlation index (i.e., the closer r is to 1.00 or -1.00) the stronger the relationship between the variables. For example, correlations near $-.20$ or $.20$ would usually be called "weak" relationships, correlations closer to $-.50$ or $.50$ would be called "moderate," and correlations around $-.70$ or $.70$ (and greater) would be called "strong."

As indicated previously, much of the research on the relationship between cheating and achievement has been correlational. In the survey administered by Baird (1980), students were asked directly, "How often have you cheated in college?" The correlation between their responses and self-reported GPAs was $-.34$. The value of $-.34$ indicates a weak-to-moderate inverse relationship between self-reported cheating and GPAs. The correlation of $-.34$ reveals that there is a slight tendency for students with *lower* GPAs to confess *more* cheating, and vice versa.

Antion and Michael (1983) compared both self-reported GPAs and actual scores on a psychology final examination with incidence and amount of cheating in a group of 148 community college students. The researchers were able to examine actual cheating using the technique of allowing students to self-score their final examinations that had previously (but unknown to the students) been scored by the instructor. Incidence of cheating was defined as a student's self-scored performance being discrepant from the actual score from the instructor's scoring of the test. Amount of cheating was defined as the degree of the discrepancy. Antion and Michael found a significantly inverse relationship between self-reported GPA and cheating and an inverse relationship between actual score on the final and cheating. This was true whether the criterion was incidence or amount of cheating.[3]

Similar results have been observed by others using the same self-grading method of investigation. Bronzaft, Stuart, and Blum (1973) and Fakouri (1972) observed the inverse relationship between grades and cheating in samples of undergraduates; Vitro (1971) documented the inverse relationship in a sample of 70 female college students. Gardner, Roper, Gonzalez, and Simpson (1988) found significantly more cheating by students with lower test grades among 245 students enrolled in a college psychology course; Bunn, Caudill, and Gropper (1992) found similar results in a survey of 476 economics students.

When students are simply asked about their cheating behaviors in surveys (as opposed to studies such as those above in which cheating is actually observed), the results are the same. A negative correlation between self-reported cheating and self-reported GPA was found at both of the 10-year intervals of one longitudinal

---

[2]More accurately, the most common correlation index used to express the relationship between GPA and cheating is known as the Pearson product–moment correlation. This index is a measure of the strength of the linear relationship between two continuous variables. Thus, a correlation of $.00$ may not mean that there is no relationship between two variables but rather that the relationship is not well described by a straight line. For example, if students with very high and very low GPAs were found to cheat extensively, whereas students with moderate GPAs did not cheat at all, the variables would clearly be related but in a U-shaped fashion. However, the Pearson product–moment correlation for this case would yield an index of $r = .00$ because the relationship is not linear.

[3]As a humorous aside, Antion and Michael also reported the occurrence of some *really* bad cheaters: There were eight students whose self-scored number correct deviated from their actual score but in a way that their self-scored marks were lower.

study (see Diekhoff et al., 1996; Haines et al., 1986). Graham et al. (1994) found a weak correlation ($r = -.22$) between admitted cheating and self-reported GPA in a sample of Midwestern college students; Moffatt (1990) reported a slight negative relationship in a survey of 232 students at Rutgers University; Mixon (1996) found a small but significant inverse relationship in a sample of 157 business administration majors; and Brandes (1986) found more cheating by students with lower grades in a sample of California elementary school students.

Expressing the association between GPA and cheating in terms of percentages (as opposed to correlations) highlights the degree of the relationship. For example, in a survey of 378 graduate and undergraduate students at a U.S. university, Scheers and Dayton (1987) found that "substantially different estimates of [self-reported] cheating behaviors occur at the various GPA levels.... The most dramatic variation in the estimates occurred in Statement 5 where the percentage of students who admitted copying on examinations ranged from 21% at the highest GPA level to 86% at the lowest GPA level for the covariate model" (p. 66).

In one of the earliest studies investigating the relationship between achievement and cheating, Drake (1941) used the method of self-scoring to identify actual cheating behavior and compared discrepant scores with the students' actual grades (unaffected by cheating). Drake found a clear relationship between cheating and grades among the 126 female college students involved in the study. Drake concluded with what might be called the Marxist theory of cheating:

> Considering the true averages of the students, unaffected by the attempts to cheat, no A student cheated, 4 per cent of the B students, 23 per cent of the C students, 75 per cent of the D students, and 67 per cent of the F (failure) students cheated. From this it may be inferred that the poorest students tend to cheat the most; that is, they tend to cheat in proportion to their needs. (p. 419)

The negative relationship between cheating and achievement as measured by grades has also been observed in international contexts. In their study in Great Britain, Newstead et al. (1996) reported "a systematic decrease in the range of cheating as achievement level increased" among a sample of college students (p. 234). In a study involving more than 1,000 respondents, Rost and Wild (1994) found that German high school students who indicated greater amounts of self-reported cheating had lower grades in both German language and mathematics.

Overall, the research can be summarized unequivocally. Cheating is inversely related to achievement: Students with lower grades are more likely both to report cheating on tests and to actually engage in the behavior, whereas students with higher achievement are less likely to do either. The relationship is only slight to moderate, but it is one of the most consistent among the demographic variables.

Age and Year in School

The background characteristics of student age and year in school are obviously related: older students tend to be more advanced in terms of grade level. The relationship between age and year in school and cheating is somewhat difficult to summarize because other characteristics of the student population change as students progress through the grade levels. For example, factors such as previous (poor) achievement, lack of motivation or effort, and economic support result in some students dropping out of a cohort as it passes from eighth grade into high school, from high school to college, or from college to graduate study. Thus, as students progress through the American educational system, they not only get older but are also, as a group, more able, more motivated, more economically well-off, and so on.

As described in chapter 2, the rates of cheating increase from the elementary school to high school years. In Brandes' (1986) study of California 6th and 11th graders, a significantly higher incidence of cheating was reported for the high schoolers. Feldman and Feldman (1967) found more cheating by 12th-grade boys compared with 7th-grade boys, although they found similar cheating rates for girls.

Cheating appears to reach a peak in high school. Most comparative studies have found that cheating rates stabilize or decline as students move from high school to college. Students' self-reports of cheating in high school and college show significantly less cheating in college (S. F. Davis et al., 1992) In Baird's (1980) survey, 84.5% of the students reported cheating while they were in high school, whereas 75.5% reported cheating in college.

On the other hand, *within* the college years, cheating appears to increase as students move from the freshman to senior years. Moffatt (1990) found more cheating among upperclassmen; J. Harp & Taietz (1966) found a greater incidence of cheating by juniors and seniors. One study even found increased cheating over the course of a single semester (Gardner et al., 1988). In that study, students were given directions to complete a weekly study guide without the use of the textbook. The study guides were reviewed to determine the extent to which the directions were followed; cheating was defined as study-guide answers that exactly matched wording found in the textbook. The amount of cheating was variable from week to week but generally increased over the semester.

A few studies have tried to disentangle the effects of age and year in school. These studies have all been at the college level, where the ages of students at a particular level can vary substantially. The findings from these studies reveal that older students tend to cheat less than their younger classmates. The survey administered by Graham et al. (1994) found that cheating was slightly related to being a traditional-aged college student, noting a correlation of −.27 between age and reported cheating. Newstead et al. (1996) also found more cheating among younger students compared with their older college classmates.

In Haines et al.'s (1986) survey, age was found to be the best predictor of cheating. In that study, age was correlated with cheating, with admitted cheaters coded "0" and noncheaters coded "1." The correlation of .40 indicates that older students were somewhat more likely to be noncheaters and vice versa. The mean age of the group that admitted cheating was 20.3 years; the mean age of the noncheaters was 25.6 years. These findings were replicated in the 10-year follow-up to their study (Diekhoff et al., 1996).

Finally, not only are younger students more likely to be cheaters in college, but they are also more likely to be perceived as such by their classmates. In a study of these perceptions by Franklyn-Stokes and Newstead (1995), students reported perceiving their peers who were over 25 years old to be less likely to cheat compared with students in the 21- to 24- or 18- to 20-year-old age groups. Newstead et al. (1996) hypothesized that this may be due to the fact that the older, nontraditional students tend to be more intrinsically motivated or more advanced in moral development.

Fraternity and Sorority Membership

Motivated, perhaps, by legends regarding the vast files of illegal tests maintained by members of Greek societies, or simply by experience, scholars have examined potential relationships between membership in a fraternity or sorority and engaging in cheating. The disdain for this "opportunity structure" has been articulated in scholarly terms. J. Harp and Taietz (1966) investigated "the anti-intellectual theme within the fraternity system" (p. 368). Their skepticism about the academic integrity of fraternities is thinly veiled in their findings: "Although only 20 per cent of the students regarded themselves as intellectuals, 42 per cent of these resided in fraternities" (p. 368).

As it turns out, the campus lore is correct: Cheating is more common among students who are members of fraternities or sororities than those who are not (so-called independents; Diekhoff et al., 1996; Haines et al., 1986; Moffatt, 1990). In the first large-scale study of the cheating differences between Greek societies and independents, Bowers (1969) concluded that "the more closely students are associated with a fraternity or sorority, the more likely they are to cheat" (p. 109).

One of the earliest studies on the subject in a sample of college students identified cheating by 36% of Greek students compared with 16% of those who were not members of a fraternity or sorority (Drake, 1941). Nearly 30 years after Drake's study, Stannard and Bowers (1970) examined cheating in a sample of 697 Greek students and 950 independents at 58 colleges and found that cheating rates had increased to 58% for the Greeks and 51% for the independents. Approximately 25 years later, in a survey of 1,793 students at seven different institutions, cheating was again found to be both increasing and more common among both fraternity members (86%) and sorority members (82%) compared with independents (67%) (McCabe & Bowers, 1996). These percentages reflect the same trend of increasing cheating as has been documented in higher education generally.

The nature of cheating by fraternity and sorority members has been summarized by Baird (1980), who concluded that:

> members of college fraternities or sororities admitted more frequent cheating in college than nonmembers, and in more of their courses. These differences were reflected in a greater probability to cheat on more types of tests and to use different methods. Fraternity–sorority students were more likely to engage in cooperative techniques (copying assignments and tests, allowing others to copy work, at taking tests for other people) than were independents. In addition, fraternity–sorority students admitted to more high school cheating than independents. (p. 519)

Finally, one of the most interesting findings related to cheating by fraternity and sorority members is found in the work of Stannard and Bowers (1970). Contrary to what might be predicted from the wealth of evidence about the relationship of Greek membership to cheating, the authors found that as the proportion of Greek membership on a campus rises, levels of cheating actually decrease. The decrease was found to apply in both Greek and independent student populations.

Religious Beliefs, Instruction, and Practice

Like membership in a fraternity or sorority, it might seem that religious belief ought to be related to cheating: Students professing adherence to an established moral system might be predicted to engage in less cheating than those who do not profess such convictions. The reality is that religious belief, instruction, and practice affect cheating in different ways.

Contrary to the expectation, research has, for the most part, found no relationship between cheating behavior and simple identification with a religion. Sierles et al. (1980) found a negligible relationship between incidence of cheating and religious preference in a study of 428 medical school students. Nowell and Laufer (1997) also found no relationship between religious preference and cheating in their sample of economics students. (In their study, religious preference was simply coded as "present" if the student expressed a religious preference or "absent" if the student did not.) Likewise, whether a student claimed membership in any church was found not to be related to cheating in a study by Knowlton and Hamerlynck (1967). R. E. Smith, Wheeler, and Diener (1975) asked a group of 440 undergraduate students to identify themselves as religious, nonreligious, atheist, or Jesus people and gave them opportunities to cheat on an examination and to volunteer for an altruistic task (working on a project that would help mentally retarded children). The researchers found no differences among the groups in terms of engaging in cheating on the test or not, students' magnitude of cheating, and willingness to volunteer to help the children.

Formal ethical instruction may not be beneficial either, although the findings are inconclusive. Atkins and Atkins (1936) provided brief ethical instruction to college students on the day of a test and found a reduction in observed cheating behavior. However, college students who read about morality before taking a vocabulary test cheated more than students who read an irrelevant passage (Dienstbier, Kahle, Wiliss, & Tunnell, 1980), Ames and Eskridge (1992) found that college students who had completed an entire ethics course were *less* likely to classify specific cheating behaviors as cheating than students who had not. Also, in a study conducted with sixth graders in Israel, students who attended religious public schools in which formal religious instruction was provided actually had higher incidence of cheating on a maze completion task than students who attended secular public schools in which no such instruction was provided.

Corcoran and Rotter (1987) found that female college students who rated higher on a moralism measure actually cheated more than those who scored lower on moralism under test conditions in which the risk of being caught cheating was low. Forsyth and Berger (1982) classified 80 female college students according to polar ethical positions: relativism versus absolutism, and idealism versus pragmatism (see Fig. 6.1). Although they found a similar lack of resistance to cheating on a test in each of these groups, they did identify interesting tendencies for various combinations of ethical ideology and moral behavior. So-called *nonrelativistic idealists* (upper right quadrant of Fig. 6.1) tended to engage in greater self-devaluation, *exceptionists* (lower right quadrant) reported increased happiness the more they cheated, and *subjectivists* (upper left quadrant) exhibited greater fear of being caught cheating.

Church attendance, too, may be negatively related to honest behavior on tests. In one study, students who reported that they attended church more frequently were significantly more likely to change their answers on a self-graded test (Hetherington & Feldman, 1964). Students identified as cheaters (i.e., those who changed their answers) reported attending church an average of 32.7 days per year, whereas noncheaters reported attendance of only 14 days per year. (Of course it can be speculated that, because these findings are based on self-reported data, students who have been identified as having cheated on a test may not have given accurate responses regarding their church attendance either.)

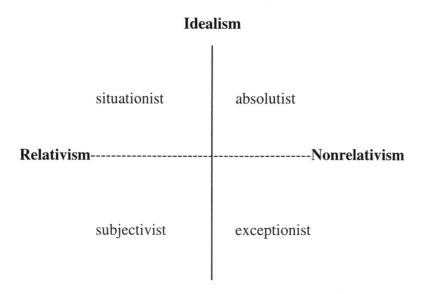

FIG. 6.1. Ethical ideology and moral behavior. Adapted with permission from "The Effects of Ethical Ideology on Moral Behavior," D. R. Forsyth & R. E. Berger, 1982, *Journal of Social Psychology, 117*(1), p. 53. Reprinetd with permission of the Helen Dwight Reid Educational Foundation. Published by Heldref Publicatins, 1319 18th St. N.W., Washington DC 20036-1802. Copyright © 1982.

On a more positive note, religious belief does appear to affect attitude toward cheating. In one study, 443 teacher education students at Indiana State University were administered a questionnaire to determine their standing on a scale of religious conservatism. The students were also asked their opinion of the statement "Cheating on an examination is justified when others are also cheating and raising the [grading] curve of the class." A majority of students identified as religious liberals and a majority of students identified as religious conservatives disagreed with the statement, with religious conservatives rejecting the statement most often (Clouse, 1973). In another study, students who indicated a high degree of involvement in religious activity were more likely to identify listed cheating behaviors as dishonest and less likely to believe that cheating is justified in given situations (Sutton & Huba, 1995).

Other Demographic Correlates

A number of other background characteristics of students have been investigated for their possible relationship to cheating on tests. These variables have been studied much less frequently than the big five, in some cases a variable has been of interest to only a single researcher. Consequently, inferences of relationship involving these variables are necessarily more tentative. Table 6.1 summarizes a number of the other demographic variables that have been studied.[4] Where corre-

---

[4]One background variable—the student's major field of study in college—is not included in the list, despite having been included in a substantial number of studies. Information on this characteristic was summarized previously (see chap. 2).

TABLE 6.1

Miscellaneous Demographic Correlates of Cheating

Variable	N	Grade Level	Type of Data	r^a	Finding: Increased Cheating Associated With …	Citation
Artistic and literary interests	1,500	College	Self-report		Score on Cultural Sophistication Scale is decreased	Centra (1970)
Birth order	78	College	Observed		Student is firstborn	Hetherington & Feldman (1964)
Employment	380	College	Self-report	−.22	Student works full time	Haines et al. (1986)
	474	College	Self-report		Student works full time	Diekhoff et al. (1996)
	311	College	Observed		Student works full or part time	Nowell & Laufer (1997)
Ethnicity	1,534	Grades 9–12	Self-report		Students are White, rather than Hispanic, Asian, or other ethnic minority; no difference for White vs. Black students	Calabrese & Cochran (1990)
	322	College	Self-report		No difference between White and Black students on behaviors perceived to be cheating	Sutton & Huba (1995)
	285	Grades 6–8	Self-report		No difference between majority (White) and nonmajority students	Anderman et al. (1998)
	143	College	Self-report		No correlation between ethnicity and cheating	Sierles et al. (1988)

Variable	N	Level	Method	r	Finding	Citation
Extracurricular participation	200	College	Self-report		No correlation with engaging in cheating; however greater participation related to stronger disapproval of cheating	Baird (1980)
	380	College	Self-report	.12	Involved in varsity sports	Haines et al. (1986)
	474	College	Self-report		Involved in varsity sports	Diekhoff et al. (1996)
Family structure	865	Grades 5–9	Self-report		Reduced susceptibility to peer pressure for students biologically intact families.[b]	Steinberg (1987)
Financial support for education	380	College	Self-report	.17	Parents are source of financial support	Haines et al. (1986)
	474	College	Self-report		Parents are source of financial support	Diekhoff et al. (1996)
	480	College	Self-report		Parents pay for college education	Graham et al. (1994)
	474	College	Self-report		Student has a scholarship	Diekhoff et al. (1996)
Full-time student status	474	College	Self-report		Attending school full time	Diekhoff et al. (1996)
Housing status	480	College	Self-report		Living in on-campus housing	Graham et al. (1994)
Intramural sports participation	380	College	Self-report	.27	Involved in intramural sports	Haines et al. (1986)
	474	College	Self-report		Involved in intramural sports	Diekhoff et al. (1996)

(continues)

TABLE 6.1 (continued)

Variable	N	Grade Level	Type of Data	r^a	Finding — Increased Cheating Associated With ...	Citation
Law violation and rule breaking	123	College	Self-report		Student admits to having committed a felony	Heisler (1974)
	60	Preschool	Observed		Rule-breakers more lenient toward cheating;[c]	Ross & Ross (1969)
	60	College	Self-report	.48	Students who admit greater cheating on tests report greater rate of dishonest behavior on the job.	Sims (1993)
	1,534	Grades 9–12	Self-report	.15 –.20	Students who have been arrested	Calabrese & Cochran (1990)
Marital status	380	College	Self-report	–.33	Student is unmarried	Haines et al. (1986)
	474	College	Self-report		Student is unmarried	Diekhoff et al. (1996)
Parental education	285	Grades 6–8	Self-report		No relationship to parents' education level	Anderman et al. (1998)
Parental style	70	College	Observed		Student reports either extremely punitive or lenient parental style	Vitro (1971)
Plagiarism	115	College	Self-report	.70	Student engages in plagiarism	Roig & DeTommaso (1995)
Political beliefs	445	College	Self-report		No difference between political liberals and conservatives on circumstances justifying cheating	Clouse (1973)

	1,500	College	Self-report		No relationship to political liberalism/conservatism	Centra (1970)
	1,500	College	Self-report		More lenient attitude toward cheating associated with lower SES	Centra (1970)
Socioeconomic status	366	High school	Observed	.14	Increased SES (by father's occupation)	Leveque & Walker (1970)
Transfer student status	143	College	Self-report		Number of medical schools attended; being a transfer student	Sierles et al. (1980, 1988)
	148	College	Observed		Being a transfer student	Antion & Michael (1983)

[a]When a correlation is reported, it is statistically significant ($p < .05$); otherwise no relationship is inferred.

[b]In this study, susceptibility to peer pressure was measured using a conformity scale consisting of 10 situations in which a student indicated how he or she would respond to various antisocial situations, of which "cheating on a exam" was only one.

[c]Rule breaking was defined in this study of preschool students as cheating on a maze test in which the only way for the child to successfully walk through a maze was to step over one of the barriers.

lations have been reported in a particular research report, the values of the correlations appear in the table. As before, positive values indicate that higher standing on the background variable is related to a greater incidence, likelihood, or probability of cheating, and negative values indicate that a higher standing on the variable is associated with decreased cheating. Regardless of whether a correlation is reported, a description of the relationship is provided. Citations to the studies on which the relationships are based appear in the final column of the table.

Although tentative, a few conclusions can be drawn from Table 6.1. Several related variables predict an increased likelihood of cheating on tests, at least at the college level. For example, participation in extracurricular activities (such as varsity sports), living on campus, and having a scholarship may all be tapping into a similar student profile, and each of these characteristics is associated with increased incidence of cheating. Also, the increased incidence of cheating associated with possession of a scholarship may fall under a more general category of support for education. When the support for education comes from "outside" sources—whether parental or institutional—the incidence of cheating is increased.

In the previous section, we saw that older students are less likely to cheat on tests. As Table 6.1 illustrates, this finding may be related to a general conclusion about older, nontraditional, or more mature students; students who would be considered nontraditional because of their age, students who attend college part time, and those who pay for their own education appear to be less likely to cheat on tests. One oft-investigated demographic characteristic—SES— appears to have no relationship to cheating.

The most powerful predictors of cheating on tests appear to be inappropriate or illegal practices in other contexts. For example, students who admit to plagiarism are highly likely to admit cheating on tests. The relationship extends beyond the school house door and spans all age levels: Research on correlates of cheating shows that children who break the rules in a maze game, medical students who are dishonest in their care of patients, and employees who admit to stealing office supplies are all more likely to cheat on tests and have more lenient attitudes toward cheating.

PSYCHOLOGICAL CONSTRUCTS

Early social scientists suspected that innate characteristics or learned personality dispositions would predict deviant behaviors of various kinds. One of the most intuitive psychological constructs thought to influence cheating on tests was intelligence. More than 40 years ago, researchers reported that students who had been identified as cheaters had slightly lower IQs than noncheaters (e.g., Gross 1946). One of the earliest studies of the relationship between intelligence and cheating bore the straightforward title "Mental Test Traits of College Cribbers" (Brownell, 1928). The author found that the mean IQ of a group of identified cheaters was somewhat below average.

However, surprisingly few studies on the relationship of cheating and intelligence have been published. Instead, as research on the topic progressed, more studies began to include achievement variables (e.g., grades, GPA, and test performance) rather than measured IQ, perhaps in part because of the greater relevance of achievement and the strong relationship between aptitude and performance. As discussed previously, lower achievement is consistently associated with an increased tendency to cheat.

Level of moral reasoning or moral development might seem to be another variable that, on the surface, would be related to cheating. Early studies that examined level of moral development (usually using the moral development stages hypothesized by Kohlberg, 1964) and observed cheating by college students found that greater cheating was associated with less advanced stages of moral development. However, more recent studies, and those involving elementary and secondary school students suggest that any relationship between moral reasoning stage and behavior is slight or nonexistent.

Table 6.2 illustrates that a variety of other psychological constructs have been studied for their possible association with cheating. The table presents numerous studies categorized by the particular psychological variable of interest. In some cases, a variable appears to have been of interest to a single researcher (e.g., conformity or procrastination). For studies such as these, the relationship between the construct of interest and cheating is presented; however, given the paucity of evidence, one can derive only the most tentative conclusions about the true relationship. In other cases, a fairly substantial amount of evidence has been amassed by numerous researchers investigating the same relationships (e.g., learning orientation or perceived risk of detection). For these constructs, much more confident conclusions can be reached. A summary of these conclusions is presented in the following paragraphs.

The highly mixed results for the relationship between cheating and achievement motivation suggest that the true relationship may be near zero. A related construct—Type A personality—has also demonstrated no consistent relationship to cheating. In the 1980s and 1990s, increased attention has been paid to notions of self-concept and self-esteem. Covington (1992) has suggested that cheating may simply be a natural manifestation of the human need to maintain self-worth: "From the self-worth perspective, cheating qualifies as part of the unhealthy legacy that results from having tied one's sense of worth to achieving competitively" (p. 91). However, there is mixed evidence on this point as well; three different studies have shown cheating associated with increased self-esteem, decreased self-esteem, and no relationship to self-esteem.

On the other hand, more refined investigations of learning–grade orientation—a construct related to achievement motivation—have revealed a fairly strong predictive association: Students whose motivation for performance is to earn a grade (as opposed to learning) are significantly more likely to report engaging in cheating to accomplish that goal. In one study (Huss et al., 1993), a correlation of $r = .38$ between grade orientation and reported cheating was found—one of the strongest of the psychological predictors. Other reasonably strong predictors of cheating include variables that are related to the learning–grade orientation dichotomy. Among them are the extent to which a student is motivated by extrinsic factors, an external locus of control, and the presence of an incentive to cheat.

Constructs that appear to have at least a moderate relationship to cheating include an increased sense of alienation or discontent with schooling and the degree to which a student has a heightened level of general anxiety related to performance in school, although specific anxiety about testing probably has little to no relationship to cheating. Students identified as cheaters also appear, in general, to be more extroverted and sociable. These characteristics may also be related to need for approval. Most studies have shown a positive relationship between cheating and need for approval; in one of them, need for approval was

TABLE 6.2
Psychological Correlates of Cheating

Variable	N	Grade Level	Type of Data	r^a	Increased Cheating Associated With ...	Citation
					Finding	
Achievement related						
Achievement motivation	154	College	Observed		No relationship to achievement motivation	Roig & Neaman (1994)
	113	Grade 5	Observed		High achievement motivation for males	Johnson & Gormly (1972)
Learning vs. grade orientation	1,500	College	Self-report		Apathy toward cheating associated with decreased motivation to achieve high grades	Centra (1970)
	154	College	Self-report		No relationship between learning or grade orientation and lenient or condemnatory attitude toward cheating	Roig & Neaman (1994)
	220	College	Self-report	.38	Grade orientation	Huss et al. (1993)
				−.26	Learning orientation scores	
	183	College	Self-report	.20	Grade orientation	Weiss et al. (1993)
				−.17	Learning orientation scores	
	943	College	Self-report		"Ends" as opposed to "means" reasons for cheating	Newstead et al. (1996)
	154	College	Self-report		No relationship to lenient or condemnatory attitudes toward cheating	Roig & Neaman (1994)

Variable	N	Grade level	Measure	Correlation	Description	Citation
Need for achievement	197	Grades 10–12	Self-report	−.35	Decreased need to achieve in school	Rost & Wild (1994)
	51	College	Observed		Higher need to achieve	Johnson (1981)
	33	College	Observed		Decreased need to achieve	Schwartz et al. (1969)
Test importance	611	Grades 5–6	Observed		Greater perceived importance of test to student when probability of success is low	Vitro & Schoer (1972)
	190	College	Observed		No significant relationship to test importance	Houston (1977b)
Affiliation	33	College	Observed		Greater need for affiliation	Schwartz et al. (1969)
Alienation	1,534	Grades 9–12	Self-report	.11–.20	Increased dislike for school[b]	Calabrese & Cochran (1990)
				.07–.14	Increased perception that teachers are unfair	Calabrese & Cochran (1990)
				.10–.20	Increased perception that school is unfair	Calabrese & Cochran (1990)
	197	Grades 10–12	Self-report		Lower contentment with school	Rost & Wild (1994)
	120	College	Self-report		Higher level of anomia	Newhouse (1982)
	149	College	Self-report		Higher level of anomia	Tom & Borin (1988)
	154	College	Self-report	−.35	Increased level of alienation[c]	Roig & Neaman (1994)
Anxiety						
Achievement anxiety	148	College	Observed	.20	Increased anxiety about school performance	Antion & Michael (1983)

(continues)

TABLE 6.2 (continued)

Variable	N	Grade Level	Type of Data	r^a	Finding: Increased Cheating Associated With ...	Citation
	111	Grades 10–11	Observed	.45	Increased anxiety about performance	Shelton & Hill (1969)
	285	Grades 6–8	Self-report	.19	Increased worry about school	Anderman et al. (1998)
Test anxiety	117	College	Observed		No relationship to test anxiety	Bronzaft et al. (1973)
	25	College	Observed		No relationship to test anxiety	Heisler (1974)
	112	College	Self-report	.38(women), .35(men)	Increased test anxiety	Smith et al. (1972)
Attitudes and perceptions	143	College	Self-report	.16	More cynical attitude toward cheating	Sierles et al. (1988)
	698	College	Self-report		Less condemning attitude toward cheating; increased perception of frequency of cheating of others	Knowlton & Hamerlynck (1967)
	5,904	College	Self-report	.51	Increased perception of cheating by others	McCabe & Trevino (1993)
	474	College	Self-report		Increased percpetion of cheating by peers	Haines et al. (1996)
	154	College	Self-report	.23	Less condemning attitude toward cheating associated with lower GPA	Roig & Neaman (1994)
	149	College	Self-report		Decreased perception of severity of cheating	Tom & Boren (1988)
	474	College	Self-report		Decreased perception of guilt as a deterrent	Haines et al. (1996)

Variable	N	Level	Method	r	Finding	Reference
	474	College	Self-report		Decreased perception of stigmatization of cheating	Haines et al. (1996)
	22	College	Observed		Engaging in cheating associated with view that it is distinctive, inconsistent, and low consensus	Forsyth et al. (1985)
	24	Grade 4	Observed		Perception of being justly priviledged or unjustly deprived	Stephenson & White (1970)
	220	College	Observed		Increased resentment toward test constructor(s)	Dienstbier et al. (1980)
	193	Grade 6	Observed		Decreased valuing of honesty by student	Homant & Rokeach (1970)
Cognitive Strategies	285	Grades 6–8	Self-report	−.18	Less frequent use of deep-level cognitive strategies (i.e., divergent thinking, problem solving)	Anderman et al. (1998)
				.31	More frequent use of self-handicapping strategies	Anderman et al. (1998)
Conformity	78	College	Observed		Increased level of achievement through conformity	Hetherington & Feldman (1964)
Intelligence	30	College	Observed		Decreased IQ score	Brownell (1928)
	153	College	Observed	.32[d]	Decreased IQ score	Hoff (1940)
	366	High school	Observed	−.40	Decreased IQ score	Leveque & Walker (1970)
Intrinsic vs. Extrinsic Motivation	228	Grades 5–6	Observed		Expectation of reward for high performance on test	Lobel & Levanon (1988)
	91	College	Self-report	.38	Intrinsic reasons for cheating	Blackburn & Miller (1996)
Introversion vs. Extroversion	30	College	Observed		Extroversion	Brownell (1928)

(continues)

109

TABLE 6.2 (continued)

Variable	N	Grade Level	Type of Data	r^a	Increased Cheating Associated With ...	Citation
					Finding	
	60	Grades 6–7	Observed		Increased extroversion and neuroticism	Keehn (1956)
	880	College	Observed[e]		Increased extroversion	Singh & Akhtar (1972)
	80	Grades 4–5	Observed		No relationship to introversion or extroversion	Stephenson & Barker (1972)
Locus of Control	148	College	Observed		No significant relationship	Antion & Michael (1983)
	51	College	Observed		External factors reported as causes of cheating	Forsyth et al. (1985)
	69	College	Self-report		External factors reported as reasons for cheating	Wang & Anderson (1994)
	218	College	Observed		Test of chance (vs. skill) for students with external locus of control	Kahle (1980)
Machiavellianism	72	College	Observed		Increased Machiavellianism in impersonal competition and decreased Machiavellianism in personal competition contexts	Cooper & Peterson (1980)
	127	K	Observed[f]		Increased for first and only children of high-Machiavellian mother; decreased for first and only children for whom both parents are high-Machiavellian	Dien (1974)
	76	Grade 6	Observed[f]		No relationship to Machiavellianism of parents	Dien & Fujisawa (1979)

	N	Population	Method		Finding	Citation
	91	College	Observed		No relationship to level of Machiavellianism	Flynn et al. (1987)
Moral Reasoning and Development	221	High school	Observed		No relationship to moral reasoning level	Bruggeman & Hart (1996)
	80	Grades 2–3	Observed		Moral reasoning at the realism stage	Coady & Sawyer (1986)
	71	College	Observed		Lower level of moral reasoning	Forsyth & Scott (1984)
	152	College	Observed		Lower level of moral reasoning	Leming (1978)
	35	College	Observed		Lower level of moral reasoning	Schwartz et al. (1969)
Need for Approval	91	College	Observed		Higher need for approval	Millham (1974)
	148	College	Observed	$-.06 - -.10$	Decreased need for approval	Antion & Michael (1983)
	25	College	Observed	$-.52$	Reduced fear of negative evaluation[g]	Dickstein et al. (1977)
	228	Grades 5–6	Observed		Increased need for approval	Lobel & Levanon (1988)
Neuroticism	60	Grades 6–7	Observed		Increased neuroticism and extroversion	Keehn (1956)
	440	College	Observed[a]		Increased neuroticism and extroversion	Singh & Akhtar (1972)
Neutralization	98	College	Self-report	.62	Increased neutralization	Daniel et al. (1991)
	190	College	Self-report		Increased neutralization	Daniel et al. (1994)
	474	College	Self-report		Increased neutralization	Haines et al. (1986)
	380	College	Self-report		Increased neutralization	Diekhoff et al. (1996)

(continues)

111

TABLE 6.2 (continued)

Variable	N	Grade Level	Type of Data	r^a	Finding — Increased Cheating Associated With ...	Citation
Procrastination	115	College	Self-report	.23	Increased procrastination	Roig & DeTommaso (1995)
Repression	78	College	Observed		Increased score on MMPI repression scale	Hetherington & Feldman (1964)0
Responsibility	78	College	Observed		Decreased score on responsibility scale	Hetherington & Feldman (1964)
Reward vs. Punishment	91	College	Observed		Desire to avoid punishment increases	Flynn et al. (1987)
	110	College	Observed		When incentive is present for low self-monitoring students	Covey et al. (1989)
	80	Grades 2–3	Observed		When incentive to cheat is present	Coady & Sawyer (1986)
	228	Grades 5–6	Observed		Anticipation of reward for good performance	Lobel & Levanson (1988)
Risk	194	College	Observed		Reduced risk of detection	Corcoran & Rotter (1987)
	5,904	College	Self-report	– .27	Reduced certainty of being caught	McCabe & Trevino (1993)
	611	Grades 5–6	Observed		Lower risk of detection on highly important tasks with low expectation of success	Vitro & Schoer (1972)
	120	College	n/a		Test performance higher for students with expectation of being able to cheat on a test	Houston (1977a)
	60	Grade 6	Observed		Lower risk of detection	Hill & Kochendorfer (1969)

Self-concept

Category	N	Grade level	Method	Effect size	Finding	Study
Academic self-concept	197	Grades 10–12	Self-report		Lower academic self-concept	Rost & Wild (1994)
Self-esteem	45	College	Observed		Decreased self-esteem	Aronson & Mettee (1968)
	276	College	Observed		Increased self-esteem	Jacobson et al. (1969)
	228	Gardes 5–6	Observed		No relationship to self-esteem[h]	Lobel & Levanon (1988)
Self-monitoring	110	College	Observed		Increased self-monitoring when incentive is available	Covey et al. (1989)
Social comparison	60	Grade 6	Observed		Knowledge of peer performance	Hill & Kochendorfer (1969)
	111	Grades 10–11	Observed		Knowledge of peer performance (for high-anxiety students only)	Shelton & Hill (1969)
Sociability	78	College	Observed		Increased sociability	Hetherington & Feldman (1964)
	27	College	Observed		Increased social participation	Johnson & Gormly (1971)
Success vs. Failure	190	College	Observed[i]	.49	Increased anticipation of success	Houston (1977b)
	45	College	Observed[c]		Moderate expectation of success; decreased cheating for high and low expectation of success	Houston (1978)
	611	Grades 5–6	Observed		Lower expectation of success	Vitro & Schoer (1972)
	197	Grades 10–12	Self-report	.37	Increased motivation to avoid failure	Rost & Wild (1994)
	32	College	Observed		Initial success	Houston & Ziff (1976)
	91	College	Observed		Initial failure	Millham (1974)

(continues)

TABLE 6.2 (continued)

Variable	N	Grade Level	Type of Data	r^a	Finding — Increased Cheating Associated With ...	Citation
Trust	60	Grade 5	Observed		Decreased level of trust in others	Doster & Chance (1976)
Type A vs. Type B personality	220	College	Self-report		No relationship to Type A personality or behaviors	Huss et al. (1993)
	183	College	Self-report	−.16	Fewer Type A behaviors	Weiss et al. (1993)
	168	College	Observed		No relationship to Type A personality or behaviors	Davis et al. (1995)
	80	College	Observed		Opportunity to cheat for Type A personality or behaviors	Perry et al. (1990)
Work Ethic	357	College	Observed		Students with high work ethic persisted twice as long as students with low work ethic before cheating	Eisenberger & Shank (1985)

Note. GPA = grade point average; K = kindergarten; MMPI = Minnesota Multiphasic Personality Inventory; n/a = not available.

[a]When a correlation is reported, it is statistically significant ($p < .05$); otherwise no relationship is inferred.

[b]The range of correlations reported in the Calabrese and Cochran (1990) study are for nine specific cheating behaviors, ranging from taking a test for another student and copying from another student to more innocuous behaviors, such as "talking to a teacher after a test to try to get on their good side to get a higher mark" (p. 71).

[c]The dependent variable in this study was self-reported condemnatory attitude toward cheating, not self-reported or actual cheating.

[d]Correlation is between IQ scores and scores on a measure of honesty.

[e]Extroversion–neuroticism scale was administered to 440 students suspected of cheating on a final examination and 440 not suspected of cheating.

[f]In this study, cheating was defined as rule breaking in an (unknowingly) monitored independent game situation.

[g]Because participants in this study may have discerned that its intent was to detect cheating, the unexpected negative correlation may actually support the idea that those students who fear negative evaluation by others may have avoided cheating to a greater degree than those who fear negative evaluation less.

[h]However, high self-esteem students who had low need for approval cheated significantly less.

[i]In this study, cheating was detected as a statistically improbable occurrence of answer similarities between examinees seated near each other and defined as the difference between incorrect answers in common with near-seated students and incorrect answers in common with distant-seated students.

conceptualized as slightly differently—as the desire to avoid (or fear of) negative evaluation—and a correlation of $r = .52$ was observed (Dickstein, Montoya, & Neitlich, 1977). The earlier findings by Shelton and Hill (1969), who found an increased level of cheating by highly anxious students but only for those who were actually aware of the performance of their peer group, support the notion that cheating may, in part, be done to avoid negative evaluation and the attendant aversive social consequences.

The strongest predictors of cheating on tests, however, appear to be the student's own perceptions about cheating. In one study, a correlation of $r = .51$ was found between students' self-reported cheating behaviors and their perceptions of the cheating behavior of others (McCabe & Trevino, 1993). Similarly, students who have more lenient attitudes toward cheating are also likely to report actually engaging in cheating more often than students who have more condemnatory attitudes toward cheating. Additionally, students' perceptions of the risk of being caught are related to their likelihood of engaging in the behavior: As one would expect, the greater the perceived risk of being caught, the lower the likelihood of cheating.

An even stronger predictor of self-reported cheating is termed *neutralization* or *externalization*, that is, the degree to which a person believes that cheating is justified by, for example, pervasive cheating on the part of others. Daniel et al. (1991) found a correlation of $r = .62$ between degree of neutralization and self-reported cheating; other studies have shown similar results (e.g., Forsyth, Pope, & McMillan, 1985; Knowlton & Hamerlynck, 1967). Results for these constructs are consistent with the tendency for cheating to be associated with an external locus of control. Whereas those who cheat on tests believe that others do so as much or more than they do, the converse also appears to be true; investigations of trustingness and trustworthiness reveal that students who tend to trust others engage in cheating less frequently.

Finally, one relationship that is not presented in Table 6.2 seems interesting enough to warrant a brief mention. A study conducted by Monte and Fish (1980) examined the cheating behaviors of 100 female undergraduate students who were given various tasks to complete in situations where the possibility of cheating existed and could be detected by the investigators. The students were questioned afterward about their cheating. Students who cheated on the tasks tended to deny cheating and to give externalizing reasons for their behavior. In a follow-up study with the same students, Monte and Fish specifically asked students to cheat and to indicate where, why, and how they had done so. Remarkably, in addition to cheating as directed, it was found that one third of the students cheated on additional items (above and beyond those they indicated they had cheated on) and denied doing so.

Overall, many personality variables have been examined for potential relationships between psychological constructs and cheating. After administering a multitude of personality batteries to their sample of 78 college students and measuring the extent of their cheating in three different contexts, Hetherington and Feldman (1964) attempted to synthesize all of their findings, concluding that "cheaters appear to exhibit a set of behaviors similar to those produced by maternal overprotection" (p. 214).

Unfortunately, conclusions based on currently available research do not suggest a synthesis nearly so tidy. As noted above, a few of these variables appear to have a moderately strong relationship to cheating. Most have only a slight relationship. Even in studies using multiple regression to gain additional predicting power by including numerous variables, the variability in cheating is explained better by the combination of variables left unmeasured and unexamined than by the constellation of demographic and personality variables included in the regression (see, e.g., Antion & Michael, 1983). In the end, perhaps the best summary of the relationship of psychological constructs and cheating is that offered by the earliest researchers on the topic, Hartshorne and May (1928), who observed that there did not appear to be strong evidence supporting any particular personality or character issue that could predict cheating with any reasonable certainty.

CLASSROOM INSTRUCTIONAL AND ENVIRONMENTAL FACTORS

In contrast to the demographic characteristics, personality traits, and behavioral dispositions that a student brings to the testing situation, there are also classroom and school factors that cannot be ascribed to the student, nor are they under his or her control. For the most part, these factors are variables associated with the size and type of classroom or school the student attends, the classroom environment, the teacher's instructional methods, personal characteristics of the teacher, and characteristics of the test the student takes.

These variables are frequently viewed by students as a major reason that cheating occurs. In one survey in which college students were asked to identify the factor most responsible for frequent cheating, they rated "instructor shortcomings" first (42%), followed by characteristics of the testing environment (i.e., the physical setting of the classroom; 35%), and characteristics of the test (23%; Knowlton & Hamerlynck, 1967). Table 6.3 provides a compilation of these and other classroom- and instructor-related variables and their association, if any, to cheating on tests.

Table 6.3 reveals that many of the school, classroom, instructor, and testing factors that might intuitively be presumed to be related to cheating are in fact related in predictable ways. Larger classes, free seating, poor proctoring or supervision of the test, inexperienced faculty, the opportunity to cheat, and take-home tests are all associated with increased cheating. Elementary and secondary schools that emphasize high achievement witness more frequent cheating than schools that do not stress performance as much, and, at the college level, there is more cheating at larger state and private institutions than at smaller ones. In preparation for a test, an undistracted learning environment may serve to reduce the amount of cheating, and a warning about the penalties for cheating immediately before a test appears to deter the behavior.

On the other hand, although the evidence is limited, there does not seem to be any relationship between cheating and when a student turns in a test (i.e., early in a class period or later). The study by Houston (1976a) suggested that use of multiple test forms, in which the same questions and answers are randomly positioned on two different versions, does not reduce cheating. (Interestingly, however, as we learn in chap. 9, this method is perceived to be highly effective by students.) Going beyond multiple forms and scrambling both questions and answer choices on a multiple-choice test does seem to reduce cheating.

TABLE 6.3

Classroom and Instructional Correlates of Cheating

				Finding[a]	
Variable	N	Grade Level	Type of Data	Increased Cheating Associated With...	Citation
Class size	209	College	Observed	Increased class size	Nowell & Laufer (1997)
	232	College	Self-report	Increased class size	Moffatt (1990)
Classroom management style	588	Grades 4–6	Observed	"Referent power" condition; decreased cheating with "coercive power" condition	Houser (1982)
Competition type	72	College	Observed	No relationship to personal or impersonal competition situations	Cooper & Peterson (1980)
Course content	49	College	Self-report	Course content perceived by students as meaningless and uninteresting	Steininger et al. (1964)
Faculty rank	209	College	Observed	Courses taught by nontenure-track faculty	Nowell & Laufer (1997)
Instructional quality	189	College	Self-report	Lower (student-) perceived instructional quality	Steininger (1968)
	91	College	Self-report	Lower (student-) perceived instructional quality	Blackburn & Miller (1996)
	49	College	Self-report	Lower (student-) perceived instructional quality	Steininger et al. (1964)
Learning conditions	40	College	Observed[b]	Distracting learning conditions	Houston (1976c)
Opportunity to cheat	72	College	Observed	Increased opportunity to cheat	Cooper & Peterson (1980)

(continues)

TABLE 6.3 (continued)

Variable	N	Grade Level	Type of Data	Finding: Increased Cheating Associated With ...	Citation
School characteristics					
Achievement levels	45	Elementary schools	Self-report	Higher scoring schools on state mathematics test	Brandes (1986)
	105	High schools	Self-report	Higher scoring schools on state mathematics test	Brandes (1986)
	285	Grades 6–8	Self-report	Perceived high-performance school climate	Anderman et al. (1998)
School type	221	High school	Observed	No relationship to religious or public school type	Bruggeman & Hart (1996)
	1,534	Grades 9–12	Self-report	Attendance at private school	Calabrese & Cochran (1990)
	218	College	Self-report	Attendance at larger state and private institutions (vs. smaller private colleges)	Davis et al. (1992)
Other	31	Medical schools	Self-report	No relationships to region of the country, tuition cost, public or private funding, age of school, or annual amount of research dollars	Baldwin et al. (1996)
Test-related					
Proctoring	110	College	Observed	Decreased level of surveillance by proctor	Covey et al. (1989)
	160	College	Self-report	Unproctored examination	Sierles et al. (1988)

(continues)

	n	Level	Method	Description	Reference
	152	College	Observed	Reduced supervision	Leming (1978)
	49	College	Self-report	Instructor leaving room during examination	Steininger et al. (1964)
Seating	323	College	Observed[b]	No relationship to seating in front or rear of room	Houston (1976b)
	323	College	Observed[b]	Students seated next to each other (vs. to the front or to the rear)	Houston (1976b)
	197	College	Observed[b]	Decreased cheating when seated in alternate columns	Houston (1986a)
	260	College	Observed[b]	Free (vs. assigned) seating	Houston (1986a)
	88	College	Observed[b]	Increased acquaintance with student seated nearby	Houston (1986a)
	119	College	Observed	Seating next to a student who cheats	Sherrill et al. (1970)
	110	College	Observed	Ease of viewing answers available to be copied	Atkins & Atkins (1936)
Test content	49	College	Self-report	Test content perceived to be based on senseless detail	Steininger et al. (1964)
Test directions	135	Grades 4–6	Observed	Test directions do not include a warning about cheating	Fischer (1970)
	312	College	Observed[b]	Test directions included severe threat about cheating and only for middle-achieving students	Houston (1983b)
	107	College	Observed	Test directions included threat of sanction for cheating	Tittle & Rowe (1973)
Test forms	102	College	Observed[b]	No relationship to use of single vs. multiple test forms	Houston (1976a)

TABLE 6.3 (continued)

Variable	N	Grade Level	Type of Data	Finding — Increased Cheating Associated With …	Citation
	54	College	Observed[b]	Decreased cheating when both arrangement of questions and answers are scrambled	Houston (1983a)
Test format	54	College	Observed	Take-home test format	Marsh (1988)
Test weight	190	College	Observed[b]	No relationship to weight of test (10% vs. 40% of course grade)	Houston (1977a)
	323	College	Observed[b]	No relationship to whether test counts toward grade	Houston (1976b)
Turn-in order	323	College	Observed[b]	No relationship to turning in test early or late	Houston (1976b)

[a] When a correlation is reported, it is statistically significant ($p < .05$), otherwise no relationship is inferred.

[b] In these studies, cheating was "observed" via statistical detection techniques.

Evidence on cheating summarized by Steininger (1968) indicated that the least cheating occurs in classrooms in which students perceive the course material to be new and interesting, the professor to be "good," and the tests to be meaningful and easy. The worst contexts are those in which the course material is perceived to be meaningless and uninteresting, the professor to be "poor," and the tests to be hard and based on senseless detail. Schab (1972) reported that the top three student-identified courses in which the most cheating occurs are, as might be predicted, math, history, and science.

Two studies that are not summarized in the table warrant description in some detail because of the light they shed on school-related factors that may influence cheating on tests.

In the first study, Evans and Craig (1990a) asked 601 junior high school through college students their perceptions of classroom and instructor variables that they believed to be related to cheating. Although this evidence is about their perceptions (as opposed to evidence that links these variables to actual cheating), the results are informative to the extent that the students' beliefs are related to their actions. According to Evans and Craig (1990a):

> the strongest attributions throughout the entire sample (75% or better) linked cheating to required (vs. elective) courses, courses that cover difficult and large amounts of material, and tests that examine for material that is not covered in class. In terms of sheer percentage figures, younger students were more likely than college students to endorse variables such as "curve grading" and being in classes with mostly "smart students." Yet a sizable majority of students at all levels (65% or better) also implicated a lack of clarity about reasons or purposes for learning as a factor conducive to cheating. (p. 334)

In the second study (Genereux & McLeod, 1995), the researchers examined two different kinds of cheating—planned and spontaneous—a distinction studied previously by Hetherington and Feldman (1964). However, Genereux and McLeod identified factors that, according to the sample of 365 college students, were most influential in increasing or decreasing the likelihood of both types of cheating. The circumstances rated highest are shown in Table 6.4.

Table 6.4 clearly illustrates that, at least in terms of students' views, numerous factors under the control of the teacher have the potential to contribute to an increased or decreased likelihood of cheating. It is important to be specific about this point; the results shown in Table 6.4 portray what students *say* would increase or decrease various types of cheating. Because the data on which these results are based are self-reported, it is uncertain if the circumstances are related to actual behavior. However, at least according these students, factors such as the perception that an instructor doesn't care about cheating, the perception that a test is unfair, and the perception that the proctoring is poor are likely to increase the amount of cheating in a classroom. Seating students apart during testing, the use of essay tests, and stiff penalties are among the factors students report as likely to decrease the amount of cheating.

The good news is that these factors are elements of classroom life that a teacher can manipulate rather easily. Ironically, although these classroom environmental and instructional factors may be some of the most predictive and most under the teachers' control, they have been the least researched, considerably less than, for example demographic variables such as gender and age, over which educators have no control.

TABLE 6.4

Top Five Circumstances Related to Planned and Spontaneous Cheating

Rank	Circumstances That Increase Cheating	Circumstances That Decrease Cheating
	Planned Cheating	
1	Student perception that instructor doesn't care about cheating	Punishment for cheating (e.g., expulsion)
2	Student financial support depends on grades	Essay examination format
3	Student perception that test is unfair	Student perception of high instructor vigilance during examination
4	Student perception of low instructor vigilance during examination	Student perception that test is fair
5	Direct effect of course grade on student's long-term goals	Course material highly valued by student
	Spontaneous Cheating	
1	Student financial support depends on grades	Punishment for cheating (e.g., expulsion)
2	Student perception that instructor doesn't care about cheating	Essay examination format
3	Direct effect of course grade on student's long-term goals	Student perception of high instructor vigilance during examination
4	Student perception of low instructor vigilance	Students seated far apart during examination
5	Student perception that test is unfair	Student perception that test is fair

Note. Adapted with permission from "Circumstances Surrounding Cheating: A Questionnaire Study of College Students," by R. L. Genereux & B. A. McLeod, 1995, *Research in Higher Education, 36*(6), p. 692.

OTHER

In the literature describing correlates of cheating on tests, a few variables have been studied that are not easily lumped into the three categories previously reviewed. For lack of a clear categorization of these variables, I group them as simply "other," although logical arguments could be made to locate them in the other three categories or to organize them according to another framework altogether.

An interesting fact about these variables is that many of them have surprising relationships to cheating. One such variable is absence from class. One might hypothesize that there would be a strong positive relationship here: The more a student was absent from class, the more he or she would be likely to cheat. In what appears to be the only study of this variable, no relationship was found (Black, 1962). Similarly, in the previously mentioned research by Genereux and McLeod (1995), factors such as an unreasonable workload assigned by the instructor and enrollment in a required (as opposed to elective) course were not mentioned by students as being among the strong inducements to cheat.

There are other relationships that are surprising because of the strength of the correlations between the variables. A study of 366 male high school students' performance on a geometry test by Leveque and Walker (1970) revealed a correlation of $r = .38$ between teachers' ratings of their students probable cheating and the students' actual cheating on the self-graded test, suggesting that teachers may know their students better than researchers (or their students!) might expect.

Across all the categories of correlates of cheating described so far, the most consistent and strongest predictors of cheating behavior have not yet been mentioned. These include previous cheating and observing others cheat. A logistic regression analysis by Bunn et al. (1992) found that whether or not a student reported having cheated in college was significantly related to also reporting having seen other students cheat and to the student's impression of the percentage of other students who cheated. In a sample of 157 business majors, Mixon and Mixon (1996) found that the best predictors of whether a student cheated were (a) observing others who cheat, (b) knowing other students who cheat, and (c) a student's perception of the degree of cheating that occurs. Mixon (1996) observed that "the determinants of habitual cheating behavior are much the same as those that relate to having cheated at least once" and that "habitual cheating behavior is ... positively related to having seen others cheat and associating oneself with individuals who routinely cheat on exams and/or written work" (p. 199). Similar results were reported by Haines et al. (1986) and by Diekhoff et al. (1996) regarding the relationship of cheating to students' perceptions of the number of other students who cheat. In the Diekhoff et al. (1996) study, reported cheating was strongly related to the belief that "a majority of students approve of cheating" (p. 495).

Witnessing the cheating of other students go unpunished is also a powerful factor in predicting whether a student will cheat. One of the earliest studies of this relationship revealed that one of the two major reasons that students said they cheated was that they had seen others get away with it (W. W. Ludeman, 1938). More recently, Heisler (1974) demonstrated that students cheat significantly less if they have witnessed another person being caught cheating; this effect was not as strong if the person caught cheating was perceived to be treated leniently.

As with countless other human behaviors, a very strong predictor of future behavior is past behavior. The same holds true for cheating: Previous cheating is associated with a greater likelihood that a student will cheat on the test at hand. The foundational study on college cheating conducted by Bowers (1964) showed that 64% of the students who reported cheating in high school went on to cheat in college; conversely, 67% of those who said that they had not cheated in high school reported a continuation of their honest behavior in college. More recently, in a study involving a group of physicians, Baldwin et al. (1996) concluded that "the best single predictor of whether someone is likely to cheat during the first two years of medical school is whether he or she has cheated before" (p. 270). This finding confirms the relationships reported in earlier studies that found correlations of $r = .38$ between cheating in high school and cheating in college (Sierles et al., 1988), and $r = .58$ between cheating in college and cheating in medical school (Sierles et al., 1980).

Finally, in any discussion of the correlates of cheating, the effect of honor codes should be examined. Because there are various types of honor codes, because investigations of their efficacy have only begun fairly recently, and because they are most closely related to the topic of *preventing* cheating, a discussion of honor codes is deferred until chapter 8.

CONCLUSION: A LONG-WINDED EPILOGUE
ON CORRELATES OF CHEATING

In considering how to thoroughly treat the topic of cheating, the notion of correlates might seem—at one level—to be highly relevant. I suspect that the following statement will be regarded as highly unusual by many readers and may not survive the editorial eyes of a nervous publisher. Nonetheless, I feel compelled to admit it: With few exceptions, it seems to me that much of what we currently know about the correlates of cheating provides little useful information. I believe that the interested reader—that is, the reader interested in preventing, detecting, or responding to cheating on tests—will almost certainly not make much progress toward those goals by studying the demographic or psychological correlates of cheating, although, as we shall see in chapter 8, knowledge of classroom environmental and instructional correlates may be quite helpful. In practical terms, I suppose what this means is that the value of a chapter on correlates of cheating is only marginal.

I beg the reader's indulgence at this point of plain contradiction. Obviously, a treatment of correlates of cheating *has* been included despite reservations about its value; this goes without saying for the reader who has delved this far into this chapter. However, I believe that some caution is in order as test makers and test givers consider how knowledge of correlates can inform the daily activities of teaching and testing. To fully explicate the reasons for urging caution, a brief digression on the aims of social science research follows. Then, in closing, I return to the question of the value of information about correlates and proffer an admittedly guarded justification for attention to factors related to cheating.

A Brief Digression on the Aims of Research

Researchers in all fields have traditionally viewed scientific inquiry as directed toward three aims: understanding, prediction, and control. These aims can (though they need not) be viewed as sequential. For example, investigation of a phenomenon begins with simple description, with the aim of *understanding* the context or behaviors under study. This is not to say that the task of describing any phenomenon—especially social or behavioral events—is simple. On the contrary, unless prompted in rare cases by revelation or inspiration, scientific progress most often begins with sustained, careful, precise, and disciplined observation. Frequently, these observations lead to identification of key variables involved and generation of hypotheses about how those variables interact—in short, to a better understanding of the phenomenon, or a beginning understanding where none existed before.

Building on accumulated descriptions, researchers then proceed to frame and test hypotheses about the relationships for which they have nascent understandings. This second order aim of research is often referred to as *prediction*. The understandings of variables and their relationships permit researchers to devise experimental situations in which the predicting power of their understandings can be tested. A more thorough understanding of the variables and relationships usually results in more accurate predictions and attempts at improved description and more precise predictive hypotheses. When the understandings do not permit accurate predictions, researchers are usually prompted to seek additional, more thorough, or clearer description to refine and retest their hypotheses—or, in most cases, to do both.

Assuming that a wealth of descriptive information has been amassed, that predictive hypotheses have been framed, and that dependable regularities in the relationships between variables have been identified, researchers often strive to achieve the highest aim of empirical activity—*control*. In education, for example, researchers have not been content to document the differential physiological, social, or pedagogical factors involved in developing reading comprehension. Nor would it be completely satisfactory to merely acquire the ability to predict which kindergartners will become fluent readers and which will not. The ultimate aim would surely be to develop reading materials, contexts, or methods and adapt these to the unique circumstance represented by each individual kindergartner, with the certainty that the combination would result in literacy for every student.

Correlates of Cheating: The Aim of Description

The information in the preceding sections on correlates focused, primarily, at the level of description. Researchers have studied cheating behavior and its relationship to a host of personal and contextual variables. As we have seen, all the usual suspects have been rounded up, including gender, age, ethnicity, intelligence, grades, and so on. However, knowing what we now know about these correlates, we must ask the critical questions that follow every discovery of predictable relationships between variables. These questions include "So what?" and "What should we *do* now that we know this?"

For example, what would we do if we knew that girls cheated more than boys? What should be done if we know that there is more cheating on independent projects than on tests? If there is more cheating in math than in science? More cheating by high school seniors than juniors? More by Catholics than Protestants? Or, combining these, what if there is more cheating by senior girls on math projects in Catholic schools?

Actually, the question is not really what would we do, but what would we do *differently*? Recalling the aims of social science research, it is one thing to know that certain characteristics are related to each other in quantifiable ways (i.e., prediction). However, the next logical step is to use this knowledge to alter situations so that the frequency of beneficial outcomes is increased or the frequency of undesirable outcomes is reduced—that is, to exert some control. The important point is this: Demographic characteristics and psychological constructs cannot be controlled, and attempting to manipulate them would be unethical or at least questionable. For example, if heightened test anxiety were shown to be related to increased cheating, it might be appropriate to introduce practices that would serve to reduce students' test anxiety. (Of course, this assumes that no other, unforeseen, or untoward consequences also follow from external manipulation of students' test anxiety—an assumption that is highly questionable; see Dunn, 1999.) On the other hand, even if it were demonstrated that level of extroversion was the strongest predictor of cheating behavior, it would be highly unethical to manipulate that personality characteristic in order to reduce cheating—or likely for any other reason.

All of this leaves social scientists with classroom environmental and instructional factors as the variables that have the greatest potential. Although these variables include some of the strongest predictors and are the most likely to be controlled—both practically and ethically—they are also among the least researched, considerably less than, for example demographic variables such as gender and age, over which educators have no control. It is easy enough to call for more research on the relationships between instructional and assessment practices and cheating. We know plenty about who cheats, how often, and why. We now need to know more about how to prevent cheating or, at the least, to investigate the nexus of sound pedagogy that deters inappropriate academic behavior in our schools. We turn to this issue in chapter 8. First, an overview of how cheating is detected is presented in the following chapter.

✦ S E V E N ✦

Detecting Cheating on Tests

It has been found that the presentation of data to the student before any accusation has been made, providing the instructor is convinced they are conclusive, is the best way to meet the situation. Some of the students who have been interviewed in this way have been kept from becoming violent.

—Bird (1929, p. 347)

As long as there have been tests, it is likely that there has been cheating on them. With tongue in cheek, Frary (1993) suggested that the problem traces back to one of the most high-stakes tests of all time, the test administered in the Garden of Eden. On that test, Eve chose A for apple; Adam copied, in spite of a strict warning and omnipresent and omniscient proctoring. God had conclusive observational data, and the evidence was irrefutable.

Frary's (1993) observation highlights the fact that all kinds of tests are susceptible to cheating by some method. Although cheating, in the form of copying on multiple-choice tests, has received the most attention, other formats are not immune to the problem. The cheating garment illustrated in chapter 3 shows how, centuries ago, cheating could be accomplished on a lengthy essay examination under strict supervision.

More recent interest in detecting copying on tests coincided with the development of the multiple-choice format.[1] The multiple-choice item was introduced as one of several objective formats in an attempt to advance the practice of testing. Although the term *multiple-choice* was not used, an early textbook for teachers argued that these "new type" items should be used because "teachers' judgments of the mentality of students are faulty" (Buckingham, 1926, p. 146). In addition to reducing subjectivity and bias in scoring, the new multiple-choice format promised to make testing more efficient in terms of time and cost, to increase content coverage, to make scoring of tests easier and faster for teachers, and, ultimately, to increase the validity of decisions based on test scores.

The benefits of multiple-choice items came at a cost, however. Whereas it was difficult for a test taker to look over the shoulder of another student and copy even a single entire essay answer, it was quite easy to copy responses to a large number of multiple-choice items. Likewise, a cheat sheet for an essay question could contain a few key dates or facts that might be helpful to a test taker in putting some details into an essay response. However, even with prior access to the essay questions, the necessary organization, analysis, and complexity of thought required to construct an acceptable essay answer could not easily be reduced to fit on a scrap of paper or the palm of the hand. Moreover, prior access to the essay question would at least force the potential cheater to do the background work necessary to answer the question—that is, to actually *learn* something. By comparison, cheating on a multiple-choice item could be accomplished (by copying during the test) without any preparation whatsoever or (by obtaining prior information from another student) simply by writing down and concealing a list of letters corresponding to the correct answers (i.e., without even having seen the questions).

Thus, cheating on an essay test was not only difficult, it was (and is) easier to detect. This fact is humorously illustrated in a cheating anecdote that has probably circulated in many variations, one of which appears here.

> A young Marine Corps captain and an Army captain, having just left the service, were interviewing for the same job in the accounting department of a large company. Both applicants, having the same qualifications, were asked by the department manager to take a 10-item test. On completion of the test, both men were informed that they had each missed only one question. The manager said to the Marine, "Thank you for your interest, but we've decided to give the job to the Army captain."
>
> The Marine asked, "And why are you doing that? We both got nine questions right! The manager explained, "We made our decision not on the number of correct answers, but on the question you missed."
>
> "And just how would one incorrect answer be better than the other?" asked the Marine.
>
> "Simple," replied the manager. "The Army captain answered Question Number 5 with 'I don't know.' You wrote down, 'Neither do I.'"

---

[1]Although the reference here, and subsequently, is to multiple-choice item formats—the issue is more accurately described as concerning *select-type* formats—that is any format in which the test taker responds by choosing from among alternatives that are already provided—as opposed to *supply-type* formats, in which the test taker must construct his or her own response. Multiple-choice items happen to be the most frequently used and recognized select-type format. Others include true–false items, alternate choice items, and matching items. The same observations that follow in this chapter about multiple-choice items apply, in general, to all other select-type formats.

In contrast to the comparative ease of detecting cheating on an essay test, identical student performance on an multiple-choice test is not obviously cheating. The reasons why two test takers might give identical responses to a set of multiple-choice items are numerous. For example, they might have studied the content together, reasoning through potential questions in the same way. Similar prior educational experiences could account for their having the same answers. Simply learning the material to be tested will result in numerous common right answers, whether a pair of test takers has studied together or not. On a more technical note, the probability associated with selecting *one* of the answer choices on a multiple-choice item is quite high; the chances are one in four that an examinee who guesses blindly will choose a particular option when the question has four choices. Given these odds, it is very likely—even when there is no possibility of cheating—that two examinees could select the same response for an item merely by guessing. Of course, those odds decrease as the number of questions increase. For example, the probability that two test takers will produce identical answers by guessing on a 20-question test is less than the probability of identical answers on a 10-question test; the probability of identical answers on a 30-question test is even smaller, and so on.

There is also a technical distinction that must be made between random selection of answer choices (i.e., guessing) and informed selection of answers. When two test takers do not choose randomly but choose on the basis of *some* information or knowledge, their chances of answering identically—without cheating—are quite good. Table 7.1 shows two such cases. The first question in Table 7.1 shows a multiple-choice question that is so poorly constructed that even test takers who have minimal knowledge about the topic can rule out two of the answer choices as being obviously incorrect. For this item, the odds of answering correctly become 50/50 if the test taker does not choose randomly but chooses between the only remotely plausible answers (C and D) after ruling out the others. The odds of answering correctly the other item shown in Table 7.1 are even better. The flaw in Item 2 is a grammatical clue. In this case, test takers with sharp eyes for singu-

---

TABLE 7.1
Relationship Between Item Characteristics and Probability
of Correct Responses

---

1. In the story you just read about automobile repair, what did the author recommend as a good source of reference materials for students who wanted to learn more about the topic?

    A. a bakery

    B. the library

    C. the newspaper

    D. a local mechanic

2. Combinations of elements that do not contain carbon are called:

    A. an isotope

    B. an inert element

    C. inorganic compounds

    D. a radioactive substance

lar–plural agreement can answer correctly without any knowledge of the topic whatsoever. Several other multiple-choice item construction flaws can increase the chances of two examinees answering an item the same way, even when no cheating has been committed.

It is probably obvious that the multiple-choice item construction flaws illustrated in Table 7.1 as well as other potential flaws, don't apply to the case of essay item formats (although they have their own potential problems). The important point is that the multiple-choice format introduced unforeseen difficulties in making the inference that cheating has occurred. Especially in the case of essay questions that required extended responses, identical answers by two test takers were so unlikely that they could be considered prima facie evidence of academic dishonesty;[2] however, with multiple-choice items, identical responses were much less conclusive evidence of cheating. When those responsible for giving tests realized the comparative ease of cheating on tests using the new format, the importance of detecting cheating was also realized. Although some of the methods for detecting cheating described in the following section can be used to detect cheating on various kinds of tests, the majority of the methods developed over the past half century—in fact, *all* of them—are intended to detect cheating on multiple-choice tests.

METHODS OF DETECTING CHEATING ON TESTS

The strategies for detecting cheating on any test can be classified as either *observational* or *statistical*. As implied by the terms themselves, observational methods rely on a human observer to make an inference that cheating has occurred from either the behavior of a test taker (e.g., the glance of one test taker in the direction of another) or physical evidence (e.g., documents containing the wording of essay answers or confiscated cheat sheets). Statistical methods address cheating by evaluating whether the probability of students' answers being identical is sufficiently smaller than the probability of similar answers occurring by sheer chance alone. If, for example, the probability of a given set of identical examinees' responses were calculated to be only 1 in 100,000 times due to chance, then the reverse is also true: The chances are 99,999 in 100,000 that the identical responses were *not* due to chance.

Observational Methods of Detecting Cheating

Can you tell a cheater just by looking at him or her? In its early years, social science pursued the commonly held belief that certain characteristics of people could be discerned just by examining their physical features. The work of Paul Broca (1861, cited in Gould, 1981) on intelligence is one example. Broca and other craniometrists pursued the idea that the physical size of the brain, volume of the cranium, shape of the skull, and so on might be related to human intellectual func-

---

[2]In making a statement that asserts the obviousness of cheating when two examinees produce identical responses to an essay item, I am contradicting my own personal experience. I once observed three graduate students produce lengthy, identical responses to five essay questions on a carefully proctored final examination. Although I considered this to be prima facie evidence, the students involved (as well as, sadly, a nervous college administrator) asserted that the strings of several hundred words in common could have happened by chance.

tioning. Cesare Lombroso's (1887, cited in Gould 1981) work in the field of criminology is another example. Lombroso searched for what he called the "stigmata"
of criminal behavior and claimed to have found them in such physical manifestations as tattoos, facial features, and sensorimotor capabilities. The following is
Lambroso's expert testimony regarding the obvious criminal features of a man
standing trial for murder:

> [The man] was in fact the most perfect type of the born criminal: enormous jaws, fron-
> tal sinuses, and zygomata, thin upper lip, huge incisors, unusually large head (1620
> cc) ..., tactile obtuseness and sensorial manicinism." (Gould, 1981, p. 138)

As work in the areas of intelligence and criminology progressed, the notion that
a person's features revealed his or her character or that physical appearance could
be used to predict human behavior were handily dispelled. However, direct observation of a person—and his or her behavior during a test—has remained a primary
source of evidence in matters of cheating on tests. According to Theresa Semel,
who oversees cases of suspected cheating on the American College Testing (ACT)
Assessment, an official investigation of suspected cheating is never initiated without some sort of observational evidence (i.e., a student's complaint that another
student used unauthorized materials, a test administrator's report of a missing
test booklet, or a proctor's report of having observed one student copying from another). If, as Semel claims, observational evidence is so vital for initiating an investigation of cheating, then the dependability of human observation is a question of
critical importance.

Unfortunately, research on the topic indicates that human observations are no-
toriously fallible. Perhaps the most convincing arguments against relying on what
a person says he or she observed are found in legal literature. As in the classroom,
eyewitness accounts continue to be relied on as a source of evidence in the courtroom. However, an accumulating body of literature suggests that human observations are subject to many biasing influences and cannot unequivocally be accepted
at face value. Elizabeth Loftus, a behavioral scientist, has conducted an ongoing
line of research into the dependability of human observations and has applied her
findings to eyewitness testimony in legal proceedings. It is easy to see how her
conclusions can be readily applied to observational evidence of cheating on tests:

> The problem can be stated rather simply: on the one hand, eyewitness testimony is
> very believable and can wield considerable influence over the decisions reached by a
> jury; on the other hand, eyewitness testimony is not always reliable. It can be flawed
> simply because of the normal and natural memory processes that occur whenever
> human beings acquire, retain, and attempt to retrieve information. (Loftus, 1979, p. 7)

In her investigations, Loftus has explained the psychological mechanisms that
lead to inaccurate perceptions of events. Although these mechanisms are normal
aspects of human cognition (her research does not address perjured testimony),
the consequences of innocent perceptual interpretations often lead to findings of
guilt. In their book on eyewitness testimony, Cutler and Penrod (1995) reported
that estimates of erroneous convictions for serious criminal offenses (e.g., murder,
rape, and robbery) range from 0.5% to 5% per year. Applying these estimates to the
approximately 1.5 million convictions per year for serious offenses results in 7,500
erroneous convictions, using the lowest estimate (i.e., 0.5%) for error rates! At least

in the legal system, this problem is beginning to receive increased attention (see, e.g., Hamilton, 1989; Taylor, 1983).

The psychological basis for inaccurate eyewitness testimony is readily translated into the context of testing. For example, consider the case of two students, Jim and Sarah, both of whom are taking a final examination in chemistry. The examination is long (1.5 hours, 100 questions) and comprehensive, covering all of the semester's material. Jim, a junior, works conscientiously and intensely, as the teacher knows he has all semester long. Jim has readied himself for the examination by keeping up with all the assignments and readings over the semester. In his attempt to ensure that his 3.9 GPA isn't harmed, he "pulled an all-nighter" to maximize his preparation. About 1 hour into the test, at the end of one section of the test that calls for intense mathematical work, the teacher notices that Jim pauses and averts his eyes from the test.

Sarah also pauses during the test and stares. Sarah is an energetic sophomore, what would be called "perky." Sarah is not an outstanding student in terms of her GPA. In the chemistry class, she has performed poorly over the semester and needs a good grade on the final to pass the course. Socially, Sarah has many friends and is very active in many campus activities and organizations. Over the preceding weekend, she did not have time to study for the final examination; her responsibilities as an event chairperson for the Kappa Kappa Lambda sorority on campus have, in fact, precluded her from spending as much study time as she might have liked throughout the semester. As Sarah pauses and stares during the test, the instructor notices that the stare appears to be in the direction of Candi, one of several KKΛ sisters in the large chemistry lecture hall.

As is obvious in these stereotyped biographical sketches, prior information about a student has the potential to taint observations. Was Jim's staring an attempt to enjoy a moment's relief from the tedious computations? Was he staring at another students test or just "into space?" Was Sarah also just trying to relieve eye strain from an hour's worth of close attention to small print, tiny subscripts, and detailed information, or was she straining even harder to see how Candi had answered Question 68? Are the students' prolonged stares blank or baleful? The chemistry professor, not having the time to investigate all circumstances that might be cheating, and possessing other information about each student that she considers relevant to her observations, decides to confront Sarah about her behavior during the examination. The confrontation and the professor's suspicions rattle Sarah. She loses her ability to concentrate on the remainder of the examination, performs poorly overall on the test, and fails the course.

Perhaps if Sarah had been more proficient at cheating, she might not have aroused the instructor's suspicion. As seen in chapter 3, in comparison with some of the other ways of cheating, Sarah's looking at her friend's paper is, well, sophomoric. Assuming that Sarah and Candi actually conspired to cheat, a prearranged set of hand signals or a pen-clicking code would have been considerably more difficult to prosecute. In fact, even if the professor were suspicious of Sarah and Candi's behavior, she would probably think long and hard about going to the chemistry department's academic affairs committee on the basis of the observational "evidence" of Sarah scratching her nose or Candi clicking her pen.

A real-life case involving a student at the University of Alabama underscores the difficulty of using—and differential weight placed on—observational methods. An English instructor observed one of her students looking at another student's paper on three different tests over the course of the semester. According to the Director of University Relations at the University of Alabama, the instructor made "*just* [italics added] a visual observation.… Apparently, what [the student] did was look at the desk next to him while another student was working on his paper, and that's what she observed. He did not have a cheat-sheet or anything like that" (Howard, 1986, p. C1). The director was further quoted as saying:

> There was the least amount of evidence in connection with that particular incident. The difference is that the first two times he admitted [cheating]. And with the third, he said he was not cheating. Again, *there was no hard evidence* [italics added]. There was only "I saw you doing this" and "No, I was not doing this." The dean made the decision of "Let's just make a withdraw–pass from the course and make him take it again. (Howard, 1986, p. C1)

A Limited Arsenal.   The repertoire of observational methods of detecting cheating is severely limited. Whether positioned at the front of a large lecture hall, seated behind a desk, or strolling up and down the aisles of a classroom, cheating is detected (when it is) by a test giver who sees a test taker doing something that raises suspicion. Essentially, observational methods consist of simply watching examinees to detect movements, actions, or behaviors that are clearly prohibited or are inferred to be performed for the purpose of cheating.

Textbooks in the field of educational measurement give advice on observation that is correspondingly simple and limited. One leading textbook on testing recommended that, when giving classroom tests, the teacher should be in the room and be alert while the test is being given: "The best way to detect cheating is to observe students during the examination—not by being preoccupied at one's desk" (Mehrens & Lehmann, 1991, p. 158). The observational method called proctoring (or invigilating) remains the single most widely practiced method for detecting cheating on tests.

When cheating is suspected through observational methods, an instructor faces the dilemma of how to confront the behavior. Options include (a) ignoring the behavior, (b) delaying further investigation until after the examination is completed, and (c) confronting a student during the test. As we shall see in the next chapter, the first option—ignoring it—is the most common. The second option can reinforce a perception that the instructor doesn't care about cheating. It also assumes that recollections of the event on the part of the instructor and the suspect are accurate and consistent over time. The third option—confronting a test taker during an examination—also carries risks. Asking a test taker if he or she is cheating can cause an innocent student to become nervous, upset, and unable to give focused attention for the remainder of the testing period. Any disruption caused by a confrontation can also cause anxiety and distraction for other students.

The best approach to a situation in which cheating is suspected is to recognize that observational methods are high inference. Discussing the possibility of cheating with a test taker during an examination should be done in a way that does not accuse the person of cheating. Instead of asking a student "Are you cheating?" or immediately confiscating a test, a teacher might say, "You may not realize this, but the way you have been looking in that direction makes it appear as if you are looking at another student's paper." Guilty students will recognize this as a warning and may be persuaded to desist; innocent students will understand the possible misinterpretations of their behavior and be grateful for the gentle reminder.

Countermeasures.   According to some researchers, those who cheat on tests have not only developed advanced methods for doing so, but also sophisticated methods for avoiding suspicion. Albas and Albas (1993) summarized the results of their 17-year research project at a large provincial university in Canada, with data on more than 300 students. The authors' work was, primarily, intended to document the prevalence and variety of innocent students' attempts to avoid their instructors' suspicion of cheating. They recognized, of course, that the methods they described also can be used to suppress suspicion of cheating by those who actually do it—a tactic they call "impression management" (p. 451). A few of the methods they describe include the following:

Staring.   "A favorite strategy is to keep their eyes fixed on the invigilators [i.e., test proctors]. The theory is that if the invigilators see students looking at them, they could not possibly be looking at anybody or anything else" (p. 455). "Students report that if they drop a pencil or some other object and have to stoop to pick it up they keep their eyes on the invigilator rather than on the object they are trying to pick up in much the same way as touch typists keep their eyes on the copy rather than the keys" (p. 456).

Smiling.   "One young woman reports that she smiles ingenuously at the invigilator and moves her eyebrows up and down a few times because as she says, 'no cheater would be comfortable enough to do a goofy thing like that'" (p. 455).

Mourning.   "One young male student indicates: 'I've given the invigilators a sort of 'help me, I'm stuck' look, hoping that it may have made them feel sorry for me and so cancel out any thoughts they may have had that I might be cheating" (p. 455)

Organizing.   "Under such circumstances the management of these materials [i.e., unauthorized books, notes, formulae] has to be elaborate and intensive in order to convince invigilators that they are not being used illicitly. One man states that he piles these materials on the floor beside his desk with the ones pertaining to the course and might be of any use at the bottom. " (p. 456).

Seating.   Albas and Albas referred to the idea that "physical locations become inured with social identities" and that students are cognizant of these associations. For that reason, one of the students they interviewed reported that "Since trouble makers (cheaters included) tend to cluster at the back of the room, I stay away from there" (p. 457). Albas and Albas (1993) also documented that "some students sit directly in front of the invigilator so that they can be ostentatiously innocent," whereas others "avoid seats beside the well known high achievers because they may be suspected of trying to copy from them. Also avoided are seats next to known cheaters" (p. 457).

All of these behaviors by students are intended to counter the natural human tendency to interpret behavior. As Albas and Albas (1993) have illustrated, in some cases students who are innocent of cheating engage in impression management in order to avoid an incorrect inference of cheating by the instructor or proctor. In other cases, students who are cheating engage in the same behaviors to diminish the possibility of an observer making the correct inference.

Like the hypothetical situations involving Jim and Sarah, a surprisingly large percentage of cases rely on human inferences about students' overt behaviors and putatively objective eyewitness accounts. As mentioned earlier, in the case of the ACT Assessment, nearly all cheating investigations are initiated as a result of some information or observation. In the context of elementary, secondary, and postsecondary education, observation constitutes, almost exclusively, the method by which cheating is detected. As has been illustrated in the case of Jim and Sarah, collateral information about the student has the potential to influence human observations and the subsequent acceptance or rejection of the belief that cheating has occurred.

Summary

Those who administer tests have a professional obligation to maintain minimum standards necessary to ensure a fair testing process. Fairness includes protecting honest examinees from having the products of their preparation, effort, and thinking taken by another. It also includes safeguarding the intended inferences based on the test scores; that is, the validity of the test scores. An inappropriately inflated test score, arrived at through cheating, does not permit those who use test scores for decision making to arrive at accurate conclusions regarding the test taker's ability or competence.

As in legal proceedings, observational evidence (i.e., eyewitness testimony) is highly persuasive. However, as we have seen, the credibility of observation relies on human interpretation of behavior and events. On the one hand, when observation is relied on to detect cheating, the testimony of an independent witness who actually saw cheating occur is highly desirable. On the other hand, the testimony of a professor who says, "I saw Sarah looking at Candi's paper," may be the least dependable testimony of all—certainly not because the professor would be lying about the matter but because of the high degree of inference involved, the well-established unreliability of our perceptions, and the necessity of human processing of those perceptions through filters and preconceptions. As we have also seen, the jury is *not* out on the question of how much faith should be placed in direct observation. Eyewitness observations aren't as good as we might presume, although observation is by far the most frequently relied on evidence of cheating and often as persuasive—or even more so—than other kinds of evidence. In many circumstances, some method of substantiating our observations—or, at least, making the conclusions based on those observations less subjective—is needed.

Statistical Methods of Detecting Cheating

Although numerous statistical methods have been developed for detecting cheating, all of them share a common feature: They are predicated on virtually the same set of carefully stated assumptions and conventions in the field of statistics. Indeed, in presenting these methods, it is important to note that it is inaccurate to say that they are methods of *detecting* cheating. Two qualifications are in order. First, like observational methods, statistical methods are incapable of detecting anything other than some occurrence that is out of the ordinary or different from other occurrences. (In order to appreciate this qualification, a short introduction on the logic of hypothesis testing is presented below, followed by a more detailed explication of a few of the statistical methods.) Second, statistical methods are capable of detecting only one or two forms of cheating; namely, answer copying—which statistical methods have demonstrated good ability to reveal—and impersonation—for which statistical methods have been largely unsuccessful. How they are able to provide evidence that these behaviors have occurred is the subject of the remainder of this chapter.

The Logic of Hypothesis Testing and Statistical "Proof"

In the social sciences, investigations about the reality of external events are frequently pursued using the conventions of what is called *hypothesis testing*. A hypothesis is a testable assertion about the nature of reality. For example, suppose that a researcher wanted to find out whether coaching and test preparation courses like Kaplan or Princeton Review had a positive effect on students' test performance. The researcher might establish two hypotheses: the so-called *null hypothesis* and an *alternative hypothesis*. The null hypothesis is known as the "hypothesis of no effect." In our example, it would state something like "There is no difference in the average SAT scores for students who complete a test preparation course compared with those who do not." Of course, the researcher may not believe that the null hypothesis is true. In fact, he or she may be committed to the notion that test preparation programs are actually helpful.[3] In that case, the researcher would be hoping to gain support for the alternative hypothesis, which might say something like "The average performance of students who have participated in a test preparation course *is greater than* the average performance of those who have not."

Strictly speaking, the researcher could not *prove* the alternative hypothesis. However, the researcher could *disprove* the null hypothesis (which said that there is no difference). A statement like a null hypothesis can be disproved merely by finding an instance in which the statement is not true. For example, a botanist could claim that "there are no four-leaf clovers." It would not require acres of four-leaf clovers to disprove the assertion that there are none of them; it would take just one. Similarly, if the researcher could show that the performance of a group of students is better when they have participated in a test preparation course, then an instance has been discovered in which the claim of "no difference" must be rejected.[4]

Let us imagine a hypothetical experiment that a researcher could design to study the effects of test preparation. If it were ethically and practically possible, students could be randomly assigned at the start of the study to two groups of, say, 100 students each. Random assignment would help ensure that the groups were comparable at the beginning of the experiment; that is, one group did not contain a

---

[3]In fact, it has been demonstrated that coaching and test preparation programs do boost test scores (see Becker, 1990). The reasons may have something to do with (a) the fact that students are simply exposed to a more prolonged study of the *content* (e.g., math or English) or just more of it; (b) the programs' emphasis on *processes* (i.e., thinking and analysis skills that the student may not have acquired during his or her formal schooling); (c) the psychological boost of confidence that students might have if they perceived that they had "an edge" or an advantage as a result of participation in the program; or (d) a combination of these factors.

[4]Of course, it should further be recognized that the researcher has not demonstrated *why* the students who attended the test preparation course performed better, merely that they have. Answering that research question—perhaps the more interesting one—may well be the next line of investigation that this researcher (or others) pursue.

higher percentage of students who were high achieving, more motivated, or some other characteristic that could cause differential performance on the SAT. One group (the treatment group) would be assigned to attend test preparation courses; the other group (a control group) would not. At the end of the study, all 200 students would take the SAT and their average levels of performance would be compared.

In comparing the performances of the treatment and control groups, it is unlikely that their average scores would ever come out to be *exactly* the same. Even if there were, in truth, no effect of participating in a test preparation course, two groups of 100 students would be likely to have different means. If the group that did not attend the test preparation course averaged, say, 500 on the verbal section of the SAT and the group that had attended the prep course averaged 510, we might conclude that a difference that small between the groups could have happened by chance. Maybe the treatment group, by the luck of the draw, had one really smart student in it, a student whose extremely high SAT verbal score pulled that group's average up to 510. An average difference of just 10 points would not be large enough to conclude that the difference was caused by something other than sheer chance.

However, we can think of other differences that would be so large we would be unwilling to say that they happened by chance alone. What if the treatment group averaged 550? 600? 750? A difference in average performance between the treatment group and the control group of 250 points (on the SAT scale, which only goes from 200 to 800) would be fantastic. If the null hypothesis were really true, the chance of observing a 250-point difference would be so infinitesimal as to make the hypothesis of no effect thoroughly untenable. The same logic and conventions support the use of statistical detection of cheating.

Statistical Models

A classification system for approaches to detect cheating was suggested by Saupe (1960), who categorized methods as *chance* or *empirical*.[5] Chance methods compare an observed pattern of responses by a pair of examinees (one or both of whom are suspected of cheating) to a known distribution, such as the binomial or standard normal distribution (see Fig. 7.1). In this way, it can be said that chance methods have an "external" frame of reference. Empirical methods compare the probability of an observed pattern of responses by a pair of examinees to a distribution of values derived from other, independent pairs of students who took the same test. Distributions of empirical indices for suspected copiers are compared to distributions of statistics obtained under conditions where cheating could not have occurred, usually from pairs of examinees seated so far apart during a test that copying would be impossible. In this way, empirical methods can be viewed as having an "internal" frame of reference. In the following sections, a few examples of these models are provided and explicated in as nontechnical a manner as possible. The few equations necessary to illustrate each type of model are drawn from the earliest work on statistical detection methods and can easily be manipulated by nearly anyone with a faint recollection of high school mathematics. These illustrations, however, serve only to introduce the general area of statistical detec-

[5]This classification system was later refined by Hanson, Harris, and Brennan (1987), who further distinguished between models based on direct and indirect adjustments.

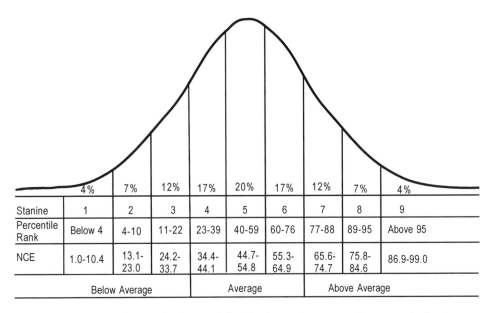

4%	7%	12%	17%	20%	17%	12%	7%	4%

Stanine	1	2	3	4	5	6	7	8	9
Percentile Rank	Below 4	4-10	11-22	23-39	40-59	60-76	77-88	89-95	Above 95
NCE	1.0-10.4	13.1-23.0	24.2-33.7	34.4-44.1	44.7-54.8	55.3-64.9	65.6-74.7	75.8-84.6	86.9-99.0

Below Average	Average	Above Average

FIG. 7.1. The standard normal distribution (NCE = normal curve equivalent).

tion methods and do not represent the state-of-the-art in this area. Indeed, in evaluating the possibility of cheating in actual practice, the methods illustrated should not be relied on. The reader interested in additional information is referred to Appendix A, which contains a more extensive and detailed discussion of current methods.

Empirical Methods. The earliest published works describing empirical methods for detecting cheating were authored by Bird (1927, 1929) and Crawford (1930). Bird suggested examining the number of common errors for a pair of examinees, one or both of whom are suspected of cheating. In his 1927 article, Bird described the case of four students identified as possibly having cheating by observation of their activities during an examination. The test consisted of 149 items, a mix of multiple-choice, true–false, analogy, matching, and completion formats. The four suspects showed 17, 25, 28, and 31 errors in common with the students from whom they were suspected of copying. In comparison, Bird found the average number of errors in common for other pairs of students not suspected of cheating to be only 4.0. Bird reported that an academic affairs committee "considered the quantitative records to be irrefutable and did not at any time raise questions which concerned the accuracy of the proctors' observations." Although all four students denied having cheated, three of them "quickly confessed guilt when confronted with the evidence" (Bird, 1927, p. 261).

Crawford (1930) suggested a similar procedure for detecting cheating, although his treatment of the problem was more thorough, including advice on "How to know which papers to suspect" (p. 776), "How to know whether there has been copying on a pair of suspected papers" (p. 778), "How to know which is the original and which is the copy" (p. 779), and "How to get confessions from guilty pupils" (p. 780). Crawford described his statistical procedure as follows:

(1) Count the total number of errors in the two suspected papers. (2) Count the number of errors in the two papers that are in pairs or are identical. (3) Find the percentage of identical errors by dividing the number of paired errors by the total number of errors of all kinds in the two papers. (4) Find the percentage of identical errors for a number of other papers chosen at random from the class group or for a number of papers from different parts of the room. (5) See how the suspected pair of papers compares with the pairs chosen from the rest of the class. (6) If desired, use statistical techniques to determine whether the suspected pair of papers is significantly different from the other pairs chosen from the room. (pp. 778–779)

A more recent, successful, and widely used empirical method is Angoff's (1974) B-index. The B-index identifies outliers in the distribution of the number of common wrong answers for pairs of test takers, after grouping test takers into strata based on the product of each pair's number of wrong answers. This method, and other more recent developments in statistical detection are examined more completely in Appendix A.

Chance Methods. Over time, methods of detection have moved away from empirical approaches and toward so-called chance methods. In fact, none of the approaches described in the preceding paragraphs are in use today. Instead, all of the approaches currently in use compare various statistics to known probability distributions. A thorough explication of these methods is beyond the scope of this book. However, the following paragraphs provide an introduction for the interested reader; complete details on each procedure can be found in the references provided.

The first chance method mentioned by Saupe (1960) was developed by Dickenson (1945), though his method was still based on numbers of incorrect answers in common. Dickenson defined the probable percentage of errors as

$$IE = (C - 1)/C^2, \tag{1}$$

where C represents the number of answer choices. For example, for a four-option multiple-choice item, $IE = (4 - 1)/4^2 = 3/16 \cong .19$. He then defined the maximum number of common errors as:

$$IE_{MAX} = 2(T_1P_1 + T_2P_2 + T_3P_3 + ...). \tag{2}$$

In Equation 2, values of T represent the number of a certain type of item in a test (e.g., T_1 might represent the number of true–false items, T_2 might represent the number of multiple-choice items, and so on). Values of P are the values of IE for each item type, calculated using Equation 1. An illustration of Dickenson's method applied to a test consisting of 45 true–false items, 20 four-option multiple-choice items, and 15 matching items (for which a list of 20 options is provided) would give the following value as the maximum number of permissible common errors:

$$IE_{MAX} = 2[40(.25) + 20(.19) + 15(.05)] \cong 29. \tag{3}$$

Using Dickenson's method on a test consisting of 80 items in the proportions described, the papers of two students who had 29 errors in common would be suspected of having those errors in common due to cheating.

Another method, developed by Anikeef (1954), compared the observed number of identical incorrect responses to the quantity Np, where N represents the number of incorrect responses by an examinee suspected of cheating and p is the reciprocal of the number of options in the test items (e.g., for four-option multiple-choice items, p = 1/4 = .25). Anikeef's method is easily illustrated. Suppose that a test taker is suspected of cheating on a 20-item test composed of four-option multiple-choice items. Overall, the suspected student answered 10 items incorrectly, 8 of them identically to another student. In this case, the statistic Np = (10)(.25) = 2.5. That statistic is compared with the binomial distribution with a mean of Np and a standard deviation of $[Np(1 - p)]^{.2}$. In this case, the mean and standard deviation are 2.5 and 1.36, respectively. Two standard deviations above the mean is set as the limit of probable occurrence due to chance; for these data, that value would be approximately 5.22. Because the observed number of identical errors, eight, is more than two standard deviations above the mean, the inference that the identical errors were arrived at independently as a result of random guessing is judged to be highly implausible. In a trial of his method using real data, Anikeef found that his index was fairly poor at identifying copying with any certainty. It was most effective at identifying large-scale copying, which he defined as one examinee copying over 16% of the answers from a single, adjacent test taker.

In addition to providing a classification scheme, Saupe (1960) introduced his own method, which was based on the statistical technique called *regression*. Saupe was the first to incorporate both correct and incorrect identical responses; this resulted in a potentially more powerful method of detection, taking advantage, conceptually, of additional data about the examinees' performance. Because the number of common right or wrong responses for a pair of examinees depends on their total number of correct and incorrect responses, Saupe proposed using regression to predict, for each pair of examinees, the number of common right and wrong responses from the product of the pair's total score and number of items answered incorrectly in common. Saupe developed two indices that, using the standard error of estimate for the regression equation, could be used to identify correspondence of right and wrong answers for a pair of examinees that constituted highly unusual or "outlier" performance—that is, correspondence of right and wrong answers beyond what would reasonably be expected between a pair of independent (i.e., noncheating) test takers.

Current Methods. Again, the methods described above are presented only to provide historical background on statistical detection methods and to illustrate the differences between the two primary approaches. Empirical methods can be used when distributions of indices for suspected copiers can be compared to indices derived from circumstances in which copying could not have occurred. This requirement cannot usually be met in typical classroom situations, but can be accomplished in large-scale testing contexts in which tests are administered at geographically separated locations. Chance methods, therefore, are required whenever it is not possible to identify a sufficient number of test takers who could not have copied. Much additional work has been done in the area of statistical methods and the reader should consult Appendix A for information about the variety of current approaches. One of these alternatives is worth mentioning here, however, if only because of the sheer volume of tests to which it is regularly applied and, consequently, the number of test takers affected by its use.

The statistical method of detecting cheating that is probably used most often today is called the K-index, which is used by Educational Testing Service (ETS). Estimates published in the *New York Times* (Nordheimer & Frantz, 1997) reveal a large volume of testing by ETS, including more than 2 million administrations of the SAT (Part I), 1.7 million administrations of the Preliminary SAT, 630,000 administrations of the GRE, 540,000 administrations of the Advanced Placement (AP) exam, and 230,000 administrations of the GMAT. In total, ETS administers more than 9 million tests annually, making ETS the largest potential user of statistical methods for detecting cheating.

The K-index is "used at ETS to assess the degree of unusual agreement between the incorrect multiple-choice answers of two examinees" and "is an estimate of the 'chance probability' that two examinees would agree as much or more as they did agree on their incorrect answers" (Holland, 1996, pp. 4–5). A history of how ETS handles what the test maker refers to as "scores of questionable validity," has been written by Saretsky (1984). Saretsky noted that, over the years, one of the most significant changes in ETS policies and procedures has been the "development, application, and increased reliance on statistical indices" used to identify possible cheating (p. 13). He reported that the K-index can be traced to the work at ETS of Frederick Kling, who developed the index in 1979. Saretsky credited the availability of statistical methods of detection and advancing computer technology as significantly increasing the number of potential cheating cases brought before the ETS Board of Review.

Unfortunately, the K-index has not been the subject of published, comparative analyses of its performance, so it is unknown whether it performs better, worse, or about the same as other available alternatives. One of the only sources of information on the K-index is Holland's (1996) analysis. In his evaluation, Holland concluded that the K-index performs well in some circumstances, but "the fact it did not yield a conservative estimate of the real agreement probability in every case studied here [e.g., on the SAT Verbal test] suggests that it may be wise to consider a few modifications of the current use of the K-index" (p. 33).

The indices used on the ACT Assessment program, the so-called AJ and AS statistics, are even less well documented than those in use at ETS, and research documenting how they compare with other indices has not been published in measurement journals.

Summary

Of all the available statistical methods for detecting cheating, several have been shown to be reasonably powerful in terms of detecting "true" copying while safeguarding against overidentification of copying (i.e., the problem statisticians refer to as Type I errors or "false positives"). Of the indices in current use, g_2, developed by Frary, Tideman, and Watts (1977), and described in Appendix A, has numerous technical advantages and has withstood comparative scrutiny in several published research reports. Unlike indices that rely only on common numbers of errors, which can bias results when overall ability is not accounted for, the g_2 index incorporates information from common right answers as well. D. M. Roberts (1987) has concluded "the statistical method developed by Frary et al. (1977) appears to be the most sensitive to correctly separating cheaters from non-cheaters in multiple-choice testing situations" (p. 77). The newest index, $\tilde{\omega}$, developed by Wollack (1997), and also described in Appendix A, may hold the greatest promise for the future, as it appears to have the advantages of the g_2 index and can be used with relatively small or large sample sizes. Ironically, the indices used most frequently—those used by the ACT Assessment program and the SAT—have received only scant attention. A considerable amount of additional research is needed on these methods.

Hi-Ho, Trigger, Away!

One of the fairly nontechnical issues surrounding the use of statistical methods to detect cheating is the use of what has been called a *trigger*. A trigger is a rule or event that defines when a statistical analysis for potential cheating should be initiated. It might seem reasonable to analyze *all* examinees' performances on a given test and flag those for whom a large index (e.g., B, K, $\tilde{\omega}$, g_2, etc.) is obtained. However, legal and technical implications argue against such a practice. For example, as can be seen in all of the research studies, every cheating index produces its share of false positives—cases flagged as cheating in which no cheating occurred. Dwyer and Hecht (1996) have summarized the professional advice regarding the use of statistical detection methods:

> Our position, which is supported by both the courts and statisticians, is that one should never accept probabilistic evidence as sufficient evidence of cheating merely because a pattern of answers is deemed to be statistically improbable. In every case, reasonable competing explanations should be evaluated, limitations of the mechanical detection strategies must be taken into account, and the inherent variability in the reliability and validity of test design and administration of all but the most rigorous of standardized tests must be considered. (p. 133)

Thus, it would seem prudent that the weight of statistical evidence only be brought to bear when some other circumstances—that is, a trigger—provide a reason for flagging cases for subsequent statistical analysis. Angoff (1993; see also Holland, 1996) suggested several triggering mechanisms in the context of large-scale testing, such as the SAT:

> In all these instances of cheating, there should be an event that triggers off the investigation—sometimes (usually) the observation that the student's score is improbably higher than that earned on an earlier administration. Or, the student's score is out of line with school grades, sometimes the proctor reports having observed that the student was seen copying from or communicating with another student, sometimes the report from another student who claims having witnessed the cheating, etc. (p. 3)

For security reasons, large testing organizations like ETS and ACT avoid providing details about their procedures for detecting and investigating cheating. However, it seems that both of these organizations rely, to varying degrees, on triggering mechanisms such as those described above. For example, although ETS uses score gains to trigger a statistical analysis, ACT does not (Semel, 1997). Among experts in psychometrics and statistics, there is little disagreement with the notion that statistical evidence should never be used to trigger an investigation into suspected cheating. Instead, statistical methods should be used to corroborate other evidence of improper activity. D. M. Roberts (1987) summarized the prevailing professional opinion:

> In any situation where there is a suspicion of cheating, the primary source of evidence should be observational. If there is corroborative evidence based on some sound statistical method, it still should be viewed as a secondary source of information. To rely on statistical evidence alone when no observational evidence is available is not only considered poor practice … but requires the prosecution to prove charges of cheating based only on a probability. (p. 79)

Commercially Available Software to Detect Cheating

Regarding the purchase of a Ford Model T, it was said that a customer could have any color that he or she wished, so long as it was black. The same state of affairs holds true with respect to commercially available software to detect cheating. As of this writing, a single software package is available, called Scrutiny! (Advanced Psychometrics, 1993). The program, developed by Advanced Psychometrics, Inc., of North Bay, Ontario, Canada, is distributed by Assessment Systems Corporation (ASC) of St. Paul, Minnesota. As of this writing, the suggested price of Scrutiny! was $399.

One advantage of Scrutiny! is that it is designed to operate on a typical personal computer. According to the manual accompanying the program, the software requires a Windows 3.1, Windows 95, or higher operating system; 1 megabyte of hard disk space is required for installation of the program; a total of 7 megabytes of free disk space is recommended for data files, temporary files, and output files; and a minimum of 4 megabytes of RAM is required (ASC, 1995). These specifications would permit Scrutiny! to run on nearly any desktop or laptop computer.

Scrutiny! uses the error similarity analysis (ESA) method of identifying potential cheating developed by Bellezza and Bellezza (1989; see Appendix A). This fact also marks Scrutiny's greatest drawback. The weaknesses of the ESA method have received attention in the professional literature. For example, Frary (1993) has observed that the method (a) fails to use information from correct response similarity, (b) fails to consider total test performance of examinees, and (c) does not take into account the attractiveness of wrong options selected in common. Also, both Bay (1994) and Chason (1997) found that ESA was the least effective index for detecting copying of the methods they compared.

The manual for Scrutiny! provides a thorough introduction to the logic of detection and accurate advice regarding appropriate cautions for interpretation and use of the results. However, the manual does diverge from generally accepted professional advice in recommending "screening test center results from multiple-choice or true–false tests for instances of probable copying" (ASC, 1995, p. 1). Although the manual indicates that all of the reports generated by Scrutiny! "are intended to be interpreted by users who have not been trained in the areas of statistics or psychometrics" (p. 1), given the relative sophistication of the procedure involved and the serious consequences that can be associated with the inference that cheating has occurred, some training in these areas also would be desirable.

To prepare for a Scrutiny! analysis, the user can import data saved in a standard test (i.e., ASCII) format using any common word processor. A data preparation utility automatically performs necessary formatting to ASCII files, certain optical mark reader files, and files from other ASC programs. The first record in the data file must contain the answer key for the test items. Items of any select-type format using between 2 and 10 response alternatives can be analyzed, and the program permits up to nine information fields for alphabetical or numerical user-supplied information, such as test site, examinee identification number (up to nine characters), and examinee seat location. A data-editing utility permits on-screen cleanup and editing of the data file. Scrutiny! also permits the user to enter a seating plan, which can be used in conjunction with identified examinee seat locations to corroborate the suspicion of cheating.

The manual reports that a Scrutiny! analysis performed on responses to a 60-item test from 100 examinees, using a 486-processor-based computer running at 66MHz took 24 seconds; the same analysis performed on a Pentium-processor machine running at 233MHz took approximately 5 seconds. Analyses of longer or shorter tests, involving more or fewer examinees, using less or more advanced computers would take more or less time, respectively.

Three reports result from a Scrutiny! analysis. A "Scoring Report" provides total group results and scored test results for each examinee, including the items each examinee answered incorrectly, the examinee's rank, and the number of items omitted. An "Item Analysis Report" gives the difficulty of each test item and the number of examinees who selected each of the options for the items, along with the minimum and maximum obtained scores, the mean and median scores, the standard deviation and skewness of the scores, and three estimates of score reliability (coefficient alpha, K-R 20, and K-R 21). Along with this abundance of information, it would seem that Scrutiny!'s programmers could have easily provided more complete item analysis (perhaps including biserial or point-biserial discrimination indices) and the more frequently encountered item difficulty index, p, in addition to the delta index provided. A "Suspicious Similarities Report" identifies examinees whose performance has been flagged by the ESA procedure as having exceeded the program's default criterion of $p \le .0001$, reflecting odds of less than 1 in 10,000 that the observed common errors were due to chance alone. Finally, a visual portrayal of the results is generated. One such graphic, produced from the sample data that accompanies the program, is reproduced in Fig. 7.2.

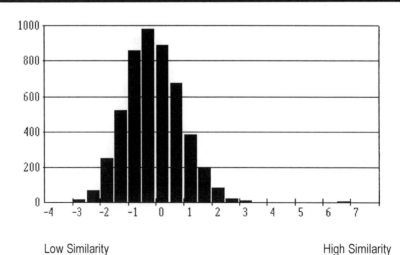

FIG. 7.2. Sample graphical output from Scrutiny! showing number of answer similarities expressed in Z-scores.

Overall, Scrutiny! is easy to use and provides the only commercially available method of investigating suspicions of answer copying. The documentation provided with the software gives complete technical information on the product and its use; relevant policy and professional cautions are also covered. Although Scrutiny! may provide a defensible method of gathering evidence to support a suspicion of cheating triggered by some other method (e.g., observation), it should not be used as a screening tool. Given the documented inadequacies of the ESA method and the availability of superior statistical approaches, Scrutiny! should probably not be used in high-stakes testing situations. Refinements in this software, and development of other commercial products to fill the need for cheating-detection software, would likely be welcomed by researchers and testing practitioners.

Problems With Statistical Methods of Detecting Cheating

It is a stark contrast. On one hand, statistical methods for detecting cheating are becoming more sophisticated, powerful, and available. On the other hand, the usefulness and applicability of those methods seem to be diverging from the reality of societal perceptions of what constitutes evidence and from current and future testing practices.

As evidenced by phenomena such as the dramatic increases in participation in mega lotteries and the O.J. Simpson trial, the general public seems inured to data related to probability and chance. Interestingly, statistical evidence regarding the improbability of an occurrence is frequently interpreted to mean just the opposite: The fact that lightning hit the same person twice at some time in the past is *proof* that it could happen today. Analogously, in the minds of many people, a 1 in 5 million chance that two examinees *could* have answered identically by chance alone is *proof* that cheating should not be suspected. If the lightning could hit, you must acquit.

Even statisticians and others who appreciate the weightiness of probabilistic statements—perhaps especially those people—recognize the limitations of statistical methods (see, e.g., Klein, 1992). They recognize the possibility of improbable events, that other factors can produce similarity of response patterns, and that statistical methods can be performed inaccurately. A few of the other technical limitations of statistical methods include the following:

1. *Applicability.* The statistical methods described in this chapter are useful almost exclusively for detecting one student copying from another. The methods cannot detect the use of cheat sheets, impersonation, electronic communication, and other (perhaps more common) forms of cheating. In addition, direct copying may be one of the least frequently practiced forms of cheating; statistical methods to detect this form of cheating may be straining the gnat and allowing the camel to pass.

2. *Sensitivity.* Each of the methods identified in this chapter fails to identify rather extensive cheating in some to many cases. In addition to their limited applicability to cheating by copying, the type of copying most likely to be identified by statistical methods might be called the "dumb and dumber" type—that is, wholesale copying of 50% or more of the responses of a more able student seated nearby. In Cizek (1996), I observed,

that's a hefty amount of copying. This seems like the equivalent of a driver's license test that only screens out people who have head-on collisions during the test. Sure, it's good to keep such folks off the road, but it would also seem that a *valid* driver's test—like a valid test of answer copying—would do much more. (p. 4)

According to Hanson et al. (1987), the large-scale type of cheating that can be detected easily by current statistical methods is not nearly as common as the occasional copying of an answer or two or a string of, at most, five answers. Bellezza and Bellezza (1989) noted that for copying to be detected on a typical five-option multiple-choice test, the test should be long and difficult enough so that the average number of errors is 15 or more. They stated that "even under these optimal conditions, cheating will not be detected if a student copies only a few answers" (p. 154). In another study involving one of the most accurate and advanced statistical detection methods, Wollack and Cohen (1998) found that "when only 10% of the items [in a test] were copied, most copiers went undetected" (p. 150). Unfortunately, it is a demonstrated reality that the types of cheating most frequently used in real testing situations is least likely to be detected by statistical methods.

Finally, although current methods strive to reduce the probability of false identifications of cheating, they are not eliminated. Attempts to develop indices that are highly sensitive to detecting "true" cheating invariably end up identifying an increased percentage of innocent persons as well.

3. *Cheater and Cheatee.* Frary et al. (1977) concurred that very small-scale copying, such as only one or two items, will have a very small chance of detection. However, they also demonstrated that the particular combination of cheater and "cheatee" and, specifically, the degree to which their ability levels are similar can make a difference. They observed that an additional factor that influences whether cheating will be detected is the particular combination of the ability levels of the persons involved. Frary et al. found that, "for example, if a moderately good student copies extensively from someone who gets over 90 percent correct, a relatively low [index of copying] may well result" (p. 253).

4. *Format Limitations.* Over the past 5 to 10 years, there has been increased criticism of the multiple-choice format and other select-type item formats. At the same time, there has been a return to more extended-response formats (e.g., essay) and performance assessments, coupled with an increasing popularity of portfolio assessment. The validity of the criticisms and defenses of the multiple-choice format is another issue. However, it is reasonable to speculate that the multiple-choice format will be used less and less often in the future, especially in elementary and secondary education. Thus, although the methods for detecting cheating presented in this chapter are appropriate for use with select-type items, it is unclear how or if they can be adapted to other formats. Nearly all available methods will *not* be able to be readily applied to emerging assessment formats; current methods will become increasingly irrelevant as the multiple-choice format itself becomes increasingly irrelevant to educational assessment (Cizek, 1996).

5. *Triggers.* If, in most cases, observational or other evidence is required to flag an examinee's test performance for statistical analysis, two issues arise. As becomes evident in the next chapter, proctors miss an awful lot, so a downward bias exists in the number of cases identified for further statistical analysis. This means that the number of true incidents of cheating that *might* be revealed by statistical methods is destined to be smaller than it could be.

6. *Relevance.* As noted in Cizek (1996), currently available statistical methods for detecting cheating are almost exclusively relevant to the context of large-scale testing, that is, those situations in which a test is administered to hundreds or thousands of examinees. Although some of the methods can be used with as few as 100 examinees, this still means that statistical methods are not suitable for use in the vast majority of classrooms, where the number of students taking a given test is usually 30 or fewer. The most advanced—and most powerful and accurate—methods are almost certainly out of the question when it comes to classroom use, and some researchers in the area of statistical detection methods have recognized this fact. For example, Bellezza and Bellezza (1995) observed that the "problems of classroom teachers differ from those of national testing organizations, and the resources available to teachers are often limited;" they concluded that "statistical analyses of cheating have not focussed on the needs of the classroom teacher" (p. 182). Wollack and Cohen (1998) noted that the usefulness of one of the advanced methods of detection is limited, "particularly in the classroom, because most teachers do not have a set of precalibrated items" (p. 144). What Wollack and Cohen did not say is that most teachers do not have any idea what "a set of precalibrated items" is. It is also unlikely that classroom teachers will develop the desire to learn the fundamentals of item response theory (IRT) necessary to understand item precalibration, nor is it likely that they would see the relevance of IRT for their classroom assessment practices.

Despite these numerous and serious limitations, a strong case can be made for the continued—even broadened—use of statistical methods. First, it must be admitted that advanced statistical detection methods such as those described in Appendix A are highly accurate, dependable, and powerful tools for detecting certain types of cheating. If computing resources, class sizes, knowledge, and desire to detect academic dishonesty exist, the technology to do so is available. Three additional compelling reasons supporting the use of statistical methods have been articulated by Frary and Olson (1985):

1. The use of statistical methods is preventative. Students who may be tempted to cheat may be dissuaded from doing so if they believe that there is a regular check for unusual response patterns.
2. The use of statistical methods demonstrates the teacher's concern about the problem of cheating and his or her commitment to address it. According to Frary and Olson, many instances of cheating may arise, in part, when it appears that no one is concerned about the problem.
3. The longitudinal use of statistical methods can provide a unique perspective. According to Frary and Olson, the identification of testing irregularities using statistical methods is far more convincing as evidence in the context of years of data in which such aberrations had not occurred.

Professional Guidelines Related to Detecting Cheating

As mentioned previously, it is commonly recommended by experts in testing that statistical methods of detecting cheating not be used to initiate an investigation of suspected cheating but as one way of acquiring corroborating evidence. In addition to these recommendations, formal guidelines for the testing profession exist that speak to situations related to cheating. For example, the *Code of Professional Responsibilities in Educational Measurement* (NCME, 1995) recommends that those who administer tests should "take appropriate security precautions before, during, and after the administration of the assessment" (Guideline 4.3, p. 5) and "avoid any conditions in the conduct of the assessment that might invalidate the results" (Guideline 4.7, p. 5). Those who score assessments are advised to "ensure the accuracy of the assessment results by conducting reasonable quality control procedures before, during, and after scoring" (Guideline 5.2, p. 5).

Foremost among these professional guidelines is the *Standards for Educational and Psychological Testing* (American Educational Research Association [AERA], American Psychological Association [APA], & NCME, 1985). The *Standards* is a collection of statements and explanatory text that are intended "to provide a basis for evaluating the quality of testing practices as they affect the various parties involved" (p. 1). The individual guidelines listed in the *Standards* are classified as either primary or secondary. Primary standards are described as "those that should be met by all tests before their operational use and in all test uses, unless a sound professional reason is available to show why it is not necessary, or technically feasible, to do so in a particular case" (p. 2). Each of the standards listed in the following paragraphs is classified in the *Standards* as primary.

One of the guiding statements (Standard 15.3) deals directly with the obligation of those who give tests to prevent cheating. It states "Reasonable efforts should be made to assure the validity of test scores by eliminating opportunities for test takers to attain scores by fraudulent means" (AERA, APA, & NCME, 1985, p. 83). Conscientious observation during a test certainly reduces, although would not eliminate, the opportunities for cheating referred to in Standard 15.3. To the extent that test takers are aware that statistical methods may be used to identify or corroborate improbably similar responses, the use of such methods would also comport with the intent of the standard.

Of course, there is also a corresponding obligation on the part of the student to attain test scores by acceptable means. The 1985 version of the *Standards* is currently being revised, and consideration is being given to adding language related to test takers' obligations. Such language might recognize, for example, that test takers have a responsibility to abide by the guidelines for testing set forth by the test giver and that unauthorized giving, receiving, or reproducing unauthorized materials or information about a test is unethical and improper.[6]

The *Standards* also address the obligations of test givers to describe the methods used to detect cheating when actions affecting a student (e.g., accusation of cheating or cancellation of test score) are contemplated. Standard 16.7, in which the phrase "test irregularities" is intended to cover copying, use of crib notes, impersonation of one test taker by another, and so on, states,

> Under certain conditions it may be desirable to cancel a test taker's score or to withhold it because of possible testing irregularities, including suspected misconduct. The type of evidence and procedures used to determine that a score should be canceled or withheld should be explained fully to all test takers whose scores are being withheld or canceled. (AERA, APA, & NCME, 1985, p. 86)

---

[6]Of course, even if such language were added, it may have little effect. The revised *Standards* would continue to be influential among those who develop and administer tests, but it is unlikely that test takers would feel bound by these requirements.

Clearly, Standard 16.7 requires that the methods used and the results of those methods that suggest an inference of cheating should be explained to those who are suspected of cheating. Standard 16.8 requires that test takers should be notified of the reasons for suspicion and that any investigation should be conducted expeditiously in order to protect the interests of the examinee.[7] In addition, Standard 16.9 implies that, when cheating is suspected, test givers have an obligation to search out not only evidence that corroborates the suspicion of cheating, but also evidence that would refute the possibility. According to Standard 16.9:

> test takers should be given advance warning and an opportunity to provide evidence that the score should not be canceled or withheld. All evidence considered in deciding upon the intended action, including evidence that might lead to a contrary decision, should be made available to the test taker on request. (AERA, APA, & NCME, 1985, p. 86)

Finally, Standard 16.10 requires that "all available data [bearing on the question of a suspect test score] judged to be relevant should be considered" (AERA, APA, & NCME, 1985, p. 87). In the explanatory text accompanying Standard 16.10, specific reference is made to statistical methods of detecting cheating:

> Allegations of testing irregularity that involve copying are sometimes based on a comparison of the distractors chosen by two test takers on items answered incorrectly by both. This method should not be used as the sole basis for decisions since it ignores other evidence that might indicate that copying did not take place. Reasonable efforts should be made to obtain contrary, as well as supporting, evidence to settle the matter of irregularity as well as the validity of the questioned score. (p. 87)

CONCLUSIONS

Evaluations of methods for detecting cheating on tests yield two conclusions. First, observational methods of detecting cheating, though necessary, can be unreliable. Second, statistical methods—useful adjuncts to observational methods—can corroborate suspicions of cheating, although the problem of false identifications (i.e., Type I errors) is ever present, as are failures to identify all instances of cheating (i.e., Type II errors).

Evaluations of the statistical methods reveal that powerful and promising methods of detecting cheating exist. However, stepping back from the technical evaluations and considering the bigger picture suggests that, on the whole, methods of detecting cheating are woefully inadequate for taking a bite out of this crime. With respect to observational methods, as we see in the next chapter, few students who admit to cheating on tests report that they are caught. To be precise in describing the statistical methods presented in this chapter, it is important to admit that none of the methods actually *detect* cheating; rather, they can provide evidence that challenges the hypothesis that cheating has *not* occurred and should be

---

[7]The guidelines presented in Standards 16.7, 16.8, 16.9, and 16.10, as presented in the 1985 version of the *Standards*, are limited to "educational admissions and licensing and certification applications" (AERA, APA, & NCME, 1985, p. 86). It is not known whether this limitation will also be included in the forthcoming revision of the *Standards*.

used only when a suspicion of cheating is triggered by some other information. Statistical methods cannot yield proof of guilt or innocence.

Furthermore, statistical methods currently lack broad acceptance by educators, perhaps because of their computational complexity and absence of intuitive appeal. Statistical methods are severely limited to objective (e.g., multiple-choice) testing situations involving fairly large numbers of examinees, and they are efficacious primarily when cheating consists of exact copying by a low-ability examinee of lengthy strings of answers from a high-ability examinee. Because most educational testing situations involve fairly small class sizes, increasing use of alternative testing formats (e.g., portfolios), and, increasingly, less testing altogether, statistical methods of detection seem destined to drift toward even less frequent use.[8]

Ultimately, it is most important to recognize that both types of evidence of cheating—observational and statistical—require subjective human judgment about whether cheating has occurred. In the end, the conclusion that cheating has occurred is almost always probabilistic and requires inference. To some people, the evidentiary weight of 1 in 100,000 odds or a teacher's direct observation of an examinee looking at another student's test paper overwhelmingly indicates that cheating has occurred; to others, the odds are proof that similar answers could have happened by chance, and eyewitness testimony is infamously undependable.

Furthermore, although both kinds of evidence have value, by definition, *evidence* is gathered only *after* a crime has been committed. As the proverb goes, an ounce of prevention is worth a pound of cure. In the case of cheating on tests, it is far preferable to prevent cheating from occurring than to attempt to detect it. Shortly, we will examine the best hope for addressing cheating—prevention. First, however, to further demonstrate the value of prevention, the next chapter examines some ways of responding to cheating once it has been discovered.

---

[8]This conclusion may not apply in some education-related contexts, such as licensure and certification testing. These contexts differ from classroom situations in that the former involve duties of public protection from incompetent practice. In these situations, professional licensure, certification, and regulatory agencies acknowledge a greater necessity to ensure valid scores and to minimize potential legal actions arising from a failure to ensure valid test content, administration, and interpretations. Also, because these testing situations frequently involve parameters suitable to statistical detection (e.g., large numbers of examinees and lengthy, objective-format tests), professional licensure and certification agencies may be much more likely to retain—or even expand—statistical detection of cheating.

✦ E I G H T ✦

Responding to Cheating

People cheat because it's really easy to cheat, really easy to get away with. And in high school, the cheaters always win. They don't get caught and they are the ones getting 100 on exams when the non-cheaters are getting 80s and 90s. Cheaters do win.
　　　　　　　　　—Connecticut high school student (cited in Stansbury, 1997c, p. 1)

I haven't caught someone cheating in my classes in years. I'm sure kids do things with homework, but as for cheating during tests, I do not see it.
　　　　　　　　　—Connecticut high school teacher (cited in Stansbury, 1997c, p. 1)

A respected scholar in the area of instruction, Kenneth Eble, attempted to describe the art of teaching, including his philosophical perspectives on the relationship between teachers and students, pedagogical methods, and pragmatic tips for addressing practical problems in the classroom. His book, *The Craft of Teaching*, attempted to address these topics as thoroughly as possible. Naturally, a comprehensive work would include testing and the issue of cheating on tests; Eble's (1988) perception of these was that they constitute the "grubby stuff and dirty work" of teaching (p. 123).

Eble is not alone in sizing up the situation in that way. Responding to cheating is perhaps one of the most distasteful, time-consuming, and undervalued tasks that a teacher can face. A number of factors contribute to this; they are addressed in the following pages. First, the evidence regarding student and faculty responses to cheating is presented, as are institutional responses to academic dishonesty. This

151

information is intended to serve as a transition to the next chapter, which describes how students, teachers, and institutions can work to prevent cheating. As will become clear in the next pages, the generally ineffectual and spotty responses to cheating make prevention all the more important.

STUDENT RESPONSES TO CHEATING

It is perhaps misleading to entitle this section "Student Responses to Cheating." A better title might be "Student Nonresponses to Cheating" because it more accurately reflects the state of affairs. There is no doubt that students see instances of cheating all around them. However, students appear to be both understanding and fraternal. Much more frequently than not, observed cheating goes unreported, apparently because students who do not cheat know what it is like to be in the other person's shoes or because of a tacit prohibition against ratting on a fellow student. In some cases, some students overlook cheating because the "teacher just seems to deserve it."

Research has documented the magnitude of the problem. When college student affairs personnel were asked about what they *think* students do when they observe other students cheating, nearly three fourths of them (72.8%) said that "students look the other way when they see someone cheat" (Aaron & Georgia, 1994, p. 87).

As it turns out, the perceptions of administrators are fairly accurate. Schab (1972) identified what he called a culture of "no squealing" in his survey of 1,629 high school students. Approximately 88% of the respondents said that they would not report it if they observed a friend cheating. Demonstrating that propinquity does not matter that much, 80% said they would not report cheating by another student even if he or she were *not* a friend. In addition to being an official stance of the U.S. military, the policy of "don't ask, don't tell" appears to be operative at the high school level.

A study by Centra (1970) at the college level corroborates the findings at the high school level. Centra surveyed 1,500 freshmen drawn from 37 institutions across the United States and asked them how they would respond to witnessing another student cheat. Table 8.1 shows that, of six possible responses to cheating, the preferred response was to do nothing (46%). The least appealing action was to report the incident (5%); coincidentally, and perhaps supporting a hypothesis of student apathy toward cheating, reporting the incident was tied for last place with the nonreponse rate for the survey. In another survey, Baird (1980) found that 40% of the students said they did not disapprove of cheating, 29% of those who admitted cheating said they never felt guilty about it, and 75% of the total group said that cheating was "a normal part of life." When asked how they would react to observing another student cheat on a test, 80.5% of the students said they would do nothing; only 1% indicated that they would report the incident.

Another study asked students who had actually observed cheating how they had responded to the incident (as opposed to asking students how they would respond to a hypothetical incident). Of the 776 college students surveyed, 74% said they had witnessed cheating during an examination. Among these students, the most common response to cheating was "see no evil": The study found that more than half of those who had witnessed cheating (53.1%) said they had ignored the incident; another 37.5% did not report it but did "mention it to their friends," and less than 1% said they had reported the incident to the instructor (Jendrek, 1992, p.

TABLE 8.1
Responses of College Freshmen to Witnessing Cheating

Response	%
Do nothing	46
Express concern to the student privately	25
Action would depend on who the student was	12
Report the cheating to the teacher or other authority, but not reveal the student's name	7
Report the incident, naming the student	5
No response	5

Note. Reprinted with permission from "College Freshmen Attitudes Toward Cheating," by J. A. Centra, 1970, *Personnel and Guidance Journal,* *48*(5), p. 368.

262). When asked why they had not reported the incident, the most common response was that "it's the student's problem, not mine" (35.2%); a smaller percentage said that, "it's the professor's problem, not mine" (6%); and 14.8% said that they just didn't want to get involved (p. 264). These responses differed by students' overall performance: The reason of "not wanting to get involved" was given more frequently by higher GPA students; lower GPA students were more likely to say it was the professor's problem.

Interestingly, nearly half of the students who had witnessed cheating did not even answer Jendrek's (1992) survey question regarding their actions in response to having observed cheating. This finding corroborates the hypothesis that most students are simply apathetic about cheating by their peers. Jendrek also asked students to describe their feelings associated with observing a fellow student cheat. Given the choices of admiration, anger, disgust, indifference, and sorrow, the most frequently reported feeling was indifference. This general lack of concern on the part of students mirrors a general institutional apathy about cheating. One survey of college officials found that only 15.2% reported that their institutions attempt to assess the extent of academic dishonesty on their campuses (Aaron, 1992).

It is certainly an open question whether apathy is a new feature of students' attitudes toward cheating or simply a newly discovered one. However, changes in testing and grading practices may be contributing to decreasing student concern about cheating on tests. For example, in the past, *norm-referenced* grading systems (i.e., "grading on the curve") were a common feature in many classrooms. Under such a system, in which a fixed percentage of As, Bs, Cs, and so on would be awarded, there is a greater sense of competition and a student knows that his or her grade can be adversely affected by the inappropriately high score of a student who cheats. Although its use has waned in recent years, norm-referenced evaluation does serve to motivate students to report academic dishonesty by others. Norm-referenced evaluation has increasingly been abandoned in favor of *fixed-standard* evaluation systems (e.g., 92%–100% correct = A, 83%–91% correct = B, 74%–82% correct = C, and so on) in classrooms at all levels. An unintended consequence of this movement may have been the elimination of a strong motivation for reporting cheating.

In conclusion, a review of what is known about students' responses to cheating yields one of the tidiest summaries in the social sciences. There are three well-established elements that contribute to the summary. First, as we learned in chapter 2, there is plenty of cheating. Second, as Evans and Craig (1990a) have observed in elementary and secondary schools (though the observation applies to other settings as well), "students usually know when cheating occurs in class" (p. 331). Third, as we have seen in this chapter, students commonly ignore cheating when they do observe it. Of course, *some* cheating is reported by students. However, given the infrequency of student reporting of cheating, the conclusion of Alschuler and Bliming (1995) seems accurate: "Whistle blowers hardly make a dent" (p. 124).

FACULTY RESPONSES TO CHEATING

According to Murray (1996), "students report that they rely on faculty to stop their classmates from cheating and express disappointment in the professors who let them get away with it" (p. 42). Although it is clear that students perceive much cheating going on around them, incidents of cheating are also observed directly by teachers or proctors, if they are on the lookout for cheating. Whether reported by a student or directly observed by a teacher, those responsible for giving tests are then faced with the question of how *they* will respond to possible cheating. We now turn to how cheating is handled by those who bear at least partial responsibility for ensuring fair assessment conditions and practices.

In contrast to students' claims and research evidence that cheating is ubiquitous, it appears that very few cheaters are actually caught in typical classroom testing situations. Fewer still face any consequences for the behavior. In addition to the previously mentioned movement toward more fixed-standard grading systems (which is probably a minor factor) the fact that detection and prosecution of cheating are so rare may contribute greatly to the frequency of cheating on tests.

First, it is useful to consider the discrepancy between rates of admitted cheating and the numbers of students who are actually caught. Fishbein (1994) described a survey of a representative sample of 232 students at Rutgers University in New Brunswick, New Jersey, in 1990. Of those students, 45% admitted to cheating occasionally and 33% were described as "hard-core" cheaters (i.e., those who admitted to cheating in eight or more courses in their academic careers). With more than 33,000 students on the Rutgers campus, even if only the so-called hard-core cheaters were caught, and even if each of the hard-core cheaters were caught in only one of the eight courses they cheated in, the number of cheating cases at Rutgers would be approximately 11,000 annually. However, according to Fishbein, fewer than 80 cases of cheating are typically reported in a given year.

The results of the Rutgers survey are comparable with the findings of other studies. In a survey of 380 undergraduates, Haines et al. (1986) found that 54.1% of the students admitted cheating, whereas only 1.3% reported *ever* being caught. Similarly, in a study involving 364 engineering students, 56% of the students admitted cheating, but only 3% said they had been caught (Singhal, 1982). Singhal also found that more professors were considerably more likely than students to have reported an instance of cheating (21% vs. 7%).

Of course, most faculty members realize that cheating is a problem and that most cheating goes undetected and unreported. In one survey of 337 faculty members at a mid-sized state university, 93% of the respondents agreed or strongly agreed with the idea that "academic dishonesty is a problem at this university"

(Jendrek, 1989, p. 405). Sixty percent of those surveyed reported they had personally witnessed cheating on an examination (although male faculty members were significantly more likely to say they had witnessed cheating than female faculty members[1] and more tenured faculty members said they had witnessed cheating than nontenured faculty members). The survey also asked faculty members how they had responded to personally witnessing cheating: 67% said they discussed it with the student only, 33% reported it to the department chairperson, 20% met with the student and the chairperson, 8% said they ignored it altogether. In a more recent study, Graham et al. (1994) found that although "the percentage of faculty that have caught a student cheating is high (78.7%), only 9% penalized students for cheating" (p. 258).

The response of ignoring cheating may be related to grade level and may be becoming even more frequent. One researcher asked elementary and high school students how their teachers responded to cheating when they observed it. Only 4.3% of the elementary school students said that their teachers "do nothing" compared with 20.2% who said that observed cheating was ignored at the high school level (Brandes, 1986, p.3). The headline for a front-page article in the APA newspaper, the *Monitor*, wondered whether psychology professors are "turning a blind eye to cheating" (Murray, 1996, p. 1). The article cited a 1990 study that revealed that 20% of a sample of 482 psychology professors admitted ignoring "strong evidence of academic dishonesty on at least one occasion" (p. 42).

RESPONSES BY TESTING ORGANIZATIONS

Companies whose business is testing have a keen interest in maintaining their reputations for delivering high-quality products. Perhaps their most valuable "product" is a test result that can be confidently interpreted as faithfully representing a test takers' performance. This means that testing companies have a large stake in ensuring that cheating is dissuaded, detected, and prosecuted. On the other hand, the same self-interest can prompt testing companies to downplay the extent or seriousness of cheating. For example, a recent *New York Times* article reported that when the large testing corporation ETS suspected cheating on one of its tests for school administrators, "the testing service decided to keep it quiet" (Frantz & Nordheimer, 1997, p. A1).

While downplaying publically the pervasiveness and effects of cheating, large testing companies also recognize the importance of responding to cheating. The perception, at least, of the certainty of being caught, along with stiff penalties for cheating, serves to dissuade cheating on the part of test takers and reassure consumers of the companies' services (e.g., college admissions officers, licensing and regulatory boards, and credentialing agencies). In addition to reports of

---

[1]There are also apparently gender differences in prescribing punishment for cheating. In a study in which 194 college students recommended punishments for hypothetical cases involving cheating on a test, men were found to recommend more severe punishments than women (Lewis & Hartnett, 1983). Woodridge and Richman (1985) found that more severe punishments were recommended for men who cheated than for women who cheated. (These authors also found that harsher punishment was recommended for White men than Black men.) In another study involving 120 undergraduate students, although both men and women were equally severe in recommending punishment for male cheaters, men were more lenient than women in prescribing punishment for female cheaters (Richey & Fichter, 1969).

downplaying the seriousness of suspected incidents of cheating, there are public indications of vigilence. For example, another news item regarding ETS estimated that approximately 1,800 investigations of suspected cheating are initiated each year related to another of its tests, the SAT (DePalma, 1992).

A committee established to study the entire test security process at ETS documented the company's method of response to potentially invalid test scores (Crocker, Geisinger, Loyd, & Webb, 1994). ETS' first response is to withhold reporting of any suspected score (when the triggers for determining if a test taker's performance is questionable correspond with those described in chap. 7). Next, all suspect test performances are referred to a Test Security Office, which collects all available evidence related to the suspected score. Sources of evidence include any of the following: test registration materials, test booklets, answer sheets, handwriting samples, analysis of the number of erasures, and statistical analysis of answer similarities with other test takers. If two or more of the sources of evidence support the suspicion of cheating, the matter is referred to an internal ETS Board of Review. The Board of Review consists of 18 senior ETS employees, although for any specific case a subset of 3 Board of Review members is empanelled to consider the evidence. After a holistic consideration of the evidence, including, if necessary, additional information, the Board of Review determines whether substantial evidence exists to support withholding a score. If any one of the three members determines that there is insufficient evidence, the score is released. Othewise, if all three members agree that there is sufficient evidence to question the appropriateness of a test taker's result, the committee withholds the score and offers the examinee one of several options described in the next section. A similar process is used by the NBME, a large organization specializing in licensure and certification testing in the medical professions (NBME, 1988).

PENALTIES FOR CHEATING

When a student is caught cheating, the consequences are usually related to the context and seriousness of the offense. Penalties can range from an informal conversation between an instructor and student to a grade penalty, loss of credit on an assignment, cancellation of a test score, expulsion from school, loss of a professional license, revocation of certification, or, in some cases, fines and incarceration. These penalties pale in comparison with those for cheating on the Chinese civil service examinations. Miyazaki (1963/1981) described an instance of suspected cheating in 1858 involving a test taker, Lo Hung-i, and various governmental officials responsible for maintaining the integrity of the examination. Apparently, Lo's test paper was replaced during an elaborate scoring process with a paper of higher quality. The substitution was made possible with the cooperation of an associate examiner. An investigation uncovered a plot by an associate examiner to mark some candidates' papers as passing despite "violations of form" and acceptance of bribes by the son of another examination official. According to Miyazaki:

> Chief Examiner Po Sui, Associate Examiner P'u An, Candidate Lo Hung-i, the official who had made the arrangements for Lo, and the son of Associate Examiner Ch'eng T'ing-kuei were sentenced to death. In the case of Ch'eng T'ing-kuei himself the death penalty was commuted and his punishment was lowered by one degree, to banishment to a distance of three thousand *li*, or about one thousand miles, from Peking. Although the assistant examiners were not involved in the plot, they were

heavily punished for negligence in not uncovering the malfeasance of their colleagues. The graduates who had written the answers containing violation of form were stripped of all previous academic credentials, and the examination administrators who had not noticed what was happening were penalized in the same way. Even the high official who had ordered the investigation after the case was uncovered was punished on the grounds that the procedure had been lax.... [T]his scandal caused a great sensation throughout the land, and for a while the examinations were conducted honestly. (p. 63)

Today, when students in the United States have been asked to judge the appropriate penalty for cheating on a test, most respond by recommending considerably more moderate penalties. In Schab's (1972) study of 1,629 high school students, most students recommended a failing grade on the test as the appropriate punishment. Less than 10% favored options that were either more or less severe, such as calling parents, failing for the entire grading period, or probation (although 6% did favor making the offending student wear a sign around his or her neck that read "CHEATER!"). In their survey of more than 6,000 college students, S. F. Davis et al. (1992) reported that "the most popular 'punishment' suggested by our respondents was for the instructor to tell students to keep their eyes on their own paper" (p. 19).

Related studies have compared the severity of penalties for cheating recommended by students and those judged appropriate by faculty members. One such study compared 252 students' and 180 faculty members' recommended punishments for a student who was caught cheating; in this study, faculty said they would assign harsher punishments than the students did (D. M. Roberts & Toombs, 1993). Students who are caught cheating a second time would receive even harsher penalties, at least in the opinion of professors. Substantial proportions of engineering faculty and students at Arizona State University who responded to a survey by Singhal (1982) said that second-time cheaters should be expelled, with faculty (86%) considerably more inclined than students (38%) to recommend the harshest punishment.

Actual (as opposed to recommended) penalties for cheating vary widely among institutions. In their survey of sanctions imposed for academic dishonesty, S. Cole and McCabe (1996) reported that "at many schools, a first violation receives a written reprimand and probation. Other schools impose a suspension of one or more quarters, perhaps sometimes with work or monetary penalties" (p. 72). The authors detailed two of the most severe sanctions—those at the University of Virginia and Stanford University. At Virginia, a student found to have committed a serious act of intentional cheating was expelled; at Stanford, the penalty for a first violation included "a one-quarter suspension, a failing grade in the course, a 40-hour work penalty, and a $100 financial penalty" (p. 73). In the context of national tests, such as the SAT, the penalty for cheating can also be severe. In 1992, a Montgomery County, Maryland, judge fined a teenager $5,000 and sentenced him to 6 months in jail for lying under oath when the boy said he had not cheated on his college admissions test but later admitted that he had paid a college freshman $200 to take the test for him (Jennings, 1992a, 1992b).

College admissions testing programs, including tests such as the SAT and the ACT, are a special case. These tests primarily involve high school juniors and seniors, although they are administered under much more highly secure and controlled circumstances than any other tests high school students are likely to have taken. Those responsible for these tests (the College Entrance Examination Board and ETS, and American College Testing, respectively) have responded to cheating in various ways ranging from ignoring evidence that cheating may have occurred to prosecution in the courts. However, for this type of testing, too, the typical penalty is comparatively lenient. In 1993, William Angoff, a distinguished research scientist at ETS, summarized the five options available when cheating was suspected: (a) outright cancellation of score; (b) the opportunity to take the test again to substantiate the questioned score; (c) the opportunity to offer verifiable information (e.g., having been sick when taking the first test) that would explain a large score gain; (d) submission of all the evidence to the colleges and universities to which the student is sending the scores, and allowing them to decide on the validity of the scores; and (e) submission of all the evidence to an arbitration board, which would then decide on the validity of the score (Angoff, 1993, p. 3). Although information on exact numbers of cheating cases and how they are handled is not available from ETS, retaking the test appears to be the most common response recommended by the test maker (DePalma, 1992).

The recommendation to offer a retake as a preferred response to suspected cheating is supported by independent scholars outside large testing companies. Frary et al. (1997) who have developed various statistical indices and strongly support their use, have suggested that retaking the test is the most acceptable way to proceed and that retakes should be *required* when statistical evidence provides a strong indication that cheating has occurred:

> We suggest that if test scores are intended to be reliable indicators of ability, then [students identified as possible cheaters by means of statistical methods] should be required to retake the test under closely supervised conditions. Such a rule would be analogous to the procedure used in a tennis match when a line judge calls a ball out and then changes his mind. Rather than legitimizing the bad call, the point is replayed. The harm to the player who would have won the point is undeniable but unavoidable. Correspondingly, when individuals produce test results that cannot reasonably be believed to be reliable indicators of their abilities, they should retake the test. We believe the modest, undeserved burden that would occasionally fall on entirely innocent persons is a small price to pay for the reduction in ill-gotten gains. (p. 255)

Some interesting research on the appeal and effects of retaking examinations was conducted by Faulkender et al. (1994), who studied a cheating incident involving approximately 550 students in three sections of an introductory college-level psychology course. Although numerous cheating-prevention measures were taken (e.g., random seating, attentive proctoring, alternate forms, and photo identification), extensive cheating was detected when it was learned that a test had been stolen from the printing shop, copied, and distributed before the day of the test. It was decided that all students–both those who had cheated and those who had not cheated—would be required to retake an alternate form of the test. Faulkender et al. compared the attitudes toward retake procedures of the psychology students involved in the *actual* cheating incident with those of students enrolled in an algebra course who were given information about a *hypothetical* cheating incident. They found that students who were faced with retaking a test because cheating had been detected (i.e., the psychology students) held more favorable attitudes toward retesting than students who had not experienced the cheating (i.e., the algebra students). According to Faulkender et al., the psychology students "reported that they would be more satisfied with retakes in the future than math students expected to be in the same situation" (p. 214).

Across all school settings, the harshest penalty for cheating is normally expulsion from the institution. When this measure is taken, there is little concern for remediation on the part of the student, although at least one desirable outcome—the prevention of future instances of cheating by the student at the particular institution—is attained. By contrast, the most lenient response to cheating—a discussion of the act between a student and an instructor—is intended to foster understanding and more honest behavior on the part of the student, although this response is not as effective in ensuring that the student will not cheat in the future. Given Jendrek's (1989) finding that a discussion between the instructor and a student suspected of cheating was the most frequently invoked measure for responding to observed cheating, it is clear that the most common response to cheating is the more lenient and remedial of the sanctions that could be administered.

The most lenient response mentioned in the literature on cheating (although it is uncertain how frequently this response occurs) involves praising a student for honesty if he or she admits to cheating when confronted. What little evidence that is available on this point suggests that such a response is counterproductive. For example, Winston (1978) conducted an intensive study of elementary school boys who had been labeled *noncompliant* because of cheating on tests, among other behaviors. As might be predicted from behavioral theory, when praise was the response to admitting cheating, the boys continued to cheat, although they were also more willing to admit doing so. However, when praise for admitting cheating was accompanied by punishment for having done so, the boys still continued to cheat, but no longer admitted it. In another study involving 245 college students, positive reinforcement for admitting cheating increased the frequency of admissions but did not change the rate of cheating (Gardner et al., 1988). That study also found that most students who were offered counseling after being identified as having cheated chose not to participate; even among those students who did choose to take part in the counseling sessions, participation was found to have no effect on subsequent cheating behavior.

Students suspected of cheating might receive a lenient response because of other considerations altogether, such as whether or not the student smiles. In a study of 151 undergraduates, participants were given information about and shown photographs of fictitious students who had been caught cheating and were asked to recommend punishment. Results showed that cheaters who smiled were treated significantly more leniently than nonsmilers (LaFrance & Hecht, 1995). In another study of locus of control and recommended punishments, students who accepted responsibility for cheating (i.e., those with an internal locus of control) were judged more favorably than students who offered an excuse for their behavior (Wallis & Kleinke, 1995). Synthesizing these results with the findings reported earlier, one might give the following advice to a student suspected of cheating: Smile, admit personal responsibility, be female, and hope that the instructor is male, is nontenured, and has had a previous (negative) encounter with university academic dishonesty procedures.

INSTITUTIONAL FACTORS

The survey by S. F. Davis et al. (1992) revealed more than 90% agreement with the proposition that faculty members *should* care about whether or not students cheat on an exam. However, although a clear majority of faculty members either acknowledge the pervasiveness of cheating or have personally witnessed it, institutional forces can militate against a faculty member's decision to respond to cheating in a formal way. These forces may explain why previously cited research has found that most faculty members who observe cheating tend to handle those situations in comparatively lenient, idiosyncratic ways that fall outside of established procedures for doing so.

This lack of congruence between institutional policies on academic dishonesty and faculty responses to cheating was documented by Jendrek (1989), who found that only 20% of faculty members who had observed cheating had complied with mandated procedures that called for an initial meeting with the student and department chairperson. Because most faculty indicated that they did not follow the prescribed procedures, their reasons for not doing so (and their reasons for handling the incident the way they did) were of interest. The most common reasons included the following: "I wasn't 100% sure that the student was cheating," "Wandering eyes are difficult to prove," "It wouldn't help," "It was a large class and I couldn't deal with the magnitude of the problem," "I'm not callous: the student simply succumbed to temptation," "It was the first time the student cheated," "The chairperson told me to do it this way," and "It's the action stated in the syllabus" (Jendrek, 1989, p. 404).

Overall, faculty reactions to cheating illustrate two important issues. First, as has been described in a previous chapter, it is difficult to "prove" (or even make a strong case) that cheating has occurred, especially for educators who, at all levels, generally receive little or no training or advice in how to prevent, detect, or respond to cheating. This problem, however, may be more easily remedied than the second issue, which compounds the first and consists of an (unintended) organizational climate that effectively dissuades educators from dealing with cheating. In the arena of higher education, Alschuler and Bliming (1995) have summarized the grim realities of the institutional context:

> The disincentives for faculty enforcement are powerful.... Elaborate institutional judicial procedures designed to insure constitutionally guaranteed due process often act as deterrents to faculty because they are so time consuming and usually adversarial.... Universities, for their part, do not provide highly paid teams of prosecutors. Frequently, faculty members' efforts to maintain academic integrity outside of established university policies expose them to litigation.... Academic integrity weighs on one side. Hassles, diversion of time better spent on teaching or research, lack of institutional support, and possible exposure to litigation weigh on the other.... When faculty members are not supported by the judicial board, they usually do not file charges of academic dishonesty again, and often advise colleagues not to file. (p. 124)

These observations have been corroborated by other researchers. Lipson and McGavern (1993) investigated faculty responses to cheating at MIT. They asked faculty who indicated that they never took any action when they suspected cheating the reasons for their inaction; 42% said that the cheating wasn't serious, 87% indicated that "cheating was difficult to prove" (p. 22), and 13% said that the procedures established for dealing with cheating seemed ineffective. In a study involving 16 colleges, McCabe (1993) also found a reluctance on the part of faculty members to respond to cheating. Some faculty failed to take action in cases of suspected cheating because they believed that the penalties for cheating were too severe, although other faculty members thought that the penalties were too lenient, given the amount of effort required to pursue a case of cheating. Other faculty members simply believed that generating the extent of proof necessary to prove cheating was "almost impossible" (p. 655). One faculty member reported that day-to-day demands left little time for even grading, much less for examining students' work for possible cheating. Overall, McCabe found that "over half (55%) of the faculty participating [in the study] felt that the typical faculty member on their campus would not be willing to devote any real effort to documenting suspected incidents of student cheating" (p. 655). The reluctance of faculty members in McCabe's study to respond to cheating is even more significant, given that the colleges he studied were limited to those that had instituted honor codes. Presumably, faculty members who implement an honor code to deal with cheating would be more, not less, likely to pursue institutional mechanisms for responding to cheating. McCabe labeled his findings "disturbing" (p. 654).

CONCLUSIONS AND RECOMMENDATIONS

What can be concluded from the evidence related to how students, faculty members, and institutions respond to cheating? First, self-report data reveal that sizable majorities of students admit to having cheated. Second, both self-report data and a review of institutional records indicate that only a minuscule fraction of those who cheat are caught. Third, among those few who are caught, most experience a conversation with the instructor as the most serious penalty. Only a fraction of a fraction of the cases of suspected cheating are handled according to established guidelines. Finally, although there is little hard data, logic and anecdotal evidence suggest that, of those suspected of cheating who experience treatment according to established procedures, at least some are exonerated. For many, exoneration might be the correct outcome. However, the point is that, in contrast to the overwhelming instances of both reported and admitted cheating, only a handful ever reach disposition according to current procedures in place at most academic institutions. The vast majority of cheating goes without detection or response.

As we have seen, both student and faculty apathy about the problem of cheating account, at least in part, for this state of affairs. Additionally, the cumbersome and unpredictable nature of formal procedures for addressing cheating often serves to dissuade educators and administrators from following them and may contribute to a disinterest in maintaining academic integrity.

Although some students may not comprehend the nuances of what constitutes plagiarism, nearly all students know that copying or paying a confederate to take a test for them constitutes cheating, and that it is wrong. Although rates of cheating may have increased, trepidation on the part of students about engaging in cheating and the willingness to respond to cheating on the part of teachers and administrators have waned. In longitudinal surveys comparing students' attitudes toward cheating in 1984 and 1994, Diekhoff et al. (1996) concluded, "It appears that 1994's students are more cognizant of the immorality of cheating, but care less!" (p. 492). The current situation presents a chicken-and-egg problem: Has the rise in cheating weakened the resolve of test givers to respond to the behavior, or has an increasing reluctance to pursue cheating precipitated an increase in the activity?

Additional research may help answer this question. Part of the answer, however, may simply lie in the facts that so few cases of cheating are detected and that responses to cheating (when detected) are unpredictable, and in most cases, are sufficiently lenient as to constitute nonresponse. Research has demonstrated that the strongest deterrents of cheating are embarrassment and fear of punishment (see, e.g., Diekhoff et al., 1996). Among students who show high neutralization (i.e., those who attribute their cheating to reasons such as "Everyone else is doing it," "The test was too hard," or "I had to do it to keep my scholarship"), the most effective deterrents are "the formal, institutional consequences of being caught (i.e., threat of receiving an F, being dropped from the course, or fear of the university reprisal)" (Haines et al., 1986, p. 346). In another study, Moffatt (1990) examined the reasons students gave for *not* cheating: The primary reason given for avoiding academic dishonesty was the fear of being caught.

Overall, these results indicate that when students (accurately) perceive that the chances of being caught are slim and the further chance of harsh punishment is nearly nil, then current responses to cheating will serve, at best, to maintain high rates of cheating and, at worst, may actually contribute to further increases. It is also clear that both students and faculty need support when responding to the problem of cheating. Students require encouragement to report cheating and guidance about what constitutes cheating and how to avoid engaging in the behavior. Effective interventions for students with a habit of cheating are not currently available. Developmental work in this area may prove useful for counseling students who have adopted cheating as a means of coping with academic demands, time stresses, and pressure for good grades.

Faculty members need encouragement for implementing and maintaining high standards of academic integrity, assistance in consistently communicating those standards to their students, and support for tackling the "grubby stuff and dirty work" that responding to cheating often entails. All of these initiatives might result in more consistent and efficacious response to cheating. However, the most prudent avenue for addressing cheating is still likely to be prevention.

✦ N I N E ✦

Deterring Cheating
An Ounce of Prevention

A certain seminary student was taking the final examination in Introduction to New Testament Studies, a course taught by a professor with a reputation for very difficult tests and stingy grading. While distributing the final examination, the professor announced to the class "You may look upward for inspiration, or downward for concentration, but not to the side for information."[1]

T he theology professor's warnings regarding cheating illustrate an attempt to prevent cheating from happening. Individual teachers and institutions have tried various means of preventing cheating, including exhortations like this professor's. However, throughout history, their attempts have not been overwhelmingly successful. In Miyazaki's (1963/1981) review of 1,400 years of examinations in Imperial China, the success of attempts to prevent cheating is summarized in this way:

> As do all examiners, they labored to keep the tests fair and the testings honest, going to great lengths in their perpetual struggle against cheating, although to the very end the contest of wits remained a draw. (p. 7)

---

[1]This story is another example of an urban legend that has probably been passed around with variations of the course title or other minor details. I do not know the source of this version, but would gladly attribute it if the source is ever located.

Preventing cheating is valuable in its own right: as one strategy for promoting more valid testing, more accurate conclusions about test takers' knowledge and skills, and more appropriate decisions about certification, remediation, instruction, placement, and so on. Additionally, the relatively infrequent detection of cheating and erratic responses to cheating suggest that prevention of academic dishonesty is apt to be the more efficacious route to addressing the behavior.

A variety of approaches to preventing cheating have been tried. These approaches can be classified according to the level within the educational system responsible for their implementation. At one level, individual students often participate in preventing cheating. For example, the practice of covering one's answers to test questions with a separate sheet of paper is a common method that students use to prevent other students from cheating; students hunching over their tests or choosing a seat away from other test takers to prevent unapproved viewing of their work are other examples. These behaviors can be observed in students from elementary school through college. Sometimes students do these things at the direction of their teachers; just as frequently, however, they are likely to do so out of their own concerns about cheating.

At the group level, teachers and others who give tests can implement strategies to deter cheating. As we saw in chapter 6, strategies demonstrably related to decreased cheating include pedagogical approaches (e.g., the overall environment that a teacher creates well in advance of giving a test and the specific instructional approach used by a teacher). An instructional setting that minimizes distractions while learning is taking place and course content that is perceived by students to be meaningful and interesting are environmental factors that are related to reduced cheating and can be fostered continuously. At the highest level, institutions can implement policies and procedures aimed at preventing cheating.

The balance of this chapter provides an overview of methods used by individual teachers and institutions to prevent cheating on tests. The chapter concludes with a discussion and examples of honor codes—a specific and increasingly popular method of preventing cheating—and an appraisal of their effectiveness.

CLASSROOM-LEVEL PREVENTION STRATEGIES

Many effective prevention strategies specifically target the test administration conditions established in the classroom when the test is given. For example, tests can be administered to smaller groups of students, even when the class size is large; students can be seated in ways that minimize student proximity and opportunities to cheat; attentive proctoring can be implemented; and test directions can include clear and specific information about the impropriety of and penalties for cheating. Each of these actions taken at the time of a test has been shown to prevent cheating.

These actions are also considered effective by test takers themselves. According to surveys of student opinion, a test that is perceived to be fair (i.e., one that uses constructed-response formats) and the perception that the instructor is both vigilant and inclined to mete strong punishment for cheating are factors that prevent cheating (S. F. Davis et al., 1992; Genereux & McLeod, 1995). A survey by Hollinger and Lanza-Kaduce (1996) asked students to rate 20 cheating prevention strategies—what they called "countermeasures." Table 9.1 shows the percentage of students rating each strategy as either effective or very effective.

TABLE 9.1

Students' Perceived Effectiveness of Cheating Prevention Strategies

Rank	Strategy	% Rating Strategy as "Effective" or "Very Effective"
1	Scrambled test forms	81.6
2	Small classes	69.8
3	Using several proctors during examinations	68.4
4	Unique make-up examinations	68.4
5	Using two or more test forms	66.6
6	Providing study guides	54.8
7	Using more essay questions	54.6
8	Making old examinations available for review	52.4
9	Verifying student identity prior to exam	46.9
10	Giving different assignments	42.8
11	Assigning specific topics for term papers	30.2
12	Using specially marked answer booklets	29.5
13	Putting student names on test booklets	28.4
14	Assigning seats for examinations	26.9
15	Checking footnotes in student papers	26.4
16	Give more in-class tests, fewer take-home tests	23.7
17	Permitting only pencils to be brought into exam room	22.7
18	Not allowing anyone to leave during an examination	22.1
19	Give more take-home tests, fewer in-class tests	17.5
20	Provide a telephone hotline to report cheating	16.0

Note. From "Academic Dishonesty and the Perceived Effectiveness of Countermeasures: An Empirical Survey of Cheating at a Major Public University," by R. C. Hollinger & L. Lanza-Kaduce, 1996, *NASPA Journal,* 33(4), p. 301. Copyright © 1996. Reprinted with permission.

Proctoring

Proctoring is the most frequently recommended strategy for preventing cheating, and the effectiveness of conscientious proctoring in preventing cheating cannot be overemphasized. It has been shown to both decrease actual cheating directly (preventing the behavior by means of a physical presence) and to decrease cheating indirectly by conveying an expectation that academic integrity is highly valued. Effective proctoring simply requires that the test giver remains attentive during the test by actually observing students, staying in and walking around the room, and keeping an eye out for behaviors that would arouse suspicion of cheating, such as those described in chapter 3. Monitoring of students while they are taking a test is also good instructional practice. Before a test, an instructor should announce that he or she will be circulating around the room and will be available to answer questions about test directions, ambiguous test questions, and so on. If the true purpose of a test is to get accurate information about what students know or can do, instructional responsibility does not end when a test begins.

However, many test givers view proctoring as (a) an unfortunate duty that they would rather not perform at all and (b) demeaning to both themselves and their students. As a result, some instructors choose to simply leave their students alone during testing and consider testing time to be time "off duty." One professor described the serious approach to proctoring taken in Saudi Arabia, then compared that with his own testing procedures:

> At my college in the United States, if I have to proctor an examination, I do little more than look up from my reading, distribute a few stern glances about the room, and perhaps get up to stroll in order to keep awake. (Caesar, 1983, p. 64)

Even worse, there exists, to a great extent, a remnant of 1960s moral relativism that causes some instructors to shun proctoring. Trabue's (1962) story of a teacher, one James P. Pendleton, who was faced with an instance of cheating in his class, illustrates this point:

> When he wanted to discipline a student for cheating, he was told that he was imposing his moral code on students who came from lower brackets of society and that this was unfair. Addressing ethical and moral attitudes would interfere with teaching subject matter. [Further, skill in cheating could even be considered beneficial because his] students were going into the business world and if trained to be honest would have the hardship of false orientation to overcome. (p. 311)

Overall, attentive monitoring of testing situations is an effective prevention strategy. On the other hand, it must be recognized that it is possible for a proctor to be "excessively vigilant," creating an environment of suspicion, mistrust, and anxiety for test takers. One study into the effects of proctoring on the test performance of 120 college students found that, in moderately crowded testing conditions, the use of proctors discouraged cheating but was also associated with increased student anxiety levels and decreased scores on examinations (McElroy & Middlemist, 1983). As described previously, Albas and Albas (1993) also documented the lengths to which students will go to avoid being suspected of cheating. When anxiety detracts from students' ability to demonstrate their true level of knowledge or skill on a test, proctoring can serve to reduce, rather than enhance, the validity of test scores. Proctoring should be approached in a nonthreatening way, as a normal part of the learning environment. In actual implementation, then, proctoring is not nearly so simple as watching test takers during an examination but must be approached as a natural part of the overall classroom environment a teacher creates.

Other Individual Prevention Strategies

Proctoring is most effective in preventing cheating on tests involving traditional formats, such as essay examinations and multiple-choice tests. Other prevention strategies must be tailored to the type of assessment used and the grade level, and consideration of how to prevent cheating must begin long before the day of the test. For example, among other prevention strategies, Frary and Olson (1985) recommended that students be informed that statistical methods of detecting cheating will be used on all examinees' papers on all tests. Although such a recommendation may be effective in discouraging cheating, it would likely be effective primarily at upper grade levels, would require resources and training not possessed by most classroom teachers, and would be limited to tests using objective-type formats.

A number of other writers have suggested prevention strategies that individual test givers can implement or adapt to nearly any level (see Jacobs & Chase, 1992; Kibler & Paterson, 1988; Moss, 1984). Many of the frequently recommended strategies are not innovative but correspond with what common sense and experience would dictate. The Top 10 suggestions are discussed here.

Define Cheating and Encourage Honesty. As simple as it seems, one strategy that has been shown to be effective in preventing cheating is to discuss cheating with students and encourage them to be honest. It has been demonstrated that explicit and recurring encouragement, modeling, and valuing of honest behavior are effective methods in reinforcing the initial discussions. On the other side of the coin, it has also been suggested that cheating is prevented by informing students that the test giver will be on the lookout for it. Specifically, knowledge that an instructor will be reviewing essay questions for unusually similar responses or analyzing multiple-choice tests using cheating-detection software can discourage students from cheating.

In individual classes at any level, a first step in preventing cheating is the straightforward discussion of the behavior. At the beginning of a school year in elementary school or at the first class meeting of a college course, students should be informed about what constitutes acceptable and unacceptable actions. Many students can rightly claim that they did not know—or were never told—that certain actions constitute cheating. At the college level, instructors can include appropriate cautions regarding cheating in a course syllabus or provide students with copies of institutional guidelines on academic dishonesty.

Design Good Tests. It has been shown that tests that are overly difficult or perceived as trivial encourage cheating. According to one Connecticut student who encountered an opportunity to cheat, "it was a pretty quick decision once the opportunity was given to me…. And it didn't bother me at all. I didn't feel bad about it because I thought [the quiz] was pointless" (Stansbury, 1997c, p. 1). According to another student, tests based on recall alone foster cheating: "The rationale is, if you are going to be able to look it up in a book anyway in life, you shouldn't be tested on memorization of math formulas" (Stansbury, 1997b, p. 1).

In addition to facing many "pointless" and poorly constructed tests, many students have been inculcated with the notion that testing is a contest in which the goal of the test maker is to outwit, trick, or deceive them. Good testing provides a fair, accurate, and efficient measurement of what a student knows or can do. Good testing consists of first preparing students by teaching the content that will be tested and of crafting test questions that are straightforward, challenging, unambiguous, and of reasonable difficulty and that address the content that was taught. When testing is perceived to be fair, cheating is less likely to occur.

Where appropriate, good tests also include questions or tasks that involve the so-called higher order cognitive skills. These cognitive skills include processes such as application and synthesis; these are contrasted with lower order processes, such as recall and recognition. The use of test questions that require higher order thinking skills diminishes the usefulness of cheat sheets.

Use Constructed-Response Formats.   Constructed-response formats, such as essays or short-answer questions, are those in which students must supply an original response (as opposed to selecting from a list of choices). Because they require more extensive responses than marking a choice (as in a multiple-choice format), they reduce the possibility of cheating by copying in class.

Consider Varied Assessment Formats.   In addition to constructed-response formats, a variety of other assessment approaches can be used. For example, performance assessments require students to actually demonstrate their knowledge or skill. Instead of testing students with a multiple-choice test that asks them to identify the picture showing a parallel circuit, a teacher can provide students with batteries, switches, wires, light bulbs, and so on, and ask them to construct a parallel circuit. Likewise, traditional oral examinations and interviews may be less efficient means of understanding students' levels of knowledge and skill, but these methods remain some of the most informative and immune to cheating available. Not enough is known about how another innovation in assessment—portfolio collections of student work—may be susceptible to cheating (Wheeler, 1993).

Avoid Situations That Encourage Cheating.   Directions for take-home examinations that prohibit the use of outside resources or discussion of questions with other students are obeyed, by definition, only by students who do not cheat. Many students find take-home examinations to be an irresistible occasion for cheating, and, by their nature, take-home examinations are completed under circumstances over which the test giver has little or no control or ability to verify that administration directions were followed. Research on take-home examinations has demonstrated that students who are administered take-home tests perform better than those who took the same test under controlled, in-class conditions (Marsh, 1988; Weber, McBee, & Krebs, 1983). In the Marsh study, students who took the take-home version of the test also performed significantly worse on a subsequent surprise test over the same material. The conclusion seems clear: Under take-home conditions, test results are nearly meaningless as indicators of students' independent performance abilities; to interpret or represent the results in that way is professionally irresponsible and technically indefensible.

On the other hand, take-home tests can offer clear advantages to the extent to which they represent a less anxiety-producing situation for students, and they can promote greater student learning. To achieve these desirable results, teachers should realize that not all tests must count for a grade. Take-home tests can be assigned as independent opportunities for students to test their own knowledge. Teachers can, if they choose, "score" take-home tests and provide students with feedback on their performance to help guide their learning. It is reasonable to assume that students will be more likely to follow take-home test directions when the results are not tied to their overall grade in a course.

Another practice—students' self-grading of tests—offers opportunities for an instructor to reduce time spent grading and for students to gain the benefit of quick feedback on their performance. Unfortunately, self-grading also offers a strong temptation to cheat and little ability to control or detect cheating. At the college level, asking student assistants (i.e., graduate assistants or teaching assistants) to grade the papers or tests submitted by other students presents the same risk associated with "asking the mice to guard the cheese." As with take-home examinations, self-grading may be a useful pedagogical strategy but introduces invalidity when used for assessment. Further, having assistants grade papers deprives the instructor of valuable opportunities to see common errors, understand students' strengths and weaknesses, and gain information for planning continuing instruction or remediation.

Research by Shaughnessy (1989) involving 367 students enrolled in colleges of business, education, arts and sciences, and fine arts indicated that, although proportionally few students who cheat on tests actually devise plans to do so ahead of time, students are likely to take advantage of a situation that permits easy cheating if one arises. Thus, the best advice is to avoid placing students in situations (e.g., proximity during testing or using take-home examinations) that heighten the temptation and opportunity to cheat.

Maintain Test Security. Prevention of cheating includes careful preparation and storage of test materials. When possible, instructors can personally duplicate copies of test materials; unauthorized access to test materials is frequently obtained when tests are sent to be copied at a campus print shop by a student aid. Unauthorized advance copies of a test can easily be obtained from wastepaper baskets; thus, when making copies of tests, extra copies and materials such as "ditto masters" should be discarded in such as way as to eliminate the possibility that these materials can be accessed by an unauthorized person. Likewise, copies of previously used examinations—particularly those bearing students' responses, those with correct answers written on them during grading, or those completed as answer keys—should be kept in a secure location, especially if some test questions will be reused on subsequent occasions. Of course, making up a new test for each occasion would also help reduce the potential for cheating by accessing old test materials.

Where appropriate, old forms of tests that may be of instruction value or might provide a legitimate method of helping students prepare for an upcoming test can be made available to students. If practice tests or old tests are made available, they should be equally accessible to all students.

Before the day of a test, new examination materials should be kept in a location to which access is restricted. Copies of these materials should not be left unattended on a desk, in an unlocked file cabinet, on an accessible computer, in a secretary's work basket, and so on.

Control the Testing Situation. To the extent possible, teachers should reduce the potential for unauthorized communication or materials to be used in a testing situation. Students should be directed to place extra books and materials under their desks, to turn in all materials used during a test, and to remove baseball caps, sunglasses, pagers, headphones, and so on. Test givers can provide necessary paper for performing calculations, booklets for recording answers, and pencils. The number of copies of a test prepared before the test should be recorded and an accounting of all materials should be completed when the examination is finished.

Additionally, several practices have been shown to reduce cheating that occurs during a test. For example, the common practice of seating students with an empty seat between test takers reduces opportunities for direct viewing of another student's test paper. Alternative forms of a test, distributed so that students seated near each other have different test forms, has been shown to be effective in reducing copying.

Know the Test Takers.   In large classes at the college level and on large-scale credentialing tests, a less able student can arrange to have a more able student take the test for him or her. Whenever possible, test givers should know the people who will be taking a test. In many large-scale contexts, this is accomplished by having test takers verify their identification in order to take the test.

At the classroom level, personal familiarity with students is not only desirable from the standpoint of fostering healthy teacher–student relationships, but it may also help deter cheating by identifying those who are not authorized to participate in a testing situation. Additionally—and possibly more important—students may be less likely to cheat when the level of anomie between student and teacher is reduced.

Plan for the Unexpected.   Although, by definition, a test giver cannot plan for all unforeseen situations, some potentially compromising situations can be predicted and procedures and responses to them can be determined in advance. For example, all teachers should have a plan for how (or if) make-up tests will be conducted, and these guidelines should be announced to students at the beginning of a school year or course. Some students cheat on tests by simply being "ill" on the day of a test and hoping that information about the test from another student will be useful. A policy that does not permit tests to be made up eliminates this possibility of cheating in this way; however, such a policy may not always be reasonable or easy to enforce equitably. To reduce the potential for this type of cheating, one can require any make-up testing to be completed within a specified number of days after the absence and use an alternate form of the test. For situations in which a multiple-choice test is scheduled, knowledge that a make-up test will consist of essay questions can sometimes prompt students who would otherwise be "ill" to make miraculous recoveries in order to take a test at the regularly scheduled time.

Understand What Students Face.   One of the most frequently cited reasons students give for cheating is self-imposed or external pressure for high grades. Those who give tests need to understand these pressures and assist students in dealing with them, which can necessitate creative or flexible examination procedures. One creative method has been proposed by Blinn (1993), who, as part of her regular testing procedures, arranges a portion of the test room with extra desks and added room between seats. When a student is faced with either the temptation to cheat or a concern that another may be cheating from him or her, the student may reseat him or herself in the designated area of the room with "no questions asked."

INSTITUTIONAL APPROACHES TO PREVENTING CHEATING

Institutionally, prevention of cheating is addressed by promoting a general valuing of academic integrity within an institution and by using specific policies that both define cheating and detail consequences for violations of institutional guidelines. One significant example of a general environmental context shown to be related to preventing cheating is an institutional culture in which the primary goal of schooling is perceived by students to be learning, as opposed to grades. Because the desire to get a higher grade is the most frequently mentioned reason for cheating, to the extent that students perceive a diminished importance of grades, a corresponding reduction in incidence of cheating is likely to occur.

Specific policies about cheating have a twofold effect. They contribute to an overall environment in a school, school system, or society; they also explicitly define inappropriate behaviors and prescribe procedures and penalties for misconduct. To the extent that students are aware of and understand these specific policies, cheating may be prevented by them in much the same way that it is deterred by specific instructions regarding cheating given before a test or by perceptions regarding the severity of penalties. The content, awareness, and enforcement of these institutional policies, then, are key to their effectiveness.

Policies and Procedures

First, it is necessary to understand the extent to which institutions actually have policies and procedures in place. Only one study has been conducted to investigate the existence of policies at the elementary and secondary school level. In that study, Brandes (1986) asked 77 elementary and 72 high school staff members in California public school districts whether their districts had a cheating policy. One hundred percent of the elementary staff and 78.4% of the high school faculty members said, "No." This finding should be interpreted cautiously, not only because it is the only study of its kind, but also because the findings may indicate only if these educators *were aware of* their districts' policies, not necessarily whether the districts actually had policies.

Nonetheless, it is clear that *some* elementary and secondary schools have policies. Table 9.2 shows one such policy from a middle school in San Marino, California. Unfortunately, because of the lack of research at the precollegiate level, it is not known whether policies like the one shown in Table 9.2 are typical of policies at other schools or even whether other schools commonly have any policy at all.

The situation is reversed at the college level, where quite a bit is known about the extent and content of cheating policies. Overall, it appears that academic integrity policies and procedures covering cheating can be found on nearly all campuses. In 1989, Aaron (1992) surveyed 175 chief student affairs personnel from a random sample of higher education institutions representing 45 states and the District of Columbia and including public colleges and universities (41%), private colleges (25.2%), and public community colleges (25.2%). Aaron found that, overall, 95.4% of the institutions reported having an academic integrity code and 98.3% indicated that their institutions had specific procedures for handling allegations of academic misconduct. Although it is reasonable to infer that nearly all institutions of higher education have guidelines in place that address cheating on tests; the extent to which these guidelines are known and followed is another question.

To address that question, Aaron (1992) also asked chief student affairs officers how academic integrity guidelines are disseminated to students. The methods used most frequently were publication in a student handbook (79.4%), inclusion in a college catalog or orientation program (42.3%), and through a separate brochure (30.3%).[2] Actual inspection of 200 four- and two- year U.S. college catalogs (four randomly selected from each state) found that 55% contained specific statements or policies on academic dishonesty (Weaver, Davis, Look, Buzzanga, & Neal, 1991).

---

[2]The percentages reported by Aaron (1992) can exceed 100% because respondents were permitted to indicate more than one dissemination method.

TABLE 9.2
Excerpts From Huntington Middle School Cheating Policy

You are cheating if you:

- Copy, fax, or duplicate assignments that will each be turned in as an "original"
- Exchange assignments by print-out, disk transfer, or modem, then submit as "original"
- Write formulas, codes, key words on your person or objects for use in a test
- Use hidden reference sheets during a test
- Use programmed material in watches or calculators, when prohibited
- Exchange answers with others (either give or receive answers)
- Take someone else's assignment and submit it as your own
- Submit material (written or designed by someone else) without giving the author/artist name and/or source (e.g. plagiarizing, or submitting work created by family, friends, or tutors)
- Take credit for group work, when little contribution was made
- Do not follow additional specific guidelines on cheating as established by department, class, or a certain teacher.

Students caught cheating on any assignment (homework, tests, projects) will be referred to our Assistant Principal. The school-wide citizenship grade will be lowered at least one grade and the parents will be called. Subsequent offenses may result in a "D" or "F" in citizenship, suspension, removal from elected positions and honorary organizations, the inability to participate in school activities, and similar consequences.

Note. From Huntington Middle School Cheating Policy, by H. E. Huntington Middle School, San Marino (CA) Public Schools.
  Available: http://www.san-marino.k12.ca.us/~heh/binderreminder/cheatpolic.html. Reprinted with permission.

Aaron (1992) also found that only 7.4% of the sample reported that faculty members addressed policies on academic integrity in their classrooms or course syllabi. A similar conclusion was reached by Maramark and Maline (1993) who observed that "faculty rarely discuss rules on academic dishonesty in their classrooms" (p. 2). There are, of course, exceptions to the general pattern of avoiding discussion of academic dishonesty in college classrooms. In a survey of 48 faculty members at a private Catholic college, 64.3% of the respondents reported that their course syllabi contained a statement on cheating (Graham et al., 1994).

Overall it appears that dissemination of cheating policies to students occurs at a distance from the scene of the potential crime. Policies tend to be well represented in catalogs and handbooks, which are probably not thoroughly read (or even uniformly possessed) by students. Policies are poorly represented in the locations students actually inhabit and where testing occurs (i.e., classrooms).

For disseminating academic integrity guidelines to faculty members, the student handbook is again a primary mechanism. According to Aaron (1992), 17.7% of the respondents indicated that the student handbook was used to convey policy information to faculty, although the most frequently cited vehicle (43.4%) was a faculty handbook. Importantly, 21.1% said that there was no special dissemination of academic integrity guidelines to faculty members. Aaron also found that, during the academic year, specific development programs focusing on academic integrity were fairly uncommon: 30.4% of respondents indicated that such programs existed for faculty, and 16.1% said they existed for students.

Of course, even saturation of the student body or faculty with copies of a document describing guidelines related to academic integrity would not ensure that these groups are aware of, or follow, prescribed guidelines or procedures. In a subsequent publication, Aaron and Georgia (1994) observed that 40.9% of the same college and university administrative personnel perceived that "faculty are unaware of guidelines for handling academic dishonesty," and 62.3% reported that "faculty members take decisions regarding academic integrity into their own hands without utilizing established procedural guidelines" (p. 88).

Another facet of cheating that requires additional study is the content of policies concerning academic dishonesty. Kibler (1993b) has suggested that preventing cheating requires a three-part strategy consisting of (a) an environment that values academic integrity, (b) specific policies that address academic integrity, and (c) ongoing educational programs to promote academic integrity (see Fig. 9.1). Kibler recommended that, at the college level, interventions designed to prevent cheating should approach the problem from a student development perspective. His advice seems appropriate for interventions targeting precollegiate levels as well, although it may not be appropriate for deterring cheating on professional, licensure, or certification testing contexts.

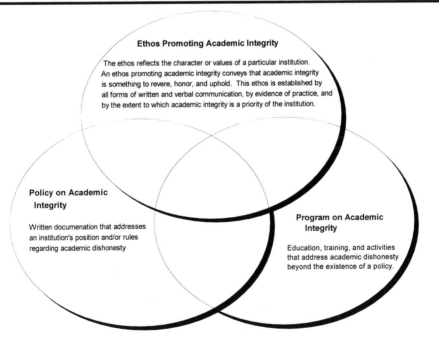

Ethos Promoting Academic Integrity

The ethos reflects the character or values of a particular institution. An ethos promoting academic integrity conveys that academic integrity is something to revere, honor, and uphold. This ethos is established by all forms of written and verbal communication, by evidence of practice, and by the extent to which academic integrity is a priority of the institution.

Policy on Academic Integrity

Written documenation that addresses an institution's position and/or rules regarding academic dishonesty

Program on Academic Integrity

Education, training, and activities that address academic dishonesty beyond the existence of a policy.

FIG. 9.1. Kibler's model for addressing academic integrity. From "A Framework for Addressing Academic Dishonesty From a Student Development Perspective," W. L. Kibler, 1993, *NASPA Journal, 31*(1), p. 12. Copyright © 1993. Reprinted with permission of the National Association of Student Personnel Administrators.

Kibler has also summarized what he and other researchers believe to be the most important elements of any cheating policy. According to Kibler (1993a), a sound policy should

- be clearly written,
- provide opportunities for open discussion and dialogue,
- include equitable adjudication procedures,
- result in consistently applied sanctions, and
- be reinforced by ethical behavior of faculty and other personnel (pp. 263-264).

In addition to Kibler's (1993a, 1993b) suggestions, a few other commentators have recommended what should be included in effective cheating policies. Unfortunately, no research has actually examined the content of cheating policies. Further, no comparison of extant and recommended content of cheating policies at either the precollegiate or collegiate levels has been conducted, nor has research on the effectiveness of proposals such as Kibler's been conducted. These topics represent another gap in what we know about cheating.

Honor Codes

For two reasons, the subject of honor codes deserves special attention in any treatment of cheating. First, although it has been shown that both institutions and individual educators tend to avoid confronting cheating, honor codes—a specific approach to dealing with the problem of cheating—have received increased attention since the late 1980s. Second, honor codes are unique in that they are designed not solely to prevent or respond to cheating, but also represent a more comprehensive way of addressing cheating by emphasizing both prevention and response and by spreading responsibility for deterring cheating among all involved in the academic community.

What Is an Honor Code?   At an abstract level, an honor code has been defined as "the proclamation and legislation of the intentions of a community of persons united in mutual agreement to oppose those inclinations and strategies that they might otherwise give in to and adopt to further their individual ends" (Hein, 1982, p. 4). At a more specific level, an honor code is a set of principles, privileges, and procedures designed to promote a climate of academic integrity. The principles articulate why an honor code is needed, provide examples of honorable academic behavior, and enumerate which behaviors fall outside the boundaries of acceptable behavior. The privileges afford students greater responsibility for maintaining an environment of academic integrity and freedom from scrutiny by proctors during examinations. Procedures are established for obtaining students' formal affirmation of the code and for pursuing alleged violations.

A typical honor code consists of several dimensions. According to two of the leading proponents of honor codes, an effective code would, at minimum, contain the following elements: (a) unproctored examinations, (b) a pledge to abide by standards of academic integrity, (c) mandatory reporting of infractions of the code, and (d) existence of an institutional judiciary system for addressing violations of

the code (McCabe & Trevino, 1993, p. 530).[3] Honor codes differ from more traditional codes of conduct in two essential respects: (a) the increased role that students play in the prevention and adjudication of cases of academic dishonesty,
and (b) an increased sense of mutual agreement about the need for academic integrity in the particular educational community (Nuss, 1996).

Footer (1996) stated that "a good code provides a means by which institutions
educate students and everyone involved in the community about what is acceptable behavior and what is not" (p. 20). To help accomplish this educative function,
Footer has suggested that a code contain a number of additional elements, including a list of prohibited behaviors and possible sanctions, primary attention to fundamental fairness, and specification of procedural aspects of the disciplinary
process. Footer's suggestions are also unique in that they not only stress the importance of what is in an honor code but also how one is developed. Her suggestions on constructing a code include involving all constituencies, using
widespread implementation and training, and conducting trial implementation of
a draft code prior to full enactment.

Honor codes also differ from other approaches to preventing cheating by situat-
ing responsibility for maintaining an environment of integrity with a group of
people, as opposed to asserting individual responsibility only. Implicitly, it is hypothesized that individuals will be more likely to behave honestly when maintaining academic integrity is a group responsibility—including the requirement that
peer misconduct be reported. An explicit test of this hypothesis was performed by
Trevino and Victor (1992), who studied groups of college students and restaurant
employees. They found that, when group members suffered negative consequences as a result of an individual's misconduct, misconduct was more likely to
be reported.

In addition to addressing the problem of cheating within a social context, honor
codes may also adopt a developmental perspective. Kibler (1993b) has recommended that honor codes are best created and implemented with the understanding
that developmental levels of students play a role in how well the elements of a code
are comprehended by students and how easily they are able to perceive a correspondence between the provisions of an honor code and their own behavior. Kibler
(1993b) asserted that students are "at different places developmentally and should
not be considered a homogeneous group" (p. 11). Because of this, he believes that an
effective honor code is an essential part of a comprehensive strategy to promote the
moral development of all students. Kibler's strategy uses a five-pronged approach:
intervention, communication, training, faculty assistance, and disciplinary policies.
Details related to these five aspects are shown in Table 9.3.

Examples of Honor Codes and Academic Integrity Policies.   Honor codes
are rare at the elementary and secondary school levels, but an increasing number
of postsecondary institutions have adopted them. It is important to note, however,
that an honor code is merely one component of an overarching policy commitment
to academic integrity. Numerous examples of academic integrity policies can be
found, and several authors have reviewed existing policies and have provided
model academic integrity policies or frameworks based on distillation of their critical elements (see, e.g., Brown & Buttolph, 1993; Sabloff & Yeager, 1989; Stoner &

---

[3]Cole and McCabe attribute these elements to the work of B. Melendez, *Honor Code Study* (Cambridge, MA: Harvard University College of Arts and Sciences, 1985).

TABLE 9.3

The Place of Honor Codes in a Comprehensive Academic Integrity Initiative

Major Elements	Components
Honor Code	(a) Disseminated, in writing, to all students and faculty
	(b) Describes student and faculty responsibilities for promoting academic integrity
	(c) Requires student and faculty commitment to the code
	(d) Contains definitions of prohibited behaviors
	(e) States consequences for violations
	(f) Describes methods for reporting violations
Communication	(a) Academic integrity discussed at student orientation, first meeting of every course, faculty, and graduate assistant training
	(b) Statements on academic dishonesty and integrity printed in admissions application materials, faculty application materials and handbook, catalogs, students handbooks, course schedule booklets, course syllabi, and examinations
	(c) Written information disseminated to students includes definition of academic dishonesty and why it is prohibited, expectations and responsibilities of students and faculty, and procedures for reporting violations
	(d) Correspondence sent to students and faculty which: provides data on academic dishonesty; describes efforts to reduce academic dishonesty; and lists and solicits suggestions for improvements in policies and practices
	(e) Efforts to promote academic integrity and case results released to media, campus press, etc.
Training	(a) Provide training on academic honesty to all teachers, including definitions of academic dishonesty, prevention strategies, methods of handling violations, sanctions, and classroom and testing conditions that promote academic integrity
Faculty Assistance	(a) Provide proctoring services where necessary
	(b) Provide case assistance to faculty when violations are reported, including appropriate policies and procedures, expectations, and strategies for gathering and presenting evidence
	(c) Recognize faculty members who properly handle cases of academic dishonesty

Disciplinary Policies

(a) Disseminate academic policies in writing to all students and faculty

(b) Develop communication policies for addressing academic dishonesty

(c) Establish and maintain a code of conduct that contains the following: a statement that academic dishonesty is prohibited and why; definitions of academic dishonesty; assurance that anonymous reports of dishonesty are accepted and pursued; simple, equitable procedures for addressing violations; established due process guidelines; a list of possible sanctions and who has the authority to implement them; a disciplinary records policy; and test administration policies that promote academic integrity

Note. From "A Framework for Addressing Academic Dishonesty From a Student Development Perspective," W. L. Kibler, 1993, *NASPA Journal, 31*(1), pp. 14–15. Copyright © 1993. Adapted with permission.

Cerminara, 1990; Toenjes, 1990; Weaver et al., 1991). One such model has been developed by Risacher and Slonaker (1996) based on their review of policies at institutions belonging to the National Association of Student Personnel Administrators (NASPA). This model and another developed by Pavela (1988a) are provided in Appendix B.

Likewise, a number of examples of honor codes are available, and those interested in developing an honor code at an institution where one does not currently exist may find the examples and experiences of other institutions to be helpful. As Footer (1996) stated:

> There is absolutely no need to craft a code from the whole cloth. There are many fine models available for institutions to use.... Review other good examples—beg, borrow, and steal—but be careful to attribute the ideas of others lest you find yourself guilty of plagiarism. (p. 30)

One example of an honor code that is particularly straightforward, and typical of the no-nonsense approach of the institution from which it derives, is the honor code used at West Point. The code simply states that "a cadet will not lie, cheat, or steal, nor tolerate those who do."[4] Two other examples of honor codes, from Duke University and the University of New Mexico School of Medicine, are presented in Table 9.4.

Who Has Honor Codes?   As noted earlier, nearly all institutions maintain established policies and procedures for dealing with academic dishonesty. However, comparatively few institutions have honor codes; those institutions with honor codes are limited almost exclusively to colleges and universities and to a few private precollegiate institutions. A key reason for this is that public elementary and secondary schools are legally obligated to serve all students, whereas college attendance is viewed as a privilege. Thus, a key aspect of honor codes—the threat of banishment from the academic community because of cheating—could not be enforced in public schools.

At the postsecondary level, honor codes are found most often in schools that prepare students for health-related occupations. One study of 31 medical schools found that a majority ($n = 21$, 65%) had honor codes (Baldwin et al., 1996). Likewise, a survey of all 75 pharmacy schools in the United States revealed that nearly half of those responding (25 of 57) had honor codes and that 3 more were developing one.

The situation is quite different outside the health professions. In a survey of 55 American Association of Universities (AAU) institutions, only 6 of the 44 institutions that responded to the survey had honor codes. Honor code institutions tended to be private, well established (all of the institutions with honor codes had been in existence prior to 1900), and located (with the exception of Stanford University) in the southeastern United States (Sabloff & Yeager, 1989).

Although many of the elements of an honor code described earlier are present where an honor code exists, not all honor codes are identical, and not all contain all of the elements. In a study conducted by Melendez (cited in S. Cole & McCabe, 1996), 32 of 71 colleges surveyed could be categorized as having an honor code, as judged by their having at least one of the four criteria listed by Cole and McCabe;

---

[4]This, and additional information about honor codes in the U.S. military education system, is available at http://www.usma.edu/Committees/Honor/info/main.htm

TABLE 9.4

Examples of Honor Codes

University of New Mexico School of Medicine[a]

Every student is expected to abide by the highest standards of honorable conduct in academic matters. Dishonest action in connection with tests, quizzes, or assignments, whether in the classroom or out, generally will be cause for dismissal from the university.

Any suspected incidence of cheating should be handled by direct faculty-to-student interaction. Should the issue not be settled to the satisfaction of all concerned, the problem can be taken to an ad hoc committee appointed by the dean. The committee will make recommendations to the administration.

This code will be presented to all students at the time of their first registration at this institution, and they will be requested to sign a statement that they have read the policy; the signed statement is to be made a part of the student's personal record.

Duke University[b]

As a student and citizen of the Duke University Community:

I will not lie, cheat, or steal in my academic endeavors. I will forthrightly oppose each and every instance of academic dishonesty. I will communicate directly with any persons I believe to have been dishonest. Such communication may be oral or written. Written communication may be signed or anonymous. I will give prompt and written notification to the appropriate faculty and the Dean of Trinity College or the Dean of the School of Engineering when I observe academic dishonesty in any course. I will let my conscience guide my decision about whether my written report will name the person or persons I believe to have committed a violation of this Code. I will join the undergraduate student body of Duke Unversity in a commitment to this Code of Honor.

[a]Reprinted with permission from "Cheating by Students: Findings, Reflections, and Remedies," by R. E. Anderson & S. S. Obenshain, 1994, *Academic Medicine, 69*(5), p. 332. Copyright © 1994.
[b]From Duke University Undergraduate Code of Honor, by Duke University.

only 1 of the institutions had all four elements. The Duke University Honor Council lists 11 institutions in addition to itself as having honor codes: Davidson College; University of Virginia; University of North Carolina, Chapel Hill; Washington and Lee University; Stanford University; University of California, Davis; West Point Military Academy; Vanderbilt University; University of Pennsylvania; Colorado College; and California Institute of Technology.[5]

Research on the Effectiveness of Honor Codes. Indisputably, the aims and content of honor codes are admirable. The questions remain, however, whether honor codes actually prevent cheating, identify a greater number of instances of cheating, or are more effective in responding to cheating. At least at the college level, evidence bearing on the effectiveness of honor codes is somewhat discouraging.

[5]This list is found at http://www.vanderbilt.edu/HonorCouncil/honor.htm.

The research on medical school honor codes concluded that the existence of a medical school honor code "does exercise some effect on cheating behavior, but the effect is not large" (Baldwin et al., 1996, p. 272). Vines (1996) reported that most pharmacy schools with honor codes (88%) were moderately to extremely satisfied with them and that on at least one measure—plagiarism—schools with honor codes had far fewer instances of that behavior than had been reported at noncode schools. Only 7% of students at the University of Alabama School of Medicine, where an honor code is in force, indicated that they had observed an honor code violation (Brooks, Cunningham, Hinson, Brown, & Weaver, 1981).

A number of investigations of the effectiveness of honor codes have been conducted outside medical schools. These studies date back to the 1935 work of Campbell, who compared cheating on examinations under two conditions (proctored exams and honor system) at a single university. Campbell found a reduced incidence of cheating among the honor system students (cited in McCabe, 1993, p. 649). Another study, conducted with samples of undergraduate sociology students at Brigham Young University, examined rates of actual cheating, which had been detected by permitting students to self-score tests that had, unbeknownst to the students, previously, been scored by the experimenter (Canning, 1956). The study spanned 5 years and included samples of students that took tests before the university implemented an honor code, while one was being developed, and after an honor code was instituted. Over the 5-year period, rates of cheating were found to have decreased by 63%, with the average amount of cheating decreasing from an average of 12.3 points per test to and average of 8.2. Overall, the author concluded that the implementation of an honor code may have been responsible for a reduction in cheating, although it is also possible that after 5 years, word leaked out among students about the self-grading procedure.

However, since the earliest studies of honor codes, a consistent finding is that the effects of honor codes are mixed. On the positive side, the existence of a code heightens awareness of the issue of cheating and communicates the stated intent of the institution and individual students to abide by high standards of ethical behavior. As has been shown in previous chapters, this public affirmation of the value placed on honesty can make, by itself, a contribution to an environment of greater academic integrity. There is some evidence that this public affirmation is associated with reduced levels of cheating. K. M. May and Loyd (1993) compared universities with honor systems and those without. In a survey of students at those institutions, they found that only 9% of students attending a university with an honor system admitted to cheating on a major examination compared with 23.7% of students at noncode universities who admitted doing so. Similar results were found for cheating on quizzes (7.9% vs. 22.1%) and assignments (17.5% vs. 34.2%). When asked about cheating in any form, 23.7% of students at code schools said they had cheated compared with 54.1% of students at noncode schools. Table 9.5 shows similar data from a survey of 2,240 college students reported by McCabe and Bowers (1994).

A recent comparison of self-reported cheating at code and noncode schools was reported by McCabe and Trevino (1993), who surveyed a total of 6,096 students from 31 U.S. colleges and universities. Fourteen institutions with honor codes and 17 schools without codes participated in the study. Students were asked to indicate how frequently they had engaged in various cheating behaviors using a scale ranging from 1 (*never*) to 4 (*many times*). Behaviors included, for example, using crib notes and copying from another student during a test. The authors found that

TABLE 9.5
Comparison of Admitted Cheating Among Student at Honor Code and Noncode Colleges

	% Admitting Engaging in Behaviors	
Behavior	Honor Code Schools	Noncode Schools
Copied from another student on a test of exam	13	29
Helped another student cheat on a test	11	29
Used crib notes on a test or exam	10	25

Note. Adapted with permission from "Academic Dishonesty Among Males in College: A Thirty Year Perspective," by D. L. McCabe & W. J. Bowers, 1994, *Journal of College Student Development, 35*(1), p. 7.

self-reported cheating differed significantly, with more cheating admitted at noncode schools than at schools with an honor code. These findings mirror the results of a similar study conducted nearly 30 years earlier by Bowers (1964; see also McCabe & Bowers, 1994).

On the negative side, it is more accurate to say that we know only that *admitted* and *self-reported* cheating are reduced at schools with honor codes, not that actual cheating is diminished. All of the available evidence on the question of the effectiveness of honor codes comes from anonymous surveys on which students are asked to confidentially report on their own behavior. Given the strong sanctions in place for violations of honor codes, it seems reasonable that students attending schools with codes would be less likely—possibly far less likely—to admit cheating, even on anonymous surveys. Additionally, given the high value placed on academic integrity at honor code institutions, the socially desirable response to researchers polling about the extent of cheating would be to indicate that it rarely occurs. Thus, a thoroughly plausible—though yet uninvestigated possibility—is that the presence of an honor code merely masks the problem of cheating by dissuading reporting of the behavior.

Some evidence from research on honor codes suggests that this hypothesis may be on target. Part of the problem may be that, recognizing the strong sanctions associated with violation of an honor code, students are reluctant to report cheating by themselves or others. For example, K. M. May and Loyd (1993) found that only 2.8% of students surveyed at code schools said that they had been accused of an honor code violation; of these, none had been found responsible. In the previously mentioned study of medical school students by Brooks et al. (1981), in which 7% of students reported observing honor code violations, only 2% of the those who had observed violations actually submitted a report of the suspected infraction. At a medical school in which an honor code was in place, students were questioned about cheating on several examinations (Sierles et al., 1988). On one of the examinations (behavioral science), 15 students indicated they had witnessed cheating, an occurrence that, according to the honor code, a student is obligated to report. However, of the 15 students who had witnessed cheating, only 2 said they had reported it. Even in cases in which the cheating was reported, the report most often took a nonspecific form, such as "I saw another student cheating, but I won't name him" (Sierles et al., 1988, p. 710). The authors concluded that students showed less support for the honor system privately than would be expected from the public support for the system evidenced by their signing of the honor pledge.

One related study provides the only direct evidence of the effectiveness of honor systems (Gardner et al., 1988). In that study, a complete honor system was not in place; however, students were asked to sign an honesty pledge affirming that they had not used certain prohibited materials (e.g., a textbook) to complete a homework assignment. The experimental design permitted the researchers to verify whether the students had in fact complied with the prohibition and to make comparisons with a group of students who had not taken the honesty pledge. The results were expressed frankly:

> The honesty pledge had no effect on cheating.... Even though class members participated in developing the honesty pledge and discussed its purpose, analysis of individual data showed that no subject decreased his or her cheating percentage immediately subsequent to signing the honesty pledge. (p. 549)

McCabe (1993) found that faculty members, too, are reluctant to report students for academic dishonesty at institutions with honor codes. This reluctance to report cheating partly can be attributed to the fact that some faculty do not accept the idea of an honor code and that others believe that the sanctions for violations of the code are too severe. Also, there is a strong inclination on the part of many faculty members to reject institutional procedures for handling cheating. McCabe (1973) found that "faculty who observe student cheating are generally reluctant to get involved in the designated campus judicial process. They prefer instead, as one respondent put it, 'to keep the problem local' and deal directly with the student" (p. 653).

Why Are Honor Codes Effective?   Where honor codes are effective, some research has been conducted to find out why. The mere presence of an honor code is insufficient to explain generally higher levels of academic integrity. The keys to the effectiveness of honor codes seem to lie more in spreading responsibility for academic integrity among all persons involved and in heightening sensitivity to issues of academic integrity, which results from increased communication about academic integrity that usually accompanies adoption of an honor code. These keys have been described by S. Cole and McCabe (1996):

> The presence of an honor code typically is accompanied by other characteristics that combine to have a strong, positive impact upon the campus climate or culture experienced by students and faculty. Three of these characteristics seem especially important. First, the vast majority of honor code schools involve students (and often faculty members) in responding to possible violations. This involvement creates a higher visibility for academic integrity issues and concerns. Second, although students and faculty scrupulously respect the privacy rights of students accused of academic dishonesty, they do discuss with their peers and colleagues the types of offenses that occur, the reasons behind the offenses, and the penalties imposed. This results in a high level of campus discourse about the state of student academic integrity. Finally, student and faculty involvement and higher visibility are usually accompanied by a stronger commitment to education and prevention. (p. 70)

Lowry (1996) suggested that two additional components may be required for honor codes to be effective. The first is institutional size, about which Lowry said: "The community [the honor system] attempts to serve must be small and personal. Not only does the idea of being more easily caught act as a deterrent to cheating, the idea that in doing so one betrays one's 'family' also diminishes the appeal of the activity" (p. 6). The second is a shared sense that all members of the academic community are inclined to act honorably. According to Lowry, "There must be a consensus among faculty, administration, and students that the school is a better place because it has an honor code, and that when in doubt, the initial presumption is one of trust that the code is being honored" (p. 6).

These hypotheses find some support in the research on honor codes. First, concerning the shared commitment to reporting cheating demanded by honor codes, McCabe and Trevino (1993) found that the presence of an honor code was positively related to an increased certainty of being caught engaging in acts of academic dishonesty. Second, regarding the increased dissemination and awareness of the rules of conduct prescribed by honor codes, the authors found a positive correlation between the existence of an honor code and the understanding of policies related to academic dishonesty. Third, they found that reduced cheating was related to the presence of severe penalties for cheating—penalties of the type associated with violations of an honor code. Finally, with respect to the hypothesized effect of an academic community, the authors found that, where honor codes existed, students had a greater perception of honesty on the part of their peers.

Together, these results are capable of explaining even the presumably contradictory findings of Gardner et al. (1988), who found no immediate effect of signing an honor pledge. Clearly, research is needed to determine whether self-reported decreases in cheating under honor systems reflects a real reduction in the behavior or merely a reduction in reporting. However, it is possible that, if honor codes are proven to reduce actual cheating, the effect may be attributable to a long-term change in individuals brought about by extended exposure to a culture of academic integrity.

PREVENTING CHEATING BY THOSE WHO GIVE TESTS

Preventing cheating by those who give tests is a particularly underresearched topic. It is ironic that much attention has been given to preventing cheating by individual students—behavior that can cause a single score to be of questionable validity—and so little attention has been paid to cheating by those who give tests, which can invalidate the scores of entire groups of students. Even more troubling is the fact that cheating by those who give tests has been documented on tests that are used to make important judgments, such as student competency tests or licensure and certification examinations. The issue of cheating on tests by those who give them has received virtually no attention in the area of professional licensure, certification, or credentialing examinations, although anecdotal reports suggest that bribery of test administration officials and other unethical activities almost certainly occur. Clearly, regulatory boards have conflicting interests in ensuring valid test scores and in avoiding dissemination of the methods and extent of breaches of test security. Without more careful investigation and open discussion of this issue, advances in preventing cheating will lag.

On another front—large-scale student achievement testing in American public schooling—there is a greater degree of openness in addressing the issue of preventing cheating. As of 1997, 48 of the 50 states have state-mandated student achievement testing programs (Roeber, Bond, & Connealy, 1998). These programs involve millions of students and hundreds of thousands of educators. Such programs are frequently referred to as high stakes because the consequences for students can be great; for example, performance on state-mandated tests can be tied to graduation or promotion. The stakes can also be high for educators when aggregated student results are interpreted as reflecting on an individual teacher's performance or on the overall level of educational quality at a given school or in a given school district. In some places, specific rewards or sanctions for educators are tied to their students' performance on mandated tests. Because of these factors, the temptation for educators to cheat and the reality of its occurrence cannot be ignored.

Many states have specific regulations that address cheating by educators (and others) and outline harsh sanctions for doing so. One survey of state departments of education revealed that a majority of states with student achievement testing programs had laws or regulations regarding security of test materials and test preparation and administration practices (Mehrens, Phillips, & Schram, 1993). For example, the Ohio Revised Code states that "no person shall reveal to any student any specific question that the person knows is part of a [state-mandated] test ... or in any other way assist a pupil to cheat on such a test" (Amended Senate Bill 230, 1996). Subsequent sections of the Ohio Revised Code indicate that violation of this regulation is a misdemeanor and is grounds for termination of employment, regardless of whether the offender is a teacher or a nonteaching employee. Any teacher found to have violated the regulation faces a mandatory 1-year suspension of his or her teaching license. Beyond revealing specific questions, state standards for the ethical use of tests also prohibit a range of unethical and inappropriate practices, including the following:

(1) any preparation activity that undermines the reliability and/or validity of inferences drawn from the assessment results;

(2) any practice that results solely in raising scores or performance levels on a specific assessment instrument without simultaneously increasing the student's achievement level as measured by tasks and/or instruments designed to assess the same content domain;

(3) any practice involving the reproduction of actual assessment materials, through any medium, for use in preparing students for an assessment;

(4) any preparation activity that includes questions, graphs, charts, passages, or other materials included in the assessment instrument or in a parallel form of the instrument, and/or materials that are paraphrases or highly similar in content to those in actual use;

(5) preparation for the assessment [that] focuses primarily on the assessment instrument or a parallel form of the instrument, including its format, rather than on the objectives being assessed;

(6) any practice that does not comply with, or has the appearance of not complying with, statutory and/or regulatory provisions related to security of assessment instruments used in schoolwide or districtwide programs; and

(7) any practice that supports or assists others in conducting unethical or inappropriate preparation activities. (Standards for the ethical use of tests, 1995, C1-C7)

Of course, the existence of regulations prohibiting an activity does not guarantee that cheating by those who give tests will not occur. The survey of state testing practices by Mehrens et al. (1993) revealed that 36 of 41 state testing programs received reports of breaches of test security in the 1989–1990 academic year. The most frequently reported incidents involved missing test materials, teachers providing test questions to students before the test, and failures to follow test administration procedures (e.g., deviating from directions or permitting additional time). Sanctions for confirmed violations were also generally lenient; the authors noted that "the most common sanction for the confirmed irregularities was that a formal letter was sent to the violators but that no *legal* action was taken" (Mehrens et al., 1993, p. 8).

The so-called *Lake Wobegon Report* (Cannell, 1989) deals exclusively with the ways in which educators take advantage of loopholes in testing regulations, manipulate tests and testing conditions, and flat out cheat in order to make exaggerated or false claims about student performance on tests. The title of the report derives its name from the mythical town in Minnesota, described by storyteller Garrison Keillor, in which "all the women are strong, all the men are good looking, and all the children are above average" (Cannell, 1989, p. 4). The claim—by all 50 states—that their pupils performed above the national average on norm-referenced standardized tests was exposed by Cannell as largely the result of unethical testing practices. After some initial controversy, Cannell's charges were broadly accepted by testing specialists and formed the basis for changes in test development practices and increased attention to test security.

Beyond just identifying the scandal, Cannell (1989) also suggested numerous measures that could be taken to limit the amount of cheating by those responsible for giving high-stakes tests. Table 9.6 shows Cannell's list of suggestions, some of which have been implemented (particularly those in the purview of test publishers), although the implementation status of others is uncertain. Other testing specialists have made similar suggestions (see, e.g., Canner, 1992; Masonis, 1987). The problem remains, however, that little or no research has been done to document the extent to which these recommendations are being followed or how effective they have been in reducing cheating by those who give tests.

CONCLUSIONS AND RECOMMENDATIONS

Preventing cheating on tests is as multifaceted as the methods and reasons for the behavior. Prevention strategies span a continuum ranging from mainly mechanical to purely principled. No single approach to preventing cheating can be invoked as the "best" approach, and no research has been conducted to allow comparative statements regarding which methods are better than others. It is unlikely, as long as there are tests, that all cheating can be prevented. However, one thing is certain: Awareness and acknowledgment of the problem of cheating is a necessary, though not sufficient, step toward reducing the frequency and effects of cheating.

At the practical level, what might be called mechanical methods have been found to be somewhat helpful. These methods are used by many teachers and are familiar to most students. These methods include providing seating arrangements during testing that are not conducive to cheating, using alternate test forms, and maintaining adequate security for test materials prior to testing. Slightly more ac-

TABLE 9.6
Recommendations for Limiting Cheating on Large-Scale Student Achievement Testing Programs

1. States and school districts should adopt policies that clearly forbid school personnel to look at high-stakes test questions except as needed during administration.

2. Testing should be done in the fall, as early as possible, preferably in September.

3. High-stakes test booklets should be sealed individually and then shrink-wrapped in class-size packets.

4. Tests should not be given to teachers until the day of testing and should be turned back in after that day's testing is completed.

5. States should have test-monitoring teams.

6. Volunteer test proctors should be requested from the community if resources are not available to hire a reputable testing firm to administer the tests.

7. All children, including special-education and bilingual students, should be tested and their scores reported with their current grade level.

8. Equivalent tests should be randomly substituted in those school districts with suspiciously high test scores.

9. New test forms should be purchased every year by those districts that can afford it.

10. Answer sheets should be scanned by the company that scores the test, both for suspicious erasures and for cluster variance (i.e., suspicious class groupings of similar responses).

11. Scores should be reported in normal curve equivalents (NCEs) using the most current national norms available.

12. Current annual norms calculated from a representative national sample of current users should be used in all schools, and all publishers doing business in any school district in a state should be required to sell them instead of old norms.

13. Parent report forms should be required to clearly state the limitations of norm-referenced tests.

14. Test publishers and scoring companies should be required to report achievement results yearly to the state department of education for all of the publisher's tests used in a state.

15. Test and curriculum-alignment committees should be disbanded.

16. Writing tests should be administered along with multiple-choice tests.

17. Test-preparation books should not be allowed in schools.

18. Those who sell high-stakes group-achievement tests should be liable for punitive damages for selling tests whose norms are more than 2 years old; selling tests whose norm sample has not been approved by the state in which the test is used; selling tests that are unsealed; selling tests that do not clearly forbid teachers from reading the test, except as needed for listening subtests; selling tests whose norm tables do not report NCE scores; selling tests whose administration manuals do not specify appropriate security measures; and willfully withholding evidence of testing irregularities form responsible state officials.

Note. From *The Lake Wobegone Report: How Public Educators Cheat on Standardized Achievement Tests* (p. 37), by J. J. Cannell, 1989, Albuquerque, NM: Friends of Education. Copyright © 1989. Adapted with permission.

tive methods that test givers can use include developing and enforcing rules related to materials that are permitted during tests and maintaining participation in the testing process through attentive proctoring.

Changes in the structure of a course and changes in the content of tests can also help reduce cheating. Teachers should create tests that are perceived to be fair, challenging, and reflective of the content of the course. Course content, too, should be meaningful and relevant to students (see Steininger, 1968). Contrary to what might be predicted, changing course requirements to demand *higher* degrees of effort, work ethic, and persistence on the part of students have been shown to reduce cheating (Eisenberger & Masterson, 1983; Eisenberger & Shank, 1985). The stereotypes of the elementary school teacher who each year requires students to do a research project on the same topic and of the college professor whose lecture notes (and tests!) have yellowed from age are too commonly real to be humorous.

In the near future, technological advances may reap practical benefits toward the reduction of cheating on tests. For example, computer-based testing eliminates many of the opportunities to cheat that are inherent in paper-and-pencil tests. Computer-adaptive testing, involving random selection of test items for individual test takers and essentially unique test forms for each examinee, makes some forms of cheating (e.g., copying) impossible while creating avenues for dishonesty (cf. Emerson, 1974; Gershon & Bergstrom, 1995). Although computer-based testing is still not widely used, there is some evidence that this technology will be effective. In one study, students who took a computer-based test achieved lower scores than those who took a traditional in-class exam, suggesting that the lower scores on the computer-based test may be attributable to reduced opportunities to cheat (Sloss, 1995). Another technological innovation, called "distance learning," in which instruction and assessment can be conducted over long distances and without the actual presence of a teacher, creates new challenges for preventing cheating.

The format of tests—especially the use of open-ended questions (such as in essays or performance assessments) and the avoidance of tests that may encourage cheating (such as take-home examinations)—can contribute to a reduction in cheating. Increasing the frequency of tests and decreasing the value of any single test can serve to reduce the incentive for students to cheat on any individual test. Providing students with information about grading and evaluation procedures in advance of test administration is helpful; even simply announcing that the instructor will review tests for possible cheating can deter the behavior. It might come as a surprise to some educators and students, but the fact is that not every assignment, quiz, or test needs to be graded. A fine distinction can be made between tests that help students and teachers to understand their strengths and weaknesses and those tests that must be used for purposes of accountability, grading, or documenting achievement.

Communication about honest and dishonest behavior is surely critical to deterring cheating. Information about relevant definitions, guidelines, policies, and procedures must be disseminated to faculty as well as students (Brilliant & Gribben, 1993). Perhaps the biggest reasons that honor codes show promise of reducing cheating is that they unashamedly communicate about the value of academic integrity and make upholding a high standard of honest behavior a responsibility of the entire academic community. This process takes advantage of a strong, positive variety of peer pressure. As McCabe and Bowers (1996) have noted, a strong influence of peer disapproval can make a healthy contribution to promoting honest behavior.

In addition to encouraging honest behavior, students should be informed about specific consequences for cheating. Although educators surely want to promote ethical behavior for its own sake, they must also recognize the reality that a major reason many students give for not cheating is the fear of getting caught (Moffatt, 1990). The research evidence on this point is clear: Cheating is prevented when the penalties for cheating are understood by test takers (Leming, 1980), when stronger penalties are more effective deterrents than weaker ones (Houston, 1983b), and when potential cheaters are dissuaded from doing so if they observe another student being caught and punished for violating the rules (Heisler, 1974). These factors explain why recommendations to increase the number and profile of cases handled by established procedures in the short term (Fishbein, 1994) may actually decrease the number of such cases in the long term.

At the principled end of the continuum, those who give tests should not shy away from addressing the ethical superiority of honest behavior in all situations. It is an unfortunate artifact of some moral education theories popularized in the 1960s and 1970s that many educators have come to believe that direct instruction about right and wrong is somehow inappropriate. Attempts to identify common values and the introduction of character education in many schools at the close of the 1990s are evidence of a repudiation of the misinterpretation that all ethical systems—or none at all—are equally acceptable.

Along these lines, direct instruction about cheating is surely appropriate, and examples about how to do it are available.[6] Such instruction would begin with specific definitions of what constitutes honest and dishonest academic behavior. At the college level, Brilliant (1996) has described the importance of presenting students with a document that defines cheating and how to engage them in a discussion of academic integrity. For younger children, research has demonstrated that even general discussion about honesty or instruction about the meaning of the term *honesty* and training in self-admonitions to be honest were effective in promoting honest behavior (Casey & Burton, 1982; Fischer, 1970; Houston, 1983c).

However, as the research on honor codes highlights, placing the burden of eliminating cheating entirely on the shoulders of individual test takers or test givers is not likely to be as efficacious as heightening general awareness about the problem, implementing systemic changes, infusing the educational environment with a concern for integrity, and construing responsibility for integrity as the province of everyone in the learning community. Promoting this type of environment—an ethos of ethical behavior surrounding teaching, learning, and testing—is the focus of the final chapter of this book.

---

[6]A particularly comprehensive and well-conceived resource on character education principles and practices is found in a book by Wynne and Ryan (1997).

✦ T E N ✦

Legal Issues
and Cheating

A certain professor decided to cross-examine four students he suspected of cheating in an innovative manner. The students had attended an all-weekend party and on Monday were ill prepared to take the final examination scheduled for that morning. After spending the entire day on Monday cramming for the test, all four showed up at the professor's office on Tuesday morning with a plausible story. They claimed that they had driven home for the weekend to visit a friend who was ill, but, on their return trip, their car got a flat tire and they had no spare; they spent the night in a hotel, had the tire repaired in the morning, and were unable to make it back to campus in time for the final examination. To the students' surprise, the professor agreed to give them a shortened version of the final examination, if they would be able to take it immediately. Sensing triumph, the students agreed and the professor seated them in opposite corners of a large examination room. The professor then wrote their single final examination question on the blackboard: "Which tire?"[1]

Unfortunately for these students, the odds of all four of them guessing the same tire are minimal. In the case of legal issues surrounding cheating on tests, the level of protection afforded to students who are accused of cheating is also fairly

---

[1]This story is one of many such stories about cheating. An Internet source that provides a taxonomy of urban legends traces one version of the story to an introductory chemistry class taught by Professor James F. Bonk at Duke University. The information provided at the site also indicates that the tale predates Professor Bonk and has been told in variations involving a teacher and students who cut class, a coach and players who show up late for practice or miss a curfew, and a boss and employees who report late for work (see http://snopes.simplenet.com/college/exam/flattire.htm).

minimal, but legal challenges to disciplinary actions for cheating are growing (R. N. Roberts, 1986). As Buss and Novick (1980) stated, "there was a time when students, practically speaking, did not have legal rights.... That time, undoubtedly, has passed" (p. 3). Stephen Davis, a leading researcher on cheating has sarcastically illustrated the tenor of the times: "If you've got a good lawyer, go ahead and cheat your heart out" (Stansbury, 1997a, p. 1).

The increase in the volume of litigation related to cheating has, however, also made some of the contours of students' rights and institutional responsibilities more distinguished. Generally, legal proceedings related to cheating have (a) avoided interfering with educators' academic decisions, (b) involved cases at the college and university level, (c) involved public institutions, (d) concerned cases in which a student was suspended or expelled, and (e) centered on violations of the student's due process rights.[2] The following sections of this chapter provide some information on the basis for challenges to institutional actions in response to cheating and legal issues that should be considered when an instance of suspected cheating is pursued by an educational institution.

POSSIBLE GROUNDS FOR CHALLENGING A SANCTION FOR CHEATING

When cheating is suspected, it can be responded to in many ways. In most of the case law related to cheating, a student has challenged a public college's or university's decision to suspend or expel the student. These sanctions are the two most severe ways that an institution can respond to cheating. Less severe sanctions would include placing the student on probation, assigning a failing grade in a course, or assigning a lowered grade. Three primary avenues to challenge sanctions for cheating exist, based on either contractual claims or Constitutional issues.

The first avenue of challenge to a sanction imposed for cheating may be based on an alleged breach of the conditions of a contract. Legally, a contract could exist between a person accused of cheating and the institution or organization that imposed a penalty. An explicit contract would exist if, for example, an informational brochure or registration materials produced by a testing company stated that "all information relevant to a case of suspected cheating will be considered prior to canceling or withholding an examinee's score." That contract would be violated if the company was found to have considered only incriminating evidence and failed to seek or consider evidence that would suggest cheating had not occurred.

Another avenue of challenge to sanctions for cheating involves Constitutional issues. Litigation related to cheating has most often been initiated when a plaintiff has asserted a violation of his or her due process rights. The concept of due process derives from the Fifth and Fourteenth Amendments to the U.S. Constitution.[3] The Fifth Amendment provides that no person shall be "deprived of life, liberty, or property, without due process of law." This protection applies to actions of the federal government. Similarly, the Fourteenth Amendment to the Constitution states

---

[2]A complete treatment of all the legal issues surrounding cheating is beyond the scope or intent of this chapter, which attempts only to provide readers with an introduction to the issues. The reader is referred to the work of Buss and Novick (1980) and Pavela (1988b) as starting points for more detailed examination of this topic.

[3]Many state constitutions also include procedural protections against state actions.

that "no State shall … deprive any person of life, liberty, or property, without due process of law." In the annals of American jurisprudence, there is no record of a student facing the death penalty for possessing a crib sheet, so Constitutional protections related to deprivation of *life* in cheating cases are not well developed. However, when a student is expelled or suspended for cheating, those actions can be seen as depriving the student of the Constitutional right to *liberty* (e.g., the freedom to pursue a chosen career) or *property* (e.g, one's good name or reputation). Constitutional protections of due process rights have been construed to include two elements: *substantive due process* and *procedural due process.* Unreasonableness of the sanction or of the decision-making process gives rise to challenges based on a failure to provide substantive due process. A legal challenge based on a failure to provide procedural due process can arise when a person who has been sanctioned for cheating was not afforded certain minimum elements considered necessary to receive a fair hearing.

It is important to make the distinction that Constitutional guarantees to procedural and substantive due process apply specifically to *governmental* actions. This means that publicly funded schools at any level would generally be subject to the germane Constitutional provisions and any explications or interpretations of those provisions in relevant case law. An action of privately funded institutions at any level would not be subject to challenge under Constitutional provisions of due process rights unless "to some significant extent the State in any of its manifestations has been found to have become involved in it [i.e., the private action]" (*Burton v. Wilmington Parking Authority,* 1961; cited by Buss & Novick, 1980, p. 24). Further, although private institutions are not required to follow the same Constitutional requirements as their publicly funded counterparts, both types of institutions are subject to the same obligations under contract law.

The prevalence of cheating on tests and the increasing litigiousness of American society has yielded at least one benefit: fairly well-developed case law in the area of challenges to sanctions for cheating. The three avenues most commonly pursued in such challenges—breach of contract, procedural due process, and substantive due process—are examined in the following sections.

Breach of Contract

A contractual relationship is initiated when, for example, a student pays money to take courses at a university and, in return, the university makes certain commitments. The U.S. courts have held that "the relationship between a university and a student is contractual in nature" (*Corso v. Creighton University,* 1984, p. 531). According to contract law, when a contractual relationship is established, the rights of each party are guided by both the language of a written contract (if one exists) and the reasonable expectations of the two parties. In the case of a student and a university, written contracts do not ordinarily specify the details of the relationship, although explicit commitments are often found in student handbooks, application materials, and so on. There are also implicit commitments and reasonable expectations. For example, a student would have a reasonable expectation of receiving competent instruction and fair testing and grading (both of which a university would probably be viewed as having made an implicit commitment to provide). A university also would have reasonable expectations regarding, for example, student effort, honesty, and academic integrity. It might explicitly set forth those expectations in a student handbook, policy statements, or honor code.

Legal challenges based on breach of contract are applicable at any level of the educational system, regardless of whether the institution is public or private. Typically, test takers' challenges arising from contract claims center on the failure of the institution to abide by a "contract" set forth regarding how instances of suspected cheating should be pursued. For example, a student accused of cheating would have a reasonable expectation that institutional guidelines prescribing the procedures for hearings, appeals, evidence, and so on, would be followed. When such guidelines exist, but are not followed in a particular case, the student accused of cheating could bring a claim of breach of contract.

One example of a such a case is found in *Corso* (1984). In that case, a Creighton University Medical School student was accused of cheating (and lying about it when asked if he had done so). The Creighton University Student Handbook indicated that exclusive authority concerning such issues rested with the student disciplinary committee, which was charged with handling cases potentially involving serious penalties. A trial court issued an injunction against the university's expulsion of the student from the medical school. The Eighth Circuit Court of Appeals upheld the injunction, agreeing with the lower court's determination that the medical school had failed to pursue alleged cheating against the student through the prescribed disciplinary committee. In a similar case, *Lightsey v. King* (1983), a federal district court in New York ruled that the Merchant Marine Academy could not pursue a different route to imposing sanctions against a midshipman accused of cheating on an examination when a mechanism established to decide such cases (an Academy honor council) already existed.

A high school senior, Brian Dalton, challenged ETS' good faith when the company refused to release Dalton's scores on the SAT. Dalton had taken the SAT as a junior and obtained a combined (verbal and mathematics) score of 620. Six months later, as a senior, Dalton took the SAT again and obtained a combined score of 1030. ETS suspected the highly unusual score increase was due to cheating (by having an imposter take the second test) and withheld Dalton's second set of scores. Dalton sued ETS for breach of contract. Haney (1993) provided several reasons why a breach of contract claim could be made by Dalton, including the failure of ETS to follow professional guidelines for appropriate testing practices, which Dalton would have reasonably expected ETS to follow. For example, Haney cited Standard 16.10 of the *Standards for Educational and Psychological Testing* (AERA, APA, & NCME, 1985), which requires that, in college admissions testing contexts such as the SAT taken by Dalton, "all available data judged to be relevant should be considered" (p. 87) when a testing irregularity (e.g., cheating) is suspected.[4] The published standard is annotated with a comment that explains that "reasonable efforts should be made to obtain contrary, as well as supporting, evidence to settle the matter of the irregularity as well as the validity of the questioned score" (p. 87).

At trial, ETS presented both statistical evidence and handwriting analysis that showed discrepancies between the two test administrations. Dalton presented evidence from a proctor who said that he had seen Dalton sign in and present a photo ID prior to the second test. A previously unknown (to Dalton) student also said that he saw Dalton at the test site; the student claimed that Dalton, a White student, stood out at the test site, which contained mostly Asian and Hispanic students. Finally, Dalton argued that the first set of scores was low because he had been suf-

---

[4]In addition to college admissions testing, Standard 16.10 also covers licensure and certification testing contexts.

fering from mononucleosis at the time and, in the interval between the two tests, he had participated in a test preparation course. The New York State Court of Appeals ruled that ETS did not uphold its end of the bargain in good faith by failing to consider the evidence submitted by Dalton when it first accused him of cheating. The court stated:

> While ETS claims to have conducted a conscientious investigation regarding Dalton's explanations for the increased score, the record is utterly devoid of any showing that the ETS board considered anything other than the reports prepared by its own two document examiners which concluded that the handwriting on the May 1991 answer sheet differed from the handwriting on the November 1991 answer sheet. (*Dalton v. Educational Testing Service*, 1994, p. 744)

The *Dalton* case illustrates a principle stated earlier in this book in the chapter on methods of detecting cheating, namely, that statistical methods (even in combination with other suggestions of cheating) may not provide sufficient evidence of cheating. In the *Dalton* case, however, the conclusion that the contract between Dalton and ETS had been breached turned not so much on the limitations of statistical evidence as it did on the finding that a good-faith effort to abide by the contract obligated ETS to investigate other possible explanations for the conclusion (suggested by the statistical evidence) that cheating had occurred. This obligation has been stated clearly by Buss and Novick (1980): "A statistical test may guarantee that in the long run it will be right 9,999 times out of 10,000. But this is not enough if *available evidence* pertaining to the 10,000th case is knowingly ignored" (p. 12).

A number of other complicating factors are involved in breach of contract cases, including the problem of determining whether a contract exists between two parties and what the parties' reasonable expectations might include in specific circumstances. For example, one issue is whether both parties were able to freely enter into the contract. Buss and Novick (1980) described the case of suspected cheating on standardized tests, such as the SAT, in which one party (the test taker) usually must take the SAT if he or she wishes to apply to a particular school; no real choice exists for the student. Such an arrangement gives the other party (i.e., the organizations responsible for the SAT, ETS and the College Entrance Examination Board) considerably more power in the "negotiations" involved when the test taker decides whether or not to enter into a contractual relationship. Thus, although ETS might print specific information about its authority to cancel or withhold test scores when cheating is suspected, this explicit description of the testing company's rights under the contract may not be enforceable if "the terms [of the contract] are so unequal as not to constitute a 'bargain' at all or if there is such extreme inequality of bargaining power that free choice by one party may appear to be absent" (Buss & Novick, 1980, p. 49).

Buss and Novick described a number of other considerations involved in the establishment, enforcement, and challenge of a contractual relationship in the context of large-scale admissions and certification testing. The purpose of this section is only to introduce readers to the principles and foundation for breach of contract claims when a sanction for cheating is invoked. For a more complete and detailed treatment of contract claims, readers should consult the thorough and detailed information provided by Buss and Novick.

Procedural Due Process

Postsecondary institutions differ from public elementary and secondary schools in that the latter provide a service (i.e., education) that is deemed by many state constitutions to be a right. Attendance at public colleges and universities is widely considered to be a privilege. However, public colleges and universities act as agents of the state. Accordingly, sanctions for cheating, imposed by public colleges and universities, are, in a legal sense, governmental actions. The U.S. Constitution and numerous state constitutions do not prohibit governmental actions that deprive persons of liberty or property (or life), although they do require that certain processes are due when such deprivations are contemplated.

One principle that guides due process considerations is that the more severe the sanction contemplated, the greater procedural protections should be afforded. For example, an instructor's decision to lower a student's semester grade from a B to a C would require less protection than an institutional decision to deny a student the privilege of remaining in a program. Striking an appropriate balance between severity of the sanction and due process requirements has frequently fallen into the realm of the courts, and the primary question in the relevant cases involving sanctions for cheating has been "Precisely *which* processes are due?"

There is broad agreement that adequate procedural due process consists of at least two provisions. Two cases, one resolved by a federal appeals court and the other at the level of the U.S. Supreme Court, have guided judicial decisions for nearly 25 years. The cases of *Dixon v. Alabama State Board of Education* (1961) and *Goss v. Lopez* (1975) require that the person subject to a sanction be provided with adequate notice of the decision and the opportunity for a hearing on the matter.

Notice.   In higher education, the leading case on due notice requirements, *Dixon v. Alabama State Board of Education* (1961), held that a student who faces serious disciplinary action (e.g., suspension or expulsion) must be provided with a specific notice of any actions that may be taken against him or her. There are several requirements for the notice: It should be timely, include the proposed action and the grounds for the proposed action, indicate that the student has the right to a hearing, and be given prior to taking the disciplinary action against the student (Swem, 1987, p. 369). Mawdsley and Permuth (1986) noted that there is no requirement that any notice be given in writing, although they recommend a written notice. Further, they observed that although "there is no clear indication as to what constitutes a timely notice, it would seem that the only requirement would be a reasonable amount of time to allow a student to prepare his defense" (Mawdsley & Permuth, 1986, p. 37).

Hearing.   The Constitutional due process requirement is that persons subject to a serious penalty or sanction must be afforded an opportunity for a hearing. Although not addressed in case law, it seems logical that the first application of a fair hearing criterion would come into play when an instructor first suspects that cheating has occurred. When a policy requires that all suspicions of cheating be handled by an established panel or procedures, these should be followed. Frequently, however, there is ambiguity about how cheating should initially be addressed or the cheating is judged to be a minor infraction and a sanction less than suspension or expulsion is likely. In such cases, a faculty member or teacher might confront a student personally about the matter in an informal discussion. Even in informal "hearings" between an instructor and a student suspected of cheating, the instructor should adopt a stance of impartiality, considering all available evidence and alternative explanations that might be offered to counter the inference that cheating occurred. E. H. Stevens (1996) has recommended that, in informal situations such as those described here, "impartiality in the decisionmaker is an important factor" and that "if [the instructor] cannot rise above a personal stake in the situation, the matter should be turned over to a department head or other appropriate colleagues" (p. 142).

Assuming that a serious sanction for cheating has been recommended and notice of a formal hearing has been provided, a student suspected of cheating on a test could voluntarily decline to have a hearing and accept the sanction or penalty. A student could also attend a hearing and not participate in the proceedings. In the event of a unfavorable decision, the person suspected of cheating could also challenge the charges, the evidence, the procedures, or the proposed sanction; in such cases, a fair hearing—that is, one in which a person can appeal the proposed action to a panel or official with authority over the matter—is required.

The Supreme Court has noted that "a school is an academic institution, not a courtroom or administrative hearing room" (*Board of Curators of the University of Missouri v. Horowitz*, 1978, p. 88). Accordingly, a fair hearing in an academic setting need not resemble a legal proceeding. However, a fair hearing has been held to require an independent, objective hearing officer or panel and the opportunity for the person accused to provide his or her side of the story. Citing numerous federal cases, Buss and Novick (1980) reported that "it is well established that due process requires an impartial decision" (p. 37). Swem (1987) stated that "due process requires that hearing boards exercise independent judgment, so that they do more than ratify an administrator's evidentiary conclusions and disciplinary sanctions" (p. 371). In support of the requirement of independence, Swem referred to the case of *Lee v. Macon County Board of Education* (1974) in which the plaintiff charged that an administrative appeal that merely rubber-stamped a principal's decision was not appropriate. The court held that "formalistic acceptance or ratification of [an administrator's] request or recommendation as to the scope of punishment, without independent Board consideration of what, under all the circumstances, the penalty should be, is less than full due process" (Swem, 1987, p. 460).

Providing some clarification to the requirement for a hearing, one federal court ruled that a student accused of a disciplinary violation should also be permitted to present evidence in his or her defense (see *Esteban v. Central Missouri State College*, 1969, cited by Tauber, 1984). Similarly, another federal court ruled that there was a Constitutional obligation that a hearing panel has "an obligation to listen to [a] plaintiff's version of the facts" (*Jaska v. Regents of the University of Michigan*, 1984, p. 1250). In a review of relevant cases, Mawdsley and Permuth (1986) have concluded that a fair hearing also requires "at the very least, a minimal opportunity for the student to present evidence on his behalf and contest evidence against him" (p. 41).

In a frequently cited case, *Goldberg v. Kelley* (1970), the Supreme Court stated that "in almost every setting where important decisions turn on questions of fact, due process requires an opportunity to confront and cross-examine adverse witnesses" (p. 269). However, the *Goldberg* case involved the termination of welfare benefits and does not fully resolve whether cases involving academic matters such as cheating fall outside the boundaries of "almost every setting." Another leading case, *Dixon v. Alabama State Board of Education* (1961), addressed the same issue of cross-examination in the context of higher education. In that case, the court held that due process did not include the right to cross-examination. Finally, citing the *Jaska* decision, R. N. Roberts (1986) concluded that due process does not require that a student be permitted to cross examine accusers or witnesses.

Mawdsley and Permuth (1986) have also attempted to clarify which processes are *not* due. First, courts have generally held the belief that hearings conducted within an academic community should not be characterized by the same sort of adversarial proceedings as a courtroom. This belief has been articulated, among other places, in the *Jaska* (1984) case in which the court noted that an academic institution "cannot ignore its duty to treat its students fairly, neither is it required to transform its classrooms into courtrooms" (p. 1250). Thus, although many university policies explicitly provide that students charged with serious violations of academic or disciplinary codes may have the benefit of an attorney or other advisor present during a hearing, many others legally can (and do) preclude representation by an attorney. When representation, either by an attorney or a counsel other than an attorney of the student's choice has been provided for explicitly in policies or guidelines of the institution, then a failure to permit such counsel may be grounds for breach of contract. Mawdsley and Permuth (1986) concluded that, when not explicitly articulated in institutional policy, "there is no clear indication that constitutional due process requires the presence of an attorney" (p. 38). In a review of relevant cases, Swem (1987) reported that "several courts have rejected the assertion that due process entitles a student to legal counsel at disciplinary hearings" (p. 373), although she suggested that other, contrary, findings reveal a need for the Supreme Court to provide clarification regarding the role of counsel.

Substantive Due Process

The requirements of substantive due process are not nearly as tidy as those of procedural due process. Substantive due process requires only "fundamental fairness," and application of that principle varies necessarily according to the facts of a particular case. The concept of substantive due process requires that actions taken in response to cheating not be arbitrary or capricious and that any penalties should be uniformly applied and consistent with the severity of the offense.

First, when an established procedure exists for handling cases of suspected cheating, all cases covered by the procedure should be handled in the same way. Swem (1987) reported that this has been the finding in several federal court cases and she concluded that, "due process requires that a university consistently apply those elements of the established procedure it promulgates" (p. 367).

Second, decisions regarding penalties for cheating must not be capricious. This means that the decisions must be based on substantial evidence (Swem, 1987). A legal definition of substantial evidence was stated in the case of *Consolidated Edison Co. v. National Labor Relations Board* (1938), where the term is defined as "such relevant evidence as a reasonable mind might accept as adequate to support a conclusion" (p. 229). Buss and Novick (1980) cited a cheating case in which one student was accused of copying from another; they reported that numerous identical wrong answers indicated, prima facie, that the student had cheated and was "sufficient" grounds for a testing company to cancel the test score of the examinee (p. 57). According to legal precedents, such actions would rarely be considered arbitrary or capricious, at least in the minds of judges; the U.S. Supreme Court has held that "plainly, they may not override it [i.e., the educational decision] unless it is such a substantial departure from accepted academic norms as to demonstrate that the person or committee responsible did not actually exercise professional judgment" (*Regents of the University of Michigan v. Ewing*, 1985, p. 513).[5]

Third, although there is little or no case law regarding the appropriateness of penalties for cheating, various authors and common sense argue for the proposition that any sanctions should fit the crime. To support this viewpoint, Tauber argued (1984) that "each penalty obviously must be tailored to the offense committed" (p. 14). In many cases in which penalties have been excessive, the courts have been willing to intervene in order to correct "a manifest abuse of discretion in the imposition of a penalty ... so that justice will prevail" (*Shober v. Commonwealth of Pennsylvania State Real Estate Commission*, 1981, p. 285).

ACADEMIC QUESTIONS

It would be an oversight not to mention another unresolved (at least in the records of the U.S. court system) but important question: Is cheating on a test an academic matter? As noted at the beginning of this chapter, courts have generally tended to avoid interference with educators' academic decisions. Dwyer and Hecht (1996) observed that "American courts have been loathe to involve themselves in the academic and educational disputes, accepting as a general rule a policy of non-interference in a university's purely academic decisions" (p. 130). Purely academic decisions would include those related to grading or evaluations of a student's academic performance, suitability for continuation in a graduate program, and so on. Violations of a school's policy on hazing, drug use, or sexual harassment would likely be purely disciplinary matters. However, a difference of opinion exists as to whether procedures for handling and sanctions responding to, cheating represent purely academic matters or whether they represent student disciplinary matters. Cheating might represent a serious lapse of academic integrity and may violate an academic honor code, but, at the same time, it might be listed among many possible behaviors prohibited in student disciplinary guidelines. The court in the *Jaska* (1984) case, recognized the problem of categorizing cheating, acknowledging that it is "an offense which cannot neatly be characterized as either 'academic' or 'disciplinary'" (p. 1248), whereas a court in another case, *University of Texas Medical School v. Than* (1994), held that "a dismissal for the misdeed of cheating is a disciplinary dismissal" (p. 844).

The distinction between *academic* and *disciplinary* matters is not a trivial one. The reticence of courts to interject themselves into academic matters can be juxtaposed with the courts' willingness (some might say, eagerness) to consider student disciplinary matters. One leading case on the due process rights of students held that due process protection was required for high school student suspensions of 10 days or more (*Goss v. Lopez*, 1975); how much more protection ought to be accorded college students facing expulsions for cheating? As Tauber (1984) has summarized:

---

[5]The *Ewing* case involved a challenge by a student who was dismissed from a medical program at the University of Michigan. It is important to note that the *Ewing* case concerned a dismissal for purely academic reasons; the student involved was not suspected of cheating.

If cheating and plagiarism are categorized as disciplinary misconduct, then students are entitled to some due process—the same due a student for any other disciplinary misconduct (e.g., drinking, vandalism). If cheating and plagiarism are categorized as academic evaluations, the students are entitled to little, if any, due process! (p. 5)

It is clear, then, that how one views cheating is consequential. Extreme opinions can be seen on both sides of the issue. Tauber (1984) forcefully asserted that:

Cheating, plagiarism, and other such student acts of academic dishonesty are more legitimately classified as a disciplinary code of conduct breach (disciplinary misconduct) rather than as an academic evaluation, and as such are beyond the rights of a single faculty member to decide. (p. 1)

Whereas Tauber recommended that all instances of suspected cheating be handled as disciplinary matters, other scholars have recommended the opposite approach. For example, R. N. Roberts (1986) acknowledged that "most public universities officially treat cheating as a disciplinary matter ... [although] most do little to discourage faculty members from punishing students for cheating within the confines of their courses" (p. 374) and cited the previously mentioned *Corso* case as signaling that "the Constitution places few restrictions on a public university to designate all types of cheating as academic offenses" (p. 378). R. N. Roberts (1986) recommended that "it would seem a good policy for public universities and the courts to treat the punishment of students for cheating as a genuine academic matter" (p. 384). With respect to how cheating is classified, a clearer delineation of where academic matters end and disciplinary matters begin would be a welcome distinction, and future courts may provide some guidance on how this line should be drawn.

CONCLUSIONS AND RECOMMENDATIONS

Although some legal issues related to cheating remain unsettled, there is a reasonable amount of case law to guide the process of responding to cheating on tests. First, when an institution has promulgated policies or guidelines that delineate students' rights or the processes that apply when cheating is suspected, those policies or guidelines should be followed. In the previously cited *Than* case, a university was enjoined from prohibiting the student's graduation because it had failed to comply with its own written policy regarding how to handle suspected cheating on tests. Second, although constitutionally required processes apply primarily to cases when serious sanctions are contemplated, it seems wise to provide certain protections to test takers whenever a penalty is recommended. Although one review of cases involving cheating revealed that "the courts bend over backwards to give public universities the benefit of the doubt in their determinations of guilt or innocence of a student for cheating" (R. N. Roberts, 1986, p. 381), it is still essential that serious penalties for cheating, such as suspensions or expulsions, be accompanied by procedures sufficient to ensure that due process requirements are fulfilled. The minimum process that is due includes a notification of the action, specification of the reasons for the action, and the opportunity for the person suspected of cheating to have a hearing on the matter. One example of a model due process policy that contains these elements is provided in Appendix C.

A third recommendation (though one with little grounding in case law) also seems warranted. When a formal hearing is conducted in a cheating case, the institution or body hearing the case should produce and retain documentation of the process at each decision point. Specifically, a copy of any written notice provided to a student and the details of hearings—including the persons attending, evidence presented (supporting and refuting), decision and reasons for the decision—should be a part of any official record of the process.

Finally, it is imperative that the educative atmosphere that characterizes a school, college, or university be recognized. Certainly, courts have made this distinction, as in the *Horowitz* (1978) case, in which the U.S. Supreme Court "decline[d] to further enlarge the judicial presence in the academic community and thereby risk deterioration of many beneficial aspects of the faculty–student relationship" (p. 90). The academy–judiciary distinction might also help to guide how test givers respond to cases of suspected cheating. The primary mission of educational institutions is to inculcate knowledge and, beyond this, the wise and virtuous application of knowledge. Thus, there may be some educational benefit to handling cases of cheating (primarily those judged to be less serious) in an informal way and to use instances of cheating as opportunities for students to confront attitudes or behaviors that contravene the standards of both the academy and a just society.

✦ E L E V E N ✦

Cheating and the Ethos of Testing

Cheating undermines integrity and fairness at all levels. It leads to weak life performance. It undermines the merit basis of our society. Cheating is an issue that should concern every citizen of this country.
— Nancy Cole, president of Educational Testing Service (1998)

The stereotype I have about concluding chapters is that they are supposed to provide a tidy wrap-up and a rosy outlook for the future. I can think of many books that have closing chapters with titles like "The Five Steps to Better Communication," or "Ten Things You Can Do to Make a Difference in Your Community," or "Three Sure-Fire Ways to Cut Your Total Tax Bill." I wish that cheating were that kind of thing. It would be far easier to write a conclusion that provided a list (if one existed) of quick-fix "solutions" to the problem of cheating. The reader looking for such a list should stop reading at this point and avoid disappointment.

I can't really deliver on a rosy outlook, either. It's hard for me to imagine a glorious day ahead when cheating does not threaten testing, undermine integrity, and devalue the accomplishments of those whose achievements were attained fairly. On a somewhat positive note, however, I think that cheating on tests should be viewed in an appropriate context; namely, that cheating on tests has existed since tests were first given and great civilizations have not been decimated by it. I won't claim that cheating is a crisis; in fact, it would be an exaggeration to name it among the top ten problems facing American education today. It is simply impossible to look at literacy levels in the United States, the educational system that prepares teachers, changing cultural attitudes toward education, the lack of options for students trapped in inadequate schools, or the way education is financed and conclude that crib sheets are a major concern.

Compared with some of these more disturbing educational problems, there are plenty of concrete steps that can be taken to deter cheating on tests (see chap. 9), to detect it (see chap. 7), to appropriately respond to cheating (see chap. 8), and to avoid legal pitfalls (see chap. 10). Sure, cheating is a problem, but in addition to expressing my concern about it, I feel a strong obligation to be honest with the reader: All in all, I think that American education would get along even if cheating continued to be engaged in and responded to in the future as it is today.

So, if the formula for listing concrete steps to a brighter day can't be followed, then what? For this chapter, it seems wise to step away from concrete actions that might be taken and focus on a bigger picture. Over the course of an entire book, the details of programmable calculators, fraternity membership, g_2 coefficients, due process, and honor codes draw our vision to the pragmatic problems up close. However, this perspective can distract us from considering the larger issues that underlie cheating on tests. This chapter represents an attempt to refocus on the more distant, less pragmatic, but more important issues.

In the distance, we can see that to really tackle cheating requires facing much larger issues, such as what education is about, what tests are for, what the role of a teacher should be, and what one's view of human nature is. These issues are not usually the topics of lunchtime conversations or the subject matter of best-selling books (although maybe they should be). In my own professional life, I can attest to the fact that practical concerns, like trying to figure out if the test I am planning can be completed by my students in 60 minutes regularly occupy more time and attention than bigger questions such as "What effect will this test have on my students, my teaching, and our learning?"

I suspect that it may be normal to avoid thinking about the bigger questions, precisely because they are more consequential and compel action. Sustained contemplation about the really big issues usually results in a state of cognitive dissonance. To resolve the dissonance requires some kind of commitment; some serious commitment or change must take place. It is far easier to avoid confronting the big issues.

I remember thinking about this principle as an undergraduate student at a large state university. In the first few warm weeks of the spring semester, you could always find one or more students standing on a plastic crate preaching to whatever audience would listen in a place where students gathered between classes. The issues were inevitably big—arguably the biggest. They preached about eternity, the human spirit, our duties to God and each other, the way of salvation, the meaning of life. Many students objected to public consideration of these big questions, apparently out of the belief that such consideration should only take place in private, on a Saturday or Sunday, or in a building set aside for that sort of thing. Some students poked fun at the preachers, urging them to change to a philosophy major if they felt so strongly about the issues. Other students took up the challenge, arguing that "Jesus could not be the Messiah because...." Those arguments always seemed more like debates about whether the Green Bay Packers were better than the San Francisco 49ers, with loyal fans defending their favorite teams. As I recall, the majority of the student body simply ignored it all—the preachers, the commotion, and the big questions. But how can the big questions be ignored?

My concern in writing this chapter is that, with regard to the issue of cheating on tests, it is also easier to ignore the problem than to confront the big issues that must be addressed if we are to make a serious commitment to changing the status quo. In the following sections, I try to accomplish a difficult task: to elucidate what I believe the big issues are, while, along the way, attempting to summarize and integrate some of the knowledge we have about cheating. I think that I can do this with a realist's perspective: I do not have confidence that any ways I might suggest for addressing the big issues will lead to rapid remedies. However, I do believe that contemplating the big issues is necessary for real change to occur. It is my hope that, after reading this chapter, the reader is left with that sense of disequilibrium mentioned previously, which does not merely lead to better spacing of chairs or more attentive proctoring but to sustained discourse and action regarding how we as educators and people, and the systems we create, can be reformed.

THE STATUS QUO

Any beginning point for reform is to understand the current state of affairs. As far as cheating on tests is concerned, the picture is remarkably clear. Cheating is pervasive. It begins at the earliest levels of the American educational system and extends beyond graduate school to tests used for selection, promotion, licensure, or certification in nearly all professions. We know that it is not a uniquely American phenomenon; cheating on tests is a problem in Nigeria, the Netherlands, and Nebraska. We know that cheating occurs by both test givers and test takers, eviscerating the very purpose of testing by invalidating inferences about skill, knowledge, or ability that are always desired and frequently necessary for making important decisions. We know that age, gender, IQ, income, ethnicity, and a host of other demographic and psychological characteristics are, at best, only weakly associated with cheating; we know that there is no better predictor of future cheating than previous behavior. We know that those who would cheat on tests have developed an amazing array of methods for doing so and that the limits of human imagination are the only limits on the sophistication and variety of cheating methods that are likely to be seen in the future. We know that current methods of detecting cheating offer only modest power to identify potential cheating, and even then only a specific type of cheating, on a specific type of test, under specific and comparatively uncommon circumstances. We know that legal considerations must appropriately constrain and guide responses to suspicions of cheating.

A FEW BIG QUESTIONS

The pragmatic concerns associated with the status quo pose reasonable challenges in themselves. However, the more fundamental questions pose even bigger challenges. One of the most puzzling big-picture issues related to cheating on tests involves a glaring contradiction. There is a modest literature base that contains commentary on the seriousness of the problem, documentation of its extent and correlates, and evaluations of a number of recommendations for preventing it. The presence of this literature might be construed to suggest that there is a broad, shared concern about the problem. In fact, the same cadre of scholars has demonstrated that no such consensus exists; the conventional wisdom and common experience are just the opposite. One of the most discouraging findings about the status quo is that, at the level of individual test takers and test givers, there is a profound apathy toward identifying, detecting, or responding to cheating. This issue has been articulated just as clearly as the findings about the prevalence and determinants of cheating. In a recent study, Alschuler and Bliming (1995) considered that "the mystery is not why cheating is wrong, or why students cheat, but why there is so little passion about this massive assault on the highest values in the academy" (p. 124). This leads to the first big question: "Why are our attitudes toward cheating so schizophrenic?"

On the one hand, we protest the horror of cheating. In the various surveys cited in this book, cheating on tests is uniformly acknowledged as wrong by both students and their teachers. Cheating is described by many authors in terms that reveal our approbation: epidemic, moral decline, dishonesty, and so on. One author included a probing discussion of cheating and plagiarism in a section of his book devoted to "pressing issues" in higher education, among which were affirmative action, racism, freedom of expression, and sexual harassment (W. W. May, 1990). This is heady company for crib notes and failure to footnote.

On the other hand, we turn a blind eye to the behavior, or we act as if the behavior were not nearly so serious as our words would lead people to believe. The same research literature that documents the pervasiveness of cheating is equally clear in highlighting that the most common response to cheating—on the part of students and their teachers—is to ignore it. Even when cheating is proved, we aren't too sure what to do about it. One study showed that only a third of chief college student affairs officers believed that an institution's grading policy should include a special grade designation when failure in a course was the result of academic dishonesty (Aaron & Georgia, 1994). Among testing specialists, whose profession is devoted to ensuring the validity of scores, there is also a sense that cheating is a taboo testing topic, better left alone than thoroughly examined. One of the leading researchers on detecting cheating, Robert Frary, has reported that some of his psychometric colleagues take such a dim view of statistical methods for detecting cheating that they derisively refer to such methods as "high-tech snitching" (White, 1996). Frary has related some events surrounding an investigation of cheating at a large university, for which he performed some statistical analyses:

> The [statistical] detection of copying is a funny business. There is a lot of hostility toward it and I really don't know why. ... A number of comments were made to the instructor bringing charges to the effect that such statistics were "unethical." (Personal communication, February 29, 1996)

Hostile, or simply ambivalent, attitudes about cheating on tests are revealed in a variety of other ways. Is the purpose of education to impart information, to train students in certain thinking skills, to instill certain moral values, to prepare students for "the real world," or some combinations of these? The complexity of these questions is highlighted in the context of cheating on tests.

On the one hand, there is the common argument that accepting cheating is akin to embracing moral decline. Those opposed to such a decline might favor even more intense scrutiny of students, test administrations, and test responses. On the other hand, some writers have expressed favorable attitudes—or at least mixed feelings—about cheating. It is possible, of course, to conceptualize a position that would eschew making distinctions in students' performances, abandon standards, and eliminate grades altogether. An educational system structured along these lines might obviate the motivation to cheat—as well as the impulse to detect, deter, or respond to cheating—and would likely classify almost nothing as academic dishonesty. A less radical position has also been articulated; namely, that cheating is merely an expression of creativity, which should be valued and accepted as a legitimate manifestation of divergent problem-solving strategies (e.g., K. Davis, 1992). Others have argued that cheating is merely a trivial matter, hardly worthy of the attention it has received:

> Why should a student who copies an answer from his neighbor's test paper be considered guilty of more serious misbehavior than the student who attempts to misinform by raising his hand when the teacher asks how many have completed their homework assignment? Why is cheating on a test considered a greater breach of educational etiquette than is faking interest during a social studies discussion or sneaking a peek at a comic book during arithmetic class? (Jackson, 1968, p. 27)

It is safe to say, perhaps, that those who hold any of these positions regarding cheating retain at least some sensitivity to the arguments of those in opposing camps. For example, those who view cheating as a divergent problem-solving strategy would probably balk at having their own heart surgery performed by a cardiologist who "creatively" passed the board examination; those who favor heightened security, prevention, and detection measures surely recognize the degradation of student–teacher relationships that results from fascist testing policies and procedures.

When we take tests, are we naturally inclined to act in ways that are honest or are we all predisposed to act according to our own self-interests? Perhaps one reason for the ambivalence about cheating is that we are unsure of our own answers to this question. On the one hand, we cognitively assent to the value of honesty and integrity, at least in the abstract. On the other hand, we know the frailties of our own humanity. We tacitly acknowledge "There, but for the grace of God, go I" when confronted with a student who has cheated in order to keep a scholarship, pass a course, or balance the demands of school and job.

Those who give tests—particularly those who also teach—also wonder about how testing affects our students. The dilemma is a difficult one. After weeks or months of collaborating with students to pursue problems of common interest, a line is drawn and isolation is the order of the day. During an examination, the collaborative relationship suddenly becomes adversarial. Silence and suspicion replace communication and support. On the part of test givers, an expectation of cooperation is replaced by an expectation that cheating will occur. On the part of test takers, an expectation of candor and facilitation gives way to the uneasy feeling that testing is a terrible game in which the objective is to detect the trickiness and deceit that are built into every test question. In many students' minds, not much has changed in the hundreds of years since Miyazaki (1963/1981) described the perceived purpose of testing in China:

> Examiners sometimes posed questions so dreadfully distorted as to make them almost impossible to understand. For example … candidates would be asked to name the one place in the Analects where the three particles *yeh, chi,* and *i* occur in sequence.

When the examiners saw that no one could answer such a question, they happily called out, "We have outwitted them." (pp. 20–21)

SOME SMALL ANSWERS

The weighty questions that underlie the problem of cheating on tests deserve far greater treatment than a few sections in a concluding chapter. However, to begin the process of addressing cheating means that tentative answers to the big questions should be offered, examined, and evaluated. I offer three. I realize that the suggestions that follow will surely not solve the problem. They might, however, provide fruitful avenues for refining our thinking about teaching, testing, and learning in ways that will, in the long term, make cheating less of a problem than it is today.

Avenue 1: Raising Expectations

My interpretation of the research on honor codes is that they may be effective at deterring cheating, partly, because they communicate two things. First, honor codes do not treat cheating as a taboo topic. Each student at an honor code institution surely knows what constitutes cheating and knows that proscribed actions violate the code. Acceptance of the responsibilities of membership in the academic community could not be any more formal or explicit; at honor code institutions, the rules are in writing and the pledge is read and signed as a condition of acceptance into the community.

Second—and more important, I believe—is that honor codes communicate a sense of greater expectations. Increasingly, research and commentary on key educational issues is revealing the powerful potential of expectations. The stream began in 1968 with the publication of Rosenthal and Jacobson's classic study of "Pygmalion in the Classroom," which demonstrated that when teachers were induced to believe that their students were of high ability, their behaviors toward students and the students' subsequent performance were affected. This line of investigation, focusing on the powerful role that expectations play in shaping behavior, has recently been extended into other areas of school life and to broader social issues (see Damon, 1995; Dunn, 1999).

When integrity is the topic of open discourse, there may be an a concomitant expectation that people who talk the talk will walk the walk. When all students commit themselves formally to academic integrity, there is—perhaps minutely so—an increased sense that people will actually try to live up to those commitments. This sense could well lead students to greater expectations of trust of their fellow students. More palpably, the belief that people will try to live up to their commitments is the foundation for the absence of proctoring that marks honor systems. To a small proportion of students, freedom from proctoring may well be abused; to a larger proportion, it is likely that it communicates a higher expectation of honest behavior.

In the case of honor systems and deterring cheating, it is not yet clear how (or even if) expectations play a part. I suspect, however, that expectations will be found to play a significant part. Further, I believe that the powerful influence of expectations for behavior will be found even in the absence of honor codes. These expectations go beyond wishful thinking about students. It would be a serious

mistake to blissfully believe that people won't cheat and leave bank vaults unlocked overnight. However, to the extent that individual teachers hold up high
standards and expect students to meet them, we are likely to see students striving
to reach those standards and communities embracing them. It is almost a truism
that we are surely more likely to see behavior of greater integrity if we expect it and
act accordingly than if we expect the opposite and put our faith for the future in
retinal scans and statistical techniques to control cheating. This answer to cheating—raising the bar of our expectations—is one that can, and should, be worked
out in classrooms, by individual teachers, and in learning communities.

Avenue 2: Systemic Improvements

Many efforts are currently under way to induce improvements in the American
educational system. A number of suggestions for improving classroom environments and testing practices would be in order even if they had no effect on cheating. However, I believe that some of the systemic improvements being debated
today may, coincidentally, result in reduced cheating on tests as much as they accomplish their intended objectives. Three specific components of assessment reform are discussed in the following paragraphs.

Clarity About the Purposes of Testing.   One topic of discussion is the instructional value of tests. Many specialists in curriculum and assessment have insisted
that tests can and should do more than simply rank students or serve administrative functions such as grading. In response, the line between instruction and assessment has become somewhat blurred. Many tests no longer serve uniquely
evaluative functions but have been designed to be valuable learning experiences
for students in their own right. I think that a renewed emphasis on the instructional value of tests is timely and will, overall, be beneficial in terms of student
achievement. However, I also see the need to retain the distinction between assessments *primarily* designed to enrich student learning and tests *primarily* intended to
gauge absolute levels of performance. It seems like a good idea that tests should
provide students with engaging, real-life problems that promote critical thinking
and skills that transfer to other contexts and that tests should provide students
with information that helps refine their learning. Although such tests are highly
desirable, the need to make summary judgments about student performance will
probably always be present. Tests are still needed that can tell us who has attained
a prescribed level of knowledge to graduate from high school, practice dentistry,
or sell real estate, even if such tests do not provide rich diagnostic information or
instructional value.

In short, we must come to grips with the fact that tests have differing purposes.
The technology of testing permits tests to be *designed* to accomplish an intended
purpose quite well. But all tests cannot serve the purposes of, say, providing engaging diagnostic tasks and certifying competence equally well. The need to make
distinctions between an assessment that serves instructional needs and an assessment that serves evaluative needs will always be with us. One area for improvement will be to instill a broader understanding of the differences between purpose
and design in those who use tests.

We will also need to make these distinctions and purposes clearer to our students.
It is clear that most students cheat on tests to get a higher grade. The current cultural
ethos affecting education in the United States reinforces the notion that learning is

not nearly as important as obtaining a degree, a credential, or a job that pays a large salary. If learning is not all that important to a student's success, then pursuit of that which *is* important–that is, a higher grade—is completely logical behavior. If *learning* were the goal, we would hope that students would use every fiber and resource at their disposal to acquire learning; we cannot be totally surprised that, when *grades* are perceived to be the goal, that students behave similarly.

I believe that a primary reason students cheat on tests is that they fail to perceive the relationship between accurate identification of their strengths and weaknesses and their subsequent success, by whatever measure they choose to define it (i.e., income, vocational choice, admission to graduate school, acquisition of a credential, etc.). Classroom teaching and testing practices must move closer toward becoming supportive environments in which the focus is on helping students to recognize the value of accurately perceiving and extending their own competence. Students must come to understand that tests that faithfully reveal their strengths and weaknesses are a good thing and that such information will be used to help them improve and is in their long-term best interest.

Altered Attitudes Toward Testing.   Second, a sea change is needed regarding the attitudes of many teachers and students toward testing. Many teachers have in the past—and continue today—to use tests for other than their primary *raison d'être*, and this has contributed to invidious attitudes toward testing. Testing specialists would contend that tests exist to obtain fair, accurate, and efficient measurements of what students know or can do. This single stated purpose stands in contrast to the multiple unstated purposes that tests have frequently been asked to serve. For example, tests are sometimes used as punishments. I wonder how many readers have heard the following threat uttered in an elementary school classroom: "If you aren't going to pay attention while we review this material, then we'll just have the test right now!" Tests are also used, in a perverted sense, as negative reinforcers: "Those students who turn in all their homework won't have to take the test on Friday."

Fairness is the key concept here, and perceptions of fairness directly affect attitudes toward tests. As mentioned previously, generations of test takers (many of whom became test givers later in life) grew up in an educational ethos in which the plain intent of the test giver was to construct test questions that were convoluted, inane, trivial, or tricky. Years of exposure to an educational system in which students perceive testing to be a game in which a person must "outpsych" the teacher or "get into the professor's head" to select the correct answer or to figure out what the test question is *really* asking must have a devastating cumulative effect.

I recall one situation that stunned me. I was working for a large testing company and consulting with a group of physicians. The 10 or so doctors were reviewing potential questions for a board examination. One multiple-choice question in particular caused the group to pause before accepting it as legitimate material for the board exam. Most members of the group were silent until one of them spoke up: "This one looks pretty good, but where's the trick?" he asked. It might be germane at this point to interject that the incorrect options to multiple-choice questions are sometimes referred to as *foils*, as in "foiled again!"

Recent years have witnessed many improvements in testing. The fact remains, though, that there is still much bad testing—and bad teaching, for that matter. McCabe and Trevino (1993) reported that:

some instructors have the reputation for being so demanding or unfair that the class-room becomes a hostile arena and a test is no longer between the student and the sub-ject but between the student and the teacher. (p. 181)

According to Mary Amato (1995), now a teacher herself, cheating during her el-ementary school days could be traced to the quality of the instruction and assess-ment:

I admit it. I cheated. In fact, I cheated every Friday on multiple-choice quizzes given by my seventh-grade history teacher. So did Patty, and Susan, and Jennifer, and who knows how many others. We didn't cheat to get good grades. The tests were a cinch—straight from the dull, outdated book that we read aloud in class every Mon-day through Thursday. We cheated to relieve the unrelenting boredom that our teacher called his lesson plan. (p. 92)

I hasten to note that professional test constructors and experts in educational testing adamantly reject the notion that test questions should be tricky, and they are also unified in recommending challenging, higher order assessments. How-ever, most tests taken by students are not professionally made. As has been exten-sively documented, most educators at any level have no training in assessment; the majority of the states require no coursework in testing for licensure as a teacher or administrator in elementary or secondary education (Gullickson, 1986; Hills, 1991; J. G. Ward, 1980). As a result, American education suffers from a serious defi-ciency in the training of school personnel to administer, interpret, and use infor-mation generated by tests. As one testing specialist has observed, we are "a nation of assessment illiterates" (Stiggins, 1991, p. 535). Although I am not aware of re-search on assessment training for college and university faculty members, I also suspect that no faculty member has ever been denied tenure for writing poor mul-tiple-choice questions.

More Careful Use of Test Results.   The final component of systemic im-provement involves changing the ways we use test scores. To develop this point, it is useful to consider those large-scale, high-stakes tests administered in U.S. ele-mentary and secondary schools. These tests are frequently mandated by state leg-islatures as a way of monitoring achievement in a state or of promoting accountability in the state's educational system, or both. The tests are called *stu-dent proficiency tests* or *minimum competency tests* and were first mandated in the 1970s. I am convinced that such tests were introduced by legislators in the first place only in response to a growing lack of public confidence that grades were meaningful indicators of student learning. I have seen many such tests, the basic academic objectives that they are intended to assess, and the careful procedures used to develop them in a fair and unbiased way. My general conclusion is that they provide reliable and valid methods for measuring some of the important knowledge and skills that we would want every student to master.

I also recognize at least one problem with these tests. In many instances, scores from the tests are used in ways that go far beyond the intended purpose of provid-ing information about an individual student's strengths and weaknesses. In some locations, teachers, principals, or entire schools are rewarded for test score im-provements. In other areas, school districts are ranked according to their students' average performance on the test. I don't think that the claim is ever made this explicitly, but such uses clearly imply that some pupils perform better than others because of the quality of instruction they receive. Better teaching ought to be rewarded; poor teaching ought to be stigmatized.

A casual analysis of these uses might seem appropriate. In fact, I would concur that student performance on a test ought to reflect instructional quality to some degree; I would also agree that meritorious teaching deserves, well, merit. I would even find comparisons of overall performance among school districts to be informative. The fact that Sunnyvale district outperformed Shady Grove Consolidated means that students in Sunnyvale performed better and probably know more, on average, about the content tested than the students at Shady Grove.

The problem with the casual analysis is twofold. First, knowing that some groups of students outperform others is interesting in its own right, but there is a far more interesting follow-up question: Why? The casual analysis nearly always suggests that the causal agent is instructional quality, although evidence supporting the causal agent is almost never presented (or even gathered, for that matter). This is a problem in its own right, but there is another problem that follows from this one. Failing to ensure, or at least vigorously promote, accurate and well- supported inferences and fair use of large-scale test results, we unwittingly increase the likelihood that cheating on tests will persist.

It's a vicious cycle. Tests that were never designed to be gauges of instructional quality are used for a purpose for which they are ill suited. Educators affected by this misuse generally (and, I believe, to some extent, rightfully) resent this use. Consequently (although, I believe, wrongfully), they reject the use of the tests altogether. Educators' resentment of the tests translates into a pernicious influence on students. I have heard teachers, in preparation for an important state-mandated achievement test, announce to their students things like "We *have* to take this test today. I have no idea why the state *makes* us do this. I know we *all* wish that we could be doing *more important* things today. Let's just do it and get it over with." I don't think anyone would absolve students, teachers, or administrators for cheating, although I also think that everyone could see how cheating is fostered when perceptions and attitudes such as these are ubiquitous. Breaking the cycle will require more careful circumscription of test purposes and uses. It also demands that test results be designed and reported in ways that minimize or eliminate harmful uses and inappropriate inferences.

Avenue 3: Examining Ourselves

The activity of testing is all about examining students. We certainly examine them closely, frequently, and in multiple ways. We are able to quantify the likelihood of cheating on tests to several decimal places. It seems worth pondering whether those who give tests ought to examine us with such regularity, in such detail, and with such precision. A familiar quotation admonishes us to remove the log in our own eye before attempting to remove the speck in another's. Our own behavior as educators has a significant effect on our students. When college students hear of their professors "spinning" their research results in ways that shed a favorable light on their funding sources, when teachers hear of standardized test answer sheets being altered by administrators, and when pupils see that the state proficiency test questions they answered today are the same ones they practiced with yesterday, the strongest possible messages about cheating are being communicated. McCabe and Bowers (1996) commented on the strong influence of peer disapproval of cheating. Here is one of the big questions: How strong is the influence of those in positions of authority, respect, and leadership?

All educational activities contain a moral dimension. The very act of constituting a curriculum implicitly communicates that some things are more valuable than others. The way teachers interact with students, and the rules they set for interactions between students communicates something about the worth and dignity that others are due. The suggestion of one writer who described how crib notes can be thought of and used as a learning device (Whitworth, 1990) seems relevant at this point. So does the decision of the Lake Forest, Illinois School District, which, in the wake of a cheating scandal in which a principal was accused of cheating (see chap. 4) simply decided to phase out some of the district's testing (Silverman, 1992). We must wonder about the impact on students of redefining dishonesty as nobility. According to the president of the Josephson Institute for Ethics, "when we are not so serious, when we give warnings, we shake our fingers and go 'tsk, tsk,' the fact of the matter is we have created a culture where cheating is not regarded as a very serious offense" (Stansbury, 1997a, p. 1).

I believe that all of us who give tests—indeed, all educators, parents, and others concerned about cheating—can, if they choose, make a significant impact in the area of promoting ethical behavior simply by virtue of our own personal actions and the extent to which we stand firm in our individual resolve to model and defend ethical behavior. Even the most profound alterations in attitudes toward cheating and testing will be irrelevant if attitudinal changes are not reflected in behavioral changes. Conversely, I believe that the most significant strides toward improving ethical behavior in students will follow concrete manifestations of our own commitment to and unashamed public defense of virtuous behavior.

I conclude this book by concurring with the an answer to this big-picture issue offered by Saltman (1996). I believe that his advice provides a firm starting point for addressing cheating specifically and, more important, for meaningful education reform generally:

> All of us are in continuous search for human models. Our students are desperate to find intellectual and humane heroes. We owe that to them. Be we can only be effective when we have fulfilled our moral and ethical obligations to ourselves. (p. 5)

✦ A P P E N D I X   A ✦

Statistical Methods for Detecting Cheating

T his appendix is provided for readers who are interested in other statistical methods used to detect cheating, as well as those who seek additional technical information regarding how various copying indices are calculated. However, in keeping with the general style and audience of this book, an attempt has been made to retain a readable exposition. Although the following sections provide additional depth and breadth of coverage, the most complete source of information for any of the methods described is the literature cited. Readers who are interested in additional detail should consult the original works.

MODERN FOUNDATIONS
OF STATISTICAL DETECTION

The science and practice of statistical methods for detecting cheating have progressed substantially since the earliest methods introduced by Bird (1927) and Saupe (1960). In fact, the technology of statistical detection has advanced to the point that several dependable and accurate methods are now available. An introduction to methods introduced since 1960 is provided in the following sections.

Angoff's Methods

One of the most important contributions to statistical detection methods was made by Angoff (1974). Angoff developed and evaluated eight indices (which he labeled A through H) using variables such as the numbers of identical incorrect responses or identical correct responses as dependent variables. Angoff also tried using outcomes, such as number of common omissions, the longest common "run" of incorrect responses, and others. He used the same set of independent variables as Saupe had used, although he expanded these as well and applied his indices to data from the SAT.

Evaluating the eight indices he proposed, Angoff (1974) concluded that the B and H indices performed satisfactorily:

> Empirical tryout of the indices against known and admitted copiers permitted the elimination of three of the indices from further use. Practical considerations removed a fourth, and further statistical study eliminated two others. The remaining two [i.e., B and H] have been in operational use at Educational Testing Service for more than two years. (p. 49)

Formulas for computing each of Angoff's indices are available in his 1974 publication. The approaches are related in that each constructs bivariate distributions of differing combinations of variables, then tests whether a suspected examinee's performance deviates significantly from the mean of the observations conditioning on some function of the examinees' overall performance. For example, Angoff's B index is computed in the following manner. First, the bivariate distribution of two variables, $W_i W_j$ and Q_{ij}, is constructed for all test takers, where $W_i W_j$ is the number of items answered incorrectly by one test taker, i, times the number of items answers incorrectly by another test taker, j; and Q_{ij} is the number of items for which test takers i and j answered incorrectly by choosing the identical incorrect response. For a pair of test takers, Examinee A and Examinee B, specific values of Q_{ij} and $W_i W_j$ are calculated, symbolized Q_{ab} and $W_a W_b$, respectively. The distribution of Q_{ij}s is then examined at the interval of $W_i W_j$ corresponding to $W_a W_b$. A statistical test can then be performed to assess whether the observed value of Q_{ab} for the suspected pair of copiers is significantly different from the mean value of Q_{ij} using the following formula:

$$t = (Q_{ab} - Q_{ij}) / S_{Qij/WiWj} \tag{1}$$

Examination of Angoff's B index reveals an important innovation that would mark future developments in statistical methods: Rather than using all students in an analysis, Angoff (1993) proposed stratifying students according to their total scores. In a subsequent paper, he provided a straightforward rationale for such an approach:

> The restriction of the norm group to those scoring at the same level as the source [i.e., the person copied from] is made simply because the score level, obviously, coerces the number of incorrect responses. For example, if the source answered only 10 items incorrectly, then the number of identically marked incorrect responses by the suspected copier and the source cannot be greater than 10. Clearly, the significance of 8 such responses when the limit is 10 is different from its significance when the limit is, say 30. (p. 6)

ESA

Cody (1985) and Bellezza and Bellezza (1989) proposed procedures that are related to Anikeef's (1954) procedure using the binomial distribution. Bellezza and Bellezza's method, referred to as ESA, has achieved some popular attention, in part due to its use in the commercially available software program designed to detect cheating described in chapter 7. The following summary of the ESA approach closely follows Bellezza and Bellezza's original description of the method.

The ESA method begins by calculating, for each item, the number of times all pairs of examinees chose the same incorrect answer. On a five-option multiple-choice item, when all four incorrect options are selected by equal proportions of examinees, the probability of two examinees selecting the same wrong answer, under an assumption of random guessing, is .25. However, because all incorrect options are rarely equally plausible, the probability of an identical error is usually closer to .40. Under the ESA approach, the probability associated with a given number of common errors is shown by Equation 2:

$$[N! / (k!)(N - k)!]P^k(1 - P)^{N-k}, \tag{2}$$

where k is the number of common items a pair of examinees answered incorrectly, N is the number of items for which they had the same incorrect response, and P is as described above.

Bellezza and Bellezza (1989) illustrated the use of the ESA method in the case of two examinees, X and Y, who take a 60-item test composed of five-option multiple-choice items. Further, Examinee X makes 25 errors, and Examinee Y makes 23 errors, 20 of their errors were on the same items, and for 18 of the 20 errors they chose the same incorrect option. The probability of Students X and Y choosing 18 or more identical incorrect answers is found by using the following equation:

$$[(20!) / (18!)(2!)][(.40^{18})(.60^2)] + [(20!) / (19!)(1!)][(.40^{19})(.60^1)] +$$
$$[(20!) / (20!)(0!)][(.40^{20})(.60^0)] = .000004700 + 000000330 + .000000011$$
$$= .000005031.$$

This value shows that the probability of 18 or more identical incorrect responses is approximately 5 in 1 million. Bellezza and Bellezza also demonstrated a computationally simpler approximation using the standard normal distribution, which yields highly similar results.

Frary et al.'s Methods

In 1977, two indices of answer copying were introduced by Frary et al. Continuing the trend of using more of the available information from examinees' responses to items, Frary et al. based their indices on the total number of identical responses for each pair of examinees. The indices, which they called g_1 and g_2, are based on estimation of probabilities that an examinee would select any possible response, including correct, incorrect, and omitted answers. The g_1 index was designed to test the null hypothesis that the observed number of common responses for any pair of examinees was likely due to chance; however, as described later, subsequent evaluation of the performance of g_1 led Frary et al. to discourage its use. The g_2 index is intended to be applied when one specific examinee is suspected of copying from another. A complete illustration showing the computation of g_2 is beyond the intended scope of this book; however, the straightforward introduction to the principle underlying g_2 presented by Frary and Tideman (1997) will assist the reader in its conceptualization:

> Determination of g_2 involves considering one examinee as the potential copier and the other as the source. Option popularity and the potential copier's score are used to estimate for each item, i, the probability, p_i, of selecting the source's answer. Then Σp_i estimates the expected number of the source's (right and wrong) answers selected (in the absence of copying) by the potential copier. Also, $[\Sigma p_i (1 - p_i)]^2$ estimates the standard deviation of the observed number of identical answers.... Two g_2s are produced for each pair of examinees, one to test the hypothesis that the first copied from the second and another to test the opposite hypothesis. (p. 21)

Frary et al. (1977) applied g_1 and g_2 to data from an actual examination and found that g_2 was superior to g_1 in part because g_1 identified fewer instances of likely copying. The authors also commented on the key role of overall test difficulty—which can be manipulated by test makers—noting that "if no examinees can answer as many as 90 percent correctly, the potential for detection is greatly enhanced" (p. 253). However, they also observed that two factors associated with values of g_2 that would flag suspicion of cheating were potentially under the control of the examinee:

> The first factor is the amount of copying. Obviously, very small-scale copying (one or two items) will have little effect, though copying over 70 percent of the answers makes detection quite likely. The second factor is the choice of the examinee from whom to copy. For example, if a moderately good student copies extensively from someone who gets over 90 percent correct, a relatively low g may well result. (p. 253)

NBME Methods

Two methods of detecting copying are described in a pamphlet produced by the NBME, an organization responsible for numerous testing programs in the medical and health-related professions. Like other large-scale testing companies, NBME relies on nonstatistical triggers to initiate statistical investigation of potential cheating. According to NBME (1988) policies,

> upon receipt of an irregularity report or other information suggesting that irregular behavior has occurred, NBME staff will evaluate the information and, if indicated, conduct statistical analysis ... and gather other information designed to verify (confirm or disconfirm) the suspected behavior. (pp. 5–6)

Two statistical methods for detecting cheating have been described by NBME. The first approach is called an adjacent–nonadjacent analysis and is designed to detect whether the responses of one examinee are likely to have been copied from another examinee seated nearby. The approach is similar to that described by Schumacher (1980), who suggested a chi-square technique to evaluate the likelihood of independence of identical and nonidentical responses when examinees take a test in two parts.

The adjacent–nonadjacent analysis method requires specific test construction and test administration conditions; consequently, it cannot be implemented in situations in which these design considerations have not been implemented. The first design consideration requires that an examination be developed to consist of at least two parts. Each part should be as equivalent as possible in terms of content coverage, difficulty, and so on. Each part is administered in separate testing sessions, and test takers are randomly assigned to seat locations for each session. For example, a 300-item test might consist of two components, administered as one 150-item booklet of items in a morning testing session, followed by a break, and a second 150-item booklet of items in an afternoon session. As described by NBME (1988):

> given these pre-conditions, one would expect the response patterns of any two examinees who take the examination independently to agree with each other to about the same extent on all sections of the test, regardless of where the two examinees might be seated in the testing room.... If the two examinees are seated adjacently during one or more sections of the test and a substantially greater degree of agreement is found in their response patterns for such sections than would be expected on the basis of their performance when seated apart, it is difficult to maintain that their test-taking behavior was independent when they were seated adjacently and it is also difficult to provide a reasonable explanation for such results other than copying. (pp. 9–10)

The adjacent–nonadjacent method analyzes agreement between the examinees' responses to items they answered incorrectly. A 2×2 chi-square test for independence is performed using the data shown in Table A.1.

The chi-square test statistic is calculated as shown in Equation 3, and is compared with a tabled critical value with a predetermined alpha level and 1 degree of freedom.

$$\chi^2 = (a + b + c + d)[(ad) - (bc)]^2 / (a + b)(a + c)(b + d)(c + d) \qquad (3)$$

The second method referenced by NBME, called an *agreement analysis*, is another approach based on the binomial distribution or, in this case, the normal approximation to the binomial expansion. The method is used when one examinee is suspected of copying from a second examinee. The focus of this approach is again on the likelihood that identical responses to items answered incorrectly were ar-

TABLE A.1
Adjacent–Nonadjacent Test for Independence of Responses

Examinees' Seating Location	Number of Items Answered Incorrectly		
	Same Option Selected	*Different Options Selected*	*Total*
Adjacent	a	b	(a + b)
Nonadjacent	c	d	(c + d)
Total	(a + c)	(b + d)	(a + b + c + d)

rived at independently by the two examinees. The formula for the test statistic is shown in Equation 4, and the critical values for the test statistic are taken from a table of areas under the standard normal distribution:

$$Z = (a - pN) \: / \: [(Npq)^2],$$ (4)

where a is the total number of items answered incorrectly for which the two examinees chose the same incorrect response, p is the probability that the two examinees would choose identical incorrect answers independently, N is the total number of items answered incorrectly by the two examinees, and $q = (1 - p)$.

The calculation of p (i.e., the probability that the two examinees would choose identical incorrect answers independently) is based on the observed proportion of examinees selecting the particular incorrect option; these proportions are averaged across all N items answered incorrectly by the two examinees under study. Finally, the second NBME procedure requires that an appropriate comparison group be identified for calculating p. The use of other test takers from the same school, a sample of test takers who obtained total scores similar to the suspected copier, or another reasonably large group that took the test independently is recommended (NBME, 1988, p. 14).

Other Methods

Assorted other indices have been proposed, although evaluation has shown most of them to be impractical or unreliable and are not in widespread use (see, e.g., Aiken, 1991, Harpp & Hogan, 1993, 1996; Houston, 1976b). For example, one approach, called the *score-difference method*, was described by D. M. Roberts (1987):

> This "score-difference" method is applied when alternate test forms, with different answer keys, are administered in the same room without the direct knowledge of the examinees. The procedure involves (a) scoring each answer document using the key appropriate to the examinee's form, (b) scoring the answer document using the alternative, inappropriate keys, and (c) finding the difference between the scores obtained from the appropriate and inappropriate keys. A large difference, especially upward, is taken as evidence of cheating. (p. 77)

Neither the score-difference method nor the other methods mentioned in this section have received much attention in the literature, nor are they widely used (if at all). An evaluation of the accuracy of the score-difference method led D. M. Roberts (1987) to conclude that it "is seriously flawed and has little to recommend it" (p. 77).

Comparisons of the Commonly Used Methods

In addition to the initial evaluation of g_2 conducted by Frary et al. (1977), Frary and Tideman (1997) compared the performance of g_2 and Angoff's B index. In a study using actual test data, Frary and Tideman found that, of 82 pairs of likely copiers identified by g_2 or B, the two indices agreed on only 43 of them. Further, they found that B tended to be more effective in identifying higher scoring pairs of copiers and g_2 to be more effective at flagging potential copying by lower scoring pairs. Bay (1994) compared a new method based on compound binomial probabilities, which she called B_m with g_2 and ESA, using both real and simulated data sets. Bay showed that, on the basis of the indices' ability to detect "true positives" (i.e., real instances of cheating), all three methods were ineffective at detecting cheating in situations where 25% or less of the total number of items had been copied. However, for percentages of copying involving more than 25% of the total number of items, B_m and g_2 were about equally effective, whereas ESA was less effective than either of the other two methods by a substantial margin.

Hanson et al. (1987) compared seven indices under various simulated cheating conditions (e.g., random copying, copying strings of items of varying length, and copying only difficult items). The indices compared included g_2, B, H, Cody's (1985) method, and three other previously untested indices. Cody's method, which is similar to that of Bellezza and Bellezza (1989), was found to be least satisfactory for detecting copying. One of the new indices, a hybrid approach called CP, was judged to be best. However, Hanson et al. (1987) observed that, overall, the differences were minimal, concluding that,

> for the type of simulated copying thought to be most realistic the methods do not differ greatly in performance, and approximately 5%, 20%, 50%, 85% and 95% of the simulated copiers who copied 10%, 20%, 30%, 40%, and 50% of the items, respectively, could be detected with a false positive rate of .001. (p. iii)

RECENT INNOVATIONS IN STATISTICAL DETECTION

The most recent innovations in detecting answer copying rely on the psychometric scaling model called IRT. Under specified circumstances, IRT methods can be used to estimate the relative difficulty and other characteristics of test items, independent of the sample of examinees attempting those items, and the relative ability of examinees, independent of the particular sample of items they attempt. (For a thorough introduction to IRT, readers should consult other sources, such as Hambleton and Swaminathan, 1985 or Lord, 1980.) IRT estimates an examinee's underlying ability (symbolized θ, or "theta" in IRT) on the basis of the examinee's responses to all items on a test and the characteristics of those items (e.g., estimates of the items' difficulty levels, called b values in IRT). According to IRT, an examinee is likely to answer items correctly for which his or her estimated ability (i.e., θ) exceeds the item's difficulty and is likely to respond incorrectly on items for which the difficulty exceeded θ.[1]

One application of IRT is called *appropriateness measurement*.[2] Appropriateness measurement refers to evaluations of how well a chosen IRT model fits the responses given by an examinee (see M. V. Levine & Rubin, 1979). In theory, a person should tend to answer correctly those items for which the examinee's ability (θ) exceeds the difficulty level of the item (b). When such a pattern of performance over

---

[1]There are many subtleties of IRT that are ignored here. For example, the preceding discussion presumes that guessing is not a factor. Readers are again urged to consult the cited sources on IRT for a more complete discussion of these and other issues related to IRT.

[2]Anoher term for appropriateness measurement is *detection of aberrant response patterns*. As I have observed elsewhere (Cizek, 1996), with admitted incidence of cheating approaching 90%, it seems difficult, conceptually, to call copying "aberrant behavior." Given the high rates of admitted cheating, it is possible that a student who copies answers from a person he or she is seated next to has copied from a student who has, in turn, copied from another student.

all items in a test occurs, the person is said to "fit" the IRT model; the person's performance is considered appropriate given his or her ability level. So-called aberrant response patterns would include the responses of an examinee whose score was lower than would be predicted on the basis of his or her estimated ability level and the responses of an examinee whose score was higher than would be predicted (although, in cases of suspected cheating, only the latter case would usually arouse interest). The second type of aberrant response pattern could occur if a test taker copied and, as a result, answered very difficult items correctly (i.e., the examinee responded to items in a way that was incongruent with his or her ability estimate). Such a person's performance would not fit the IRT model well. Appropriateness measurement involves computation of an index for each examinee to describe how well his or her performance fits the model. Examination of these person-fit indices for all test takers can be used to detect cheating.

Early applications of the least sophisticated IRT model (i.e., the Rasch, or one-parameter logistic model) to the practical problem of cheating were somewhat disappointing. For example, Madsen (1987) used Rasch person-fit measures to investigate whether they might be used to identify highly able impersonators who take examinations for others and who try to avoid arousing suspicion by "faking bad" on some test items. Madsen's work showed that Rasch person-fit measures had little promise for use in this context, although he suggested that they might be used to detect other forms of cheating. However, subsequent investigations of the person-fit measures to detect cheating have demonstrated the inadequacy of this approach (see, e.g., Chason & Maller, 1996; Iwamoto, Nungester, & Luecht, 1996). Because any number of factors unrelated to cheating can result in poor person-fit (e.g., guessing, differential exposure to curriculum, or item characteristics), and because the statistical significance of person-fit indices does not depend on the similarity of responses between a suspected copier and another test taker, this method of investigating cheating has essentially been abandoned.

A second IRT-based approach has recently been introduced by Wollack (1996, 1997). Wollack's index, symbolized ω (omega), provides a way of detecting cheating that does so by identifying examinee response patterns that do not fit the underlying IRT model. Nonfitting response patterns would include cases in which the examinee's correct responses occur on items for which, given the examinee's estimated ability, correct responses would be highly improbable.

Wollack's index uses the same basic conceptualization as the index developed by Frary et al. (1977) and the derivation of ω closely parallels that of g_2 (see Wollack, 1997, pp. 307–311). However, calculation of g_2 involves estimation of the probability of a suspected copier selecting each option for an item; these estimates are calculated on the basis of the item difficulties, option difficulties, and the ratio of the suspected copier's total score to the overall mean score on the test. Wollack noted that this estimation process assumes that option discrimination values are constant across all ability levels. To address this concern, ω is calculated using an IRT approach called the *nominal response model* (Bock, 1972), in which estimates of the probability of a test taker selecting each of the options for a test item take into account that examinee's ability level.

Using simulated data, Wollack (1997) compared ω, g_2, and a variation of g_2, using sample sizes of 100 and 500 and test lengths of 40 and 80 five-option items. Item parameters were estimated from samples of approximately 20,000 examinees' responses to the items in an actual administration; these item parameters were then treated as known and used to generate item responses with ability distributed normally. Copying was simulated in three ways (random copying, copying of items of greater difficulty, and copying of strings of four consecutive responses) and in varying proportions (10%, 20%, 30%, and 40% of the total number of items), with the percentage of examinees copying held constant at 5%. The three indices were evaluated on the basis of their ability to detect true copying and Type I error rates (i.e., false identifications of copying). Wollack (1979) concluded that "$\tilde{\omega}$ was better for detecting answer copying, under all conditions simulated here, than [the other indices]. $\tilde{\omega}$ controlled the Type I error rate under all conditions ... [and] regardless of the type of copying, on an 80-item test, $\tilde{\omega}$ had good power to detect examinees who copied at least 20% of the items ... [whereas] on a 40-item test, $\tilde{\omega}$ had good power to detect examinees who copied at least 30% of the items" (p. 318). Wollack also found that, consistent with Frary et al.'s (1977) findings, the Type I error rate for g_2 tended to increase as sample size increased, although inflation in Type I error rate for g_2 observed in Wollack's simulation was not as great as that resulting from the simulation reported by Hanson et al. (1987).

In contrast to the prevalence of simulation studies, a study by Chason (1997) compared $\tilde{\omega}$ with other detection indices using the actual responses of 1,000 examinees on an 80-item certification test and with simulated copying papers inserted into the sample. Chason compared $\tilde{\omega}$, g_2, and the ESA approaches and found that $\tilde{\omega}$ and g_2 performed similarly, detecting 72% and 73% of the copying pairs, respectively. However, in nine varying conditions, the ESA procedure failed to identify cheating in three of them; in the other six conditions, ESA identified less than 20% of the cheating pairs.

CONCLUSIONS

A number of statistical methods exist for detecting cheating—copying, to be specific—on tests. Although several of the methods that have been proposed lack technical adequacy, a number of them have survived careful evaluation by those within the psychometric profession. Among the more recently introduced methods, both Frary et al.'s g_2 and Wollack's $\tilde{\omega}$ index provide defensible, reasonably accurate methods for identifying copying on tests. Use of either method involves a trade-off: Whereas $\tilde{\omega}$ offers better control of Type I error rate, g_2 detected a slightly greater proportion of copiers.

Regardless of the method selected, the issue of what weight to ascribe to statistical evidence remains. Even the best statistical evidence may be discounted by those with a dislike for any type of quantitative analysis or a distaste for detecting cheating by any method whatsoever. In light of these concerns, and other technical issues, statistical methods should be used primarily as supportive evidence to back up a suspicion of cheating, as opposed to being used as a screening tool or sole source of evidence.[3] Although statistical detection methods have found broad use in large-scale testing programs, they are not widely used in other testing contexts. This neglect is partially attributable to the affective stance toward cheating detection described earlier, as well as to technical limitations in current methods.

---

[3]Statistical methods also can be used to prevent cheating. For example, Frary has suggested that "pairs identified as likely copiers using only statistical methods can be observed systematically on subsequent tests ... [or] a pair can be advised privately of the high statistic and advised not to sit next to each other on subsequent tests" (R. B. Frary, personal communication, October 1988).

On the technical side, IRT-based approaches such as $\hat{\omega}$ require either known item parameters or sufficiently large numbers of examinees for calibration of items. Even in college classes with as many as 100 or more test takers, standard errors of item parameter and ability estimates would be disconcertingly large. This limitation of the state-of-the-art methods using IRT precludes their use in most classroom testing situations, although subsequent research by Wollack and Cohen (1998) found that $\hat{\omega}$ can detect copying when item parameters must be estimated from samples as small as 100 on tests of 40 to 80 items.

On the other hand, it is doubtful that, even in contexts with sufficient sample sizes, the best of the current detection methods could overcome the affective resistance of many test givers. These two issues—one a public relations problem and one a technical matter—will probably be the battlefields for future developments in statistical detection.

✦ APPENDIX B ✦

Academic Integrity Policy Models

SAMPLE 1[1]

An essential dimension of [*insert institution's name*] mission is to provide higher education for the intellectual, social, physical, emotional, and spiritual development of students. Faculty, students, and administrators share responsibility for accomplishing these goals. Academic integrity means honesty concerning all aspects of academic performance. Academic integrity must be fully integrated into the campus' academic environment, including norms for student life and classroom expectations. Integration is best accomplished when faculty members (faculty) and students understand and accept [*insert institution's name*] standards of academic behavior, and when the standards are uniformly and fairly enforced.

Faculty authority over the classroom and grades includes the primary charge to communicate principles of academic integrity and the consequences of academic misconduct. Expectations should be clear and the classroom should be managed to support them. Faculty need to know the following enforcement system. They are obligated to use it when academic dishonesty occurs. Enforcement supports honest students and promotes our commitment to academic integrity.

---

[1]From Risacher and Slonaker (1996). Reprinted with permission.

Students must not cheat or plagiarize. Also, they must not condone these behaviors or assist others who cheat or plagiarize. Academic misconduct not only
jeopardizes the career of the individual student involved, but it also undermines
the scholastic achievements of all students, and attacks the mission of the institution. Students are inherently responsible to do their own work, thereby insuring
the integrity of their academic records.

What Is Academic Dishonesty?

Academic dishonesty is as broad as the human imagination. The most common
forms of academic dishonesty are cheating and plagiarism.

Cheating includes:
A. submitting material that is not yours as part of your course performance,
   such as copying from another student's exam, allowing a student to copy
   from your exam; or,
B. using information or devices that are not allowed by the faculty; such as
   using formulas or data from a computer program, or using unauthorized
   materials for a take-home exam; or,
C. obtaining and using unauthorized material, such as a copy of an examination before it is given; or,
D. fabricating information, such as data for a lab report; or,
E. violating procedures prescribed to protect the integrity of an assignment,
   test, or other evaluation; or,
F. collaborating with others on assignments without the faculty's consent; or,
G. cooperating with or helping another student to cheat; or,
H. other forms of dishonest behavior, such as having another person take an
   examination in your place; or, altering exam answers and requesting the
   exam be regraded; or, communicating with any person during an exam,
   other than the exam proctor or faculty.

Plagiarism includes:

A. directly quoting the words of others without using quotation marks or in-
   dented format to identify them; or,
B. using sources of information (published or unpublished) without identifying them; or,
C. paraphrasing materials or ideas of others without identifying the sources.

If you are unsure about something that you want to do or the proper use of materials, then ask the faculty for clarification.

Resolution of Academic Dishonesty Matters

When a faculty member has reasonable cause to believe that a student has committed an act of academic dishonesty, the faculty member shall meet with the student
as soon as reasonably possible to discuss and attempt to resolve the incident. If after talking with the student, or when the student fails to meet with the faculty
member, and the faculty still believes that academic dishonesty occurred, the fac-

ulty member will assign a penalty grade. When the penalty grade is an "F" for the course, the faculty member will notify the registrar's office that the student cannot withdraw or drop the class. The final grade for the course will not be recorded by the Registrar until the date for the student to request a hearing, or appealing the decision, has passed. Students requesting a hearing, or appealing a decision shall be permitted to attend and fully participate in the course until the process is complete. The faculty may also refer the matter for disciplinary action, as discussed in the section captioned *Penalties*.

The faculty will notify the student in writing of the faculty's decision and of the student's right to a formal hearing before the Academic Dishonesty Hearing Panel (ADHP). The written notice will be either personally delivered to the student or mailed via regular U.S. mail to the student's most recent local address. The faculty will submit a copy of the letter and a confidential report of the incident to the Chair of the faculty's department, the dean of the college, and the [*insert title of chief student disciplinary officer*]. The confidential report shall outline the facts and circumstances of the academic dishonesty, including: the date, time, and location of the incident; a summary of what occurred; a description of any physical evidence, e.g., paper test, crib sheets; the names of other persons who witnessed the incident; and any other pertinent information.

Penalties

The minimum penalty grade for dishonesty in a term paper or final examination shall be an "F" for the course. Dishonesty in other required course work shall result in a minimum penalty grade of zero for that work.

When academic dishonesty includes flagrant behavior, such as having a substitute take an exam, or stealing an exam, then the faculty also shall refer the matter to the [*insert title of chief student disciplinary officer*] for disciplinary action pursuant to the Student Code of Conduct. The [*insert title of chief student disciplinary officer*] may initiate disciplinary action against a student with repeated academic dishonesty violations.

Academic Dishonesty Hearing Panel (ADHP)

Composition

The ADHP shall include five members, three faculty and two students. The faculty members shall be appointed/elected by [*insert name of faculty governance body*], for one-year terms. Additionally, there will be one faculty and one student alternate, determined in the same manner as the regular members. A faculty Chair for the ADHP shall be selected by the members of the ADHP.

Jurisdiction

The jurisdiction of the ADHP will be to conduct hearings of academic dishonesty decisions made by faculty. A student who has received such a penalty may request a hearing by submitting a written request as soon as reasonably possible, but not to exceed 14 calendar days after the faculty's written notice was personally delivered or mailed to the student.

Actions

After the hearing, the ADHP may find that academic dishonesty occurred, in which case the penalty imposed by the faculty will be affirmed; or, may find that academic misconduct did not occur, in which case the penalty imposed by the faculty member will be rescinded. Excepting, the ADHP may reduce the penalty if they find that the penalty was arbitrary, too severe, or blatantly harsh. If the penalty is rescinded, the faculty will grade the subject work, i.e., the exam, paper, project, etc., on its academic merit.

Procedural Guidelines

The ADHP shall establish its own operating procedures. While they need not be formal, they shall assure fundamental due process is provided, recognizing that a student is innocent until proven otherwise. Fundamental due process includes the following rights:

- notice of the charge, including sufficient detail to inform the student about the nature and facts of the incident;
- notice of who will present information at the hearing;
- reasonable notice of the hearing (including one continuance for good cause, at the request of the student);
- a copy of any ADHP established procedures;
- to have an individual hearing if more than one student is charged;
- to be present at the hearing;
- to face the faculty or other accuser;
- to be heard and present information;
- to an advisor;
- to question all those presenting information;
- to call on others to present information;
- to remain silent;
- to an impartial decision;
- to timely notice of the decision;
- to a record of the proceedings;
- to appeal.

The Chair of the ADHP will respond to questions about the ADHP's established procedures, and may decide procedural matters not already established by the ADHP, all with or without the advice of the other members. Otherwise, a majority vote of the five members will decide a procedural question. The Chair is the designated spokesperson for the ADHP, and is responsible for all communication on behalf of the ADHP.

A hearing will be open unless the student requests that it be closed. In an open hearing, the ADHP may limit attendance due to limitations of the physical facility, to exclude disruptive individuals, or otherwise to promote an atmosphere conducive to due process.

ADHP decisions affirming a penalty will be based on a preponderance of the evidence and a majority affirmative vote. The Chair of the ADHP will vote only to break a tie. The student may have an advisor assist with all aspects of the hearing. An advisor may be a student, a staff, a faculty, or other person, excepting a practicing attorney.

An audio record of the proceedings will be made. The ADHP shall furnish to the student written notice of its decision and the student's appeal rights. The ADHP's file of the hearing and the recording shall be retained by the [*insert title of chief student disciplinary officer*].

Student Appeals

A student may appeal an ADHP decision to the [*insert name of institution's appeals board*] according to the appeal process established in the Student Code of Conduct. [*Note: if there is no institutional appeal board, the authors suggest that the appeal be made to either the chief academic affairs officer or to the president.*]

SAMPLE 2[2]

Code of Academic Integrity

Academic dishonesty is a serious offense at the university because it undermines the bonds of trust and honesty between members of the community and defrauds those who may eventually depend upon our knowledge and integrity. Such dishonesty consists of:

Cheating
Intentionally using or attempting to use unauthorized materials, information, or study aids in any academic exercise.
Fabrication
Intentional and unauthorized falsification or invention of any information or citation in an academic exercise.

Intentionally or knowingly helping or attempting to help another to violate any provision of this *Code*.
Plagiarism
Intentionally or knowingly representing the words or ideas of another as one's own in any academic exercise.

Procedures

1. A faculty member who suspects that a student has committed an act of academic dishonesty shall:

   (a) so inform the student and [a designated administrative officer] in writing on the standard form established for that purpose; and
   (b) if authorized by [the administrative officer], accord the student an opportunity for a personal meeting to discuss the allegation and to present relevant evidence, in accordance with procedures set forth in part 3 of this *Code*.

---

[2]From Kibler, Nuss, Paterson, and Pavela (1988). Footnotes omitted; reprinted with permission.

2. Prior to authorizing a faculty member to resolve a case, [the designated administrative officer] shall agree to meet with an accused student, upon the student's timely request, in order to review pertinent procedures. In any event, [the designated administrator] will retain discretionary authority to refer a case for a hearing, to modify or clarify the charges, or to hear the case informally, consistent with the procedures and sanctions specified for cases resolved by faculty members, as set forth in parts 3–5. Hearing referrals may be made in contested or complicated cases, or upon the faculty member's request, or for other good cause. A referral to a hearing must be made if a student is subject to suspension or expulsion, or in any case in which a student makes a timely written request for a hearing. A request for a hearing will be timely if submitted in writing within ten business days after a student was given the notice required in part 1 (a) of this *Code*, either by personal delivery or by certified mail.

3. Proceedings in cases resolved by a faculty member, as specified in part 1 (b) of this *Code*, are informal and nonadversarial. The faculty member will provide the student with written notice of a scheduled meeting at least three days in advance. The purpose of the meeting will be to review and discuss the charges before a final decision is reached. Documentary evidence and written statements could be relied upon by the faculty member, as long as the student was allowed to respond to them at the meeting. Students may also be allowed to bring relevant witnesses, or be accompanied by parents or other advisors, in the sole discretion of the faculty member. Neither the faculty member nor the student will be represented by legal counsel.

4. A faculty member who is authorized to hear the case in accordance with part 3, and who determines that a student is responsible for an act of academic dishonesty, may take any of the following actions, which shall be promptly reported in writing to [the designated administrative officer], along with a brief written statement of reasons for finding the student responsible for the offense:

   (a) impose additional course requirements, including repetition of the work in question;
   (b) impose a grade of F;
   (c) impose a grade of XF, as specified in part 10 of this *Code*.

   A student found responsible for any act of academic dishonesty will also be left with a disciplinary record, which shall be maintained in accordance with policies established for all disciplinary cases. The record may be voided if the student successfully completes the university sponsored academic integrity seminar, as specified in part 10 of this *Code*, and is not found responsible for any subsequent disciplinary offense.

5. Except for the XF grade penalty, penalties imposed in accordance with parts 2 and 4 of this *Code* shall be final and conclusive and not subject to appeal within the university disciplinary system.

6. Students subject to the XF penalty, when imposed in accordance with parts 2 and 4 of this *Code*, may file a timely appeal with the Student Honor Council. An appeal will not be timely if it is received more than ten business days after the student has been given written notice of the penalty, either by personal delivery or certified mail. The Student

Honor Council will consider only written appeals, in accordance with the following standards—

(a) The XF penalty may be rescinded if it is determined to be grossly disproportionate to the offense.
(b) The case may be remanded for a hearing, in accordance with parts 7 and 8, if a deviation from the procedures specified in this *Code* were so substantial as to deny the student the fundamental requirements of due process, as defined by the courts in cases of academic discipline at institutions of higher education.

7. Students referred for a hearing shall be so notified in writing either by personal delivery or by certified mail, and will be provided with a statement specifying the charge(s). Students referred for a hearing are subject to the full range of disciplinary sanctions, including suspension or expulsion, as well as the penalties specified in part 4 of this *Code*.

8. The following procedural guidelines are applicable in academic dishonesty hearings—

(a) Students shall be informed of the hearing date and the specific charges against them at least ten days in advance.
(b) Cases shall be resolved by a hearing board administered by the [chief academic or student affairs officer]. The board will include two faculty members appointed by the [designated administrative officer] and three members of the student honor council, as provided in part 12 of this *Code*. An ad hoc board composed of two students and one faculty member may be selected by [the designated administrative officer] if it is determined that a regular hearing board cannot be convened in time to resolve a pending case promptly.
(c) A non-voting hearing officer will preside. Hearing officers shall exercise control over the proceedings to avoid needless consumption of time and to achieve the orderly completion of the hearing.
(d) The accused student may be assisted by an advisor, who may be an attorney. The role of advisors will be limited to:

(1) making a brief, relevant opening statement;
(2) suggesting relevant questions which will be directed by the hearing officer to any witnesses;
(3) providing confidential advice to the accused student;
(4) making brief, relevant statements as to any appropriate sanction to be imposed.

(e) The complainant shall be an administrative officer, designated by the university, who may not be a licensed attorney or a law school graduate.
(f) Hearings will be closed to the public, except for the immediate members of the accused student's family and for the accused student's advisor. An open hearing may be held, in the discretion of the hearing officer, if requested by the accused student.
(g) Any person, including the accused student, who disrupts a hearing or who fails to adhere to the rulings of the hearing officer may be excluded from the proceeding.

(h) Hearings shall be tape recorded or transcribed.

(i) Prospective witnesses, other than the complainant and the accused student, may be excluded from the hearing during the testimony of other witnesses. All parties, the witnesses, and the public shall be excluded during panel deliberations.

(j) The burden of proof shall be on the complainant, who must establish the guilt of the accused student by clear and convincing evidence.

(k) Formal rules of evidence shall not be applicable. The hearing officer shall give effect to the rules of confidentiality and privilege, but shall otherwise admit all matters into evidence which reasonable persons would accept as having probative value in the conduct of their affairs. Unduly repetitious or irrelevant evidence may be excluded.

(l) Accused students shall be accorded an opportunity to question those witnesses who testify for the complainant at the hearing.

(m) Affidavits shall not be admitted into evidence unless signed by the affiant and witnessed by a university employee.

(n) A determination of guilt shall be followed by a supplemental proceeding in which either party may submit evidence or make statements concerning the appropriate sanction to be imposed. The past disciplinary record of the accused student shall not be supplied to the panel prior to the supplementary proceeding.

(o) The final decision of the board shall be by a majority vote.

(p) The board will provide a brief, written statement of reasons for finding a student responsible for an offense.

9. The decision of the hearing board will be a recommendation to the [chief academic or student affairs officer]. Students will be provided with a copy of the board's decision by personal delivery or by certified mail, and will have five business days after receiving the decision to provide written comments to the [chief academic or student affairs officer]. Subsequent action taken by the [chief academic or student affairs officer] shall be final and conclusive and not subject to further appeal within the university disciplinary system.

10. The XF grade penalty specified in part 4 (c) shall be recorded on the transcript with the notation "failure due to academic dishonesty." The XF symbol may be removed, and permanently replaced with a grade of F, upon the student's written petition to the Student Honor Council. Such a petition may not be granted if the student has been found responsible for any other disciplinary offense, and will not be granted until the student has successfully completed a regularly scheduled non-credit seminar on academic integrity and moral development. All other student records pertaining to academic dishonesty will be voided in accordance with procedures established for student disciplinary cases. No student with the XF grade on the transcript will be permitted to represent the university in any extra-curricular activity, or run for or hold office in any recognized student organization.

11. A reasonable administrative fee, as established by the Student Honor Council and approved by [a designated administrative officer], will be charged to students found responsible for academic dishonesty or other

comparable disciplinary offenses. The Student Honor council may waive the fee, and substitute a community service assignment, upon petition.

12. A student honor council consisting of twelve members shall be established. Seven members of the council will be appointed by campus honorary societies and organizations designated by the [chief academic officer], in consultation with the president of the student government association. Designated student organizations will include organizations representing commuter students, residential students, students residing in fraternities and sororities, and other organizations which promote racial, cultural, and other forms of diversity on campus. The five remaining members of the council shall be selected in accordance with procedures established by the [chief student affairs officer].

The honor council has the following powers and responsibilities:

(a) To develop its own bylaws and procedures, subject to approval by the [chief academic or student affairs officer] for legal sufficiency, and compliance with the standards set by this *Code*;

(b) to serve on and constitute a majority of the university hearing board, as specified in part 8 (b) of this *Code*. Appointments to the board shall rotate among honor council members, in accordance with council bylaws;

(c) to hear appeals from cases not referred to a hearing, as provided in part 6;

(d) to review and make final decisions concerning petitions by students for removal of the XF grade penalty, as specified in part 10 of this *Code*;

(e) to establish the administrative fee, and to consider fee waiver petitions, in accordance with part 11 of this *Code*;

(f) to modify the procedural guidelines established in part 8 of this *Code*, subject to approval by the [chief academic or student affairs officer] for legal sufficiency and compliance with the other standards set by the *Code*. Two-thirds vote of all twelve council members shall be required before a proposed modification may be sent to [chief academic or student affairs officer] for final adoption;

(g) to review complaints of academic dishonesty which are either not referred to or not resolved by faculty members, in accordance with part 1. The review shall be conducted by a standing committee of three council members designated in accordance with council bylaws. If the standing committee determines that there is reasonable cause to believe that academic dishonesty may have occurred, the matter shall be referred to the [designated administrative officer], in accordance with part 2 of this *Code*. Council members who review any case in accordance with this part shall not participate in any subsequent proceedings pertaining to the case;

(h) assisting in design and teaching of the non-credit seminar specified in part 10 of this *Code*;

(i) advising and consulting with faculty and administrative officers on matters related to academic integrity standards, policies and procedures;

(j) issuing an annual report to the campus community on academic integrity standard, policies, and procedures, including recommendations for appropriate changes;

(k) additional duties or responsibilities delegated by the [chief academic or student affairs officer].

13. Both faculty members and students share concurrent authority for reporting allegations of academic dishonesty, in accordance with this *Code*. Faculty members must remain responsible for examination security, and the proctoring of examinations.

14. All applicants for admission to undergraduate or graduate programs at the university, as well as all students registering for courses, will be expected to write an honor pledge as a condition of admission.

Sample Due Process Policy

DUE PROCESS STATEMENT[1]

A. Whenever a faculty member believes that a student has performed at a failing level or has exhibited unethical or unprofessional behavior, the faculty member shall inform the student of this concern and shall propose a means of remedying the situation. If the issue can be resolved in a mutually satisfactory manner, the matter need go no further. If either the student or the faculty member is not satisfied with the outcome of the discussion, either one may request an informal hearing after notifying the other party. This request should be made to the faculty representative directly responsible for that portion of the curriculum or to the appropriate steering committee.

B. An informal hearing shall be a private discussion held in the presence of an impartial third party appointed by the responsible faculty representative or steering committee and mutually agreed upon by the student and the faculty member. The purpose of this hearing is to work out a mutually satisfactory remedy with the help of the third party.

No record of the meeting need be kept except for any remedial plan devised. That plan shall become a permanent part of the student's file.

---

[1]From Anderson and Obenshain (1994). Reprinted with permission.

In the event that either the student or the faculty member is dissatisfied with the outcome of the informal hearing or if the deficiency is of sufficient magnitude to potentially justify the student's dismissal from the school of medicine, a formal hearing will be convened before the appropriate steering committee. The request for a formal hearing should be made in writing to the chairperson of the steering committee within ten days of the informal hearing.

C. The purpose of the formal hearing is to provide a full and fair discussion of evidence concerning the allegations. The following guidelines shall apply.

1. At least ten days before the hearing, the student and the faculty member shall be given a copy of the rules and procedures that apply.
2. The student shall be allowed to inspect the entire academic medical school file including any material concerning the allegations.
3. The student shall be allowed to have an advisor present at the hearing, but the advisor will not have official standing during the hearing.
4. The hearing will be conducted before a majority of the members of the committee that is to decide a means of remedy of the allegations.
5. The student will be given the opportunity to present any relevant evidence regarding the allegations.
6. The student will be shown all evidence, including grades and narrative evaluations, that are to be considered in arriving at a decision.
7. The student will have the opportunity to question any witness who presents evidence at the hearing.
8. All recommendations resulting from the formal hearing will be based solely upon the evidence presented at the hearing.
9. A record of the meeting will be kept and the student will be given a copy of the record upon request.
10. The findings and proposed remedy will be stated in writing and transmitted to the student, the curriculum committee, and the dean.

D. If either the student or the academic unit of the faculty is dissatisfied with the outcome of the formal hearing, a written request for appeal must be made within ten days of receipt of the outcome of the formal hearing to the curriculum committee. The curriculum committee will consult with the dean of the school of medicine and an appeals hearing will be held within 30 days of the request. If necessary, the final decision is that of the school of medicine faculty.

♦ ♦ ♦ ♦

References

Aaron, R. M. (1992). Student academic dishonesty: Are collegiate institutions addressing the issue? *NASPA Journal, 29*(2), 107–113.

Aaron, R. M., & Georgia, R. T. (1994). Administrator perceptions of student academic dishonesty in collegiate institutions. *NASPA Journal, 31*(2), 83–91.

Adams, R. (1992, January 31). Kashmir cheating clampdown. *Times Higher Education Supplement,* p. 9.

Advanced Psychometrics. (1993). *Scrutiny!* [Computer software]. St. Paul, MN: Author.

Aiken, L. R. (1991). Detecting, understanding, and controlling for cheating on tests. *Research in Higher Education, 32*(6), 725–736.

Akaninwor, G. I. K. (1997). Examination malpractices in developing areas: A case study. *Studies in Educational Evaluation, 23*(3), 275–277.

Albas, D., & Albas, C. A. (1993). Disclaimer mannerisms of students: How to avoid being labeled as cheaters. *Canadian Review of Sociology & Anthropology, 30*(4), 451–467.

Alschuler, A. S., & Bliming, G. S. (1995). Curbing epidemic cheating through systemic change. *College Teaching, 43*(4), 123–125.

Amato, M. K. (1995, October/November). Confessions of a seventh-grade cheat. *Instructor,* p. 92.

Amended Senate Bill 230. (1996). *Ohio Revised Code,* 3319.151.

American Educational Research Association, American Psychological Association, & National Council on Measurement in Education. (1985). *Standards for educational and psychological testing.* Washington, DC: American Psychological Association.

Ames, G. A., & Eskridge, C. W. (1992). The impact of ethics courses on student attitudes and behavior regarding cheating. *Journal of College Student Development, 33*(6), 556–557.

Anderman, E. M., Griesinger, T., & Westerfield, G. (1998). Motivation and cheating during early adolescence. *Journal of Educational Psychology, 90*(1), 84–93.

Anderson, E. (1996, July 24). No one nails cheating manicurists. *New Orleans Times–Picayune,* p. A2.

Anderson, R. E., & Obenshain, S. S. (1994). Cheating by students: Findings, reflections, and remedies. *Academic Medicine, 69*(5), 323–332.

Angoff, W. H. (1974). The development of statistical indices for detecting cheaters. *Journal of the American Statistical Association, 69*(345), 44–49.

Angoff, W. H. (1993, April). *Considerations in the deterrence and detection of cheating.* Paper presented at the annual meeting of the American Educational Research Association, Atlanta, GA.

Anikeef, A. M. (1954). Index of collaboration for test administrators. *Journal of Applied Psychology, 38*(3), 174–177.

Antion, D. L., & Michael, W. B. (1983). Short-term predictive validity of demographic, affective, personal and cognitive variables in relation to two criterion measures of cheating behaviors. *Educational and Psychological Measurement, 43*(2), 467–482.

Aronson, E., & Mettee, D. R., (1968). Dishonest behavior as a function of differential levels of induced self-esteem. *Journal of Personality and Social Psychology, 9*(2), 121–127.

Assessment Systems Corporation. (1995). *Scrutiny!: Software to identify test misconduct.* St. Paul, MN: Author.

Atkins, B. E., & Atkins, R. E. (1936). A study of honesty of prospective teachers. *Elementary School Journal, 36,* 595–603.

Baird, J. S., Jr. (1980). Current trends in college cheating. *Psychology in the Schools, 17*(4), 515–522.

Baldwin, D. C., Daughtery, S. R., Rowley, B. D., & Schwarz, M. R. (1996). Cheating in medical school: A survey of second-year students at 31 schools. *Academic Medicine, 71*(3), 267–273.

Barnett, D. C., & Dalton, J. C. (1981). Why college students cheat. *Journal of College Student Personnel, 22,* 545–551.

Bay, M. L. G. (1994). Detection of copying on multiple-choice examinations (unpublished doctoral dissertation, Southern Illinois University, 1987). *Dissertation Abstracts International, 56*(3–A), 899.

Becker, B. J. (1990). Coaching for the Scholastic Aptitude Test: Further synthesis and appraisal. *Review of Educational Research, 60*(3), 373–419.

Bellezza, F. S., & Bellezza, S. F. (1989). Detection of cheating on multiple-choice tests by using error similarity analysis. *Teaching of Psychology, 16*(3), 151–155.

Bellezza, F. S., & Bellezza, S. F. (1995). Detection of copying on multiple-choice tests: An update. *Teaching of Psychology, 22*(3), 180–182.

Bhargava, A. (1987, June 10). Indian officials struggle to improve corruption-ridden universities. *Chronicle of Higher Education,* p. A37.

Bird, C. (1927). The detection of cheating on objective examinations. *School and Society, 25*(635), 261–262.

Bird, C. (1929). An improved method of detecting cheating in objective examinations. *Journal of Educational Research, 19*(5), 341–348.

Black, D. (1962). The falsification of reported examination marks in a senior university education course. *Journal of Educational Sociology, 35*(8), 346–354.

Blackburn, M. A., & Miller, R. B. (1996, April). *Cheating and motivation: A possible relationship.* Paper presented at the annual meeting of the American Educational Research Association, New York.

Blinn, L. V. (1993). Coping with cheating: An effective method at Michigan State that defeats cheating. *Journal of College Science Teaching, 23*(3), 173–174.

Blum, D. (1994, May 4). Six Navy football players may be expelled. *Chronicle of Higher Education,* p. A44.

Board of Curators of the University of Missouri v. Horowitz, 435 U.S. 78 (1978).

Bock, R. D. (1972). Estimation of item parameters and latent ability when responses are scored in two or more nominal categories. *Psychometrika, 37*(1), 29–51.

Bowers, W. J. (1964). *Student dishonesty and its control in college.* New York: Columbia University, Bureau of Applied Social Research.

Brandes, B. (1986). *Academic honesty: A special study of California students.* Sacramento, CA: California State Department of Education, Bureau of Publications.

Brickman, W. W. (1961). Ethics, examinations, and education. *School and Society, 89,* 412–415.

Brilliant, J. J. (1996). An intervention to decrease cheating in an immigrant population. *Journal of College Student Development, 37,* 590–591.

Brilliant, J. J., & Gribben, C. A. (1993). A workshop for faculty and counselors on academic dishonesty. *Journal of College Student Development, 34*(6), 437–438.

Bronner, S. J. (1995). *Piled higher and deeper.* Little Rock, AR: August House.

Bronzaft, A. L., Stuart, I. R., & Blum, B. (1973). Test anxiety and cheating on college examinations. *Psychological Reports, 32*(1), 149–150.

Brooks, C. M., Cunningham, R., Hinson, N., Brown, S., & Weaver, B. (1981). Student attitudes toward a medical school honor code. *Journal of Medical Education, 56*(8), 669–671.

Brown, S. M. (1998, April 2). Pagers replacing pages of crib notes. *Philadelphia Inquirer,* p. F6.

Brown, V. L., & Buttolph, K. (Eds.). (1993). *Student disciplinary issues: A legal compendium.* Washington, DC: National Association of College and University Attorneys. (ERIC Document Reproduction Service No. ED 363 186)

Brownell, H. C. (1928). Mental test traits of college cribbers. *School and Society, 27,* 764.

Bruggeman, E. L., & Hart, K. J. (1996). Cheating, lying, and moral reasoning by religious and secular high school students. *Journal of Educational Research, 89*(6), 340–344.

Buckingham, B. R. (1926). *Research for teachers.* New York: Silver Burdett.

Bunn, D. N., Caudill, S. B., & Gropper, D. M. (1992). Crime in the classroom: An economic analysis of undergraduate student cheating behavior. *Journal of Economic Education, 23*(3), 197–207.

Burton v. Wilmington Parking Authority, 365 U.S. 715 (1961).

Bushway, A., & Nash, W. R. (1977). School cheating behavior. *Review of Educational Research, 47*(4), 623–632.

Buss, W. G., & Novick, M. R. (1980). The detection of cheating on standardized tests: Statistical and legal analysis. *Journal of Law and Education, 9*(1), 1–64.

Caesar, T. P. (1983, June 1). When expert cheaters met the invigilators. *Chronicle of Higher Education,* p. 64.

Calabrese, R. L., & Cochran, J. T. (1990). The relationship of alienation to cheating among a sample of American adolescents. *Journal of Research and Development in Education, 23*(2), 65–71.

Cannell, J. J. (1989). *The Lake Wobegone report: How public educators cheat on standardized achievement tests.* Albuquerque, NM: Friends for Education.

Canner, J. (1992). Regaining the public trust: A review of school testing programs, practices. *NASSP Bulletin, 72*(545), 6–15.

Canning, R. R. (1956). Does an honor system reduce classroom cheating? An experimental answer. *Journal of Experimental Education, 24,* 291–296.

Casey, W. M., & Burton, R. V. (1982). Training children to be consistently honest through verbal self-instruction. *Child Development, 53*(4), 911–919.

Centra, J. A. (1970). College freshmen attitudes toward cheating. *Personnel and Guidance Journal, 48*(5), 366–373.

Chason, W. (1997, April). *A comparison of several classical and IRT–based methods to detect aberrant response patterns.* Paper presented at the annual meeting of the American Educational Research Association, Chicago, IL.

Chason, W. M., & Maller, S. (1996, April). *Utility of the Rasch person-fit statistic in detecting answer copying: A comparison with traditional cheating indices.* Paper presented at the annual meeting of the American Educational Research Association, New York.

Cheating found, 10,000 asked to retake exam. (1983, October 19). *Chronicle of Higher Education,* p. A20.

Cheating scandal jars a suburb of high achievers. (1992, January 1). *New York Times,* p. A32.

Christian, N. M. (1998, April 24). Taxi agency alters exam after charges of cheating. *New York Times,* p. B5.

Cizek, G. J. (1993). Rethinking psychometricians' beliefs about learning. *Educational Researcher, 22*(4), 4–9.

Cizek, G. J. (1996, April). *Detection of answer copying: Getting a focus on the bigger picture.* Discussant remarks presented at the annual meeting of the American Educational Research Association, New York.

Cizek, G. J., Rachor, R. E., & Fitzgerald, S. M. (1996). Teachers' assessment practices: Preparation, isolation, and the kitchen sink. *Educational Assessment, 3*(2), 159–179.

Clouse, B. (1973). Attitudes of college students as a function of sex, politics, and religion. *Journal of College Student Personnel, 14*(3), 260–264.

Coady, H., & Sawyer, D. (1986). Moral judgment, sex, and level of temptation as determinants of resistance to temptation. *Journal of Psychology, 120*(2), 177–181.

Cody, R. P. (1985). Statistical analysis of examinations to detect cheating. *Journal of Medical Education, 60*(2), 136–137.

Cohen, S. A., & Hyman, J. S. (1991). Can fantasies become facts? *Educational Measurement: Issues and Practice, 10*(1), 20–23.

Cole, N. (1998, November 9). Teen cheating hurts all. *USA Today*, p. A24.

Cole, S., & McCabe, D. L. (1996). Issues in academic integrity. In W. L. Merced (Ed.), *Critical issues in judicial affairs: Current trends and practice* (pp. 67–77). San Francisco: Jossey-Bass.

Colton, G. D. (1997, March). *High-tech approaches to breeching examination security.* Paper presented at the annual meeting of the National Council on Measurement in Education, Chicago.

Consolidated Edison Co. v. National Labor Relations Board, 305 U.S. 197 (1938).

Cooper, S., & Peterson, D. (1980). Machiavellianism and spontaneous cheating in competition. *Journal of Research in Personality, 14*(1), 70–75.

Corcoran, K. J., & Rotter, J. B. (1987). Morality-Conscience Guilt scale as a predictor of ethical behavior in a cheating situation among college females. *Journal of General Psychology.*

Cordiero, P. A., & Carspecken, P. F. (1993). How a minority of the minority succeed: A case study of twenty Hispanic achievers. *Qualitative Studies in Education, 6*(4), 277–290. 114(2), 117–123.

Cordiero, W. P. (1995). Should a school of business change its ethics to conform to the cultural diversity of its students? *Journal of Education for Business, 71*(1), 27–29.

Cornehlsen, V. H. (1965). Cheating attitudes and practices in a suburban high school. *Journal of the National Association of Women Deans and Counselors, 28*(1), 106–109.

Corso v. Creighton University, 731 F.2d 529 (1984).

Covey, M. K., Saladin, S., & Killen, P. J. (1989). Self-monitoring, surveillance, and incentive effects on cheating. *Journal of Social Psychology, 129*(5), 673–679.

Covington, M. V. (1992). *Making the grade: A self-worth perspective on motivation and school reform.* New York: Cambridge University Press.

Crawford, C. C. (1930). Dishonesty in objective tests. *School Review, 38*(10), 776–781.

Crocker, L., Geisinger, K., Loyd, B., & Webb, M. (1994). *Report of the panel convened to review test security processes at the Educational Testing Service in February 1994.* Princeton, NJ: Educational Testing Service.

Cumming, D. (1995, September 25). Competition, weak morals increasing cheating incidents. *Atlanta Journal and Constitution*, p. B2.

Cutler, B. L., & Penrod, S. D. (1995). *Mistaken identification: The eyewitness, psychology, and the law.* London: Cambridge University Press.

Dalton v. Educational Testing Service, 614 N.Y.2d 742 (1994).

Damon, W. (1995). *Greater expectations: Overcoming the culture of indulgence in America's homes and schools.* New York: Free Press.

Daniel, L. G., Adams, B. N., & Smith, N. M. (1994). Academic misconduct among nursing students: A multivariate analysis. *Journal of Professional Nursing, 10*(5), 278–288.

Daniel, L. G., Blount, K. D., & Ferrell, C. M. (1991). Academic misconduct among teacher education students: A descriptive-correlational study. *Research in Higher Education, 32*(6), 703–724.

Davis, K. (1992). Student cheating: A defensive essay. *English Journal, 81*(6), 72–74.

Davis, S. F., Grover, C. A., Becker, A. H., & McGregor, L. N. (1992). Academic dishonesty: Prevalence, determinants, techniques, and punishments. *Teaching of Psychology, 19*(1), 16–20.

Davis, S. F., & Ludvigson, H. W. (1995). Additional data on academic dishonesty and a proposal for remediation. *Teaching of Psychology, 22*(2), 119–121.

Davis, S. F., Noble, L. M., Zak, E. N., & Dreyer, K. K. (1994). A comparison of cheating and learning/grade orientation in American and Australian college students. *College Student Journal, 28*(3), 353–356.

Davis, S. F., Pierce, M. C., Yandell, L. R., Arnow, P. S., & Loree, A. (1995). Cheating in college and the Type A personality: A reevaluation. *College Student Journal, 29*(4), 493–497.

DePalma, A. (1992, May 2). The chase after cheaters on college-entry exams. *New York Times,* p. A1.

Dickenson, H. P. (1945). Identical errors and deception. *Journal of Educational Research, 38*(7), 534–542.

Dickstein, L. S., Montoya, R., & Neitlich, A. (1977). Cheating and fear of negative evaluation. *Bulletin of the Psychonomic Society, 10*(4), 319–320.

Diekhoff, G. M., LaBeff, E. E., Clark, R. E., Williams, L. E., Francis, B., & Haines, V. J. (1996). College cheating: Ten years later. *Research in Higher Education, 37*(4), 487–502.

Dien, D. S. (1974). Parental Machiavellianism and children's cheating in Japan. *Journal of Cross-Cultural Psychology, 5*(3), 259–270.

Dien, D. S., & Fujisawa, H. (1979). Machiavellianism in Japan: A longitudinal study. *Journal of Cross-Cultural Psychology, 10*(4), 508–516.

Dienstbier, R. A., Kahle, L. R., Wilis, K. A., & Tunnell, G. B. (1980). The impact of moral theories on cheating: Studies of emotion attribution and schema activation. *Motivation and Emotion, 4*(3), 193–216.

Dixon v. Alabama State Board of Education, 294 F.2d 150 (1961).

Doster, J. T., & Chance, J. (1976). Interpersonal trust and trustworthiness in preadolescents. *Journal of Psychology, 93*(1), 71–79.

Drake, C. A. (1941). Why students cheat. *Journal of Higher Education, 12,* 418–420.

Dunn, T. G. (1999). Policy and practical implications of theoretical advances in education. In G. J. Cizek (Ed.), *Handbook of educational policy* (pp. 273–296). San Diego, CA: Academic Press.

Dwyer, D. J., & Hecht, J. B. (1996). Using statistics to catch cheaters: Methodological and legal issues for student personnel administrators. *NASPA Journal, 33*(2), 125–135.

Eaton, T. A. (1995). The Sharp Electronic Organizer: A warning. *Journal of Chemical Education, 72,* 180–181.

Eble, K. E. (1988). *The craft of teaching: A guide to mastering the professor's art.* San Francisco: Jossey-Bass.

Eisenberger, R., & Masterson, F. A. (1983). Required high effort increases subsequent persistence and reduces cheating. *Journal of Personality and Social Psychology, 44*(3), 593–599.

Eisenberger, R., & Shank, D. M. (1985). Personal work ethic and effort training affect cheating. *Journal of Personality and Social Psychology, 49*(2), 520–528.

Emerson, P. L. (1974). Experience with computer generation and scoring of tests for a large class. *Educational and Psychological Measurement, 34*(3), 703–709.

Enker, M. S. (1987). Attitudinal and normative variables as predictors of cheating behavior. *Journal of Cross-Cultural Psychology, 18*(3), 315–330.

Erickson, M. L., & Smith, W. B. (1974). On the relationship between self-reported and actual deviance: An empirical test. *Humboldt Journal of Social Relations, 1*(2), 106–113.

Esteban v. Central Missouri State College, 415 F.2d 1077 (1969).

Evans, E. D., & Craig, D. (1990a). Adolescent cognitions for academic cheating as a function of grade level and achievement status. *Journal of Adolescent Research, 5*(3), 325–345.

Evans, E. D., & Craig, D. (1990b). Teacher and student perceptions of academic cheating in middle and senior high schools. *Journal of Educational Research, 84*(1), 44–52.

Evans, E. D, Craig, D., & Mietzel, G. (1993). Adolescents' cognitions and attributions for academic cheating: A cross-national study. *Journal of Psychology, 127*(6), 585–602.

Fakouri, M. E. (1972). Achievement motivation and cheating. *Psychological Reports, 31*(2), 629–630.

Faulkender, P. J., Range, L. M., Hamilton, M., Strehlow, M., Jackson, S., Blanchard, E., & Dean, P. (1994). The case of the stolen psychology test: An analysis of an actual cheating incident. *Ethics and Behavior, 4*(3), 209–217.

Feldman, S. E., & Feldman, M. T. (1967). Transition of sex differences in cheating. *Psychological Reports, 20*(3), 957–958.

Fischer, C. T. (1970). Levels of cheating under conditions of informative appeal to honesty, public affirmation of value, and threat of punishment. *Journal of Educational Research, 64*(1), 12–16.

Fishbein, L. (1994). We can curb college cheating. *Education Digest, 59,* 58–61.

Flynn, S., Reichard, M., & Slane, S. (1987). Cheating as a function of task outcome and Machiavellianism. *Journal of Psychology, 121*(5), 423–427.

Footer, N. S. (1996). Achieving fundamental fairness: The code of conduct. In W. L. Merced (Ed.), *Critical issues in judicial affairs: Current trends and practice* (pp. 19–33). San Francisco: Jossey-Bass.

Forsyth, D. R., & Berger, R. E. (1982). The effects of ethical ideology on moral behavior. *Journal of Social Psychology, 117*(1), 53–56.

Forsyth, D. R., Pope, W. R., & McMillan, J. H. (1985). Students' reactions after cheating: An attributional analysis. *Contemporary Educational Psychology, 10*(1), 72–82.

Forsyth, D. R., & Scott, W. L. (1984). Attributions and moral judgments: Kohlberg's stage theory as a taxonomy of moral attributions. *Bulletin of the Psychonomic Society, 22*(4), 321–323.

Franklyn-Stokes, A., & Newstead, S. E. (1995). Undergraduate cheating: Who does what and why? *Studies in Higher Education, 20*(2), 159–172.

Frantz, D., & Nordheimer, J. (1997, September 28). Giant of exam business keeps quiet on cheating. *New York Times,* p. A1.

Frary, R. B. (1993). Statistical detection of multiple-choice answer copying: Review and commentary. *Applied Measurement in Education, 6*(2), 153–165.

Frary, R. B., & Olson, G. H. (1985, April). *Detection of coaching and answer copying on standardized tests.* Paper presented at the annual meeting of the National Council on Measurement in Education, Chicago, IL. (ERIC Document Reproduction Service No. ED 262 057)

Frary, R. B., & Tideman, T. N. (1997). Comparison of two indices of answer copying and development of a spliced index. *Educational and Psychological Measurement, 57*(1), 20–32.

Frary, R. B., Tideman, T. N., & Watts, T. M. (1977). Indices of cheating on multiple-choice tests. *Journal of Educational Statistics, 2,* 235–256.

Gardner, W. M., Roper, J. T., Gonzalez, C. C., & Simpson, R. G. (1988). Analysis of cheating on academic assignments. *Psychological Record, 38*(4), 543–555.

Gay, G. H. (1990). Standardized tests: Irregularities in administering of tests affect test results. *Journal of Instructional Psychology, 17*(2), 93–103.

Genereux, R. L., & McLeod, B. A. (1995). Circumstances surrounding cheating: A questionnaire study of college students. *Research in Higher Education, 36*(6), 687–704.

Gershon, R., & Bergstrom, B. (1995, April). *Does cheating on CAT pay: Not.* Paper presented at the annual meeting of the American Educational Research Association, San Francisco, CA. (ERIC Document Reproduction Service No. ED 392 844)

Godfrey, J. R., & Waugh, R. F. (1996, April). *Students perceptions of cheating in Australian independent schools.* Paper presented at the annual meeting of the American Educational Research Association, New York.

Goldberg v. Kelley, 397 U.S. 254 (1970).

Goldsen, R. K. (1960). *What college students think.* Princeton, NJ: Van Nostrand.

Goss v. Lopez, 419 U.S. 565 (1975).

Gould, S. J. (1981). *The mismeasure of man.* New York: Norton.

Graham, M. A., Monday, J., O'Brien, K., & Steffen, S. (1994). Cheating at small colleges: An examination of student and faculty attitudes and behaviors. *Journal of College Student Development, 35*(4), 255–260.

Greenberg, B. G., Abul-Ela, A., Simmons, W. R., & Horvitz, D. G. (1969). The unrelated question randomized response model: Theoretical framework. *Journal of the American Statistical Association, 64*, 520–539.

Greene, A. S., & Saxe, L. (1992, April). *Everybody (else) does it: Academic cheating*. Paper presented at the annual meeting of the Eastern Psychological Association, Boston, MA. (ERIC Document Reproduction Service No. ED 347 941)

Gross, M. M. (1946). The effect of certain types of motivation on the honesty of children. *Journal of Educational Research, 40*, 133–140.

Gullickson, A. R. (1986). Teacher education and teacher-perceived needs in educational measurement. *Journal of Educational Measurement, 23*, 347–354.

Haines, V. J., Diekhoff, G. M., LaBeff, E. E., & Clark, R. E. (1986). College cheating: Immaturity, lack of commitment, and the neutralizing attitude. *Research in Higher Education, 25*(4), 342–354.

Hambleton, R. K., & Swaminathan, H. (1985). *Item response theory: Principles and applications*. Boston: Kluwer Nijhoff.

Hamilton, B. G. (1989). Expert testimony on the reliability of eyewitness identifications: A critical analysis of its admissibility. *Missouri Law Review, 54*(3), 732–776.

Haney, W. M. (1993, April). *Cheating and escheating on standardized tests*. Paper presented at the annual meeting of the American Educational Research Association, Atlanta, GA.

Hanson, B. A., Harris, D. J., & Brennan, R. L. (1987). *A comparison of several statistical methods for examining allegations of copying* (ACT Research Report Series No. 87–15). Iowa City, IA: American College Testing.

Harp, J., & Taietz, P. (1966). Academic integrity and social structure: A study of cheating among college students. *Social Problems, 13*(4), 365–373.

Harp, L. (1995, May 3). Academic tourney's black mark: A cheating scandal. *Education Week*, pp. 1, 14.

Harpp, D. N., & Hogan, J. J. (1993). Crime in the classroom: Detection and prevention of cheating on multiple-choice exams. *Journal of Chemical Education, 70*(4), 306–311.

Harpp, D. N., & Hogan, J. J. (1996). Crime in the classroom Part II: An update. *Journal of Chemical Education, 73*(4), 349–351.

Hartshorne, H., & May, M.A. (1928). *Studies in the nature of character: Vol. 1. Studies in deceit*. New York: Macmillan.

Haussman, F. (1988, March 18). Irate parents denounce Brazilian exam 'mafia.' *Times Higher Education Supplement*, p. 8.

Hein, D. (1982). Rethinking honor. *Journal of Thought, 17*(1), 3–6.

Heisler, G. (1974). Ways to deter law violators: Effects of levels of threat and vicarious punishment on cheating. *Journal of Consulting and Clinical Psychology, 42*(4), 577–582.

Hemmings, A. (1996). Conflicting images? Being Black and a model high school student. *Anthropology & Education Quarterly, 27*(1), 20–50.

Hetherington, E. M., & Feldman, S. E. (1964). College cheating as a function of subject and situational variables. *Journal of Educational Psychology, 55*, 212–218.

Hill, J. P., & Kochendorfer, R. A. (1969). Knowledge of peer success and risk of detection as determinants of cheating. *Developmental Psychology, 1*(3), 231–238.

Hills, J. R. (1991). Apathy concerning testing and grading. *Phi Delta Kappan, 72*, 540– 545.

Hoff, A. G. (1940). A study of the honesty and accuracy found in pupil checking of examination papers. *Journal of Educational Research, 34*(2), 127–129.

Hofkins, D. (1995, June 16). Cheating 'rife' in national tests. *Times Educational Supplement*, p. 1.

Holland, P. W. (1996). *Assessing unusual agreement between the incorrect answers of two examinees using the K-index: Statistical theory and empirical support* (ETS Technical Report No. 96–4). Princeton, NJ: Educational Testing Service.

Hollinger, R. C., & Lanza-Kaduce, L. (1996). Academic dishonesty and the perceived effectiveness of countermeasures: An empirical survey of cheating at a major public university. *NASPA Journal, 33*(4), 292–306.

Homant, R., & Rokeach, M. (1970). Value of honesty and cheating behavior. *Personality: An International Journal, 1*(2), 153–162.

Houser, B. B. (1978). Cheating among elementary grade level students: An examination. *Journal of Instructional Psychology, 5*(3), 2–5.

Houser, B. B. (1982). Student cheating and attitude: A function of classroom control technique. *Contemporary Educational Psychology, 7*(2), 113–123.

Houston, J. P. (1976a). Amount and loci of classroom answer copying, spaced seating, and alternate test forms. *Journal of Educational Psychology, 68*(6), 729–735.

Houston, J. P. (1976b). The assessment and prevention of answer copying on undergraduate multiple-choice examinations. *Research in Higher Education, 5*(4), 301–311.

Houston, J. P. (1976c). Learning and cheating as a function of study phase distraction. *Journal of Educational Research, 69*(7), 247–249.

Houston, J. P. (1977a). Cheating behavior, anticipated success–failure, confidence, and test importance. *Journal of Educational Psychology, 69*(1), 55–60.

Houston, J. P. (1977b). Learning, opportunity to cheat, and amount of reward. *Journal of Experimental Education, 45*(3), 30–35.

Houston, J. P. (1978). Curvilinear relationships among anticipated success, cheating behavior, temptation to cheat, and perceived instrumentality of cheating. *Journal of Educational Psychology, 70*(5), 758–762.

Houston, J. P. (1983a). Alternate test forms as a means of reducing multiple-choice answer copying in the classroom. *Journal of Educational Psychology, 75*(4), 572–575.

Houston, J. P. (1983b). College classroom cheating threat, sex, and prior performance. *College Student Journal, 17*(3), 229–235.

Houston, J. P. (1983c). Kohlberg-type moral instruction and cheating behavior. *College Student Journal, 17*(2), 196–204.

Houston, J. P. (1986). Classroom answer copying: Roles of acquaintanceship and free versus assigned seating. *Journal of Educational Psychology, 78*(3), 230–232.

Houston, J. P., & Ziff, T. (1976). Effects of success and failure on cheating behavior. *Journal of Educational Psychology, 68*(3), 371–376.

Howard, S. (1986, April 10). Alabama swimmer Berndt caught cheating. *Atlanta Journal and Constitution*, p. C1.

Huss, M. T., Curnyn, J. P., Roberts, S. L., Davis, S. F., Yandell, L., & Giordano, P. (1993). Hard driven but not dishonest: Cheating and the Type A personality. *Bulletin of the Psychonomic Society, 31*(5), 429–430.

Iwamoto, C. K., Nungester, R. J., & Luecht, R. M. (1996, April). *Power of similarity methods and person-fit analyses to detect answer copying behavior.* Paper presented at the annual meeting of the American Educational Research Association, New York.

Jackson, P. W. (1968). *Life in classrooms.* New York: Holt, Rinehart and Winston.

Jacobs, L. C., & Chase, C. I. (1992). *Developing and using tests effectively: A guide for faculty.* San Francisco: Jossey-Bass.

Jacobson, L. I., Berger, S. E., & Millham, J. (1969). Self-esteem, sex differences, and the tendency to cheat. *Proceedings of the 77th annual convention of the American Psychological Association, 4*(1), 353–354.

James, H. W. (1933). Honesty as a character trait among young people. *Journal of Educational Research, 26,* 572–579.

Jaska v. Regents of the University of Michigan, 597 F. Supp. 1245 (E.D. Mich. 1984).

Jendrek, M. P. (1989). Faculty reactions to academic dishonesty. *Journal of College Student Development, 30*(5), 401–406.

Jendrek, M. P. (1992). Students' reactions to academic dishonesty. *Journal of College Student Development, 33*(3), 260–273.

Jennings, V. T. (1992a, June 27). Md. teen fined $5,000 for SAT lawsuit. *Washington Post,* p. B8.

Jennings, V. T. (1992b, October 24). Teen gets six months in SAT scandal. *Washington Post,* p. A1.

Johnson, C. D., & Gormly, J. (1971). Achievement, sociability, and task importance in relation to academic cheating. *Psychological Reports, 28*(1), 302.

Johnson, C. D., & Gormly, J. (1972). Academic cheating: The contribution of sex, personality, and situational variables. *Developmental Psychology, 6*(2), 320–325.

Johnson, J., & Farkas, S. (1997). *Getting by: What American teenagers really think about their schools.* New York: Public Agenda.

Johnson, P. B. (1981). Achievement motivation and success: Does the end justify the means? *Journal of Personality and Social Psychology, 40*(2), 374–375.

Kahle, L. R. (1980). Stimulus condition self-selection by males in the interaction of locus of control and skill-chance situations. *Journal of Personality and Social Psychology, 38*(1), 50– 56.

Keehn, J. D. (1956). Unrealistic reporting as a function of extraverted neuroses. *Journal of Clinical Psychology, 12*, 61–63.

Kerkvliet, J. (1994). Cheating by economics students: A comparison of survey results. *Journal of Economic Education, 25*(2), 121–133.

Khashan, H. (1984). A study of student perceptions in a Saudi Arabian university. *Research in Higher Education, 21*(1), 17–31.

Kher-Durlabhji, N., & Lacina-Gifford, L. J. (1992, April). *Quest for test success: Preservice teachers' views of high stakes tests.* Paper presented at the annual meeting of the Mid-South Educational Research Association, Knoxville, TN. (ERIC Document Reproduction Service No. ED 353 338)

Kibler, W. L. (1993a). Academic dishonesty: A student development dilemma. *NASPA Journal, 30*(4), 252–257.

Kibler, W. L. (1993b). A framework for addressing academic dishonesty from a student development perspective. *NASPA Journal, 31*(1), 8–18.

Kibler, W. L., & Paterson, B. G. (1988). Strategies to prevent academic dishonesty. In W. L. Kibler, E. M. Nuss, B. G. Paterson, & G. Pavela (Eds.), *Academic integrity and student development: Legal issues and policy perspectives* (pp. 19–36). Asheville, NC: College Administration Publications.

King, J. (1997, August 13). Eight charged in alleged test-cheating scheme [on-line]. http://www.pathfinder.com/@@CmG8LAcA3*zFDt2y/news/latest/RB/1997/Aug13?44. html

Klein, S. P. (1992). Chance: Statistical evidence of cheating on multiple-choice tests. *New Directions for Statistics and Computing, 5*(3), 23–27.

Knowlton, J. Q., & Hamerlynck, L. A. (1967). Perception of deviant behavior: A study of cheating. *Journal of Educational Psychology, 58*(6), 379–385.

Kohlberg, L. (1964). Development of moral character and moral ideology. In M. Hoffman & L. Hoffman (Eds.), *Review of child development research.* New York: Russell Sage.

Krebs, R. L. (1969). Teacher perceptions of children's moral behavior. *Psychology in the Schools, 6*(4), 394–395.

Kuehn, P., Stanwyck, D. J., & Holland, C. L. (1990). Attitudes toward "cheating" behaviors in the ESL classroom. *TESOL Quarterly, 24*(2), 313–317.

LaFrance, M., & Hecht, M. A. (1995). Why smiles generate leniency. *Personality and Social Psychology Bulletin, 21*(3), 207–214.

Lawton, M. (1996, November 13). Alleged tampering underscores pitfalls of testing. *Education Week*, p. 5.

Lee v. Macon County Board of Education, 490 F.2d 458 (1974).

Leming, J. S. (1978). Cheating behavior, situational influence, and moral development. *Journal of Educational Research, 71*(4), 214–217.

Leming, J. S. (1980). Cheating behavior, subject variables, and components of the Internal–External Scale under high and low risk conditions. *Journal of Educational Research, 74*(2), 83–87.

Leveque, K. L., & Walker, R. E. (1970). Correlates of high school cheating behavior. *Psychology in the Schools, 7*(2), 159–163.

Levine, D. (1995, October). Cheating in our schools: A national scandal. *Reader's Digest*, 65–70.

Levine, M. V., & Rubin, D. B. (1979). Measuring the appropriateness of multiple-choice test scores. *Journal of Educational Statistics, 4*, 269–290.

Lewis, K. H., & Hartnett, J. J. (1983, March). *Sex differences in the perception of male/female unethical behavior.* Paper presented at the annual meeting of the Southeastern Psychological Association, Atlanta, GA. (ERIC Document Reproduction Service No. ED 234 316)

Lightsey v. King, 567 F. Supp. 645 (E.D. N.Y., 1983).

Ligon, G. (1985, March), *Opportunity knocked out: Reducing cheating by teachers on student tests.* Paper presented at the annual meeting of the American Educational Research Association, Chicago, IL. (ERIC Document Reproduction Service No. ED 263 181)

Lindsay, D. (1996, October 2). Whodunit? Officials find thousands of erasures on standardized tests and suspect tampering. *Education Week,* pp. 25–29.

Linn, R. L., & Gronlund, N. E. (1995). *Measurement and assessment in teaching* (7th ed.). Columbus, OH: Merrill.

Lipson, A., & McGavern, N. (1993, May). *Undergraduate academic dishonesty at MIT: Results of a study of attitudes and behavior of undergraduates, faculty, and graduate teaching assistants.* Paper presented at the 33rd annual forum for the Association for Institutional Research, Chicago, IL. (ERIC Document Reproduction Service No. ED 368 272)

Livosky, M., & Tauber, R. T. (1994). Views of cheating among college students and faculty. *Psychology in the Schools, 31*(1), 72–82.

Lobel, T. E., & Levanon, I. (1988). Self-esteem, need of approval, and cheating behavior in children. *Journal of Educational Psychology, 80,* 122–123.

Loftus, E. F. (1979). *Eyewitness testimony.* Cambridge, MA: Harvard University Press.

Lord, F. M. (1980). *Applications of item response theory to practical testing problems.* Hillsdale, NJ: Lawrence Erlbaum Associates.

Loupe, D. (1998a, June 13). Cheating inquiries abound on two key tests. *Atlanta Journal and Constitution,* p. A1.

Loupe, D. (1998b, March 24). Marist test-stealers leave school. *Atlanta Journal and Constitution,* p. B1.

Lowry, J. D. (1996). Communities of trust: A recent graduate's experience with honor codes. *Journal of College Science Teaching, 26*(1), 6.

LSU discloses cheating plot. (1992, May 15). *New Orleans Times–Picayune,* p. B4.

Ludeman, R. B. (1988). A survey of academic integrity practices in U.S. higher education. *Journal of College Student Development, 29,* 172–173.

Ludeman, W. W. (1938). A study of cheating in public schools. *American School Boards Journal, 96,* 45–46.

MacGregor, K. (1997, February 21). Cheat-proof exams in the pipeline. *Times Education Supplement,* p. 17.

Madaus, G. F. (1988). The influence of testing on the curriculum. In L. N. Tanner (Ed.), *Critical issues in curriculum: Eighty-seventh yearbook of the National Society for the Study of Education* (pp. 83–121). Chicago: University of Chicago Press.

Madsen, H. S. (1987). *Utilizing Rasch analysis to detect cheating on language examinations.* (ERIC Document Reproduction Service No. ED 287 284).

Mann, T. W. (1987). You're only hurting yourself. *Teaching English in the Two-Year College, 14*(2), 121–126.

Maramark, S., & Maline, M. B. (1993). *Issues in education: Academic dishonesty among college students* (Report No. OERI–93–3082). Washington, DC: U.S. Department of Education, Office of Educational Research and Improvement.

Marsh, R. (1988, November). *An effect of unstructured evaluation on academic integrity.* Paper presented at the annual meeting of the Mid-South Educational Research Association, Louisville, KY. (ERIC Document Reproduction Service No. ED 303 508)

Maslen, G. (1993, November 19). Five on cheating at Deakin charge. *Times Higher Education Supplement,* p. 11.

Maslen, G. (1996, October 11). Cheats with pagers and cordless radio cribs. *Times Educational Supplement,* p. 16.

Masonis, E. (1987). *Test security issues for the New Jersey High School Proficiency Test.* (ERIC Document Reproduction Service No. ED 306 2510)

Mawdsley, R. D., & Permuth, S. (1986). Plagiarism and cheating. In T. N. Jones & D. P. Semler (Eds.), *School law update, 1986* (pp. 32–46). Topeka, KS: National Organization on Legal Problems in Education.

May, K. M., & Loyd, B. H. (1993). Academic dishonesty: The honor system and students' attitudes. *Journal of College Student Development, 34*(2), 125–129.

May, W. W. (Ed.). (1990). *Ethics and higher education.* New York: Macmillan.

McCabe, D. L. (1993). Faculty responses to academic dishonesty: The influence of student honor codes. *Research in Higher Education, 34*(5), 647–658.

McCabe, D. L., & Bowers, W. J. (1994). Academic dishonesty among males in college: A thirty year perspective. *Journal of College Student Development, 35*(1), 5–10.

McCabe, D. L., & Bowers, W. J. (1996). The relationship between student cheating and college fraternity or sorority membership. *NASPA Journal, 33*(4), 280–291.

McCabe, D. L., & Trevino, L. K. (1993). Academic dishonesty: Honor codes and other contextual influences. *Journal of Higher Education, 64*(5), 522–538.

McCabe, D. L., & Trevino, L. K. (1996). What we know about cheating in college: Longitudinal trends and recent developments. *Change, 28*(1), 28–33.

McElroy, J. C., & Middlemist, R. D. (1983). Personal space, crowding, and the interference model of test anxiety. *Psychological Reports, 53*(2), 419–424.

McLaughlin, R. D., & Ross, S. M. (1989). Student cheating in high school: A case of moral reasoning vs. 'fuzzy' logic. *High School Journal, 72*(3), 97–104.

Meade, J. (1992). Cheating: Is academic dishonesty par for the course? *Prism, 1*(7), 30– 32.

Mechling, J. (1988). On the relation between creativity and cutting corners. In S. C. Feinstein, A. H. Esman, J. G. Looney, G. H. Orvin, J. L. Schimel, A. Z. Schwartzberg, A. S. Sorosky, & M. Sugar (Eds.), *Adolescent psychiatry: Developmental and clinical studies* (Vol. 15, pp. 346–366). Chicago: University of Chicago Press.

Mehrens, W. A., & Kaminski, J. (1989). Methods for improving standardized test scores: Fruitful, fruitless, or fraudulent? *Educational Measurement: Issues and Practice, 8*(3), 14–22.

Mehrens, W. A., & Lehmann, I. J. (1991). *Measurement and evaluation in education and psychology* (4th ed.). Fort Worth, TX: Holt, Rinehart and Winston.

Mehrens, W. A., Phillips, S. E., & Schram, C. M. (1993). Survey of test security practices. *Educational Measurement: Issues and Practice, 12*(4), 5–19.

Merriam-Webster's collegiate dictionary (10th ed.). (1993). Springfield, MA: Merriam-Webster.

Messick, S. (1989). Validity. In R. L. Linn (Ed.), *Educational measurement* (3rd ed., pp. 13–104). New York: Macmillan.

Millham, J. (1974). Two components of need for approval score and their relationship to cheating following success and failure. *Journal of Research in Personality, 8,* 378–392.

Mixon, F. G., Jr. (1996). Crime in the classroom: An extension. *Journal of Economic Education, 27*(3), 195–200.

Mixon, F. G., & Mixon, D. C. (1996). The economics of illegitimate activities: Further evidence. *Journal of Socioeconomics, 25*(3), 373–381.

Miyazaki, I. (1981). *China's examination hell: The civil service examinations of imperial China* (C. Schirokauer, Trans.). New Haven, CT: Yale University Press. (Original work published 1963)

Moffatt, M. (1990). *Undergraduate cheating.* New Brunswick, NJ: Rutgers University Press.

Monsaas, J. A., & Engelhard, G., Jr. (1991, April). *Attitudes toward testing practices as cheating and teachers' testing practices.* Paper presented at the annual meeting of the American Educational Research Association, Chicago, IL. (ERIC Document Reproduction Service No. ED 338 643)

Monte, C. F., & Fish, J. M. (1980). Lying true: An investigation of moral consistency in unethical behavior. *International Journal of Group Tensions, 10*(1), 130–138.

More Detroit police included in test-cheating allegation. (1997, August 7). *The Toledo Blade,* p. 12.

Moss, B. (1984). *Notes on cheating for the busy classroom teacher.* (ERIC Document Reproduction Service No. ED 243 203)

Murray, B. (1996, January). Are professors turning a blind eye to cheating? *APA Monitor*, pp. 1, 42.

Nash, I. (1989, January 27). GCSE cheats exposed by exam board. *Times Educational Supplement*, p. A1.

National Board of Medical Examiners. (1988). *National Board policies and procedures regarding irregular behavior.* Philadelphia: Author

National Council on Measurement in Education [NCME] (1995). *Code of professional responsibilities in educational measurement.* Washington, DC: Author.

New age of stealth cheating. (1995, April). *American Teacher, 79*, p. 2.

Newhouse, R. C. (1982). Alienation and cheating behavior in the school environment. *Psychology in the Schools, 19*(2), 234–237.

Newstead, S. E., Franklyn-Stokes, A., & Armstead, P. (1996). Individual differences in student cheating. *Journal of Educational Psychology, 88*(2), 229–241.

Nordheimer, J., & Frantz, D. (1997, September 30). Testing giant exceeds its roots, drawing business rivals' ire. *New York Times*, pp. A1, A24.

Norris, W. (1988, March 18). Like a lamb to the slaughter. *Times Higher Education Supplement*, p. 8.

Nowell, C., & Laufer, D. (1997). Undergraduate cheating in the fields of business and economics. *Journal of Economic Education, 28*(1), 3–12.

Nuss, E. M. (1996, February). *What colleges teach students about moral responsibility? Putting the honor back in student honor codes.* Paper presented at the annual meeting of the Institute on College Student Values, Tallahassee, FL. (ERIC Document Reproduction Service No. ED 393 346)

Oles, H. J. (1975). A leak in test security. *Psychological Reports, 37*(3), 921–922.

Pavela, G. (1988a). Code of academic integrity. In W. L. Kibler, E. M. Nuss, B. G. Paterson, & G. Pavela (Eds.), *Academic integrity and student development: Legal issues and policy perspectives* (pp. 69–77). Asheville, NC: College Administration Publications.

Pavela, G. (1988b). The law and academic integrity. In W. L. Kibler, E. M. Nuss, B. G. Paterson, & G. Pavela (Eds.), *Academic integrity and student development: Legal issues and policy perspectives* (pp. 37–63). Asheville, NC: College Administration Publications.

Payne, S. L., & Nantz, K. S. (1994). Social accounts and metaphors about cheating. *College Teaching, 42*(3), 90–96.

Perlman, C. L. (1985, March). *Results of a citywide testing program audit in Chicago.* Paper presented at the annual meeting of the American Educational Research Association, Chicago, IL. (ERIC Document Reproduction Service No. ED 263 212)

Perry, A. R., Kane, K. M., Bernesser, K. J., & Spicker, P. T. (1990). Type A behavior, competitive student-striving, and cheating among college students. *Psychological Reports, 66*(2), 459–465.

Poltorak, Y. (1995). Cheating behavior among students of four Moscow institutes. *Higher Education, 30*(2), 225–246.

Popham, W. J. (1991, April). *Defensible/indefensible instructional preparation for high-stakes achievement tests.* Paper presented at the annual meeting of the American Educational Research Association, Chicago, IL.

Popham, W. J. (1994). Educational assessment's lurking lacuna: The measurement of affect. *Education and Urban Society, 26*(4), 404–416.

Regents of the University of Michigan v. Ewing, 106 S. Ct. 507 (1985).

Richey, M. H., & Fichter, J. J. (1969). Sex differences in moralism and punitiveness. *Psychonomic Science, 16*(4), 185–186.

Risacher, J., & Slonaker, W. (1996). Academic misconduct: NASPA institutional members' views and a pragmatic model policy. *NASPA Journal, 33*(2), 105–124.

Roberts, D. M. (1987). Limitations of the score-difference method in detecting cheating in recognition test situations. *Journal of Educational Measurement, 24*(1), 77–81.

Roberts, D. M., & Toombs, R. (1993). A scale to assess perceptions of cheating in examination-related situations. *Educational and Psychological Measurement, 53*(3), 755–762.

Roberts, R. N. (1986). Public university responses to academic dishonesty: Disciplinary or academic. *Journal of Law & Education, 15*(4), 369–384.

Roeber, E., Bond, L., & Connealy, S. (1998). *Annual survey of state student assessment programs, 1997*. Washington, DC: Council of Chief State School Officers.

Roig, M., & DeTommaso, L. (1995). Are college cheating and plagiarism related to academic procrastination? *Psychological Reports, 77*(2), 691–698.

Roig, M., & Neaman, M. W. (1994). Alienation, learning or grade orientation, and achievement as correlates of attitudes toward cheating. *Perceptual and Motor Skills, 78*, 1096–1098.

Rosenthal, R., & Jacobson, L. (1968). *Pygmalion in the classroom*. New York: Holt, Rinehart & Winston.

Ross, D., & Ross, S. (1969). Leniency toward cheating in preschool children. *Journal of Educational Psychology, 60*(6), 483–487.

Rost, D. H., & Wild, K. P. (1994). Cheating and achievement-avoidance at school: Components and assessment. *British Journal of Educational Psychology, 64*(1), 119–132.

Sabloff, P. L., & Yeager, J. L. (1989). *Building a workable academic integrity system: Issues and options*. (ERIC Document Reproduction Service No. ED 304 970)

Saltman, P. (1996). Cheating prevention: Not an end in itself. *Journal of College Science Teaching, 26*(1), 5.

Saretsky, G. D. (1984). *The treatment of scores of questionable validity: The origins and development of the ETS Board of Review*. Princeton, NJ: Educational Testing Service.

Saupe, J. L. (1960). An empirical model for the corroboration of suspected cheating on multiple-choice tests. *Educational and Psychological Measurement, 20*(3), 475–490.

Schab, F. (1969). Cheating in high school: Differences between the sexes. *Journal of the National Association of Women Deans and Counselors, 33*(1), 39–42

Schab, F. (1972). Cheating in high school: A comparison of behavior of students in the college prep and general curriculum. *Journal of Youth and Adolescence, 1*(3), 251–256.

Schab, F. (1991). Schooling without learning: Thirty years of cheating in high school. *Adolescence, 26*(104), 839–847.

Scheers, N. J., & Dayton, C. M. (1987). Improved estimation of academic cheating behavior using the randomized response technique. *Research in Higher Education, 26*(1), 61–69.

Schumacher, C. F. (1980, April). *A method for detection or confirmation of collaborative behavior*. Paper presented at the annual meeting of the American Educational Research Association, Boston, MA.

Schwartz, S. H., Feldman, K. A., Brown, M. E., & Heingartner, A. (1969). Some personality correlates of conduct in two situations of moral conflict. *Journal of Personality, 37*(1), 41–57.

Semel, T. (1997, March). *Procedures for investigating test irregularities*. Paper presented at the annual meeting of the National Council on Measurement in Education, Chicago, IL.

Shaughnessy, M. F. (1989). *The psychology of cheating behavior*. (ERIC Document Reproduction Service No. ED303 708)

Shelton, J., & Hill, J. P. (1969). Effects on cheating of achievement anxiety and knowledge of peer performance. *Developmental Psychology, 1*(5), 449–445.

Shepard, L. A., & Doughtery, K. C. (1991). *Effects of high-stakes testing on instruction*. Paper presented at the annual meeting of the American Educational Research Association, Chicago, IL. (ERIC Document Reproduction Service No. ED 337 468)

Sherrill, D., Horowitz, B., Friedman, S. T., & Salisbury, J. L. (1970). Seating aggregation as an index of contagion. *Educational and Psychological Measurement, 30*(3), 663–668.

Sherrill, D., Salisbury, J. L., Horowitz, B., & Friedman, S. T. (1971). Classroom cheating: Consistent attitude, perceptions, and behavior. *American Educational Research Journal, 8*(3), 503–510.

Shober v. Commonwealth of Pennsylvania State Real Estate Commission, 435 A.2d. 285 (1981).

Sierles, F. S., Hendrickx, I., & Circle, S. (1980). Cheating in medical school. *Journal of Medical Education, 55*, 124–125.

Sierles, F. S., Kushner, B. D., & Krause, P. B. (1988). A controlled experiment with a medical student honor system. *Journal of Medical Education, 63*(9), 705–713.

Silverman, D. (1992, January 23). Lake Forest schools to downplay testing. *Chicago Tribune*, p. NW3.

Simpson, D. E., Yindra, K. J., Towne, J. B., & Rosenfeld, P. S. (1989). Medical students' perceptions of cheating. *Academic Medicine, 64*(4), 221–222.

Sims, R. L. (1993). The relationship between academic dishonesty and unethical business practices. *Journal of Education for Business, 68*(4), 207–211.

Sims, R. L. (1995). The severity of academic dishonesty: A comparison of faculty and student views. *Psychology in the Schools, 32*(3), 233–238.

Singh, U. P., & Akhtar, S. N. (1972). Personality variables and cheating in examinations. *Indian Journal of Social Work, 32*(4), 423–428.

Singhal, A. C. (1982). Factors in students' dishonesty. *Psychological Reports, 51*(3), 775–780.

Sloss, G. S. (1995). Comment: Is computer-based testing a solution to students' cheating? *Teaching Sociology, 23*, 58–59.

Smith, C. P., Ryan, E. R., & Diggins, D. R. (1972). Moral decision making: Cheating on examinations. *Journal of Personality, 40*(4), 640–660.

Smith, M. L. (1991). Meanings of test preparation. *American Educational Research Journal, 28*(3), 521–542.

Smith, P. (1987, January 9). Bribery and corruption in high places. *Times Educational Supplement,* p. 17.

Smith, R. E., Wheeler, G., & Diener, E. (1975). Faith without works: Jesus people, resistance to temptation, and altruism. *Journal of Applied Social Psychology, 5*(4), 320–330.

Spiller, S., & Crown, D. F. (1995). Changes over time in academic dishonesty at the collegiate level. *Psychological Reports, 76*(3), 763–768.

Standards for the ethical use of tests. (1995). *Ohio Administrative Code.* 3301-7-01.

Stannard, C. I., & Bowers, W. J. (1970). The college fraternity as an opportunity structure for meeting academic demands. *Social Problems, 17*(3), 371–390.

Stansbury, R. (1997a, March 4). Is cheating a) serious? b) minor? c) like, no big deal? *Hartford Courant,* p. 1.

Stansbury, R. (1997b, March 3). Technology, Internet powerful tests of integrity. *Hartford Courant,* p. 1.

Stansbury, R. (1997c, March 2). When the ends justify the means. *Hartford Courant,* p. 1.

Stanton, M. (1980). Moral judgments among students: A cross-cultural study. *Adolescence, 15*(57), 231–241.

Steinberg, L. (1987). Single parents, stepparents, and the susceptibility of adolescents to antisocial peer pressure. *Child Development, 58*(1), 269–275.

Steininger, M. (1968). Attitudes toward cheating: General and specific. *Psychological Reports, 22*(3), 1101–1107.

Steininger, M., Johnson, R., & Kirts, D. (1964). Cheating on college examinations as a function of situationally aroused anxiety and hostility. *Journal of Educational Psychology, 55*(6), 317–324.

Stephenson, G. M., & White, J. H. (1970). Privilege, deprivation, and children's moral behavior: An experimental clarification of the role of investments. *Journal of Experimental Social Psychology, 6*(2), 167–176.

Stephenson, G. M., & Barker, J. (1972). Personality and the pursuit of distributive justice: An experimental study of children's moral behavior. *British Journal of Social and Clinical Psychology, 11*(3), 207–219.

Stern, E. B., & Havlicek, L. (1986). Academic misconduct: Results of faculty and undergraduate student surveys. *Journal of Allied Health, 15*(2), 129–142.

Stevens, E. H. (1996). Informal resolution of academic misconduct cases: A due process paradigm. *College Teaching, 61*(1), 140–144.

Stevens, G. E., & Stevens, F. W. (1987). Ethical inclinations of tomorrow's managers revisited: How and why students cheat. *Journal of Education for Business, 61*(1), 24–29.

Stiggins, R. J. (1991). Assessment literacy. *Phi Delta Kappan, 72*(7), 534–539.

Stoner, E. N., & Cerminara, K. L. (1990). Harnessing the spirit of insubordination: A model student disciplinary code. *Journal of College and University Law, 17*(2), 89–121.

Sullivan, J. (1995, October 24). Cheating scandal hits Yale Divinity, wrongdoers get penance as punishment. *Yale Daily News*, p. 1.

Sumrain, I. A. (1987). Academic dishonesty: Comparing American and foreign students' attitudes (Doctoral dissertation, Oregon State University, 1987). *Dissertation Abstracts International, 48*(5–A), 1091.

Suspected cheating on M.D. licensing test. (1997, August 2). *New York Times*, p. A5.

Sutton, E. M., & Huba, M. E. (1995). Undergraduate student perceptions of academic dishonesty as a function of ethnicity and religious participation. *NASPA Journal, 33*(1), 19–34.

Swem, L. L. (1987). Due process rights in student disciplinary matters. *Journal of College and University Law, 14*(2), 359–382.

Systematic flaws found in pilot testing. (1990, December). *NOCA Professional Regulation News*, p. 3.

Tarling, L. (1985). *Taylor's troubles*. Ringwood, Victoria, Australia: Penguin Books.

Tauber, R. T. (1984, January). *Cheating and plagiarism: Matters beyond a faculty member's right to decide*. Paper presented at the annual meeting of the National Association of Teacher Educators, New Orleans, LA. (ERIC Document Reproduction Service No. ED 240 969)

Taylor, L. E. (1983). Reliability of eyewitness identification. *Trial Lawyers Quarterly, 15*(3), 10–17.

Tittle, C. R., & Rowe, A. R. (1973). Moral appeal, sanction threat, and deviance: An experimental test. *Social Problems, 20*(4), 488–498.

Toch, T., & Wagner, B. (1992, April 27). Schools for scandal. *U.S. News and World Report*, pp. 66–72.

Todd-Mancillas, W. R. (1987, November). *Academic dishonesty among communication students and professionals: Some consequences and what might be done about them*. Paper presented at the annual meeting of the Speech Communication Association, Boston, MA. (ERIC Document Reproduction Service No. ED 296 406)

Todd-Mancillas, W. R., & Sisson, E. (1987, February). *Cheating among engineering students: An analysis*. Paper presented at the annual meeting of the American Association for the Advancement of Science, Chicago, IL. (ERIC Document Reproduction Service No. ED 281 771)

Toenjes, R. N. (1990). *The UNC Charlotte code of student academic integrity*. (ERIC Document Reproduction Service No. ED 321 655)

Tom, G., & Borin, N. (1988). Cheating in academe. *Journal of Education for Business, 63*(4), 153–157.

Trabue, A. (1962). Classroom cheating—An isolated phenomenon? *Educational Record, 43*, 309–316.

Trevino, L. K., & Victor, B. (1992). Peer reporting of unethical behavior: A social context perspective. *Academy of Management Journal, 35*(1), 38–64.

20 are disciplined in test-imposter case. (1997, July 24). *The Toledo Blade*, p. 40.

Tysome, T. (1994, August 19). Cheating purge: Inspectors out. *Times Higher Education Supplement*, p. 1.

University of Texas Medical School at Houston v. Than, 874 S.W.2d 838 (Tex.ct. App.Houston [1st Dist.] 1994).

Vandewiele, M. (1980). Perception of causes of and attitudes towards cheating at school by Senegalese secondary school children. *Psychological Reports, 46*(1), 207–210.

Vines, E. L. (1996). Honor codes at schools and colleges of pharmacy. *American Journal of Pharmaceutical Education, 60*(4), 348–352.

Vitro, F. T. (1971). The relationship of classroom dishonesty to perceived parental discipline. *Journal of College Student Personnel, 12*(6), 427–429.

Vitro, F. T., & Schoer, L. A. (1972). The effects of probability of test success, test importance, and risk of detection on the incidence of cheating. *Journal of School Psychology, 10*(3), 269–277.

Walker, R. E., Wiemeler, G. E., Procyk, M. R., & Knake, W. P. (1966). The contagion of cheating. *Psychology in the Schools, 3*, 359–360.

Wallis, R., & Kleinke, C. L. (1995). Acceptance of external versus internal excuses by an externally or internally oriented audience. *Basic and Applied Social Psychology, 17*(3), 411–420.

Walshe, J. (1988, May 20). Expelled duo to get case re-examined. *Times Higher Education Supplement*, p. 10.

Wang, D., & Anderson, N. H. (1994). Excuse-making and blaming as a function of internal/external locus of control. *European Journal of Social Psychology, 24*(2), 295–302.

Ward, J. G. (1980). Teachers and testing: A survey of knowledge and attitudes. In L. Rudner (Ed.), *Testing in our schools* (pp. 15–24). Washington, DC: National Institute of Education.

Warman, E. (1994). Dental students' attitudes toward cheating. *Journal of Dental Education, 58*(6), 402–405.

Warner, S. L. (1965). Randomized response: A survey technique for eliminating evasive response bias. *Journal of the American Statistical Association, 60*, 63–69.

Waugh, R. F., Godfrey, J. R., Evans, E. D., & Craig, D. (1995). Measuring students' perceptions about cheating in six countries. *Australian Journal of Psychology, 47*(2), 73–80.

Weaver, K. A., Davis, S. F., Look, C., Buzzanga, V. L., & Neal, L. (1991). Examining academic dishonesty policies. *College Student Journal, 25*(3), 302–305.

Weber, L. J., McBee, J. K., & Krebs, J. E. (1983). Take home tests: An experimental study. *Research in Higher Education, 18*(2), 473–483.

Weil, S. (1990, August 24). Widespread cheating undermines matriculation. *Times Educational Supplement*, p. 7.

Weiss, J., Gilbert, K., Giordano, P., & Davis, S. F. (1993). Academic dishonesty, type A behavior and classroom orientation. *Bulletin of the Psychonomic Society, 31*(2), 101–102.

Weizel, R. (1997, October 19). Report indicates Conn. principal altered tests. *Boston Globe*, p. P–6.

Wheeler, P. H. (1993). *Using portfolios to assess teacher performance* (Report No. 93.7). Livermore, CA: EREAPA Associates.

White, B. (1996, April 11). "High-tech snitching" may not stop test cheaters. *Atlanta Journal and Constitution*, p. C1.

Whitworth, R. (1990). Using crib notes as a learning device. *Clearing House, 64*, 23–24.

Who's Who Among American High School Students. (1993). *Attitudes and opinions from the nation's high achieving teens: 24th annual survey of high achievers*. Lake Forest, IL: Author.

Who's Who Among American High School Students. (1994). *Attitudes and opinions from the nation's high achieving teens: 25th annual survey of high achievers*. Lake Forest, IL: Author.

Who's Who Among American High School Students. (1995). *A portrait of a generation: 25 years of teen behavior and attitudes*. Lake Forest, IL: Author.

Wilgoren, J. (1996, July 2). Firefighters retake job test. *Los Angeles Times*, p. B3.

Williams, L. (1997, September 30). School officials' scores invalid; cheating probe may cost jobs. *New Orleans Times–Picayune*, p. A1.

Winston, A. S. (1978). Experimental analysis of admission of cheating: An exploratory study. *Psychological Record, 28*(4), 517–523.

Wollack, J. A. (1996, April). *Detection of answer copying using item response theory*. Paper presented at the annual meeting of the American Educational Research Association, New York.

Wollack, J. A. (1997). A nominal response model approach for detecting answer copying. *Applied Psychological Measurement, 21*(4), 307–320.

Wollack, J. A., & Cohen, A. S. (1998). Detection of answer copying with unknown item and trait parameters. *Applied Psychological Measurement, 22*(2), 144–152.

Wooldridge, P., & Richman, C. L. (1985). Teachers' choice of punishment as a function of a student's gender, age, race, and IQ level. *Journal of School Psychology, 23*(1), 19–29.

Wright B. D., & Masters, G. (1982). *Rating scale analysis*. Chicago: MESA Press.

Wynne, E. A., & Ryan, K. (1997). *Reclaiming our schools: Teaching character, academics, and discipline* (2nd ed.). Upper Saddle River, NJ: Merrill.

Zastrow, C. H. (1970). Cheating among college graduate students. *Journal of Educational Research, 64*, 157–160.

◆ ◆ ◆ ◆

Author Index

✦ ✦ ✦ ✦

Subject Index